I0121625

Marriages of
MECKLENBURG COUNTY, NORTH CAROLINA

❦❦

1783–1868

Marriages of
MECKLENBURG COUNTY, NORTH CAROLINA

1783-1868

Compiled by
BRENT H. HOLCOMB

CLEARFIELD COMPANY

Reprinted for Clearfield Company Inc. by
Genealogical Publishing Co. Inc.
Baltimore, MD 1991

Copyright © 1981
Genealogical Publishing Co., Inc.
Baltimore, Maryland
All Rights Reserved
Library of Congress Catalogue Card Number 80-84316
International Standard Book Number 0-8063-0923-7
Made in the United States of America

INTRODUCTION

THIS VOLUME CONTAINS abstracts of all marriage bonds extant for Mecklenburg County, North Carolina. Although Mecklenburg was formed in 1763 from Anson County, the earliest extant bond dates from 1783. From the number of bonds in existence from that period forward, it is obvious that a great many have not survived. Beginning in the year 1851 the register of deeds in each county in North Carolina was required to keep a register of the marriage bonds issued. This register is extant and is still in the office of the Register of Deeds in Charlotte, the seat of Mecklenburg County. A comparison of this register and the marriage bonds for the years 1851-1867 has been made, and those entries for which bonds were not found have been included in this volume, pages 223-241. Some duplication may have resulted because of variant spellings, but the compiler would rather err on the side of duplication than omission. The marriage bonds themselves are on file at the North Carolina Archives in Raleigh. The abstracts included here were made from microfilm copies of both the bonds and the register.

As a matter of interest the reader should note that some marriage *references* may be found in other volumes by the compiler: *Mecklenburg County, North Carolina Deed Abstracts 1763-1779* and *Mecklenburg County, North Carolina Abstracts of Early Wills 1763-1790 [1749-1790]*. Also of interest are the records of the parent county, which may be found in *Anson County, North Carolina Deed Abstracts, 1749-1766; Abstracts of Wills & Estates, 1749-1795*, also by the compiler.

BRENT H. HOLCOMB, C. A. L. S.
Columbia, South Carolina

Marriages of
MECKLENBURG COUNTY, NORTH CAROLINA

1783-1868

MECKLENBURG COUNTY, NORTH CAROLINA MARRIAGE BONDS 1783-1868

Abbet, Samuel & Catherine Winchester, 11 Dec 1802; James Brient
(Brent?), bondsman; Isaac Alexander, witness.

Abernathy, C. W. & Mary A. Kistler, 25 Sept 1856; John C. Abernathy, bondsman; W. K. Reid, C. C. C., witness. married by
J. R. Pickett, min. of Gospel, 25 Sept 1856.

Abernathy, John C. & Sarah S. Hutson, 13 May 1843; Miles B. Abernathy, bondsman.

Abernathy, John W. & Martha A. Ray, 4 June 1861; Wm S. Turner,
bondsman; W. K. Reid, C. C. C., witness. married 11 June
1861 by William W. Jones.

Abernathy, Wm D. & Isabella Cole, 27 June 1860; John Farrar,
bondsman; Wm. S. Norament, witness. married 27 June 1860
by Wm. S. Norment, J. P.

Acock, John N. & Susannah Gasky, 30 Dec 1844; John M. Muse,
bondsman; N. B. Taylor, wit.

Acock, Thomas & Ursla Huddleston, 23 Oct 1814; Matthew West,
bondsman; Isaac S. Alexander, wit.

Adams, James P. & Margaret Kernes, 20 Jan 1852; T. A. Adams,
bondsman; B. Oates, C. C. C.,wit. married 20 Jan 1852 by H.
B. Cunningham.

Adams, Joel F. & Isabella M. McKenzie, 9 Jan 1861; J. M. McKenzie,
bondsman; W. K. Reid, C. C. C., wit. married 10 Jan 1861, by
A. Sinclair, Pastor Pres. Church, Charlotte.

Adams, Lewis & Mrs. Elizebeth Sanders, 25 May 1834; Eli O. Black,
bondsman; Philemon Morris, wit.

Adams, Leroy & Miss Mary Grier, 14 July 1847; Lewis S. Williams,
bondsman.

Adams, Samuel & Mathew (Martha?) Givens, 24 Jan 1799; Samuel
Givens, bondsman; Shared Gray, wit.

1

Adkins, Jackson & Lucretia J. Wilson, 19 Dec 1847; Joseph R.
Wilson, bondsman; Saml J. Lourie, wit.

Ahrens, F. W. & L. A. Henderson, 10 Dec 1857; Wm Maxwell, bondsman; W. K. Reid, C. C. C., wit. married by R. H. Lafferty,
Pastor of the Congregation of Sugar Creek, 10 Dec 1857.

Aikens, John & Ann Aikens, 3 Sept 1798; Samuel Aikens, bondsman;
Isaac Alexander, wit.

Alderson, Armstead & Peggy Hutchison, 14 Jan 1803; John Polk,
bondsman; Isaac Alexander, wit.

Alderson, Robert & Miss Nancy Smith, 20 Feb 1804; Sterling Russell, bondsman; Isaac Alexander, wit.

Alexander, Abdon & Martha J. Sloan, 27 Aug 1859; J. S. Collins,
bondsman; W. K. Reid, C. C. C., wit. married 27 Aug 1859 by
J. B. Watt, Pastor.

Alexander, Abel A. & Angeline Davis, 13 Oct 1835; Columbus Morrison, bondsman; B. Oates, C. C. C., wit.

Alexander, Abijah F. & Esther A. Ross, 6 Sept 1851; Stanhope W.
Alexander, bondsman; James Parks, wit. married 10 Sept 1851
by Walter W. Pharr.

Alexander, Abishai & Abigail McFarlin, 23 Aug 1798; Jacob McFarlin, bondsman.

Alexander, Adlai L. & Nancy Roberson, 1 Jan 1819; James Dickson,
bondsman; Isaac S. Alexander, wit.

Alexander, Alanson & Miss Harriet C. Shelby, 17 Dec 1823; Milton
Shelby, bondsman; Isaac Alexander, wit.

Alexander, Albert & Susan Alexander, 19 Dec 1846; John Hartgrove,
bondsman; Saml J. Lourie, wit.

Alexander, Amos & Mildridge Orr, 23 Dec 1797; Isaac Campbell,
bondsman; Isaac Alexander, wit.

Alexander, Augustus & Sally Glass, 13 Feb 1839; Robt Kirkpatrick,
bondsman; B. Oates, C. C. C., wit.

Alexander, Azariah & Fanny Alexander, 16 Nov 1802; Ephraim Alexander, bondsman; Isaac Alexander, wit.

Alexander, Benjamin F. & Hannah K. Wilson, 22 July 1823; Edwin
Alexander, bondsman; Isaac S. Alexander, wit.

Alexander, C. S. & Margaret Moore, 5 Apr 1845; W. A. Todd, bondsman; N. B. Taylor, wit.

Alexander, Calvin G. & Nancy Kirk, 27 March 1833; Calvin S. Weir,
bondsman; R. S. Dawkins, wit.

Alexander, Charles W. & Margaret A. Flow, 26 Dec 1861; Egbert A.
Ross, bondsman; W. K. Reid, C. C. C., wit. married 26 Dec
1861 by R. H. Lafferty, Pastor of the congregation of Sugar Creek.

Alexander, Cornelius & Mary E. Caldwell, 24 Nov 1856; Francis N.
Query, bondsman; W. K. Reid, C. C. C., wit. married 26 Nov
1856 by R. H. Lafferty, Pastor of the congregation of Sugar Creek.

Alexander, Cyrus & Rebekah Arthurs, 20 March 1797; Josiah
Alexander, bondsman; Isaac Alexander, wit.

Alexander, Cyrus J. & Elizabeth E. Sloan, 5 Jan 1853; James L.
Sloan, bondsman; B. Oates, C. C. C., wit. married 12 Jan
1853 by Walter S. Pharr.

Alexander, Cyrus M. & Martha Cole, 23 Feb 1836; Alexander McLeod,
bondsman; B. Oates, C. C. C., wit.

Alexander, Cyrus W. & Nancy Lawing, 23 June 1835; John Lawing,
bondsman; B. Oates, C. C. C., wit.

Alexander, Dan & Susanah Shelby, 11 June 1800; Andrew Wallace,
bondsman.

Alexander, Daniel & Sarah Alexander, 14 Aug 1800; the Revd. Saml.
C. Caldwell, bondsman.

Alexander, David & Rebekah Doherty, 17 Sept 1814; Thomas Kennedy,
bondsman; Isaac Alexander, wit.

Alexander, Dionisius & Harriet C. Harris, 31 Dec 1846; Richard C.
Carson, bondsman.

Alexander, Elem E. & Mary P. Hartgrove, 2 Jan 1844; James Elins,
bondsman; N. B. Taylor, wit.

Alexander, Eli & Margaret Orr, 1 April 1806; Ambrose Alexander,
bondsman; Isaac Alexander, wit.

Alexander, Eli & Margaret Alcorn, 21 Dec 1808; Ephraim Alexander,
bondsman.

Alexander, Elias & Patsey Garrison, 7 July 1800; Samuel Garrison,
bondsman; Isaac Alexander, wit.

Alexander, Evan & Agness Moore, 2 Nov 1818; John Flow, bondsman.
Isaac Alexander, wit.

Alexander, Evan Pinkny & Elizabeth C Berryhill, 24 Feb 1824;
Milton Shelby, bondsman; Isaac S. Alexander, wit.

Alexander, Ezekiel & Patsey Robison, 8 March 1806; Ozni Alexander,
bondsman; Isaac Alexander, wit.

Alexander, Ezekiel & Rachel Price, 25 March 1811; Ephraim Alexander, bondsman; Isaac Alexander, wit.

Alexander, Ezekiel & Catherine C. Houston, 20 Dec 1836; John M.
Alexander, bondsman; B. Oates, C. C. C.,wit.

Alexander, Francis & Jane McCorkle, 5 Nov 1815; William Allison,
bondsman.

Alexander, G. W. & Sarah S. Jetton, 24 Feb 1855; John N. Blythe,
bondsman; R. F. Blythe, J. P., wit. married 28 Feb 1855 by
Walter W. Pharr.

Alexander, George W. & Wilmuth A. Christenbury, 27 March 1857;
E. W. Whitlow, bondsman, W. K. Reid, C. C. C., wit. married
31 March 1857 by R. L. D. Armon, J. P.

3

Alexander, Ira & Miss Dorcus Alexander, 11 Dec 1842; N. S. Alexander, bondsman; C. T. Alexander, wit.

Alexander, Isaac F. & Lydia Campbell, 1 Sept 1830; William Wynens, bondsman.

Alexander, Isaac W. & Caroline Morrison, 8 Aug 1845; David W. Miller, bondsman.

Alexander, James & Hanah Clark, 16 Oct 1798; Isaac Alexander, bondsman; Isaac Alexander, wit.

Alexander, James & Ann Alexander, 7 July 1802; Thomas Alexander, bondsman; Ruth Alexander, wit.

Alexander, James & Martha Rogers, 14 Nov 1806; Thomas Kennedy, bondsman.

Alexander, James & Isabella Maxwell, 14 Jan 1831; William Maxwell, bondsman; B. Oates, D. C.

Alexander, James & Elizabeth Stringfellow, 26 May 1834; West Ensey, bondsman.

Alexander, James A. & Margret C. Alexander, 29 June 1816; Absalom Alexander, bondsman.

Alexander, James C. & Catharine Thomason, 24 Feb 1831; Josephus Alexander, bondsman.

Alexander, James F. & Martha McGinnis, 16 May 1859; William W. Phelan, bondsman; W. K. Reid, C. C. C., wit. married 17 May 1859 by E. F. Rockwell, V. D. M.

Alexander, James H. & M. E. Beaty, 14 May 1862; James H. Williams, bondsman; W. K. Reid, C. C. C.,wit. married 27 May 1862 by S. E. Pharr, V. D. M.

Alexander, James L. & Rosanah Blanchard, 23 Aug 1842; George Acock, bondsman.

Alexander, James L. & Catharine E. McGee, 9 Dec 1854; John S. Maxwell, bondsman; W. K. Reid, C. C. C., wit. married 14 Dec 1854 by Thomas M. Farrow, V. D. M.

Alexander, James M. & Mary L. Wilson, 9 July 1844; David Allen, bondsman; N. B. Taylor, wit.

Alexander, James N. & Mary M. Caldwell, 2 March 1858; M. M. Tyer, bondsman; W. K. Reid, C. C. C., wit. married 4 March 1854 by Danl. A. Penick.

Alexander, James P. & Sarah Bently, 18 Jan 1830; John W. Potts, bondsman; Richd S. Dinkins, wit.

Alexander, James R. & Harriet Baker, 8 Dec 1836; Samuel P. Alexander, bondsman.

Alexander, James S. & Mary Allen, 16 Feb 1836; Moses Alexander, bondsman.

Alexander, James Scott & Matilda McLean, 14 Dec 1814; John A. McLain, bondsman. Isaac Alexander, wit. (not on microfilm)

Alexander, Jas. W. & Margaret L. Reid, 17 Dec 1850; John Walker, bondsman.

Alexander, Joel B. & Cynthia Morrison, 16 Aug 1815; Carns H. Henderson, bondsman.

Alexander, John & Sarah Shelby, 15 Aug 1798; Daniel Alexander, bondsman.

Alexander, John G. & Elizabeth Lemmond, 3 April 1811; Ezel. Robison, bondsman.

Alexander, John M. & Jane F. Harris, 21 Jan 1817; James Wilson, bondsman; Isaac Alexander, wit.

Alexander, John M. & Cynthia M. Todd, 27 Dec 1854; Benjamin P. Alexander, bondsman; W. K. Reid, wit. married 28 Dec 1854, by A. B. Cunningham.

Alexander, John O. & Jane E. Lee, 17 Feb 1857; A. W. Blair, bondsman; John Walker, wit. married 17 Feb 1857, by J. M. Walker, min.

Alexander, John Ramsey & Janet Henderson, 14 Dec 1823; David A. Caldwell, bondsman.

Alexander, John S. & Susan Alexander, 18 Oct 1830; Hezekiah J. Alexander, bondsman; E. Elms, wit.

Alexander, Leander D. & Miss Margaret Parks, 31 July 1843; Rufus L. Alexander, bondsman.

Alexander, Lawson, & Jenny Berry Elliott, 6 May 1828; George Elliott, bondsman; Isaac S. Alexander, wit.

Alexander, Marcus & Malinda McClure, 21 Aug 1811; Richard McRee, bondsman; Isaac Alexander, wit.

Alexander, Marcus, & Martha Gilmor, 13 April 1822; Elam Alexander, bondsman; Isaac Alexander, wit.

Alexander, Marcus F. & Mary Johnston, 30 Jan 1844; Wm Hutchison, bondsman; N. B. Taylor, wit.

Alexander, Mathew, & Jenny Martin, 27 Sept 1810; Thomas Kennedy, bondsman; Isaac Alexander, wit.

Alexander, Mathew & Miss Margt. McKorkl, 5 Oct 1824; Aron Alexander Kenady, bondsman; K. D. Dinkins(?), wit.

Alexander, Matthew A. & Abbey M. Barnett, 15 Dec 1860; A. A. Kanady, bondsman; P. S. Whisnant, wit. married 20 Dec 1860 by R. H. Lafferty, Pastor of the congregation of Sugar creek.

Alexander, Moses & Elizabeth Orr, 28 Jan 1800; Nathan Orr Junr., bondsman.

Alexander, Moses & Margaret H. Allen, 14 Dec 1836; Robert Query, bondsman.

Alexander, Moses Mc. & Miss Margaret M. Brales, 24 July 1830; Wm. C. Corum, bondsman.

Alexander, Moses W. & Margaret M. Alexander, 6 Dec 1830; Robert F. Wilson, bondsman.

Alexander, Nathaniel & Caroline Alexander, 27 Oct 1823; Lawson H. Alexander, bondsman; Thomas J. Polk, wit.

Alexander, Ozwold & Martha Robison, 16 April 1806; Ezekiel Robison, bondsman.

Alexander, Ozwold & Hannah Park, 20 March 1809; John Park Junr., bondsman; Isaac Alexander, wit.

Alexander, Ozwold, & Mary Moore, 17 Oct 1826; Isaac Campbell, bondsman.

Alexander, R. B. & Cornelia A. Wilson; W. K. Reid, C. C. C., wit. married 19 Sept 1860, by S. C. Pharr, V. D. M. (bond missing, license dated 30 Aug 1860)

Alexander, Robert D. & Abigail B. Caldwell, 9 Feb 1829; Tho. B. Smart, bondsman.

Alexander, Rufus L. & Melissa D. Montgomery, 22 May 1844; Thomas M. Alexander, bondsman; N. B. Taylor, wit.

Alexander, S. C. & Mary H. Brown, 13 May 1857; R. D. Alexander, bondsman. married 21 May 1857 by Drury Lacy at Davidson College.

Alexander, Sample & Betsy M'Craken, 21 March 1809; Joseph Blackwood, bondsman; M. M'Linzy, wit.

Alexander, Saml. C. & Nannie R. Price, 20 March 1862; R. W. McDowell, bondsman; W. K. Reid, C. C. C., wit. married 25 March 1862 by R. Z. Johnston.

Alexander, Silas & Nancy Brown, 8 May 1846; Thomas H. Brown(?), bondsman; B. Oates, C. C. C., wit.

Alexander, Sinai & Miss Dorcus Hartgrove, 6 Jan 1843; Wm Rives, bondsman; C. T. Alexander, C. C. C., wit.

Alexander, Sinai & Clementina Hartgrove, 14 April 1853; W. W. Morrow, bondsman; married 14 April 1853 by J. W. Morrow.

Alexander, Stanhope W. & Dorcas H. Hunter, 24 Sept 1851; Silus(?) C. Hunter, bondsman; B. Oates, C. C. C., wit.

Alexander, Stephen & Isabella Shelby, 22 Nov 1797; William Alexander Junr., bondsman

Alexander, Stephen & Martha Montgomery, 8 Sept 1819; James C. Montgomery, bondsman; Isaac Alexander, wit.

Alexander, Thos. Mc. & Nancy Jeteen, 28 Jan 1845; K. F. Blythe, bondsman.

Alexander, Thomas R. & Adline J. Howell, 29 June 1861; John C. Fesperman, bondsman; W. W. Grier, wit. married 30 June 1861 by Wm. W. Pharr, minister.

Alexander, Ulysses & Jane Hunter Bath, 12 Jan 1831; Hezekiah J. Alexander, bondsman; E. Elum, wit.

Alexander, Ulysses & Milly A. Alexander, 6 June 1838; Elim Robison, bondsman; B. Oates, C. C. C.,wit.

Alexander, W. J. & Sarah A. Reid, 21 Feb 1860; Hugh Boyce, bondsman; W. K. Reid, C. C. C., wit. married 22 Feb 1860, by Lorenzo Hunter, J. P.

Alexander, William & Permelia Ferguson, 4 Jan 1844; Matthew Neagle, bondsman; N. B. Taylor, wit.

Alexander, William A. & Margaret E. Hayes, 15 Oct 1835; Samuel P. Alexander, bondsman.

Alexander, William Julias & Elvira Catherine Wilson, 2 Dec 1824; Dr. Saml Henderson,bondsman; Isaac S. Alexander, wit.

Alexander, William L. & Nancy Gray, 7 March 1835; Rufus L. Alexander, bondsman; B. Oates, wit.

Alexander, William L. D. & Catharine J. G. Johnston, 14 April 1859; Wm Caldwell, bondsman; W. K. Reid, C. C. C., wit. married 21 April 1859 by Walter S. Pharr.

Alexander, William N. & Sarah L. White, 29 Oct 1855; Thomas A. Kirkpatrick, bondsman; W. K. Reid, C. C. C., wit. married 29 Oct 1855 by J. Walker, J. P.

Alexander, William P. & Susan P. Griffith, 3 Nov 1857; John Phelan, bondsman; W. K. Reid, C. C. C., wit. married 3 Nov 1857 by F. M. Ross, J. P.

Alexander, William S. & Isabella L. Alexander, 26 Dec 1842; Amos M. Alexander, bondsman; Jas Johnston, J. P., wit.

Alexander, Wm. T. (F?) and Margaret Cochran, 31 July 1846; Wm. F. Baker, bondsman; Wm W. Dearmon, wit.

Alexander, Zadock & Miss Fenny Darnell, 4 March 1820(?); Joseph Smith, bondsman.

Algea, Robert & Jane Hayse, 5 Jan 1811; Hugh B. Hayes, bondsman.

Allen, Ambrose & Nancy Sarah Cooper, 28 Oct 1854; John A. Cooper, bondsman; W. K. Reid, C. C. C., wit. married 30 Oct 1854 by J. B. Wall, V. D. M.

Allen, David and Margarett L. Weir, 10 Jan 1826; Francis Ross, bondsman; Isaac S. Alexander, wit.

Allen, John & Dorcas M. Cochran, 17 Dec 1836; William Alexander, bondsman; B. Oates, C. C. C., wit.

Allen, John N. & Nancy Mahon, 1 Nov 1836; Leroy Springs,bondsman. B. Oates, C. C. C., wit.

Allen, Josiah & Elizebeth Baker, 18 May 1818; Austin Cook, bondsman; Isaac S. Alexander, wit.

Allen, Robert & Jenny Green, 13 Feb 1806; James Cook, bondsman. Isaac Alexander, wit.

Allen, Robert M. & Margaret M. Cook, 23 Feb 1836; William Cooper, bondsman.

Allen, Samuel & Polly Matthews, 30 Jan 1821; John Allen, bondsman;
Isaac Alexander, wit.

Allen, Thomas & Ketherine Pitman, 31 March 1810(?); Joseph Blackwood, bondsman.

Allen, William & Charlotte Robinson, 25 Sept 1834; Alexander
Cooper, bondsman; B. Oates, C. C. C., wit.

Allin, Benjn. & Ann Lawing, 14 Jan 1797; George Thomson, bondsman.

Allison, Henry & Elizabeth Clark, 10 Sept 1834; Archibald Clark,
bondsman.

Allison, Isaac A. & Mary N. Robison, 10 Dec 1855; Samuel F. Houston,
bondsman; W. K. Reid, C. C. C., wit. married 13 Dec 1855 by
R. H. Lafferty, Pastor of the congregation of Sugar Creek.

Allison, John & Eleanor Buchanan, 17 July 1799; Michael Stinson,
bondsman; Isaac Alexander, wit.

Allison, John & Nancy M. Lemons, 28 Jan 1822; Thos. Hutchison,
bondsman.

Allison, Moses G. & Mary E. Riglar, 20 Dec 1853; James S. Berryhill, bondsman. married 22 Dec 1853 by John A. Mood, Pastor
of the M. E. Church, Charlotte, N. C.

Allison, Thomas C. & Mary A. Irwin, 11 June 1859; Robt Shaw,
bondsman; W. K. Reid, C. C. C.,wit. married 12 June 1859 by
Alex. Phillippe.

Allison, William & Susan R. Alexander, 2 Nov 1814; Isaac S. Alexander, bondsman.

Anderson, J. Monroe & Margaret A. Neal, 11 Aug 1842; Saml. W.
Neal, bondsman.

Anderson, John & Sarah Irwin, 14 Sept 1811; Hugh McDowell, bondsman.
Isaac Alexander, wit.

Anderson, William W. & Jane Capps, 19 April 1841; Martin Icehour,
bondsman.

Andrew,William & Barba. Caldwell, 16 April 1792; Robert Caldwell,
bondsman; Isaac Alexander, wit.

Andrews, E. H. & Sarah A. Bolton, 16 Sept 1845; M. W. Alexander,
bondsman; Wm. F. Alexander, wit.

Andrews, Will & Peggy Houston, 20 March 1821; Arthur Stafford,
bondsman; Isaac Alexander, wit.

Archer, Wilson & Violet Worsham, 29 Oct 1853; Alfred Worsham,
bondsman; W. K. Reid, C. C. C.,wit. married 29 Oct 1853 by
Walter S. Pharr.

Armour, Samuel J. & Elizabeth E. Dewese, 21 Jan 1843; Hugh Haig-
wood, bondsman; Jas Johnston, J. P., wit.

Armstrong, John & Agness Beaty, 7 Sept 1807; William Beaty, bondsman.
Michl. M'Cleary, wit.

Arnold, George H. & Susanna Engles, 5 Aug 1812; Alexander Washim, bondsman.

Arnold, John & Margaret Greer, 14 March 1835; William N. Orr, bondsman; B. Oates, wit.

Arnold, Robert & Eliza Kerr, 13 Feb 1832; James Matthews, bondsman.

Ashley, James & Lucretia Adkins, 13 May 1851; Hugh Harris, bondsman. married 3 July 1851 by John H. Grier, J. P.

Atchison, Thomas & Jane Gainer ,17 April 1793; Aaron Griffith, bondsman.

Atchison, William & Dury Byrom, 3 May 1823; Jacob Baker, bondsman. Isaac S. Alexander, wit.

Atkins, Benjamin & Martha Buchannan, 27 May 1844; Matthew Miller, bondsman; N. B. Taylor, wit.

Austin, Jonathan & Pamelia Star, 18 Dec 1809; Allen Orr, bondsman.

Auten, Isaac & Jemima P. Peoples, 2 Jan 1834; William C. Peoples, bondsman.

Auten, John W. & Isabella McLeary, 18 May 1847; Abner S. Hunter, bondsman; B. Oates, C. C. C., wit. married 19 May 1847 by Wm Davidson.

Auten, Josiah & Margt. Berryhill, 20 Feb 1800; Samuel Berryhill, bondsman; Isaac Alexander, wit.

Auten, Will. M. & Louisa Hutchison, 26 Dec 1860; Thaddeus C. McGathey, bondsman; W. K. Reid, C. C. C. wit. married 27 Dec 1860 by J. S. Means, J. P.

Auton, Isaac W. & Margaret McRee, 31 Aug 1857; Joseph T. Love, bondsman; W. K. Reid, C. C. C., wit. married 1 Sept 1857 by G. L. Campbell, J. P.

Auton, John & Betsey Barnhill, 18 Feb 1819; Peter Auten, bondsman. Isaac Alexander, wit.

Auton, Samuel & Eliza J. Jamison, 22 Oct 1859; Robert F. Auton, bondsman; W. K. Reid, C. C. C., wit. married 25 Oct 1859 by G. L. Campbell, J. P.

Auton, Thomas J. & Sarah Watts, 1 April 1862; David Ledwell, bondsman; W. W. Grier, wit. married 3 April 1862 by Walter S. Pharr.

Badger, Samuel J. W. & Miss Jane V. C. Coldins, 25 March 1844; David Rudisill, bondsman; Jas Johnston, J. P. wit.

Baer, Griffith & Susannah Todd, 22 May 1819; Adam Todd, bondsman. Isaac Alexander, wit.

Baget, Irvin & Judy Rodden, 11 June 1818; Jethro Wilson, bondsman. Rebecca C. Alexander, wit.

Bailes, E. M. & Miss H. E. A. Fox, 7 Feb 1865; D. G. Maxwell, bondsman; married 7 Feb 1865 by T. W. Dewey, J. P.

Bailey, Hugh & Jane Todd, 11 April 1807; Joseph Todd, bondsman; Isaac Alexander, wit.

Bailey, J(ames) R. & Nancy·C. Partler, 2 Jan 1842; John A. Bollinger, bondsman.

Bailey, John F. & Elizabeth J. Watts, 17 June 1865; William W. E. Berryhill, bondsman; W. W. Grier, wit.

Bailey, Wm. M. & Elen M. Alexander, 13 Dec 1850; John L. Watson, bondsman; B. Oates, C. C. C., wit.

Bain, David & Rachel G. Robison, 4 April 1841; Levi Saunders, bondsman; B. Oates, wit.

Bain, James N. & Elisabeth B. Doherty, 29 March 1825; Jonathan Dewese, bondsman; J. Doherty, wit.

Bain, John & Polly Alexander, 3 June 1819; Josiah M. Alexander, bondsman; Jno. McLane, wit.

Bain, Samuel & Jane Hood, 20 Jan 1820(?); John Irwin, bondsman. Isaac Alexander, wit.

Baker, Aron & Jean Davis, 23 Feb 1805; Robert Davis, bondsman; Shared Gray, wit.

Baker, Abel & Susannah Dow, 4 Jan 1816; Daniel Harrison, bondsman.

Baker, Charles M. & Cynthia Hanks, 28 June 1836; William Blanchard, bondsman; B. Oates, C. C. C.,wit.

Baker, Elijah & Mary Wiley, 15 Nov 1798; James Wiley, bondsman. Isaac Alexander, wit.

Baker, Elijah Junr. & Jane C. Baker, 15 Jan 1838; Elijah Baker Senr., bondsman; B. Oates, C. C. C., wit.

Baker, G. F. & Mary Cook, 28 Nov 1860; C. L. Stanford, bondsman; P. S. Whisnant, wit. married 29 Nov 1860 by Jos. C. Nicholson.

Baker, George and Elizabeth Cook, 28 July 1817; Powel Cook, bondsman; Chas T. Alexander, wit.

Baker, Griffith--see Baer, Griffith

Baker, Isaac & Elizabeth Hooks, 15 Dec 1830; Abraham Reed, bondsman; B. Oates, D. C., wit.

Baker, Jacob, & Hannah Pelt, 21 Dec 1825; Joseph B. McDonald, bondsman; Richd Gillespie, wit.

Baker, Jacob, & Eveline Duese, 10 Jan 1832; John Bain, bondsman; B. Oates, D. C., wit.

Baker, James C. & Laura Beaty, 21 May 1861; J. B. Phillips, bondsman; W. K. Reid, wit. married 21 May 1861 by C. Overman, J. P.

Baker, James W. & Lavina Richmond, 20 May 1835; B. Oates, C. C. C., wit.

Baker, Jeptha & Rebecca R. Henderson, 18 Dec 1860; James Cunningham, bondsman, W. K. Reid, wit.

Baker, Jepthah & Eliz. Pitman, 11 March 1797; Matthew Pitman, bondsman; Isaac Alexander, wit.

Baker, Jesse & Mary Wallace, 27 Aug 1851; William Johns(t)on, bondsman; James Parks, wit. married 28 Aug 1851 by J. Walker, J. P.

Baker, Jonathan & Famson Redden, 16 Sept 1801; Jonathan Griffith, bondsman.

Baker, Michael & Rachel Griffith, 13 May 1812; John Byram, bondsman; Isaac Alexander, C. M. C.,wit.

Baker, Samuel & Rebekah Davis, 16 Dec 1804; James Davis, bondsman.

Baker, William H. & Martha A. Stephens, 2 Feb 1842; Charles M. Baker, bondsman.

Baker, William L. & Isabella Kerr, 2 May 1860; Haney F. Russell, bondsman; W. K. Reid, C. C. C., wit. married 3 May 1860 by John Walker, J. P.

Baldwin, Allen & Elizabeth Henderson, 3 June 1818; William E. McKee, bondsman; Isaac Alexander, wit.

Ballard, James & Mary Briggle, 15 Sept 1795; James Orr, bondsman. Isaac Alexander, wit.

Ballard, Jesse & Nancy Boyd, 27 Dec 1806; Green Fields, bondsman. Isaac Alexander, wit.

Ballard, John H. & Mary Ann Knowles, 3 Dec 1855; James A. Campbell, bondsman; W. K. Reid, C. C. C., wit.

Ballard, William H. & Margaret A. Reid, 1 April 1861; William E. Sizer, bondsman; W. K. Reid , C. C. C.,wit. married 2 April 1861 by Jos. C. Nicholson, J. P.

Banker, J. L. & Mary C. Erwin, 7 Oct 1844; James Mason, bondsman. C. S. Alexander, wit.

Banker, Jacob L. & Mary E. Cook, 8 Dec 1865; J. A. Allison, bondsman; Wm Maxwell, C. C. C., wit. married 30(?) Dec 1865 by Jno F. Butt.

Banker, John & _____ Goforth, 7 Jan 1813; Daniel Boyd, bondsman; Ruthy Alexander, wit.

Barham, Henry W. & Elisabeth Stephens, 6 May 1851; Jesse E. Hannon, bondsman; Saml A.Davis, J. P., wit.

Barham, Wm. A. & Martha E. Buchanon, 22 Sept 1843; C. E. Moss, bondsman.

Barker, Baily & Charity Phifer, 7 Sept 1839; Andrew Starnes, bondsman; B. Oates, wit.

Barker, Thomas & Margret Reden, 22 Nov 1846; Randle Reden, bondsman; D. Wentz, J. P., wit.

Barnes, William & Keziah Cunningham, 17 Nov 1819; Jacob Cunningham, bondsman.

Barnet , Amos & Catherine Porter, 25 Dec 1819; Thomas L. Hutchison, bondsman; Isaac S. Alexander, wit.

Barnet , John & Jane Gaston, 22 July 1795; Robert Barnett, bondsman; Isaac Alexander, wit.

Barnet , Moses & Frances Robeson, 26 Aug 1794; John Robison, bondsman

Barnet , Robert & Jennet Todd, 7 May 1789; Robert Robeson, bondsman.

Barnet , Vincent & Lucinda Potts, 6 Feb 1828; David T. Thomason, bondsman; Isaac Alexander, wit.

Barnet , Wm. G. & Margaret M. Duese, 17 Jan 1846; Joseph R. Ewart, bondsman; S. J. Lourie, wit.

Barnett, A. G. & Miss Martha McGahey, 28 Oct 1865; J. Lee Barnett, bondsman; Wm. Maxwell, wit. married 2 Nov 1865 by Walter S. Pharr.

Barnett, D. F. & Lucinda Potts, 12 Dec 1863; J. J. Price, bondsman; married 13 Dec 1863 by S. C. Alexander.

Barnett, D. W. & Mary E. Thomasson, 15 Sept 1859; John L. Parks, bondsman; W. K. Reid, C. C. C., wit. married 22 Sept 1859 by A. Ranson.

Barnett, David E. & Rebeckah Montgomery, 7 Feb 1827; James McClure, bondsman.

Barnett, Hugh M. & Patsey Johnston, 4 Jan 1819; Robert P. Johnston, bondsman; Isaac Alexander, wit.

Barnett, James G. & Deborah Montgomery, 24 Jan 1827; William Luckey, bondsman; Pearsall(?) Thompson, wit.

Barnett, John W. & Mary A. Lee, 17 Nov 1852; T. B. Withers, bondsman; James Parks, wit. married 18 Nov 1852 by S. C. Pharr.

Barnett, Marcus & Sinthey Frasure, 27 March 1826; Marshall R. McKoy, bondsman; Richd. Gillespie, wit.

Barnett, Robert C. & Margret Weeks, 27 Nov 1827; John N. Davis, bondsman; Pearsall Thompson, wit.

Barnett, Robert F. & Mary T. Sample, 9 Dec 1828; Hezekiah Alexander, bondsman; Tho. B. Small, wit.

Barnett, Thomas G. & Margret Brown, 12 Dec 1826; Ransom Gray, bondsman; Pearsall Thompson, wit.

Barnett, Thomas G. & Elizebeth Ewart, 15 Dec 1838; James Wallace, bondsman; Hugh M'Aulay, wit.

Barnett, William & Jansy Davis, 24 Oct 1812; Joseph Douglass, bondsman; Isaac Alexander, wit.

Barnhardt, Daniel C. & Mary E. Berryhill, 26 Feb 1852; Caleb A. Suther, bondsman; B. Oates, C. C. C., wit. married 26 Feb 1852 by A. G. Stacy, Pastor of the M. E. Church, South, Charlotte, N. C.

Barnhill, John & Nancy Jimmeson, 28 Feb 1816; Mathew Wallace, bondsman; Philemon Morris, wit.

12

Barnhill, Jno H. & Mary Jamison, 20 Aug 1840; Robt I. Summerville, bondsman.

Barnhill, Robert & Jane Auton, 24 Feb 1824; Samuel Martin, bondsman; Isaac Alexander, wit.

Barnhill, Robert W. & Sarah Russel, 20 Nov 1851; John H. Barnhill, bondsman; David D. Oates, wit. married 20 Nov 1851 by William Reid, J. P.

Barnhill, Thomas & Mary Phillipps, 18 Dec 1849; Thomas Harrison, bondsman; Saml. Lowrie, wit.

Barnhill, William & Elizabeth Conner, 31 Oct 1810; John Barnett, bondsman; Isaac Alexander, wit.

Barnwell, Tom & Ann Hudson, 26 Aug 1865; Lonzo Davidson, bondsman. married 26 Aug 1865 by Rev. Wm. H. Pitts, elder.

Barnycastle, John & Sarah Atkinson, 2 Aug 1822; John Emerson, bondsman; K. S. Dinkins, wit.

Barr, John C. & Eliza Orr, 13 Feb 1819; John Wilson, bondsman; Isaac Alexander, wit.

Barr, John C. & Martha C. Hadley, 9 Nov 1844; Nathan H. Orr, bondsman.

Barringer, Caleb A. & Mary G. L. Caldwell, 16 Feb 1842; Daniel N. Caldwell, bondsman.

Barry, Andrew & Jemima Sample, 15 March 1796; James Sample, bondsman.

Barry, William C. & Araminta S. Sampel, 28 Dec 1831; William Carruthers, bondsman; B. Oates, D. C., wit.

Bartaine, Richard & Sarah Strain, 2 June 1801; John Johnston, bondsman; Jno Hoey, Hugh Coffey, wit.

Bartlett, James & M. C. Griffith, 15 Oct 1860; James H. Henderson, bondsman; W. K. Reid, C. C. C., wit. 16 Oct 1860, married by Charles Overman, J. P.

Battenbury, William & Mary A. Osborne, 28 July 1859; Charles Friedman, bondsman; W. K. Reid, C. C. C., wit. married 8 Sept 1859 by G. N. Houston(?), J. P.

Baxter, Daniel & Isabella Stewart, 10 Feb 1807; William Stewart, bondsman.

Beain, Daniel & Margaret _____, 24 Oct 1788; Peter Huie, bondsman.

Beal, Benjamin & Miss Elen Blythe, 11 July 1865; A. McCoy, bondsman. married 26 July 1865 by Samuel C. Pharr.

Beall, B. L. & Jane E. Alexander, 19 July 1862; E. Nye Hutchison, bondsman. married 29 July 1862 by R. Z. Johnston.

Bean, Daniel & Sarah Ross, 29 Dec 1789; William Ross, bondsman.

Bean, Hugh & Elizabeth Hood, 3 Nov 1809; John Hood, bondsman; Isaac Alexander, wit.

Bean, John & Elizabeth Wilson, 7 March 1797; James Wilson, bondsman; Isaac Alexander, wit.

Bean, William & Mary McCracken, 12 Sept 1791; George McCracken,
bondsman; Isaac Alexander, wit.

Bear, John & Sarah Howel; J. A. Segraves, bondsman; 1 Dec 1865;
R. M. White, wit. married 1 Dec 1865 by Jno F. Butt.

Beard, Joseph & Rebecca C. Caldwell, 20 Dec 1859; John D. Barnett,
bondsman; W. K. Reid, C. C. C., wit. married 22 Dec 1859 by
A. Ranson.

Beard, Robert & Miss Mary Knox, 15 Feb 1838; Alexander H. Terrence,
bondsman; James Johnston, wit.

Beard, William L. & Francis Brown, 26 March 1834; Robert Beard,
bondsman.

Beatey,Francis M. & Ann Grier, 2 Feb 1843; W. W. Elms, bondsman.

Beatey,Henry Leny & Margaret E. Smith, 6 Oct 1857; Anderson Beaty,
William Smith, bondsmen; W. K. Reid, C. C. C., wit. married
6 Oct 1857 by Wm. S. Norment, J. P.

Beatey,James & Esther Owin, 25 Aug 1803; William Owens, bondsman.

Beatey,John & Esther Vealn, 24 Jan 1817; Jonathan Beaty, bondsman;
Isaac Alexander, wit.

Beatey,John & Isabella Clark, 12 April 1837; B. Oates, bondsman.

Beatey,William & Martha Dunn, 6 Oct 1807; Moses Green, bondsman;
Michl. McLeary, wit.

Beatey,Wm. & Isabell McCorkl, 21 April 1791; Thomas McCorkle,
bondsman; James Meek, wit.

Beaty, A. M. & Sarah Thomas, 15 Jan 1864; T. J. Walker, bondsman;
married 15 Jan 1864 by G. C. Cathey, J. P.

Beaty, Andrew & Clarissa Robison, 25 April 1864; John W. Conly,
bondsman; C. S. Alexander, wit.

Beaty, Ezekiel, & Lily Hipp, 9 June 1847; Wm Walls, bondsman;
Saml G. Lourie, wit.

Beaty, Francis & Jane Waddell, 3 Jan 1806; Joel McCorkle, bondsman.
Isaac Alexander, wit.

Beaty, James & Ellen Lintele, 14 Nov 1831; David Cowan, bondsman;
B. Oates, D. C., wit.

Beaty, James M. & Christina Sherman, 3 June 1852; William W. Quinn,
bondsman; B. Oates, C. C. C., wit. married 3 June 1852 by
Alexr. Springs, J. P.

Beaty, John & Martha Hill, _____ 179_; W. A. Heneboy, bondsman.

Beaty, John & Polly Wilson, 20 May 1806; Walter Faires, bondsman.
Isaac Alexander, wit.

Beaty, John & Sarah Cook, 17 Feb 1849; Edward H. Moss, bondsman.
B. Oates, C. C. C., wit.

Beaty, John D. & Mary J. Clark, 26 Dec 1838; William Frew, bondsman; B. Oates, C. C. C., wit.

Beaty, Joseph & Susanah McKee, 14 Aug 1798; Thomas McKee, bondsman.

Beaty, Lawson & Mary C. McLure, 20 Nov 1833; George L. McGinn, bondsman.

Beaty, Moses & Martha Campbell, 4 Nov 1794; Joseph Haynes, bondsman; Isaac Alexander, wit.

Beaty, Moses & Nancy Weathers, 1 Dec 1800; Elijah Davis, bondsman.

Beaty, Nathan & Isabella Beaty, 10 Dec 1801; James Wilson, bondsman.

Beaty, Robert M. & Mary Jamison, 7 Nov 1836; Thomas Jamison, bondsman; B. Oates, C. C. C., wit.

Beaty, Samuel W. & Elizabeth Johnston, 17 Dec 1823; Thomas T. Johnston, bondsman.

Beaty, Smith & Nancy Caroline Beaty, 23 March 1850; John W. Beaty, bondsman; B. Oates, C. C. C., wit.

Beaty, William & Margarett Byram, 16 March 1825; John McCord, bondsman; Isaac S. Alexander, wit.

Beaty, William & Caroline Rea, 1 April 1841; Robert Franklin Clark, bondsman.

Beaty, William & Miss Eliza McGee, 22 Nov 1852; P. A. Rankin, bondsman; B. Oates, C. C. C., wit.

Beaty, William P. & Cynthia Armstrong, 25 July 1839; James M'Clure, bondsman.

Beaver, H. N. & Margaret E. Flow, 8 Feb 1859, J. F. Stansill, bondsman; John Phelan, wit. married 17 Feb 1859 by Danl. A. Penick, Sen.

Beaver, John C. M. & Margaret E. White, 14 Jan 1862; M. W. Robinson, bondsman; John Phelan, wit. married 16 Jan 1862 by H. N. Pharr, pastor.

Beaver, Wm. & Margaret Young, 25 July 1843; John C. Barr, bondsman.

Bechter & A. M. Hill, 14 Feb 1866; A. Bethune, bondsman.

Becket, James & Elisebeth Orsburn, 30 Jan 1794; Samuel Becket, bondsman; Shared Gray, wit.

Becket, Samuel & Susana Osburn, 27 July 1801; John Osburn, bondsman; Andw. Walker, J. P., wit.

Belk, Samson D. & Mary Richardson, 3 Dec 1834; James P. Belk, bondsman; S. V. Simons, wit.

Bell, John & Rachel Price, 18 Dec 1792; Robert Price, bondsman.

Bell, John & Esther Davis, 12 Feb 1798; William Flin, bondsman; Isaac Alexander, wit.

Bell, John & Allice Watson, 26 April 1865; George W. Harper, bondsman.

Bell, Joseph C. & R. B. Ewart, 12 Feb 1859; R. K. Ewart, bondsman;
W. K. Reid, C. C. C., wit. 15 Feb 1859, married by Walter S.
Pharr.

Bell, Robert & Dolly Dilyard, 26 April 1808; Jacob Julien, bondsman; Isaac Alexander, wit.

Bell, Robert C. & Mary J. Ardry, 22 Aug 1854; J. M. Hutchison,
bondsman; B. Oates, wit. married 22 Aug 1854, by Rev. R. F.
Taylor.

Bell, Samuel & Miss E. A. Beard, 14 Nov 1865; M. W. Bell, bondsman.
married 28 Nov 1865 by J. R. Gillespie, J. P.

Benerman, Wm. & Elizabeth Davis, 17 Nov 1794; Benjamin Wilson,
bondsman; Isaac Alexander, wit.

Benett, Littleton, & Sarah Craton(?), 1 Jan 1808; Thomas Cole,
bondsman; Ruth Alexander, wit.

Benfield, H. S. & Jane Rice, 18 Oct 1860; Robert Kennady, bondsman;
W. W. Grier, wit. married 18 Oct 1860 by C. Overman, J. P.

Benfield, John R. & Margt C. Earnhardt, 19 Dec 1865; Wm. A. Rice,
bondsman. married 20 Dec 1865 by J. G. McLaughlin.

Benfil, Edney & Margaret Tarlton, 8 April 1859; Robert J. Sloan,
Bondsman; Jno Phelan, wit. married 14 April 1859, B. H.
Garrison, J. P.

Bennet, Abraham, & Hannah Williams, 24 Dec 1805; John Smith, bondsman.

Bennett, Perry & Ann Gilbert, 20 Jan 1854; John J. Benedict,
bondsman; W. K. Reid, C. C. C., wit. married 20 Jan 1854 by
H. M. Ross, J. P.

Benson, John Kerr & Jenney Finch, 21 Oct 1796; John Duckworth
Junr., bondsman; Jas. Conner, wit.

Benton, John & Mary Pucket, 15 March 1825; Jeby Cashon, bondsman;
J. Doherty, wit.

Benton, John & Patsey Roach, 8 May 1827; Robert Morrow, bondsman;
A. B. Jetton, wit.

Berry, Matthew (free) & Celia Reid (free), 23 Jan 1861; Robert
Berry (free), bondsman; W. K. Reid, C. C. C., wit. married
24 Jan 1861 by Wm. S. Norment, J. P.

Berry, Robert (free), & Rebecca Woodward (free), 20 Jan 1859;
Wm. T. Alexander, bondsman; W. K. Reid, C. C. C., wit. married
20 Jan 1859 by C. O. Sermon, J. P.

Berryhill, Alexander & Sarah C. Wiley, 16 July 1863; W. W. Grier,
bondsman.

Berryhill, Allison & Peggy Ann Berryhill, 11 Jan 1820; Samuel
Berryhill, bondsman.

Berryhill, Andrew & Hannah J. Love, 12 Jan 1858; K. W. Berryhill,
bondsman; W. K. Reid, C. C. C., wit. married 14 Jan 1858,
by Jos. C. Nicholson, J. P.

Berryhill, Andrew A. & Matilda Redden, 17 Dec 1833; Adam H.
Todd, bondsman; B. Oates, C. C. C., wit.

Berryhill, David F. & Elizebeth Cathcart, 8 April 1816; Arthur
Jameson, bondsman; Isaac Alexander, wit.

Berryhill, David W. A. & Minton H. Rawdon, 26 Sept 1839; John
Reed, bondsman; J. B. Kerr, wit.

Berryhill, James McRee & Elizabeth Quirey, 2 Aug 1802; Moses Swann,
bondsman; Isaac Alexander, wit.

Berryhill, James S. & Elizabeth J. Warwick, 21 Feb 1864; M. H.
Shuford, bondsman. married 22 March 1866 by R. Z. Johnston.

Berryhill, John & Catherine S. Reed, 30 March 1836; Joseph C.
Nicholson, bondsman; B. Oates, wit.

Berryhill, Joseph J. & Harriet Todd, 15 June 1825; A. Sing,
bondsman; J. M. Hutchison, wit.

Berryhill, Joseph R. & Peggy Ann Freeman, 9 April 1840; Thomas
Berryhill, bondsman; B. Oates, C. C. C., wit.

Berryhill, Michael Washington & Miss Mary Pelt, 6 Oct 1824;
Annenius Sing, bondsman; K. S. Dinkins, wit.

Berryhill, Pinkney Leroy & Laura Josey, 14 April 1857; A. W.
McCaner(?), bondsman; W. K. Reid, C. C. C., wit. married 15
April 1858 by Wm. S. Norment, J. P.

Berryhill, Samuel & Sarah Bigham, 6 Jan 1802; William Todd,
bondsman.

Berryhill, Samuel & Miss Margaret Alexander, 10 Feb 1823; Pinckney
Alexander, bondsman; K. S. Dinkins, wit.

Berryhill, Samuel & Elizabeth Rodden, 16 Aug 1825; Robert M.
Kerr, bondsman; Isaac Alexander, wit.

Berryhill, Taylor & Margaret E. Rea, 15 May 1832; Alford A.
Berryhill, bondsman.

Berryhill, Thomas P. & Cynthia M. Todd, 3 March 1821; Samuel
Berryhill, bondsman; Isaac S. Alexander, wit.

Berryhill, W. R. & Emily E. Arms, 30 Oct 1865; W. A. McGinn,
bondsman; W. Maxwell, wit. married 1 Nov 1865 by Jas C.
Chalmers, minister.

Berryhill, W. R. & Mary E. Rodden, 12 Jan 1858; Wm. R. Berryhill,
bondsman; W. K. Reid, C. C. C., wit. married 13 Jan 1858,
by Alex Cooper, J. P.

Berryhill, William Mc. & Betsey Berryhill, 23 Aug 1820; John
Freeman, bondsman; Isaac Alexander, wit.

Berryhill, William R. & Mary L. Reed, 11 Dec 1837; John N.
Sharpley, bondsman; B. Oates, C. C. C., wit.

Betterson, Phillip & Caroline Smith, 27 Dec 1865; Young Pace,
bondsman; R. M. White, wit.

Bevins, Abraham & Polly Cochran, 6 Oct 1818; Moses Bevins, bondsman. Jno. Rea, J. P., wit.

17

Bibb, Walthall & Esther Moses, 23 March 1828; James S. Morris, bondsman; Isaac Alexander, wit.

Bibb, William & Rachel Simohs, 3 Dec 1818; James J. Morris, bondsman; Isaac Alexander, wit.

Biggart, James & Jane Rea, 8 June 1836; John N. Whitesides, bondsman; B. Oates, wit.

Bigger, Allison H. & Catharine M. Smith, 24 May 1860; Matthew L. Wallace, bondsman; W. K. Reid, C. C. C., wit. married 24 May 1860 by R. McEwen, J. P.

Bigger, Robert & Catherine Thompson, 1 Jany 1788; Joseph Patton, bondsman; Saml Martin, wit.

Bigger, Robert & Rebecca Robinson, 31 July 1826; McCamy A. White, bondsman.

Bigger, William & Mary Ann Snell, 16 Jan 1802; James Bigger, bondsman.

Bigger, William B. & Mary Ann Snell, 10 Sept 1827; Volintine Faggert, bondsman; Pearsall Thompson, wit.

Biggers, Robert H. W. & Sarah H. Biggers, 14 March 1839; James Hall, bondsman; W. H. Simpson, J. P., wit.

Biggers, Francis A. & Lucinda S. Miller, 22 Feb 1853 (license only). married 1 March 1853 by C. B. Cross, J. P.

Biggers, Joseph & Sarah Snell, 23 Feb 1811; Hugh Snell, bondsman; Isaac Alexander, wit.

Biggers, Jno. W. H. & Mary Simpson, 13 Oct 1832; Charles T. Freeman, bondsman; B. Oates, wit.

Bigham, Green L. & Mary A. Hany, 11 Feb 1846; Wm. L. Suggs, bondsman; B. Oates, C. C. C., wit.

Bigham, Green L. & Mary A. Beaty, 12 April 1852; J. J. Sloan, bondsman; James Parks, wit. married 13 April 1852 by G. C. Cathey, J. P.

Bigham, Hugh & Sarah Bigham, 15 July 1795; Samuel Bigham, bondsman; Isaac Alexander, wit.

Bigham, James & Sarah Walker, 19 July 1803; Simon Van Pelt, bondsman; Isaac Alexander, wit.

Bigham, James & Mary M. Hunter, 14 Feb 1831; John Porter, bondsman; B. Oates, wit.

Bigham, James & Isabella E. Neely, 4 May 1837; Alexander Greer, bondsman; B. Oates, wit.

Bigham, John & Agness Rose, 4 Sept 1799; James Bigham, bondsman; Isaac Alexander, wit.

Bigham, Mathis & Tabitha Green, 27 Sept 1808; Moses Green, bondsman; Michl. McLeary, wit.

Bigham, Robert & Martha Young Reed, 31 Dec 1799; John Reed, bondsman; Isaac Alexander, wit.

Bigham, Robert & Jane Matthews, 31 Dec 1813; James Greer, bondsman; Isaac Alexander, wit.

Bigham, Robert & Polly Jackson, 4 Jan 1815; John Porter, bondsman; Ruthy R. Alexander, wit.

Bigham, Robert & Jane Hunter, 23 Dec 1829; Robert Porter, bondsman; B. Oates, wit.

Bigham, Robert M. & Margaret B. Berryhill, 14 April 1847; Stephen T. Berryhill, bondsman.

Bigham, Wm. C. & Jane R. Alexander, 8 May 1845; J. C. Kirkpatrick, bondsman; C. S. Alexander, wit.

Bigham, William M. & Sarah L. Rea, 6 June 1844; J. H. McGinnis, bondsman; N. B. Taylor, wit.

Bighim, Saml. & Nancy McKnight, 29 April 1818; Robert McKnight, bondsman; Isaac S. Alexander, wit.

Bingham, L. S. & Jane E. Harris, 2 Feb 1849; W. F. Taylor, bondsman.

Biram, Repton & Dolly McDowell, 30 Dec 1793; John Biram, bondsman; Edw. Waine, wit.

Bird, Charles & Betsey Sansing, 15 Dec 1834; John R. Williams, bondsman; Jas. H. Blake signed as bondsman; B. Oates, C. C. C., wit.

Bird, James & Polly Hull, 7 Jan 1811; Alexander Hodge Junr., bondsman; Isaac Alexander, wit.

Bird, John & Jane Duffy, 9 Jan 1810; John Duffy, bondsman; Isaac R. Alexander, wit.

Bird, Nelson & Polly Maculla (McCullough?), 21 May 1816; John Bird, bondsman; C. S. J. Alexander, wit.

Biren, Moses & Sally Cochran, 20 Jan 1820; Abram Biren, bondsman; Isaac Alexander, John Read, wit.

Black, Abner S. & Catherine Smith, 7 Aug 1845; Samuel M. McCall, bondsman; Isaac S. Alexander, wit.

Black, Absalon, & Jane Query, 29 June 1818; Mathew Wallace, bondsman; Isaac Alexander, wit.

Black, Cyrus & Mary Irwin, 7 Oct 1828; Mesel Hutson, bondsman; E. Elem, wit.

Black, Cyrus, & Elizabeth Harkey, 31 May 1831; Thomas J. Williamson, bondsman; Eli Springs, wit.

Black, David L. & Isabela Patten, 24 Aug 1836; Thomas B. Neely, bondsman; F. N. Ross, wit.

Black, Eli O. & Lydia C. Maxwell, 8 March 1830; Edwin W. Maxwell, bondsman; Isaac S. Alexander, wit.

Black, Ezekiel & Sarah McEwen, 26 Oct 1807; William Beaty, bondsman; Isaac Alexander, wit.

Black, Ezekiel & Delila Saunders, 30 Dec 1839; Richard Searcy, bondsman; B. Oates, C. C. C., wit.

Black, Ezekiel & Nancy Hannah Alexander, 18 July 1843; Joab A. Campbell, bondsman; C. T. Alexander, wit.

Black, George & Agness Osborn, 25 March 1800; James Osborn, bondsman.

Black, H. W. & Alvira McComb, 8 Oct 1841; Joseph H. Erwin, bondsman; B. Oates, wit.

Black, Hammelton & Margaret Robinett, 23 Oct 1810; Saml Black, Danl Hall, bondsmen; Isaac S. Alexander, wit.

Black, J. C. & Margaret K. Black, 25 Sept 1861; D. C. Bryson, bondsman; P. S. Whisnant, wit. married 26 Sept 1861 by Walter S. Pharr.

Black, James & Eliz. Shanks, 24 March 1801; John Black, bondsman.

Black, James & Peggy Black, 2 Feb 1814; Alexander Moore, bondsman; Isaac Alexander, wit.

Black, James & Miss Sally M'Comb, 12 March 1817; Evan Alexander, bondsman.

Black, James M. & Elizabeth Johnston, 19 Nov 1836; David Parks, bondsman.

Black, Joe & Sussanah Patterson, 17 March 1866; D. Archie, bondsman; Wm. Maxwell, wit.

Black, John & Mary Walker, 1 Sept 1790; Daniel McAuley, bondsman; Isaac Alexander, wit.

Black, John & Agness Wier, 10 __ 1792; James Scott, bondsman.

Black, John & Lydia Hood, 25 Aug 1802; John Spring, bondsman.

Black, John & Peggy Meek, 9 March 1803; John Walker, bondsman.

Black, John B. & Mary Ann Edwards, 2 Sept 1856; Thos. M. Black, bondsman; W. K. Reid, C. C. C., wit. married 4 Sept 1856 by R. B. Jones, M. G.

Black, Joseph B. & Jane A. Query, 16 Dec 1842; Lucius Query, bondsman (not on microfilm)

Black, Joseph Y. & Martha L. Morrow, 17 Aug 1837; A. G. Potts, bondsman; Edwin Potts, J. P., wit.

Black, Nelson L. & Sarah B. Lawson, 6 Dec 1839; H. W. Houston, bondsman; B. Oates, C. C. C.

Black, Richard & Elizabeth Partlow, 1 Jan 1805; David Partlow, bondsman; Isaac Alexander, wit.

Black, Robert & Dovey Hartt, 4 April 1808; Samuel Kerr, bondsman; Isaac Alexander, wit.

Black, Samuel & _____, 24 Aug 1819; Eli McCall, bondsman.

Black, Samuel & Elizabeth M'Auley, 26 Jan 1822; Thomas McCall, bondsman; Isaac Alexander, wit.

Black, Thomas A. & Miss Margaret J. Houston, 28 Jan 1854;
R. B. Weddington, bondsman; W. K. Reid, C. C. C., wit.
married 31 Jan 1854 by S. C. Pharr, V. D. M.

Black, Thomas M. & A. E. McCauley, 11 March 1858; W. Morris,
bondsman; W. K. Reid, C. C. C., wit. married 11 March 1858
by J. M. Walker, Min.

Black, Thomas O. & Miss Francis Greble, 1 March 1823; William
Greble, bondsman; K. S. Dinkins, wit.

Black, Thomas O. & Selia Irwin, 2 Jan 1828; Samuel B. Hays, bondsman.

Black, Wm. & Mary Anne Johnston, 13 July 1792; Daniel McAuley,
bondsman; Isaac Alexander, wit.

Black, William & Mary Irwin, 20 Feb 1793; Theophilus A. Canon,
bondsman; Isaac Alexander, wit.

Black, William & Elizabeth Meacham, 22 July 1801; Joshua Parks,
bondsman; Isaac Alexander, wit.

Black, William Senr & Margaret Niel, 22 Sept 1801; James Wallis,
bondsman; Mary A. Wallis, wit.

Black, Wm & Amelia Black, 26 Jan 1807; Wm Johnston, bondsman;
Wm Beaty, wit.

Black, Wm & Eliza Jane Aiken, 11 Feb 1861; Robert Gibbon, bondsman;
W. K. Reid, C. C. C., wit. 19 March 1861 E. F. Rockwell,
V. D. M.

Black, William C. & Miss Maggie A. Ross, 25 May 1866; Leonidus
Pearce (Pierce), bondsman; W. Maxwell, wit. married 1 Feb
1866 by R. Z. Johnston.

Black, William J. & Ms. Matildy Flow, 30 Dec 1824; James Brown,
bondsman; Philemon Morris, wit.

Black, William L. & Rachel M. Wentz, 22 Jan 1841; Eli C. Greer,
bondsman; B. Oates, wit.

Black, Wm. M. & Miss E. M. Hannon, 11 May 1865; George W. Bright,
bondsman. married 16 May 1865 by W. J. Hayes, J. P.

Black, Hugh & Margret Boyd, 30 March 1808; Aaron Baker, bondsman.

Blackburn, John A. & Jane Todd, 9 Oct 1850; John L. Watson, bondsman; B. Oates, C. C. C., wit.

Blackley, Thomas H. & Mary H. Morrow, 20 Sept 1838; William L.
Black, bondsman; James Johnston, wit.

Blakely, Thomas H. & Jane Gilden, 31 March 1862; Thos T. Johnson,
bondsman; W. K. Reid, C. C. C., wit. married 3 April 1862 by
B. H. Garrison, J. P.

Blackwelder, Alfred & Matilda Berryhill, 22 Dec 1858; John M.
Shelby, bondsman; W. K. Reid, C. C. C., wit. married 23 Dec
1858 by W. H. Neal, J. P.

MECKLENBURG MARRIAGES 1783-1868

Blackwelder, David M. & Lucy Hagler, 23 Dec 1857; Elias M.
   Crowell, bondsman; W. K. Reid, C. C. C., wit. married 24
Dec 1857 by Alex Cooper, J. P.

Blackwelder, Isaac W. & Nelly Hagler, 30 Aug 1856; David M.
   Blackwelder, bondsman; W. K. Reid, C. C. C., wit. married 6
Sept 1856 by Alex Cooper, J. P.

Blackwelder, John & Elizabeth Wentz, 8 Nov 1851; Volentin
   Wentz, bondsman; James Parks, wit. married 12 Nov 1851 by
W. Neal, J. P.

Blackwelder, Moses & Ann Kerr, 29 Jan 1850; Samuel Thornberg,
   bondsman; James Park, wit.

Blackwood, Gideon & Ann Blackwood, 14 Nov 1811; Joseph Blackwood,
   bondsman; Isaac Alexander, wit.

Blackwood, Joseph & Peggy Haynes, 17 April 1824; Andrew Clark,
   bondsman; Isaac Alexander, wit.

Blaekley, James & Martha Walker, 29 ___ 1793; John Miller, bondsman; Isaac Alexander, wit.

Blain, Jasen & Nancy Eaks, 3 Nov 1808; Voluntine Parish, bondsman.

Blair, James G. & Piety Hooks, 27 Nov 1819; Samuel Blair, bondsman;
   Isaac Alexander, wit.

Blair, James G. & Margaret Query, 12 Feb 1849; John Q. Lemmond,
   bondsman; B. Oates, C. C. C., wit.

Blair, J. T. & Elisabeth L. Parks, 26 Sept 1853; P. M. Morris,
   bondsman; W. K. Reid, wit. married 27 Sept 1853 by R. H.
Lafferty, Pastor of the Congregation of Sugar Creek.

Blair, John & Agness Smith, 8 Oct 1799; William Stewart, bondsman.

Blair, John & Elizabeth Snell, 26 March 1800; Robert Donaldson,
   bondsman; Isaac Alexander, wit.

Blair, John M. & Susan J. Crowell, 8 April 1861; J. W. Brown,
   bondsman; W. K. Reid, C. C. C., wit. married 9 April 1861
by Allan McCorquodale.

Blair, Laird & Margarett C. Orr, 24 July 1833; James Hennigan,
   bondsman; Isaac S. Alexander, wit.

Blair, Laird & Mary Ann Wilson, 20 Aug 1838. no bondsman or wit.

Blair, Milton & Caroline Alexander, 31 March 1831; John Snell,
   bondsman; Wm. V. Barr(?), wit.

Blair, Saml & Eliza Alexander, 26 Nov 1823; Richard McRee, bondsman;
   Isaac S. Alexander, wit.

Blair, Samuel M. & A. J. Query, 19 Feb 1850; Washington Blair,
   bondsman; James Parks, wit.

Blake, James H. & Margaret A. Davidson, 13 Sept 1820; Duncan
   Campbell, bondsman; Isaac Alexander, wit.

Blakely, Hugh & Rebecca Peoples, 21 Dec 1843; Hugh D. Ewart,
   bondsman.

Blakely, Thomas & Taripa Huster, 8 Oct 1812; Robert Ross, bondsman; Sam. C. Caldwell, wit.

Blakely, William & Martha Pippens, 17 Dec 1852; Hugh Blakely, bondsman; Jas. Johnston, J. P., wit. married 21 Dec 1852 by James Johnston.

Blakely, William J. & Mary J. Cook, 8 Jan 1866. married 8 Jan 1866 by Jno F. Butt.

Blakley, J. A. & E. J. Solomon, 25 March 1863; Henry W. Caldwell, bondsman. married 26 March 1863 by T. W. Dewey, J. P.

Blakly, Daniel A. & Margaret C.Monteich, 25 March 1837; Samuel A. Baird, bondsman; B. Oates, wit.

Blalock, William & Louiza Shepherd, 6 July 1840; Thomas Boyd, bondsman.

Blanchard, Thomas G. & Elizabeth Andrews, 15 March 1841; Andrew Walsh, bondsman; B. Oates, wit.

Blanchet, Thomas & Rosanna Rodden, 8 Sept 1805; William Rodden, bondsman; Isaac Alexander, wit.

Blankenship, Samuel H. & Miss A. Alexander, 3 Dec 1859; Joseph B. Boiles, bondsman; J. R. Daniel, wit.

Blankenship, Samuel H. & Adaline Hoover, 8 Aug 1854; William O. Moss, bondsman; W. K. Reid, C. C. C., wit. married 16 Aug 1854 by A. M. Watson, minister.

Blaylock, Isom & Margaret Wilson, 21 May 1839; Sinai Alexander, bondsman; James T. J. Orr, wit.

Blelock, Willis & Tabitha Darnell, 29 Dec 1806; William Darnell, bondsman.

Blount, George W. & Jane Cox, 2 Sept 1850; J. D. Boyte, bondsman; James Parks, wit.

Blount, James & Louisa Ann Norment, 17 May 1826; Clark Weddington, bondsman; Isaac Alexander, wit.

Blount, John & Jane L. Crump, 14 Sept 1864; Wm Maxwell, wit. married 17 Sept 1864 by R. M. Ewen, J. P.

Bluford, William & Suckey Stow, 20 Dec 1803; Solomon Stow, bondsman; Isaac Alexander, C. M. C., wit.

Blyth, Samuel & Patsey Bonds, 9 May 1803; George Bonds, bondsman; J. Wallis, wit.

Blythe, George S. & Elizabeth Allen, 5 Dec 1865; J. W. McCoy, bondsman. married 5 Dec 1865 by Jno F. Butt.

Blythe, Robert & Mary Crenshaw, 11 Oct 1865; Wm. L. Blythe, bondsman; married 12 Oct 1865 by Jno F. Butt.

Blythe, Saml. & Izzabella Nantz, 8 Jan 1822; Joseph Walker, bondsman; Isaac S. Alexander, wit.

Boal, Thomas & Abigail Orr, 27 Feb 1799; William Tasey Orr, bondsman.

23

Boals, Addison P. & Jane Irwin, 1 March 1825; John Houston, bondsman; Isaac Alexander, wit.

Boatwright, James & Martha Alexander, 4 Sept 1845; S. W. Boatwright, bondsman; Wm. F. Alexander, wit.

Boatwright, John & Margaret Ann Porter, 26 May 1832; Andrew H. Porter, bondsman; W. Elms, wit.

Boatwright, S. Washington, & Cynthia Robeson, 10 April 1834; Franklin Lewis, bondsman; B. Oates, C. C. C., wit.

Boatwright, S. W. & Mary Porter, 8 Jan 1846; Wm. K. Reid, bondsman; B. Oates, C. C. C., wit.

Bootwright, Samuel & Nancy Weathers, 1 Aug 1792; Reuben Weathers, bondsman; Isaac Alexander, wit.

Bodkin, John & Polly Sandford, 25 Sept 1828; Joseph Graham, bondsman; Alex. R. Jetton, wit.

Boggs, Asahel & Esther McCay, 25 Jan 1792; Beaty McCoy, bondsman. Wm. B. Alexander, wit.

Bohanon, Robert & Elizabeth Glover, 1 Dec 1824; George Bohanon, bondsman; Isaac S. Alexander, wit.

Bonds, James & Peggy Morrow, 27 April 1802; David Morrow, bondsman; J. Wallis, wit.

Bost, Hiram A. & Margaret P. Bready, 5 Feb 1854; B. B. Eidston, bondsman; James Johnston, wit. married 23 Feb 1854 by E. F. Rockwell, V. D. M.

Bost, John M. & Ann H. King, 17 March 1855; M. L. Bost, bondsman; John Phelan, wit. married 22 March 1855, by Danl A. Penick.

Bostwick, William M. & Caroline Graham, 21 Feb 1817; John Campbell, bondsman.

Bowden, Elzy & Manerva Keziah, 4 Jan 1865; Nathan M. Carter, bondsman; married 4 Jan 1866(sic), by T. W. Dewey, J. P.

Bowdon, Arthur S. & Elizabeth Smith, 31 March 1832; K. D. Dinkins, bondsman.

Bowdon, John & Margaret Randolph, 6 Nov 1817; Ephraim Kendrick, bondsman.

Bowie, Benjamin & Eleanor Moore, 25 Oct 1827; William Moore, bondsman; Pearsall Thompson, wit.

Bowman, Saml Majr. & Mrs. Margt. Wilson, 12 July 1801; Capt. John Henderson, bondsman.

Boyce, Elam B. & Sarah Ann Hunter, 26 Sept 1841; Marens Alexander, bondsman.

Boyce, Hugh & Rossannah D. Hunter, 10 April 1856; S. A. Boyce, bondsman; W. K. Reid, C. C. C., wit. married 10 April 1856 by J. M. Walker, Min.

Boyce, S. A. & Sarah E. Walker, 9 Nov 1848; M. C. L. McLeod, bondsman; J. Walker, wit.

Boyce, William & Emeline Walkup, 8 Jan 1852; Robert C. Bell, bondsman.

Boyd, Andrew & Sarah Dunbarr, 18 Dec 1793; John Coughren, bondsman.

Boyd, Benjamin P. & Terza Red, 11 Nov 1839; William Alexander, bondsman.

Boyd, Daniel & Patsy Parish, 15 Sept 1812; Voluntine Parish, bondsman; Isaac S. Alexander, wit.

Boyd, Daniel & Elizebeth Simral, 1 June 1822; Hugh Simrel, bondsman.

Boyd, H. B. & Margaret E. Helms, 2 Oct 1865; Jeremiah Clontz, bondsman; Wm. Maxwell, wit. married 4 Oct 1865 by J. S. Reid, J. P.

Boyd, James & Elizabeth J. Smith, 10 Oct 1831; Benjamin Smith, bondsman; B. Oates, D. C., wit.

Boyd, John J. & Nancy J. Knox, 12 Jan 1859; S. C. Youngblood, bondsman; W. K. Reid, C. C. C., wit. married 20 Jan 1859, by J. B. Watt, Pastor.

Boyd, Joshua D. & Allona L. Smith, 28 Dec 1826; James M. Hutchison, bondsman; Pearsall Thompson, wit.

Boyd, Thomas & Susanna Darnell, 19 Dec 1796; John Mitchell, bondsman.

Boyes, John & Isabella Kirkpatrick, 27 Dec 1800; Hugh Kirkpatrick, bondsman; Isaac Alexander, wit.

Boyes, William & Nancy Scott, 4 Oct 1833; William Reid, bondsman.

Boyle, William & Mary Blackwood, 15 Nov 1797; Andrew Lawing, bondsman.

Boyles, William & Elizabeth Berry, 31 Jan 182_; John Reid, bondsman; Isaac Alexander, wit.

Boyte, Josiah & Mary Acock, 4 July 1839; Robert Simpson, bondsman; W. H. Simpson, J. P., wit.

Bracher (Bradshaw), Solomon, & Elisebeth Givens, 1 Aug 1797; Hance McCain, bondsman; Shared Gray, wit.

Bracket, Benjamin & Margaret J. Wilson, 25 Jan 1837; John Williamson, bondsman.

Bradford, James & Melinda Wallace, 12 Dec 1835; William S. Wallace, bondsman; B. Oates, C. C. C., wit.

Bradley, Evan B. & Elizebeth _____, 12 Feb 1799; James Davis, bondsman;

Bradley, Francis & Martha Henderson, 12 Aug 1836; William W. Price, bondsman.

Bradley, James A. & Elizabeth Houston, 30 Oct 1810; Alexander Stinson, bondsman; Isaac Alexander, wit.

Bradshaw, William & Ann Winchester, 8 Aug 1800; Thomas Winchester, bondsman; Geo Ford, Will Houston, wit.

Brady, John McKnitt, & Jean Mitchell, 1 Feb 1796; John Erwin, bondsman; Isaac Alexander, wit.

Branch, Armsted & Miss Sarah Dinkins, 18 March 1824; John Dinkins, bondsman; K. J. Dinkins, wit.

Brandon, James A. & Mary E. Carothers, 15 Jan 1841; William A. Todd, bondsman.

Brandon, John & Jane H. Carothers, 20 Nov 1840; Jas. S. Carothers, bondsman.

Brantley, Cordy Franklin & Nancy M. C. Holden, 21 May 1859; William W. Ferrell, bondsman; W. K. Reid, C. C. C., wit. married 25 May 1859 by R. L. D. Arman(?), J. P.

Bratton, R. M. & Mary A. Serrence, 23 April 1849; E. C. Davidson, bondsman; Saml. J. Lourie, wit.

Bratton, S. E. & Letitia A. Torrence, 7 Sept 1847; J. Alexander Fox, bondsman; Saml. J. Lourie, wit.

Brawley, Wm. J. & Isabella M. York, 24 Aug 1855; C. H. Elms, bondsman; W. K. Reid, C. C. C., wit. married 30 Aug 1855 by Walter S. Pharr.

Brawly, James G. & Mary E. Brawly, 22 Nov 1858; Samuel C. Hagan, bondsman; R. F. Blythe, wit. married 22 Nov 1858, by R. F. Blythe, J. P.

Brevard, John F. & Margaret J. Conner, 15 Aug 1820; Henry W. M. Conner, bondsman.

Brevard, Thomas & Sarah Letters, 1 March 1804; Lewis Jetton, bondsman; Archd. Cathey, J. P., wit.

Brewer, N. Alex. F. & A. M. Black, 1 Aug 1842; C. E. Moss, bondsman.

Brewer, Thomas F. & Harriet E. Oehler, 24 Feb 1866; D. M. Oehler, bondsman. married 1 March 1866 by E. F. Rockwell, V. D. M.

Bryan, James & Sarah A. Robison, 16 Nov 1850; Samuel P. Alexander, bondsman; B. Oates, C. C. C., wit.

Briard, Andrew R. & Mary F. Baker, 12 June 1858; James A. Elms, bondsman; W. K. Reid, C. C. C., wit. married 14 July 1858 by P. Nicholson.

Bridges, Benjamin & Nancy Caborn, 27 Feb 1816; John Brumbley, Adlai Alexander, bondsmen.

Brigman, George W. & Martha Ann Neal, 13 March 1866; Saml. Lourie, bondsman. married 13 March 1866 by Jno F. Butt.

Brigman, John & Fanny Christenbery, 30 Sept 1856; Stephen Hipp, bondsman; W. K. Reid, C. C. C., wit. married 9 Oct 1856 by R. L. D. Armor, J. P.

Brigman, John J. & Mary Jane Watts, 30 Oct 1860; John Stowe, bondsman; W. K. Reid, C. C. C., wit. married 1 Nov 1860 by Walter S. Pharr.

Brinkley, Thomas & Sarah Jane Lancaster, 25 June 1861; William
Wedlock, bondsman; W. W. Grier, wit. married 25 June 1861
by C. Overman, J. P.

Brinkley, William & Clarissa Stuart, 15 Jan 1828; James A. Deaton,
bondsman; A. B. Jetton, wit.

Brint, James & Sarah Wynes, 11 Sept 1802; William Luckey Junr.,
bondsman.

Britton, E. H. & Rebecca S. Meetze, 26 Sept 1860; Neill Wilkinson,
bondsman; W. K. Reid, C. C. C., wit. married 27 Sept 1860 by
Richd. H. Griffith, minister of the Gospel.

Britton, J. Evans & Margaret E. Elms, 8 Jan 1861; Neil Wilkinson,
bondsman; P.S. Whisnant, wit. married 8 Jan 1861 by Richd.
H. Griffith, minister of the Gospel.

Bronson, Edward M. & Sarah Ann Orr, 6 March 1813; William Faires,
bondsman; Isaac Alexander, wit.

Brooks, William & Cartharine M. Clontz, 21 Nov 1833; James Carelock,
bondsman.

Broom, Alce & Elizabeth Yarbrough, 13 Aug 1840; Shared Yarbrough,
bondsman; Wm. Bill, J. P., wit.

Broom, Troy & Selena Thompson, 6 Dec 1840; Noah Helmes, bondsman;
Wm. Bill, J. P.

Brown, A. F. & Lucretia Hall, 12 Dec 1860; E. P. Hall, bondsman;
P. S. Whisnant, wit. married 13 Dec 1860 by R. F. Blythe, J. P.

Brown, Adams, & Jenny Morrow, 28 April 1801; Elias Crockett,
bondsman; J. Wallis, wit.

Brown, Alfred & Lydia Smith, 14 Nov 1865; J. L. Stevens, bondsman.
married 14 Nov 1865 by Jno. F. Butt.

Brown, Allen H. & Nancy C. Jamison, 22 Aug 1838; Robert Mc. Jamison, bondsman.

Brown, Andersor & Nancy Hamet Cashon, 28 May 1854; Joseph McQuay,
bondsman; W. K. Reid, C. C. C., wit. married 23 May 1854
by G. L. Campbell, J. P.

Brown, B. F. & Miss Anna Barnett, 3 Oct 1865; E. L. S. Barnett,
bondsman; Wm. Maxwell, wit. married 10 Oct 1854 by H. B.
Pratt.

Brown, Benjamin & Jane Herren, 9 June 1809; Josiah Brown, bondsman.

Brown, Benjamin & Erixley McCauley, 7 Jan 1828; Thomas G. Barnett,
bondsman; Tho. B. Smartt, wit.

Brown, Benj. F. & Mary Jamason, 20 May 1843; Wm. J. Jamison,
bondsman.

Brown, Benjamin G. & Elizabeth M. Thompson, 2 Aug 1858; Joseph
Thompson, bondsman; W. K. Reid, C. C. C., wit. married __
Aug 1859 by J. B. Watt, Pastor.

Brown, Charles & Mary S. Kirkpatrick, 4 Sept 1848; Tho. H. Brem,
bondsman; Sam. J. Lourie, wit.

Brown, Daniel & Mary Polk, 24 Dec 1794; John Reed, bondsman.

Brown, David & Mary Gibbons, 25 Oct 1804; John Brown, bondsman;
J. Wallis, wit.

Brown, Eli & Nancy P. Freeman, 5 Nov 1832; Joseph Berryhill,
bondsman; Isaac Alexander, wit.

Brown, Enoch & Patsey Wilson, 18 March 1813; Joseph Haynes, bondsman; Isaac Alexander, wit.

Brown, Gabriel & Polly Ferrell, 22 Dec 1813; William Ferrell,
bondsman; Almira M. Alexander, wit.

Brown, J. F. & Mary F. Alexander, 7 Sept 1865; S. L. Hucks, bondsman. married 7 Sept 1865 by S. C. Pharr.

Brown, James & Agness Walker, 7 Oct 1795; Hugh Walker, bondsman;
Isaac Alexander, wit.

Brown, James & Jean Jemison, 10 Feb 1797; John Jamison, bondsman;
Jas. Conner(?), wit.

Brown, James & Nancy Smith, 28 Feb 1804; Adam Brown, bondsman; J.
Wallis, wit.

Brown, James C. & Sarah Jane McLeen(?), 29 Aug 1859; Joseph H.
Beard, bondsman; W. K. Reid, C. C. C., wit. married 1 Sept
1859, by Walter S. Pharr.

Brown, James G. & Mary J. Hall, 30 Aug 1860; John B. Flannagan,
bondsman; W. K. Reid, C. C. C., wit. married 4 Sept 1860
by J. Rumple, V. D. M.

Brown, James H. & Sarah J. Freeman, 28 July 1828; Wm. K. Reid,
bondsman; Pearsall Thompson, wit.

Brown, James H. & Hannah E. Alexander, 1 Dec 1857; S. A. Kirkpatrick, bondsman; W. K. Reid, C. C. C., wit. married 3 Dec
1857, by R. H. Lafferty, Pastor of the Congregation of Sugar Creek.

Brown, James J. & Amelia E. Edwards, 5 Jan 1857; James R. L. Hill,
bondsman; W. K. Reid, C. C. C., wit. married 8 Jan 1857 by
R. L. D. Armor, J. P.

Brown, James J. & Sarah A. Worsham, 30 July 1861; Wm. F. Boyls,
bondsman; Wm. Patterson, wit. married 30 July 1861 by
R. F. Blythe.

Brown, James W. & Meranda E. Ray, 19 Oct 1848; John K. Red, bondsman.

Brown, James W. & Margaret C. Blair, 22 Dec 1860; J. W. Herren,
bondsman; W. K. Reid, C. C. C., wit. married 25 Dec 1860 by
J. C. Chalmers, Minr.

Brown, John & Marthew Maxwell, 17 Dec 1792; William Brown, bondsman; James Meek, wit.

Brown, John & Betsey Sharpe, 22 Dec 1802; William Walker, bondsman;
Isaac Alexander, wit.

Brown, John C. & Sarah A. Patterson, 13 Dec 1854; S. W. Alexander,
bondsman; W. K. Reid, C. C. C., wit. married 13 Dec 1854 by
S. C. Pharr, V. D. M.

Brown, John G. & Eli Merchant, 2 April 1833; Thomas Russell, bondsman; B. Oates, D. C., wit.

Brown, John M. & Manica Kerr, 7 April 1832; James G. Flennikin, bondsman.

Brown, John W. & Mary Herron, 5 Feb 1828; Allen Heren, bondsman; Thomas B. Smart, wit.

Brown, John W. & Mary A. J. Black, 23 Sept 1851; A. J. Hamlet, bondsman; B. Oates, C. C. C., wit. married 24 Sept 1851 by Lorenzo Hunter, J. P.

Brown, John W. & Ann C. Griffith, 8 Jan 1853; J. B. Griffith, bondsman; B. Oates, C. C. C.,wit. married 13 Jan 1853 by S. C. Pharr.

Brown, Josiah & Levina Fieser, 19 June 1814; Benjamin Brown, bondsman; Isaac Alexander, wit.

Brown, Josiah & Sarah A. Smith, 4 Oct 1825; John W. Brown, bondsman; Richd. Gillespie, wit.

Brown, M. H. & Martha J. Edwards, 9 Dec 1865; D. M. Oehler, bondsman; married 14 Dec 1865, by S. C. Pharr.

Brown, Murrell & Mary Suckey, 24 July 1840; Henry Conner, bondsman.

Brown, Peter & Sarah Putman; 29 April 1800; Jepthah Baker, bondsman; Wm. M'Call, wit.

Brown, Robert & Elizabeth Bryson, 28 March 1794; Francis Yourees, bondsman; Isaac Alexander, wit.

Brown, Samuel & Katharine Jamison, 31 March 1801; John Jamison, bondsman; Jno Harris, J. P., wit.

Brown, Silas W. & Jean Ormond, 19 March 1816; James Porter, bondsman; John Rea, J. P., wit.

Brown, Stanhope, & Margaret C. McGahey, 5 Dec 1853; William T. Mc-Gahy, bondsman. married 8 Dec 1853 by J. Wilson, J. P.

Brown, Stanhope H. & Jane Caldwell, 25 Oct 1856; Wm. J. Killough, bondsman; W. K. Reid, C. C. C., wit. married 25 Oct 1856 by Walter S. Pharr.

Brown, Thomas & Henrietta McIntosh, 12 Oct 1865; Lonzo Davidson, bondsman; Wm. Maxwell, wit. (license states parties are colored) married 18 Oct 1865 by George Everhart, Rector, St. Peters, Charlotte, N. C.

Brown, William & Miss Jane Haynes, 12 April 1800; Joseph Haynes, bondsman; Isaac Alexander, wit.

Brown, William & Betsey Cristenberry, 4 Dec 1819; James Ferrell, bondsman; Isaac Alexander, wit.

Brown, William & Martha A. Monteith, 29 Oct 1839; Joseph E. Brown, bondsman;

Brown, William A. & Margaret Reed,12 Oct 1847; M. W. Freeman, bondsman; B. Oates, C. C. C., wit.

Brown, William A. & Sarah H. Johnston, 6 Aug 1861; Samuel F. Houston, bondsman; W.K. Reid, C. C. C., wit. married 8 Aug 1861 by A. Ranson.

Brown, William N. & Miss Elizabeth Flannagan, 19 Sept 1835; Samuel Orr, bondsman.

Brown, William P. & Harriet C. Heron, 28 April 1846; William J. Jamison, bondsman; S. S. Lourie, wit.

Bruks, John & Patsey Cuthbertson, 26 Nov 1825; John Cuthbertson, bondsman; Isaac Alexander, wit.

Bryan, Aaron M. & Mary Houston, 14 Feb 1837; William Carson, bondsman; B. Oates, wit.

Bryan, Matthew & Levina Pitman, 25 July 1810; Thomas Sprott, bondsman.

Bryant, Henry & Miss Julia S. Parks, 6 May 1865; D. J. Rea, bondsman. married 11 May 1865 by R. Z. Johnston.

Bryant, Sidney & Amelia R. Hipp, 16 Aug 1860; John W. Auton, bondsman; P. S. Whisnant, wit. married 16 Aug 1860, by Wm. S. Norment, J. P.

Bryce, John Y. & Miss Julia C. Jones, 29 June 1855; J. M. Davidson, bondsman; W. K. Reid, C. C. C., wit.

Bryson, James & Anne Doherty, 11 March 1799; John Henderson, bondsman; Jno Harris, J. P., wit.

Buchanan, Charles & Betsey Simmons, 8 May 1821; Isaac Alexander, wit; William Simmons, bondsman.

Buchanan, Green A. H. & Hannah J. McKnight, 3 Aug 1846; Smith Beaty, bondsman; S. J. Lourie, wit.

Buchanan, James & Mary Potter, 27 Dec 1794; John Stewart, bondsman.

Buckhanon, Hugh & Susan Rose, 20 Dec 1803; Samuel Philips, bondsman.

Bullinger, Abel & Harriet Partlow, 12 July 1832; James B. Neely, bondsman; R. S. Dinkins, wit.

Burford, Benjamin & Nancy Persons, 1 March 1797; Bartlett Meacham, bondsman; Ruthy Alexander, wit.

Burnett, William & Matilda Carolina Alexander, 10 Dec 1811; Francis Alexander, bondsman; Isaac Alexander, wit.

Burney, E. L. & Martha H. Henderson, 25 Sept 1851; S. N. Weddington, bondsman; C. A. Henderson, wit. married 1 Oct 1851 by Samuel B. O. Wilson, V. D. M.

Burnnet, P. M. & Eliza Fincher, 12 Oct 1841; J. M. Stewart, bondsman.

Burns, Laird & Jean Williams, 30 Jan 1801; David Starns, bondsman; Jno Hoey, J. P., Fredrick Starns, wit.

Burns, Samuel A. & Elizebeth Harris, 27 Aug 1851; John W. Moore, bondsman; James Parks, wit. married 26 Aug 1851 by John Hunter.

Burroughs, J. C. & Margaret E. Spratt, 13 Aug 1860; Jno. P. Heath, bondsman; W. K. Reid, C. C. C., wit. married 14 Aug 1860 by James B. Watt, V. D. M.

Busby, Wm & Mary Morrow, 5 March 1812; Robert Morrow, bondsman.

Bynam, William & Margaret Vinty, 27 Dec 1797; Valentine Vinty (Vintz?), bondsman; Isaac Alexander, wit.

Bynum, John W. & Nancy Gallant, 4 Aug 1828; Robert J. Dinkins, bondsman; Pearsall Thompson, wit.

Byram, Beverly & Sally Williamson, 13 April 1807; Mathew Bryan,Jr., bondsman.

Byram, Henry & Mary Cook, 8 Jan 1803; David Griffith, bondsman; Isaac Alexander, wit.

Byram, James & Hannah Williamson, 26 Sept 1808; Isaac Beaty, bondsman; Isaac Alexander, wit.

Byram, James & Elizabeth E. Glover, 1 Jan 1839; Robert Porter, bondsman.

Byram, James & Margaret Hannon, 13 June 1844; John M. Porter, bondsman.

Byram, John P. & Catherine L. Kerr, 23 March 1838; Robert Porter, bondsman.

Byram, Joseph & Catharine Griffith, 17 Feb 1818; James C. Griffith, bondsman; Rebecca C. Alexander, wit.

Byram, Robert J. & Caroline Sharp, 3 Sept 1829; George W. Williamson, bondsman; A. Cooper, wit.

Byram, Upton & Peggy Porter, 15 June 1807; William Cook, bondsman; Isaac Alexander, wit.

Byram, William & Katharine Cook, 5 Dec 1792; Robert Cook, bondsman; Isaac Alexander, wit.

Byram, William & Jean Page, 11 Dec 1809; Jepthah Baker, bondsman; Isaac Alexander, wit.

Byram, William & Nancy Walker, 18 March 1818; Alexander Cooper, bondsman; Isaac S. Alexander, wit.

Byram, William & Mary Condre, 20 Sept 1825; Joseph Byram, bondsman; Isaac S. Alexander, wit.

Byrom, John & Dolly Byrom, 23 May 1791; John Beaty, bondsman; Isaac Alexander, wit.

Byrong, William & Miss Catherine Bryan, 28 Feb 1824; Robert Sterling, bondsman.

Caine, Elisha & Catharine Lewis, 6 Feb 1805; Francis Lewis, bondsman; Adam J. Springs, wit.

Caldwell, Alexander & Sarah Davison, 9 Oct 1794; Joseph McKnitt Alexander, bondsman; Isaac Alexander, C. M. C., wit.

Caldwell, Amos & Dinah Wilson (coloured), 18 Sept 1865; Columbus White, bondsman. married 21 Sept 1865 by E. F. Rockwell, V. D. M.

Caldwell, Andrew & Margaret M. Querry, 12 Feb 1823; Jeremiah Howie, bondsman.

Caldwell, Andrew H. & Sarah A. Williamson, 26 March 1844; Jno M. M. Caldwell, bondsman.

Caldwell, C. F. & Margaret E. Wilson, 29 Nov 1856; N. Johnston, bondsman; W. K. Reid, C. C. C., wit. married __ Dec __ by R. H. Lafferty, Pastor of the Congregation of Sugar Creek.

Caldwell, Charles & Mary Parks, 23 Nov 1865; Saml Grier, bondsman.

Caldwell, Charles & Mary Caldwell, 23 Nov 1865; Wm Maxwell, C. C. C.

Caldwell, D. S. & Martha J. Wilson, 6 Aug 1851; G. L. Gibson, bondsman.

Caldwell, D. S. & E. L. Neely, 14 May 1862; Albert Wilson, bondsman; W. K. Reid, C. C. C., wit. married 14 May 1862 by R. H. Lafferty, Pastor of the Congregation of Sugar Creek.

Caldwell, Daniel & Izabella Shields, 18 Jan 1826; Jeremiah Howie, bondsman.

Caldwell, Daniel G. & Harriet C. Alexander, 26 Feb 1861; Robert N. Caldwell, bondsman; W. K. Reid, C. C. C., wit. married 28 Feb 1861 by R. H. Lafferty, Pastor of the Congregation of Sugar Creek.

Caldwell, David & Mary Smith, 29 June 1791; Stephen Alexander, bondsman; Jno Allison, wit.

Caldwell, David A. & Mrs. Martha Caldwell, 12 Dec 1836; Wm. B. Alexander, bondsman.

Caldwell, David T. & Harriet E. Davidson, 13 March 1826; Joshua D. Boyd, bondsman; Isaac Alexander, wit.

Caldwell, Derick & Easter Alexander, 17 Oct 1865; Isreal Caldwell, bondsman; R. M. White, wit. married 21 Oct 1865 by _____.

Caldwell, Edward & Ann E. Terrence, 11 Aug 1826; Andrew Caldwell, bondsman; A. B. Jetton, wit.

Caldwell, Franklin & Miss Sarah Caldwell, 19 Feb 1864; Henry W. Conner, bondsman; R. M. White, wit. marriage license to Franklin Caldwell and Miss Sarah Reid; married 21 Feb 1864 by W. B. Withers, J. P.

Caldwell, G. W. & M. E. Alexander, 30 Jan 1866; J. K. Alexander, bondsman; Wm. Maxwell, wit. married 1 Feb 1866 by H. B. Pratt.

Caldwell, Green W. & Jane N. McComb; Henry B. Williams, bondsman.

Caldwell, Hugh M. & Martha A. S. Ker, 19 Oct 1857; W. L. Caldwell, bondsman; married 20 Oct 1857 by J. Rumple.

Caldwell, J. C. & Lilla A. Henderson, 23 June 1856; S. N. Weddington, bondsman; H. P. Helper, wit. married 1 July 1856 by Drury Lacy.

MECKLENBURG MARRIAGES 1783-1868

Caldwell, J. L. & Hannah C. Neely, 28 June 1841; James Bigham, bondsman.

Caldwell, J. M. & C. N. Cochran, 1 Jan 1862; W. L. Caldwell, bondsman; W. K. Reid, wit. married 2 Jan 1862 by J. G. McLaughlin.

Caldwell, James & Patsey _____, 2 May 1801; John Black, bondsman; Jas. Conner, wit.

Caldwell, James & Minty Parks, 12 Aug 1816; Robert Caldwell, bondsman.

Caldwell, James & Mary Dixon, 23 Feb 1831; John M. McLean, bondsman.

Caldwell, James F. & Barbara M. McCracken, 29 Dec 1852; J. W. Blair, bondsman.

Caldwell, James M. & Margaret C. Moore, 15 Jan 1851; Thomas C. Allison, bondsman; B. Oates, C. C. C., wit.

Caldwell, Jeff & Amanda Hanley, 1 Jan 1866; married 2 Jan 1866.

Caldwell, John & Margarette Howie, 25 Feb 1823; Jeremiah Howie, bondsman; Isaac S. Alexander, wit.

Caldwell, John D. & Martha Kerr, 6 March 1855; married 6 March 1855 by W. H. Neal, J. P.

Caldwell, John H. & Jane C. Query, 2 Jan 1860; Saml. W. Caldwell, bondsman; W. K. Reid, C. C. C.,wit. married 5 Jan 1860 by J. G. McLaughlin.

Caldwell, John N. & Ruth Jane Alexander, 27 Jan 1857; R. N. Caldwell, bondsman; W. K. Reid, C. C. C., wit. married 29 Jan 1857 by R. H. Lafferty, Pastor of the Congregation of Sugar Creek.

Caldwell, Joshua J. & Drusilla J. Kelly, 6 Oct 1857; Wm. R. Berryhill, bondsman; W. K. Reid, C. C. C., wit. married 6 Oct 1857 by Wm. S. Norment, J. P.

Caldwell, McCamy W. & Mary A. Query, 12 Dec 1854; Wm. L. Caldwell, bondsman; W. K. Reid, C. C. C., wit. married 14 Dec 1854 by Walter S. Pharr.

Caldwell, Pinckney C. Dr. & Sarah R. Wilson, 12 Dec 1831; Dr. Thomas Harris, bondsman.

Caldwell, R. H. & M. E. E. Caldwell, 26 July 1859; S. W. Caldwell, bondsman; W. K. Reid, C. C. C., wit. married 28 July 1859 by Danl. A. Penick Sen.

Caldwell, R. N. & Henrietta L. Harris, 1st Sept 1857; C. Overman, bondsman; W. K. Reid, C. C. C., wit. married 2 Sept 1857 by C. K. Caldwell, minister.

Caldwell, Robert & Mary Shields, 20 March 1819; William Andrews, bondsman; Isaac Alexander, wit.

Caldwell, Robert & Levinah Houston, 27 Dec 1819; Wm Andrews, bondsman; Isaac Alexander, wit.

Caldwell, Robert A. & Martha Cochran, 7 Feb 1855; W. L. Caldwell, bondsman; W. K. Reid, C. C. C., wit.

Caldwell, Samuel & Esther Barnett, 11 March 1818; Amos Barnett, bondsman; Isaac Alexander, wit.

Caldwell, Samuel C. & Abigail B. Alexander, 8 May 1793; John McKnitt Alexander, bondsman; Wm. B.Alexander, wit.

Caldwell, Silas & Eliza J. Cochran, 26 Aug 1864; E. P. Cochran, bondsman.

Caldwell, Thomas G. & Betsey Black, 2 May 1801; William Conner, bondsman; Jas Conner, wit.

Caldwell, William & Angelina R. Templeton, 24 March 1851; Saml N. Weddington, bondsman.

Caldwell, William L. & Margaret P. S. Caldwell, 28 Oct 1857; D. A. Caldwell, bondsman; W. K. Reid, C. C. C., wit. married 29 Oct 1857 by Jethro Rumple.

Calhoun, William & Jane Lentile, 8 Oct 1825; Joseph Kerr, bondsman; Isaac Alexander, wit.

Collins, Ross & Elizabeth Foster, 28 Aug 1821; David Stewart Kern, bondsman.

Collins, Thomas & Margaret Polk, 19 Jan 1825; Samuel Allen, bondsman; Isaac Alexander, wit.

Collins, William R. & Nancy Braly, 5 Aug 1830; Francis Ross, bondsman.

Calvin, William & Harriet Watts, 20 Sept 1836; Charles Calvin, bondsman; B. Oates, C. C. C., wit.

Campbell, Andrew M. & Mary Jane Neely, 11 Sept 1837; R. R. Taylor, bondsman; A. J. Perry, wit.

Campbell, George & Mary Russell, 24 Jan 1791; Robert Erwin, bondsman; Isaac Alexander, wit.

Campbell, George L. & Mary J. Summerville, 1 Jan 1845; John L. Todd, bondsman; N. B. Taylor, wit.

Campbell, George L. & Martha J. Brown, 27 May 1854; A. H. Brown, bondsman; W. K. Reid, C. C. C., wit. married 28 May 1854 by Alex Cooper(?).

Campbell, Isaac & Catherine Orr, 4 Sept 1799; William Wallis, bondsman.

Campbell, Isaac & Mary A. Johnston, 4 Sept 1840; B. Oates, bondsman.

Campbell, Joab & Sarah Johnston, 5 Dec 1855; Wm. H. Campbell, bondsman; W. K. Reid, C. C. C., wit. married 12 Dec 1855 by T. M. Farren, V. D. M.

Campbell, John & Matilda Polk, 2 May 1792; Samuel Polk, bondsman; Isaac Alexander, wit.

Campbell, John & Elizabeth W. Alexander, 19 Aug 1817; Elias Alexander, bondsman.

Campbell, John & Miss Nancy _____, 28 July 1823; David Harry, bondsman.

Campbell, John A. & Susan Marander Alexander, 3 March 1841; John Sample Davis, bondsman.

Campbell, John D. & Miss Susan Grier, 22 July 1834; Stephen H. Smith, bondsman.

Campbell, Marcus Mc. & Martha Jane Nelson, 19 Feb 1852; W. H. Campbell, bondsman.

Campbell, Robert & Jane Turner, 30 March 1791; Alexander Tacy(?), bondsman; J. Mc. Alexander, wit.

Campbell, William & Deborah McRee(?),3 Feb 1790; William McRee, bondsman.

Campbell, William & Ann Shoeman, 7 July 1841; Samuel A. Harris, bondsman.

Campbell, Wm. H. & Jane C. Alexander, 13 July 1858; Thomas P. Rogers, bondsman, W. K. Reid, C. C. C., wit. married 15 July 1858 by R. H. Lafferty, Pastor of the Congregation of Sugar Creek.

Campbell, William J. & Margaret E. Faris, 8 Nov 1849; S. H. Johnson, bondsman.

Cannon, Theophilus & Jane Alexander, 14 Jan 1853; Tho. H. Brem, bondsman; B. Oates, C. C. C., wit. married 18 Jan 1853 by Walter W. Pharr.

Canon, Edward J. & Jane E.Alexander, 15 Nov 1842; James T. Henry, bondsman.

Canon, James & Ann Black, 29 July 1790; John Allison, bondsman; Wm. F. Alexander, wit.

Canon, Joseph & P____ Canon, 17 Aug 1803; Joseph Canon, bondsman.

Capps, Francis & Jane Lawing, 4 Feb 1836; Nathaniel P. Gray, bondsman; B. Oates, C. C. C., wit.

Capps, Hiram T. & Sarah R. Williamson, 23 March 1840; David McEmmerson, bondsman.

Capps, James & Levina Williamson, 9 Nov 1813; John McGinn, bondsman; Isaac Alexander, wit.

Capps, James & Polly Presley, 19 May 1846; Eli P. McCarver, bondsman; B. Oates, C. C. C., wit.

Capps, James & Sarah Jane Sharpe, 13 Sept 1856; Wm. W. Quinn, bondsman; W. K. Reid, C. C. C., wit.

Capps, John & Nancy Abernathee, 2 Dec 1811; David Gilmer(?), bondsman.

Capps, Joseph & Margaret Hepworth, 7 Dec 1839; John Lawing, bondsman; B. Oates, C. C. c., wit.

Capps, Lewis & Rachael Barnhill, 22 Feb 1814; James Carigan, bondsman; Isaac S. Alexander, wit.

Capps, Thomas & Caroline Lepner, 9 Oct 1809; Samuel Stricklin(?), bondsman; Isaac Alexander, wit.

Caps, Henry & Peggy Brown, 10 July 1823; Eli Martin, bondsman.

Carlock, Cornelius & Matilda Pyron, 5 Oct 1831; Thomas Carlock, bondsman; Isaac Alexander, wit.

Carlock, Thomas & Hannah Ste---, 26 April 1831; Cornelius Carlock, bondsman.

Careter,William & Mary Bradley, 10 Aug 1838; Elam Harrison, bondsman; B. Oates, C. C. C., wit.

Carnton, James & Miss Anne Platt, 28 Feb 1817; Allen Baldwin, Robert McKenzie, bondsmen; Alexander, C. M. C., wit.

Carothers, David & Nancy Knox, 22 May 1813; Robert Knox, bondsman; Isaac Alexander, wit.

Carothers, David J. & Mary Ann Wilson, 11 Nov 1844; John J. Knox, bondsman; N. B. Taylor, wit.

Carothers, J. D. & Nancy H. Knox, 17 March 1851; Samuel M. Whitesides, bondsman. married 20 March 1851 by A. L. Watts.

Carothers, James & Elisabeth Lorance, 17 May 1791; Archibald Houston, bondsman.

Carothers, James & Peggy Swann Neely, 3 Oct 1809; John S. Neely, bondsman; Isaac Alexander, wit.

Carothers, Thomas & Ann Stewart, 10 Feb 1797; John Phillips, bondsman; Isaac Alexander, wit.

Carothers, Thomas M. & Jane L. Potts, 7 June 1856; John S. Neely, bondsman; W. K. Reid, C. C. C., wit. married 16 June 1856 by J. G. Richards.

Carothers, William N. & Sarah Cornelia Saylor(?), 24 April 1849; S. D. Carothers, bondsman.

Carr, Hugh & Jane Brown, 20 April 1802; John Kerr, bondsman; Isaac Alexander, wit.

Carr, Hugh & Jean Gardner, 5 Aug 1809; James Gardner, Eliezer Flinn, bondsmen.

Carr, William & Polly Clark, 25 May 1810; Alexander Clark, bondsman; Isaac Alexander, wit.

Carragan, Charles H. & Margaret M. Russ, 28 July 1847; James M. Gilson, bondsman; Saml J. Lourie, wit.

Carrigan, William F. & Martha A. Ewert, 30 Oct 1849; H. D. Ewart, bondsman.

Carrel, James & Martha Williams, 11 June 1800; David McDonald, bondsman

Carrel, Nathan B. & Jannett Graham, 13 Oct 1831; Pearsall Thompson, bondsman.

Carrigan, Peter & Sally Linsing, 2 July 1810; John Muns, bondsman; Isaac Alexander, wit.

Carrigan, William & Rebeckah ____, 27 Dec 1793; Andrew Herman, bondsman.

Carrthers, John & Malinda Bonson, 28 May 1810; John Netiz, bondsman; Isaac Alexander, wit.

Carrothers, Thomas Neely & Peggy Neely, 1 Jan 1813; James Carothers, bondsman; Isaac S. Alexander, wit.

Carruth, George & Miss Polly Graham, 22 Oct 1816; Robert McKenzie, bondsman.

Carson, James H. & Mary Ann Williams, 24 May 1854; James M. Hutchison, bondsman; W. K. Reid, C. C. C., wit. married 25 May 1854 by R. H. Morrison.

Carson, Richard C. & Harriet A. Wilson, 28 Nov 1835; James H. Orr, bondsman; B. Oates, C. C. C., wit.

Carter, William & Elizabeth Goodman, 15 Jan 1839; B. Oates, wit.

Carter, William & Jane Baker, 12 Sept 1851; John W. Moore, bondsman; married 18 Sept 1851.

Cash, Francis A. & Harriet Ann Bates, 18 Nov 1822; A. Little, bondsman.

Cashen, Joel & Suckey Powers, 17 Oct 1811; William Duckworth, bondsman.

Cashen, Joel & Suckey Powers, 17 Oct 1811; William Caldwell, bondsman; Andrew Johnson, wit.

Cashing, John & Dolley Tucker, 1 July 1801; Henry Conner, bondsman; Jas Conner, J. P., wit.

Cashon, Archibald & Nancy Cashon, 4 Aug 1835; Thomas Cashon, bondsman; B. Oates, C. C. C., wit.

Cashon, Burwell & Catharine B. Dewese, 14 Aug 1839; John Warshaw, bondsman; James Johnston, wit.

Cashon, David L. & Cynthia J. Hutchison, 24 Jan 1853; John J. King, bondsman; B. Oates, C. C. C., wit. married 27 Jan 1853 by R. H. Lafferty, Pastor of the Congregation of Sugar Creek.

Cashon, Hiram W. & Melissa Ferrell, 4 May 1836; Thomas Cashon, bondsman; B. Oates, C. C. C., wit.

Cashon, Jaby & Patsy Powers, 29 Aug 1810; Miles Worsham, bondsman; Isaac Alexander, wit.

Cashon, Jaby & Amelia McLeary, 5 Sept 1846; Winslow Robinson, bondsman; N. B. Taylor, wit.

Cashon, Miles D. & Harriet Barnhill, 19 April 1849; James T. Cashon, bondsman; B. Oates, C. C. C., wit.

Cashon, Peter & Gemima Cashon, 6 Oct 1812; John Cashon, bondsman.

Cashon, Thomas & Sarah Sloan, 18 Nov 1820; John Sloan, bondsman; Isaac Alexander, wit.

Cashon, Thomas & Mary L. Brown, 2 Aug 1836; L. D. Porter, bondsman; B. Oates, C. C. C., wit.

Casper, Henry W. & Mary Hannon, 15 July 1839; Robert Mc. Jamison, bondsman; B. Oates, C. C. C., wit.

Cathcart, James L. & Mary Kimbel, 6 Dec 1828; Newton Cathcart, bondsman; Pearsall Thompson, wit.

Cathcart, John & Betsey Hipworth, 19 Oct 1812; John W. Herron, bondsman.

Cathcart, John C. & Margaret E. Stewart, 16 Jan 1858; Jos. B. Boyles, bondsman; W. K. Reid, C. C. C., wit. married 19 Jan 1858 by G. D. Parks.

Cathcart, John R. & Martha E. Johnston, 16 Dec 1852; A. A. Holshouser, bondsman; Jas Johnston, J. P., wit. married 21 ___ 1852 by Saml B. O.Wilson, V. D. M.

Cathcart, Newton & Caroline Cole, 23 Feb 1829; Joseph Berryhill, bondsman.

Cathcart, Robert & Sarah J. Brown, 29 May 1834; J. W. W. Faris, bondsman.

Cathcart, William & Miss Sarah _____; Jesse H. Clark, bondsman.

Cathey,Alexander, & Esther Waddell, 17 Feb 1804; Walter Carruth, bondsman.

Cathey, Alexander & Mary Blanchard, 25 Aug 1832; Andrew Rawdon, bondsman.

Cathey, Alexander A. & Nancy H. Todd, 23 April 1860; Wm. M. Auton, bondsman. married 24 April 1860 by Stephen Wilson, J. P.

Cathey, Alfred & Christian C. Underwood, married 21 May 1856 by G. L. Campbell, J. P.   John W. Neel, bondsman; W. K. Reid, C. C. C., wit.

Cathey, Andrew & Elizabeth A. Miller, 22 April 1835; Robert Beard, bondsman; James Johnston, wit.

Cathey, Archibald & Agness Slone, 25 May 179_; James Slone, bondsman; Ruthy Alexander, wit.

Cathey, Archibald & Martha Mahan, 1 March 1843; M. H. Waddell, bondsman; C. S. Alexander, wit.

Cathey, George & _____ Wilson, 7 April 1807; Alexander Cathey, bondsman.

Cathey, George & Malinda Ticer, 10 March 1842; D. C. Vaynes(?), bondsman.

Cathey, George C. & Nancy A. Cathey, 4 Dec 1839; George S. Sloan, bondsman; B. Oates, C. C. C., wit.

Cathey, George Henry & Emily Herron, 21 Nov 1863; W. D. Tevepaugh, bondsman; Wm. Maxwell, wit. married 26 Nov 1863 by G. C. Cathey, J. P.

Cathey, Henry & Mary J. Freeman, 5 Sept 1859; William A. Freeman, bondsman; W. W. Grier, wit. married 6 Sept 1859 by G. C. Cathy, J. P.

Cathey, James A. & Jane Izabella Alexander, 17 May 1848; George
C. Neel, bondsman.

Cathey, James A. & Elisabeth Jane Clark,22 Aug 1855; Robert A.
Freeman, bondsman; W. K. Reid, C. C. C., wit.

Cathey, Jesse & Sena Rogers, 14 Feb 1810; Joseph Wilson, bondsman;
Isaac Alexander, wit.

Cathey, John & Elizabeth Calhoun, 19 March 1800; George Calhoun,
bondsman.

Cathey, John & Miss Polly Neel, 3 March 1830; Archibald M. Clark,
bondsman; E. Elem, wit.

Cathey, John & Ann M. Niell, 11 May 1846; William S. Cathey,
bondsman; B. Oates, C. C. C., wit.

Cathey, John Junr. & Eliza Eliotte, 19 Feb 1816; George Waddle,
bondsman; M. M. Leary, wit.

Cathey, John A. & Mary D. Hipp, 21 Dec 1859; John N. Lee,
bondsman; W. K. Reid, C. C. C., wit. married 22 Dec 1859 by
J. P. Ross, J. P.

Cathey, John L. & Martha A. Cathy, 24 Jan 1866; Alexander Cathey,
bondsman; married 25 Jan 1866 by ___ Pharr.

Cathey, Joseph R. & Mary Ledford, 27 April 1846; James Jamison,
bondsman.

Cathey, Sugar & Adaline Blair, 20 Jan 1862; G. C. Cathey, bondsman;
married 11 Feb 1862 by J. C. Chalmers, Min.

Cathey, William & Susan A. Todd, 16 Jan 1864; A. W. Clark, bondsman. married 17 Jan 1866 by S. C. Pharr.

Cathey, Wm. A. & Sarah A. Clark, 25 Jan 1845; Peter Fite, bondsman.

Cauthorn, John & Polly Darnell, 28 Dec 1805; Thomas Boyd, bondsman.

Caziah, William & Miss Charrity Ritch, 13 Dec 1827; Jesse Stilwell,
bondsman; Wm. Houston, J. P., wit.

Chapman, Robert P. & Rachel M. Johnston, 21 May 1860; John C.
Reed, bondsman; W. K. Reid, C. C. C., wit. married 23 May
1860, by J. P. Ross, J. P.

Chapman, Robert P. & Miss J. C. Johnston, 1 Aug 1865; Mathew
Chapman, bondsman. married 2 Aug 1865 by J. S. Maxwell,
J. P.

Chappel, Eli & Mary Carruthers, 17 Jan 1866; W. K. Reid, bondsman.

Check, Randell & _____, 26 ___ 1807; Felty Cheek, bondsman.

Cheeck, Thomas M. & Elizabeth Phillips, 11 Aug 1863; W. J.
Collins, bondsman. married 13 Aug 1863 by A. Sinclair, Pres.
Pastor.

Chesheir, Burch & Jane B. Henderson, 5 May 1829; David Parks,
bondsman.

Choat, J. M. & Margaret J. Simeral, 8 Jan 1848; F. G. Simeral,
bondsman; B.Oates, C. C. C., wit.

39

Choat, William & Rachel A. Simril, 20 Aug 1849; Saml. B. Knox, bondsman.

Christenberry, James T. & Mary Robison, 15 March 1828; William Starnes, bondsman; P. Thompson, wit.

Christenberry, Caleb E. & Mary E. Neely, 28 April 1856; J. N. Knox, bondsman; W. K. Reid, C. C. C., wit.

Christenberry, Daniel A. & Margt. R. Moon, 2 April 1845; Ralph E. Irwin, bondsman; N. B. Taylor, wit.

Christenberry, Eli A. & Margaret Harrison, 1 Dec 1857; Joseph B. Christenberry, bondsman; W. K. Reid, C. C. C., wit. 8 Dec 1857, married by Isaac Wilson, J. P.

Christenberry, John G. & Jane C. Ferrell, 14 Feb 1859; William W. Ferrell, bondsman; John Phelan, wit. married 15 Feb 1859 by R. L. De Armor, J. P.

Christenberry, John H. & Telitha Ferrell, 10 May 1843; Elisha L. D. Christenbury, bondsman; W. W. Alexander, wit.

Christenberry, Joseph B. & Abigail Simpson, 1 Dec 1857; Eli A. Christenbury, bondsman; W. K. Reid, C. C. C., wit. married 2 Dec 1857 by G. W. M. Creighton.

Christenbury, Moses & Catharine Starns, 15 March 1828; William Harris, bondsman.

Christenbury, Moses M. & Mary Jane Ferrel, 15 Sept 1859; Cordy F. Brantley, bondsman; W. W. Grier, wit. married 15 Sept 1859 by D. Henderson.

Christenbury, R. F. & Mary Ann Peoples, 6 Nov 1865; M. Harky, bondsman; Wm. Maxwell, wit. married 7 Nov 1865 by R. L. D. Armor.

Christenbury, Samuel B. & Jane Delitha Johnston, 26 April 1861; M. D. L. Moody, bondsman. married 2 May 1861 by John Hunter, Pastor of Sardis Congregation.

Christenbury, Samuel H. & Mary E. Christenbury, 10 May 1856; Elam W. Whitlow, bondsman; W. K. Reid, C. C. C., wit. married 13 May 1856 by R. L. D. Armor, J. P.

Christenbury, Wm. G. & Mary M. Oaton, 2 Jan 1856; Richard Jordan, bondsman; W. K. Reid, C. C. C., wit.

Christenbury, William P. & Mary McGarrar, 24 May 1837; Gabriel Ferrell, bondsman; B. Oates, wit.

Clanton, Drury & Eleanor Beaty, 8 May 1828; Francis M. Beaty, bondsman; P. Thompson, wit.

Clanton, John B. & Ann Walker, 6 Aug 1856; I. J. Sloan, bondsman; W. K. Reid, C. C. C., wit. married 6 Aug 1856 by Samuel C. Pharr.

Clark, A. W. & R. A. Todd, 16 Jan 1864; William Cathy, bondsman; married 17 Jan 1866 by S. C. Pharr

Clark, Allison & _____, 1 Dec 1813; John Curry, bondsman.

Clark, Almarine & Elizabeth W. Robison, 27 Dec 1848; William H.
Clark, bondsman.

Clark, Andrew & Margaret Carson, 17 Oct 1823; Samuel Bigham, bondsman; Isaac Alexander, wit.

Clark, Ezekiel W. & _____ Baker, 20 April 1821; Jacob Baker, bondsman; _____ Alexander, wit.

Clark, Henry & Sarah Dixon, 4 Dec 1857; William Clark, bondsman;
W. K. Reid, C. C. C., wit. married 4 Dec 1857 by Jos. C. N.
Nicholson, J. P.

Clark, James & Lucy Beard, 18 Sept 1805; William Simmons, bondsman;
Isaac Alexander, wit.

Clark, James & Melissa Moore, 24 Nov 1829; Amzi Moore, bondsman;
Isaac Alexander, wit.

Clark, James & Sarah M. McCorkle, 15 Nov 1836; Le Rea, bondsman;
B. Oates, wit.

Clark, James A. & Margaret J. Clark, 10 April 1849; Wm. A. Stinson,
bondsman.

Clark, Jesse H. & Jane Pemella McGilvray(?), 14 April 1825;
Zenas A. Clark, bondsman; Isaac S. Alexander, wit.

Clark, John & _____, 23 Oct 1804; Dawson Williamson, bondsman.

Clark, John & Nancy Ann Freeman, 31 March 1859; John W.McAlister,
bondsman; W. K. Reid, C. C. C., wit. Consent of Mary Freeman
for her daughter Nancy Ann Freeman to marry John Clark, 31 March
1859, wit: J. W. McAllister. married 31 March 1859 by Jos. C.
Nicholson, J. P.

Clark, John W. & Betsey Capps, 23 Nov 1848; William Elliott, bondsman; B. Oates, C. C. C., wit.

Clark, John W. & Sarah J. Robison, 2 Feb 1858; Almarine Clark,
bondsman; John Phelan, wit. married 2 Feb 1858 by G. C.
Cathey, J. P.

Clark, Jonas & Ann Alexander, 31 March 1818; George Hampton,
bondsman; Isaac Alexander, wit.

Clark, Jonas & Miss Ann Johnston, 15 Sept 1824; Jesse H. Clark,
bondsman; R. S. Dinkins, wit.

Clark, N. Allison, & Harriet S. Rockwell, 16 May 1857; E. F.
Rockwell, bondsman; W. K. Reid, C. C. C., wit. married 21
May 1857 by E. F. Rockwell.

Clark, Robert F. & Nancy Beaty, 26 Sept 1839; John Reed, bondsman;
J. B. Kerr, wit.

Clark, Robert H. & Jane Carson, 15 July 1828; Archibald Waddle,
bondsman; Pearsall Thompson, wit.

Clark, Robt. H. & Christian A. Todd, 23 Dec 1841; James H. Kerr,
bondsman; C. T. Alexander, wit.

Clark, Robert M. & Margaret S. Irwin, 18 Dec 1838; John Mason,
bondsman.

Clark, Samuel & Matilda Clark, 19 Nov 1829; James M. Secrest, bondsman; A. Cooper, wit.

Clark, Thomas B. & Nancy Sing, 21 Dec 1836; John Irwin, bondsman; B. Oates, C. C. C., wit.

Clark, William & Ann Thompson, 2 Nov 1796; William Alexander, bondsman; Isaac Alexander, wit.

Clark, William & Lucinda Montgomerv, 27 Jan 1809; James Montgomery, bondsman.

Clark, William & Fanny Cathy, 23 July 1818; Joseph Allison, bondsman; H. M. Fox, wit.

Clark, Wm. & Lucretia Tayler, 30 Aug 1845; Wm. S. Norment, bondsman; C. S. Alexander, wit.

Clark, Wm. H. & Ann A. Todd, 13 Oct 1852; James W. McGinn, bondsman; S. Lourie, wit. married 14 Oct 1852 by G. C. Cathey, J. P.

Clark, William P. & Maria Louisa Hattaway, 24 July 1816; John T. Cowen, bondsman.

Clarke, Robert & Darcas Lindsay, 27 Feb 1790; James Speers, bondsman; Isaac Alexander, wit.

Clemans, Wm. & Mary C. Collier, 21 Dec 1863; Henry S. Miller, bondsman.

Cleny, James & Esther Mc-----, 5 Nov 1822; William Scott, bondsman.

Clonts, Adam & Patsey Blair, 25 Feb 1822; Jacob Clonts, bondsman; Isaac Alexander, wit.

Clontz, Jeremiah & Mary L. Byram, 12 Aug 1864; John Trelour, bondsman; married 12 Aug 1864 by J. C. Nicholson, J. P.

Cloye, J. G. & Susan Todd, 9 Feb 1846; Mortimer Connely, bondsman; S. J. ____, wit.

Cochran, A. H. & Jane T. Harris, 21 Aug 1838; Samuel P. Caldwell, bondsman.

Cochran, A. H. & Elizabeth R. Allison, 8 Feb 1851; Wm Allison, bondsman; B. Oates, C. C. C., wit.

Cochran, Ben & Mary Davis, 1 Dec 1790; William Henderson, bondsman(?); Isaac Alexander, wit.

Cochran, Elam P. & Mary G. McGinnis, 29 Aug 1842; Thomas H. McClelan, bondsman.

Cochran, Elam S. & Mary S. Reich, 20 Sept 1858; A. H. Cochran, bondsman; W. K. Reid, C. C. C., wit. married 21 Sept 1858 by R. H. Lafferty, Pastor of the Congregation of Sugar Creek.

Cochran, Eliezer & Mahuldah Worrick, 21 July 1815; Jesse Stilwell, bondsman; Isaac Alexander, wit.

Cochran, Ezra & Miss Hannah _____, 17 Feb 1824; Levi Cochran, bondsman.

Cochran, Jesse C. & Nancy M. Faulkner, 21 Dec 1859; R. C. Mc-
Ginnis, bondsman; W. K. Reid, C. C. C., wit. married 21 Dec
1859 by J. G. McLaughlin.

Cochran, John & Darcus(?) McEwen, 3 Aug 1791; Robert Cochran,
bondsman; John Allison, wit.

Cochran, John & Jenny Chapple, 20 Aug 1795; Thomas Cochran, bondsman; James Wallis, wit.

Cochran, John & Martha Rea, 6 June 1816; Andrew Rea, bondsman;
John Rea, J. P., wit.

Cochran, John F. & Eady R. Festerman, 4 Jan 1859; William R.
Cochran, bondsman; W. K. Reid, C. C. C., wit. married 5 Jan
1859 by J. G. McLaughlin.

Cochran, Joseph & Catherine C. McKnight, 8 April 1840; James
McKnight, bondsman.

Cochran, Joseph & Martha N. Sample, 24 April 1843; Thomas H.
Brem, bondsman; C. S. Alexander, wit.

Cochran, Joseph C. & Margaret J. Porter, 30 Nov 1853; Joseph C.
Walker, bondsman; W. K. Reid, C. C. C., wit. married 1 Dec
1853 by John Hunter, Pastor of Back Creek C.

Cochran, Joseph C. & Isabella Omelia Peeples, 11 Feb 1861;
J. N. Hunter, bondsman; W. K. Reid, C. C. C., wit. married
12 Feb 1861 by A. Ranson.

Cochran, Robert B. & Elisabeth C. Query, 22 Feb 1854; Livingston
Alexander, bondsman; W. K. Reid, C. C. C., wit. married 26
Feb 1854 by John Hunter, Pastor of Back Creek C.

Cochran, Robt C. & Mijah Cochran, 1 Dec 1856; Francis N. Query,
bondsman; W. K. Reid, C. C. C., wit. married 2 Dec 1856 by
Isaac G. McLaughlin.

Cochran, Robert C. H. & Barbara P. Cochran, 21 March 1855; Robt
W. Alexander, bondsman; W. K. Reid, C. C. C., wit. married
22 March 1855 by A. Foster Quay.

Cochran, Robert L. & Miss Martha M. McGinnis, 15 Dec 1846; A. W.
Cook bondsman; S. J. Lourie, wit.

Cochran, Robert M. & Eliza McGinniss, 4 Oct 1819; Elias Snell,
bondsman; Isaac Alexander, wit.

Cochran, Rt M. & Mary J. Davis, 31 Jan 1855; James M. McKnight,
bondsman; W. K. Reid, C. C. C., married 1 Feb 1855 by John
Hunter, Pastor of Back Creek Congr.

Cochran, Thomas S. & Ms. Cathren Dulan(?), 17 Jan 1816; Elias
Stilwell, bondsman; Tho. Morris(?), wit.

Cochran, U. C. & Elizabeth Jane Hunter, 25 Nov 1846; Tho. J.
Hunter, bondsman; B. Oates, C. C. C., wit.

Cochran, Willm. & Mary McCreery, 20 Aug 1795; Thomas Cochran,
bondsman; James Wallis, wit.

Cochran, William & Lydia E. Towle, 27 Sept 1853; Robert W. Cochran,
bondsman; W. K. Reid, wit. married 29 Sept 1853 by John
Hunter, Pastor of Back Creek C.

Cochran, William & Eliza Bain, 27 Oct 1857; Wm. C. Harris, bondsman; W. K. Reid, C. C. C.,wit.

Cochran, William C. & Margaret Galloway, 16 Dec 1845; Henry H. Galloway, bondsman; B. Oates, wit.

Cochran, Wm. L. & Sarah S. McCaleb, 14 Jan 1853; Wm. B. Cochran, bondsman.; B. Oates, C. C. C., wit. married 18 Jan 1853 by Walter S. Pharr.

Cochran, Wm. R.& Margaret Nelson, 17 Sept 1863; D. A. Caldwell, bondsman. married by J. G. McLaughlin (no date).

Cochrane, Levi & Elizabeth Bibby, 14 Feb 1822; Azeriah Cochran, bondsman.

Cockran, Charles H. & Cena Cochran, 15 May 1858; R. M. Cochran, bondsman; W. K. Reid, C. C. C., wit.

Coffey, David S. & Miss Jane E. Kerr, 24 July 1843; Wm. McIlwann, bondsman.

Coffey, James & Eli--- ------, 23 May 1827; Ben Morrow, bondsman; Pearsall Thompson, wit.

Coffey, John M. & Jane Kerr, 7 Jan 1839; David Morrow, bondsman; B. Oates, wit.

Cohoon, John & Abigail McCleary, 19 Sept 1803; Samuel McLeary, bondsman.

Cole, B. J. & Mary A. J. Page, 24 Sept 1858; James F. Page, bondsman; K. W. Berryhill, wit. married 24 Sept 1858 by F. M. Ross, J. P.

Cole, John & Mary Barnett, 25 Feb 1798; Samuel Yandell, bondsman; Isaac Alexander, wit.

Cole, John & Martha Weathers, 7 Aug 1797; John Weathers, bondsman.

Cole, Reuben & Elizabeth Shepperd, 23 Nov 1829; Adam Cooper, bondsman.

Cole, Thomas Trussel & Tabiath Burnett, 29 Dec 1803; William Burton, bondsman; Isaac Alexander, wit.

Cole, William A. & Mary Ann Chaney, 30 June 1859; James R. Gordon, bondsman; W. K. Reid, C. C. C., wit. married 30 June 1859 by Thos. W. Dewey, J. P.

Collens, Eli & Dorcas Alexander, 10 Dec 1829; Samuel Meacham, bondsman; Tho. B. _____, wit.

Collier, W. J. & Miss M. J. McGilvary, 24 May 1864; T. J. Wilkerson, bondsman.

Collins, James S. & Nancy C. Sloan, 2 Dec 1856; Robert Collins, bondsman; W. K. Reid, C. C. C., wit. married _ Dec 1856 by G. D. Parks.

Collins, John F. & Laura A. Hunter, 22 Feb 1864; J. S. Collins, bondsman; married 22 Feb 1864 by J. G. McLaughlin.

Collins, Louis D. & Cynthia Black, 18 July 1810; Nazara Poole, bondsman.

Collins, Robert D. & Eliza Wilson, 22 Oct 1850; James S. Collins, bondsman.

Colvert, Robert S. & Mary Jane Massey, 20 May 1839; J. P. C. Massey, bondsman.

Conder, George & Mary Griffith, 20 Dec 1820; James C.Griffith, bondsman; A. M. Alexander, wit.

Conder, John & Emily Houston, 29 Dec 1831; Uriah Harky, bondsman; B. Oates, D. C., wit.

Conder, Lewis & Rebecca Crowel, 17 Oct 1828; Ezekiel Crowell, bondsman; E. Elms, wit.

Conder, Peter & Caroline Thompson, 26 Nov 1833; James Ritch, bondsman; P. E. Lanier(?), wit.

Conder, Philip & Sophia Byram, 23 May 1820; John Tye, bondsman; Isaac S. Alexander, wit.

Conger, John A. & Rebecca _____, 14 Dec 1822; Robert Mich, Junr., bondsman.

Connoly, John & Mary Stanford, 1 March 1790; Robert Stanford, bondsman; J. Mc. Alexander, wit.

Connell, William T. & Polly Lesley Smith, 4 March 1803; Philip Roberts, bondsman.

Conner, James & _iley Wilson, 13 Aug 1795; Patrick Johnston, bondsman.

Conner, Thomas & Margaret Colley, 15 Feb 1817; Thomas Colley, bondsman; Isaac Alexander, wit.

Conrad, William & Eliza J. Springs, 16 Aug 1859; Jas. J. Black-wood, bondsman. married 16 Aug 1859 by Richd. H. Griffith, minister of the Gospel.

Cook, Amzi & Margery Jane McGinnis, 1 Oct 1848; W. A. Cook, bondsman.

Cook, Austin & Margaret Allen, 22 Sept 1818; Charles Cook, bondsman; Isaac Alexander, wit.

Cook, Chas. & Mary Sprott, 25 Aug 1812; Jno Paschall, bondsman; Chas. T. Alexander, wit.

Cook, Daniel & Martha Brumley, 18 April 1811; Marcus Alexander, bondsman; Isaac Alexander, wit.

Cook, George A. & Tersa M. Blanshet, 23 April 1841; Andrew J. Allen, bondsman.

Cook, James & Sarah Allen, 30 Dec 1806; William Cook, bondsman.

Cook, John & Margaret Cowan, 1 May 1802; Winslow J. McRee, bondsman; Isaac Alexander, wit.

Cook, Joseph & Sophia Herron, 22 Oct 1860; W. H. Alexander, bondsman; P. S. Whisnant, wit. married 23 Oct 1860 by B. H. Garrison, J. P.

45

Cook, Powel & Hannah Baker, 29 Oct 1817; Jordan Dillerman(?), bondsman.

Cook, Robert & Tirzah Orr, 4 Aug 1814; William J. Wilson, bondsman; Robt Wilson, wit.

Cook, Robert & Rachel Baker, 12 Oct 1816; Charles Cook, bondsman; Isaac Alexander, wit.

Cook, Robert N. & Jane Byram, 27 Dec 1831; John W. Adams, bondsman; B. Oates, D. C., wit.

Cook, Thomas & Peggy Lourie, 21 Dec 1807; Wm Cook, bondsman.

Cook, W. A. & Leonora A. Reed, 5 Sept 1848; W. S. Daniel, bondsman; Saml J. Lourie, wit.

Cook, William & Eleanor Allen, 6 Aug 1810; Thomas Allen, bondsman; Isaac Alexander, wit.

Cook, William & Sally Starnes, 1 June 1835; Franklin Shaffer, bondsman; B. Oates, C. C. C., wit.

Cook, William & Marget Blackwood, 16 Oct 1835; James T. J. Orr, bondsman.

Cook, William & Sarah Herron, 31 July 1850; J. W. Kellough, bondsman; B. Oates, C. C. C.,wit.

Coontz, Samuel & Mary Weeks, 26 Aug 181_; John McCulloch, bondsman.

Cooper, Alexander, & Miss Elizabeth Stinson, 4 March 1824; William Stinson, bondsman; R. J. Dinkins, wit.

Cooper, Alexander & Elizabeth Thompson,15 Aug 1850; W. W. Elms, bondsman; James _____, wit.

Cooper, Alexander & Elizabeth D. Thompson, 20 Feb 1852; Thomas T. Johnston, bondsman. married 25 Feb 1858 by ____ Nicholson, J. P.

Cooper, James M. & Martha H. Hall, 28 May 1846; A. A. Norwood, bondsman.

Cooper, John A. & Cynthia A. Williamson, 26 Sept 1849; William O. Moss, bondsman; Saml. J. Lourie, wit.

Cooper, Joseph & Mary Leviston, 30 March 1791; George Hill, bondsman.

Cooper, N. C. & Mary A. Cooper, 11 June 1856; J. A. Cooper, bondsman; J. H. Grier,wit. married 11 June 1856 by J. H. Grier, J. P.

Cooper, Thomas & Ann E.Adams, 18 Nov 1841; C. S. Alexander, wit.

Cooper, Thomas & M. Ruth Sadler, 27 Oct 1865; W. D. Clanton, bondsman; W. Maxwell, wit. married 31 Oct 1865 by Jas. C. Chalmers, minister.

Cooper, William & Margaret H. Hunter, 19 June 1823; Thomas Cooper, bondsman; Isaac Alexander, wit.

Cooper, William A. & Ann A. Dunn, 17 Jan 1848; J. W. Henderson, bondsman; B. Oates, wit.

Coover, Solomon & Jane Davis, 6 Dec 1834; Alfred R. Wolfington, bondsman; B. Oates, C. C. C., wit.

Cornelius, H. F. & Rebecca Cathey, 6 March 1858; James P. White, bondsman; W. K. Reid, C. C. C., wit. married 10 March 1858, by T. L. Triplett.

Cornelius, James H. & Nancy J. Cathey, 3 Oct 1865; J. S. Gordon, bondsman. married 11 Oct 1865 by E. W. Thompson.

Corathers, James S. & Hannah Starr Neely, 19 Feb 1813; Joseph Whiteside, bondsman.

Cosey, John & Susy Hartwick, 17 Feb 1816; Hubart Cosey, bondsman; Isaac Alexander, wit.

Coston, James & Su--- Berryhill, 24 Feb 1808; Thomas Sprott, bondsman.

Coughorn, James & Elisabeth Orr, 19 Jan 1798; Robert Coughorn, bondsman; Shared Gray, wit.

Coulter, David & Catharine Shinn, 14 Sept 1825; William H. Winston, bondsman; Isaac Alexander, wit.

Cousar(t), John B. & Mary J. Weddington, 11 Jan 1844; S. N. Weddington, bondsman; N. B. Taylor, wit.

Cousart, John B. & Jane B. Springs, 14 Nov 1854; S. N. Weddington, bondsman; W. A. Black, wit.

Cowan, A. M. & R. C. L. Donaldson, 9 Nov 1852; Rufus A. Bready, bondsman; James Johnson, J. P., wit. married 10 Nov 1852 by Saml. B. O. Wilson, V. D. M.

Cowan, David & Frances Waddle, 20 May 1835; Middleton Lawing, bondsman; B. Oates, C. C. C., wit.

Cowan, David & Elizabeth C. Clarke, 26 Oct 1846; Middleton Lawing, bondsman; B. Oates, C. C. C., wit.

Cowan, David & Marthew Eliott, 15 March 1808; Winfield Mason, bondsman.

Cowan, William G. W. & Mary Clark, 16 Oct 1816; Joseph Erwin, bondsman.

Cox, David & Miss Martha Dunn, 6 Jan 1830; Grief Gray, bondsman.

Cox, George L. & Precila Festerman, 3 July 1865; J. F. Butt, bondsman. married 3 July 1865 by Jno F. Butt, Local Deacon.

Cox, James & Rachel Jamison, 1 May 1811; Robert Sumpter, bondsman; M. McLeary, wit.

Cox, Samuel & Deborah C. Taylor, 2 April 1832; B. Oates, bondsman.

Cox, W. L. & Miss E. J. Love, 21 June 1865; G. W. Gatlin, bondsman; married 21 June 1865 by Jno F. Butt, Local Deacon

Cox, William G. & Sarah Spears, 17 Jan 1828; Ezekiel Elms, bondsman; Thomas B. Smartt, wit.

Coxx, Samuel & Sally Jamison, 10 April 1809; William Reed, bondsman.

Craige, Alexander & Agness Huey, 9 March 1804; John Huey, bondsman.

Craig, James & Mary McKnight, 20 Jan 1796; James McKnight, bondsman; Isaac Alexander, wit.

Craig, Leander & Margaret D. Yandles, 1 Sept 1859; Milas M. Yandle, bondsman; W. K. Reid, C. C. C., wit. married 12 Sept 1859 by C. Moretz, Clerg.

Craig, Moses & Margert Erwin(?), 26 Dec 1793; David Orr, bondsman; Willm. Matthews, wit.

Craig, William & Jobil Cry, ___ 1794; James Cry, bondsman; Shared Gray, wit.

Craig, William & Jennett Campbell, 23 April 1798; Robert Campbell, bondsman.

Craige, Micheal & Pemeala Woodall, 22 Oct 1835; Archabald Forbes, bondsman; John Stilwell, wit.

Crain, Nore & Mary Vickry, 5 July 1830; John McKorkel (McCorkle), bondsman; Jo. Cunningham, J. P.,wit.

Crain, Peyton & Pruda McLain, 10 March 1823; John Cowan, bondsman.

Crawford, Thomas & Mary Davidson, 27 April 1816; Saml. W. Davidson, bondsman; Alexr. M. Alexander, wit.

Creighton, H. L. & Mary Jane Means, 16 Nov 1859; A. W. Blair, bondsman; W. K. Reid, C. C. C., wit. married 16 Nov 1859 by A. Sinclair, Pastor Pres. Church, Charlotte, N. Ca.

Creighton, Joseph M. & Jane Adams, 1 Feb 1847; Thomas A. Adams, bondsman; B. Oates, wit.

Crenshaw, D. W. & Ann Long, 29 Sept 1856; Joseph R. Cathey, bondsman; W. K. Reid, C. C. C., wit. married 29 Sept 1856 by Wm. S. Norment, J. P.

Crenshaw, Hen(d)ry & Marey Mitchel, 26 May 1801; James Little, bondsman; Andw Walker, wit.

Crenshaw, L. Berry & Marey Robertson, 2 April 1801; James Little, bondsman; Andw Walker, J. P., wit.

Creswell, David & Katharine Nance, 30 Aug 1836; James Shepherd, bondsman; John Nance, wit.

Crispo, Antonio & Milly Porter, 7 Aug 1828; William H. Folger, bondsman.

Crockett, Archd. & Debrah Willson, 12 Jan 1792; Wm Potts, bondsman; Jno Duglass, wit.

Crockett, Archibald & Esther Davis, 3 April 1820; John McQuay, bondsman; Isaac Alexander, wit.

Crocket, John M. & Levicy C. Barnett, 29 Sept 1828; John J. Dunlap, bondsman; Pearsall Thompson, wit.

Crofford, James & Sally Graham, 5 Sept 1804; John Morris, bondsman.

Crofford, James & Susannah Phifer, 28 April 1813; James Crofford Senr., bondsman; Isaac Alexander, wit.

Cross, Lewis & Kessander W. Baker, 24 Feb 1829; David McGilvray, bondsman; Isaac S. Alexander, wit.

Cross, William & Mary Ann Jamison, 7 Feb 1850; James L. McLure, bondsman; B. Oates, C. C. C., wit. married 7 Feb 1850 by Wm. Davidson.

Cross, William & Hannah Chapman, 11 Jan 1860; J. P. Ross, bondsman; W. K. Reid, C. C. C., wit. married 12 Jan 1860 by J. P. Ross, J. P.

Crowell, Adam & Eleanor Lenmond, 1 Sept 1836; H. W. Black, bondsman; B. Oates, wit.

Crowell, Colson & Lucy Stuart, 15 Feb 1849; John R. Glover, bondsman; Saml A. David, J. P., wit.

Crowell, E. M. & Mary Jane Lambeth, 23 Dec 1865; J. H. McConnell, bondsman; married 26 Dec 1865 by J. C. Chalmers, Minr.

Crowell, E. M. & Cathrine Cagle, 19 March 1829; Samuel Yandle, bondsman.

Crowell, Elisha & Catherine Crowell, 13 March 1827; Berry Hooks, bondsman; Wm. ____, wit.

Crowell, Evan A. & Katherine Long, 8 Jan 1835; William C. Tartlow(?), bondsman; Wm. H. Simpson, J. P., wit.

Crowell, George & Elizabeth Pyrant, 30 Aug 1804; William Pyrant, bondsman.

Crowell, George & Marah Griffin, 6 March 1827; Micheal Crowell, bondsman.

Crowell, Henry & Apsey Fowler, 19 Aug 1830;Ephraim Secrest, bondsman; W. Simpson, wit.

Crowell, John & Isbel McWilliams, 2 Feb 1797; Joseph McQuiston, bondsman; Reuben Stewart, John Simpson, wit. (bond in one place has the groom as Simon Crowell).

Crowell, Michael M. & Elizebeth Mcall, 31 Aug 1843; Green L. Crowell, bondsman.

Crowell, S. W. & Mary E. Stowe, 26 Oct 1865; J. B. Greer, bondsman; married 31 Oct 1865 by Jas. C. Chalmers, minister.

Crowell, Simon--see Crowell, John

Crowell, William D. & Martha Purveance, 24 May 1831; James C. Davis, bondsman.

Crowell, Wm. S. & Mary Henderson, 7 Sept 1854; James A. Elms, bondsman; married 7 Sept 1854 by J. W. Morrow, J. P.

Crump , Alfred & Peggy Janes (both free), 18 Sept 1856; Wm. W. Quinn, bondsman; W. K. Reid, C. C. C., wit.

Crump, Coonrod & Elizebeth Bobbot, 26 Nov 1840; William Roark, bondsman.

Crump, Erwin & Mary C. Helms, 29 Aug 1860; Robert McEwen, bondsman; Erwin Ferny(?), wit.   married 30 Aug 1860 by R. McEwen, J. P.

Crump, Lewis & Mrs. Omey Helmes, 1 Sept 1849; Henry J. Crump, bondsman; Philemon Morris, wit.

Cruse, Henry & Dorcas C. Alexander, 6 Jan 1847; Henry C. Owens, bondsman; Saml J. Lourie, wit.

Crye, David & Jean Elott, 12 Jan 1797; Wm Crage, bondsman; Shared Gray, wit.

Culp, Bengn. & Mary Cline, 4 Sept 1787; George Rese (Rise), bondsman; Jno Rogers, wit.

Culp, Benjamine A. & Miss Caroline Hodd, 23 May 1848; John P. Weeks, bondsman; Saml. A. Davis, J. P., wit.

Culp, Drury M. & Sarah Jane Alexander, 24 July 1841; Thomas O. Hood, bondsman; N. B. Taylor, wit.

Culp, John & Polly Ann Alexander, 22 July 1802; Augustus Alexander, bondsman; Isaac Alexander, wit.

Culp, John & Milly L. Robinson, 27 Jan 1852; James Cunningham, bondsman; Saml A. Davis, J. P., wit.

Culp, M. M. & Rachel C. Johnston, 19 Oct 1861; J. Harvey White, bondsman; W. K. Reid, C. C. C., wit.   married 6 Nov 1861 by __ Meacham, minister of the gospel.

Culp, Thomas G. & Catharine Mc. McCollum, 14 Sept 1852; John N. Kerr, bondsman; married 14 Sept 18__, by __ Patterson.

Cunningham, H. B. & Dovy A. W. Alexander, 14 April 1845; W. P. Caldwell, bondsman; C. T. Alexander, wit.

Cunningham, James & Mary Jane Red, 21 Dec 1847; John W. Blair, bondsman.

Cunningham, William & Jane Smith, 16 Oct 1805; Richard Sharp, bondsman; J. Wallis, wit.

Cunningham, William K. & Rebecca S. Swann, 10 Feb 1847; James Glover, bondsman.

Cunningham, William R. & Caroline Downes, 16 July 1830; James Parks, bondsman.

Cureton, John & Lydia L. Potts, 28 Feb 1825; Jeremiah Cureton, bondsman.

Cureton, Jeremiah & Nancy F. Potts, 15 Feb 1825; Jeremiah Cureton of Lancaster Dist., S. C. and Nancy F. Potts of Mecklenburg Co., N. C.

Curry, M. W. & Elizabeth Jane Horstler, 2 Dec 1834; Isaac Spencer, bondsman; B. Oates, C. C. C., wit.

Curry, Nixon & Dovey Caldwell, 6 Sept 1819; John McLane, bondsman.

Curry, Robert & Serah Taylor, 6 March 1792(?); Robert Slone, bondsman.

Curry, Rufus J. & Elizabeth D. Sloan, 15 Aug 183_; John M. Alexander, bondsman; James Johnston, wit.

Cuthbertson, David & Matilda Simpson, 2 Aug 1841; Jefferson Simpson, bondsman; H. Stewart, wit.

Cuthbertson, John & Margaret Simpson, 15 Dec 1804; John Simpson, bondsman; Isaac Alexander, wit.

Cuthbertson, Moses Wilson & Rachael Lucinda Russell, 25 Aug 1828; David Cuthbertson, bondsman.

Cuthbertson, William & Marey Rusel, 11 Feb 1836; James J. Rusel, bondsman; Eli Stewart, wit.

Davis, Thomas & Hanah Henderson, 17 Sept 1792; Moses Thomson, bondsman.

DeCamp, Charles & Miss M. J. Stewart, 11 Nov 1864; W. J. Kerr, bondsman.

DeWolfe, Fred. S. & Laura E. Kerr, 11 May 1864; Samuel A. Davis, bondsman; married 11 May 1864 by B. M. Palmer.

Duckworth, John Sample & Sarah Stewart, 9 Sept 1801; Geo Duckworth, bondsman; Isaac Alexander, wit.

Eagle, John & Sarah J. McGathey, 8 Dec 1856; S. W. Robison, bondsman; W. K. Reid, C. C. C. married 9 Dec 1856 by R. H. Lafferty, Pastor of the Congregation of Sugar Creek.

Eainey, A. P. & Jane S. Campbell, 30 June 1858; Henry Thomas, bondsman; W. K. Reid, C. C. C., wit. married 1 July 1858, by R. B. Jones, M. G.

Earnhart, John & Mary A. Montgomery, 21 Jan 1846; Thomas O. Earnheardt, bondsman; S. J. Lourie, wit.

Earnhart, John M. & Elizabeth A. Hunter, 1 Nov 1837; Robert B. Hunter, bondsman.

Earnheart, S. O. & Margt. Emily Hunter, 17 Feb 1847; Abner Hunter, bondsman; Sam. J. Lourie, wit.

Easley, John & Martha Brown, 26 Oct 1811; Walter Fairis, bondsman.

Easley, John L. & Mary Cnup, 15 Sept 1852; Ervin Finey, bondsman; W. C. Patterson, wit. married 16 Sept 1852 by W. C. Patterson, M. G.

Edwards, A. J. & E. M. Dearmond, 3 June 1856; A. W. Blair, bondsman; W. K. Reid, C. C. C., wit. married 5 June 1856 by J. M. Walker, Min.

Edwards, James & Sophia Miller, 29 Nov 1835; James Rowland, bondsman; Isaac S. Alexander, wit.

Edwards, John A. & Harriet M. Guyer, 15 Feb 1856; Thomas J.
Glover, and A. M. Blair, bondsmen; W. K. Reid, C. C. C., wit.

Edwards, Marcus B. & Abagail S. Dearman, 15 Dec 1836; Richard L.
Dearman, bondsman; B. Oates, C. C. C., wit.

Edwards, Matthew A. & Matilda Manson, 4 Feb 1840; no bondsman,
no wit.

Edwards, Robert M. & Margaret E. Allen, 12 July 1860; Moses
Ashley, bondsman; W. K. Reid, C. C. C., wit. married 12
July 1860 by Richd. H. Griffith, Minister of the Gospel.

Edwards, Thos. & Sarah Harris, 11 Oct 1865; Wm. Maxwell, C. C. C.,
wit; married 12 Oct 1865 by R. Z. Johnston, M.G.

Edwards, Wm. O. & Elenor J. Hovel, 1 Sept 1828; Zachariah McCawley,
bondsman; Pearsall Thompson, wit.

Eigenbrun, Isaac & Miss Carrie Cohen, 6 May 1863; Isaac Lowenstein,
bondsman. married 12 Oct 1865 by R. Z. Johnston, minister.

Eller, William & Susannah Weant, 5 Feb 1866; J. C. C. Frazer,
bondsman; Wm. Maxwell, wit. married 6 Feb 1866 by J. G.
McLaughlin.

Elliot, Henry & Elizabeth Secrest, 27 July 1842; James A. Johnston,
bondsman.

Elliott, E. O. & Martha J. E. McRee, 28 Oct 1851; E. C. Davidson,
bondsman; James Parks, wit. married 29 Oct 1851 by R. H. Lafferty, Pastor of the Congregation of Sugar Creek.

Elliott, Samuel H. & Mrs. Mary Secrast, 5 Oct 1829; James S.
Chambers, bondsman; Adam Cooper, wit.

Elliott, Samuel H. & Emma C. Archey(?), 3 Jan 1866; John C.
Grier, bondsman.

Elliott, T. B. & Ruth J. Shaw, 23 June 1856; Wm. P. Hill, bondsman;
W. K. Reid, C. C. C., wit. married 23 June 1856 by A. W.
Miller.

Elliott, Thomas Junr. & Martha Elliott, 7 Jan 1809; John B. Elliott, bondsman; Isaac Alexander, wit.

Elliotte, Hugh & Jane Jameson, 3 Jan 1807; Jonathan Griffeth,
bondsman.

Elliotte, Richard W. & Biddy E. Lawing, 15 March 1842; Baldwin
Frew, bondsman.

Elliottee, John B. & Nancy Johnston, 12 April 1847; Wm. M. Hutchison, bondsman; Saml. J. Lourie, wit.

Elwood, John & Sarah Miller, 16 Jan 1836; Thomas Davis, bondsman;
B. Oates, C. C. C., wit.

Elmes, Frederick K. & Ann Neel, 20 Jan 1821; Jesse Ck. Neel,
bondsman.

Elms, A. A. & M. E. Kee, 18 Oct 1854; J. H. Elms, bondsman; J. W.
Morrow, J. P., wit. married 18 Oct 1854 by J. W. Morrow, J. P.

Elms, C. H. & Angelina Bryant, 6 May 1858; John Phelan, bondsman. married 6 May 1858, by E. D. Meynardie, Pastor M. E. Church, Charlotte, N. C.

Elms, James A. & Malvina Blankenship, 18 Aug 1858; John P. Elms, bondsman; K. W. Berryhill, wit. married __ Aug 1858 by P. Nicholson.

Elms, William W. & Mary A. Davidson, 7 Nov 1836; B. F. Davidson, bondsman.

Emerson, David M. & Isabella Adeline Todd, 27 Dec 1838; N. S. A. Chaffin, bondsman.

Emerson, Henry & Mrs. Jane M'Comb, 25 May 1809; William Luckey, bondsman.

Emerson, John S. & Sarah Barnycastle, 1 Aug 1822; Thomas Searcy, bondsman; R. J. Dinkins, wit.

Emerson, Stephen T. & Nancy Jamison, 7 Dec 1825; Jesse Clark, bondsman; Isaac Alexander, wit.

Emerson, William & Mary Torrence, 6 June 1812; Adam Torrence, bondsman.

Emmonds, Franklin & Margaret Still, 15 Jan 1845; John B. Peoples, bondsman.

Emmons, Franklin & Mary Orr, 29 Nov 1848; James L. Porter, bondsman.

Enlow, M. L. & Lydia S. Smith, 19 Jan 1860; J. L. Stephens, bondsman; W. K. Reid, C. C. C., wit. married 19 Jan 1860 by Richd. H. Griffith, minister of the gospel.

Ensey, West & Nancy Warbritton, 15 March 1832; Andrew Harris, bondsman; B. Oates, wit.

Eppes, Elisha & Eliza Allen, 23 Jan 1854; Philip J. Russell, bondsman; W. K. Reid, C. C. C., wit. married 24 Jan 1854 by S. C. Pharr, V. D. M.

Ervin, John S. & Agnes M. McGinnis, 13 Dec 1845; Charles H. Erwin (Irwin), bondsman; B. Oates, wit.

Ervin, Wm. & Permillia McDowell, 19 June 1842; Robt W. McDowell, bondsman.

Erwin, C. M. & Editha R. S. A. Walker, 9 Oct 1855; Wm. H. Tunstall, bondsman; W. K. Reid, C. C. C., wit. married 9 Oct 1855 by A. W. Miller.

Erwin, Columbus M. & Jane A. Hunter, 2 Feb 1847; Henry S. Hunter, bondsman; Saml. J. Lourie, wit.

Erwin, Jno. J. & Sarah M. Allison, 12 Jan 1825; Joshua D. Boyd, bondsman; Isaac S. Alexander, wit.

Erwin, S. W. & Mary C. Alexander, 30 Jan 1836; William W. Elms, bondsman; B. Oates, wit.

Evans, Charles & Amanda Kirkpatrick, colored, 6 April 1866; Joe Wallace, bondsman; Wm. Maxwell, wit.

Evans, John & Hanah Chapman, 2 Sept 1799; Charles Wright, bondsman; Isaac Alexander, wit.

Evans, John & Nancy Clark, 23 July 1812; Rinehart Suther, bondsman; Isaac Alexander, wit.

Ewart, Hugh & Margret McCulloch, 22 Jan 1816; Joseph Ewart, bondsman; Isaac Alexander, wit.

Ewart, Joseph R. & Mary E. Barnett, 17 Jan 1846; Wm. G. Barnett, bondsman; S. J. Lourie, wit.

Ewart, R. K. & M. A. M. Beard, 20 Dec 1861; Thomas Y. McConnell, bondsman; W. K. Reid, C. C. C., wit. married 25 Dec 1861 by A. Ranson.

Ewing, J. H. & Martha N. Dunn, 7 Dec 1852; S. A. Roper, bondsman; B. Oates, C. C. C., wit. married 7 Dec 1852 by G. L. Campbell, J. P.

Ewing, John & Violet Hutchison, 8 Oct 1856; Colin C. King, bondsman; W. K. Reid, C. C. C., wit. married 8 Oct 1856 by David Henderson, J. P.

Ewing, Wm. A. & Jane E. McCracken, 2 Oct 1860; Wm. D. McCracken, bondsman; W. W. Grier, wit. married 2 Oct 1860 by W. M. Kerr.

Ezell, Frederic & Jensy Sprott, 23 Jan 1805; James Kerr, bondsman; J. Wallis, wit.

Ezell, Moses & Mary Bowden, 16 April 1831; Samuel Ticer, bondsman; B. Oates, D. C., wit.

Ezzell, Andrew S. & Mary Stitt (Still?), 25 Nov 1837; Joshua D. Bowden, bondsman; B. Oates, C. C. C., wit.

Ezzell, Andrew S. & Louisa M. Dunn, 1 Oct 1839; Charles E. Moss, bondsman; M. Launier, wit.

Ezzell, James A. & Sarah A. Gray, 4 Jan 1864; D. G. Maxwell, bondsman; married 6 Jan 1864 by R. Z. Johnston.

Fagert, Joseph & Sally Cathcart, 29 Dec 1817; James L. Cathcart, bondsman; Isaac Alexander, wit.

Faires, George N. & Telitha Hayes, 12 Nov 1860; W. K. Reid, C. C. C. wit. Elijah Hayes, bondsman. married 13 Nov 1860 by Lorenzo Hunter, J. P.

Faires, J. W. & Catharine Hoover, 20 June 1842; Jonathan Rea, bondsman.

Faires, J. W. W. & Margaret L. Marshall, 4 March 1836; Alexander L. Porter, bondsman; B.Oates, C. C. C.

Faires, Marcus C. & Dovey E. Shields, 21 Dec 1852; Marquis L. Garris, bondsman; B. Oates, C. C. C., wit. married 23 Dec 1852 by John Hunter, Pastor of Back Creek, Con.

Faires, Robert & Susannah Orr, 22 May 1816; Joseph S. Orr, bondsman; Philemon Morris, wit.

Faires, Robert & Mary Holms, 25 June 1822; John Brown, bondsman; Isaac S. Alexander, wit.

MECKLENBURG MARRIAGES 1783-1868

Faires, Robt W. & Susannah A. Plummer, 25 Nov 1851; Samuel F.
Houston, bondsman; B. Oates, C. C. C., wit. married 27 Nov
1851 by R. H. Lafferty, Pastor of the congregation of Sugar
Creek.

Faires, Walter & Martha Wilson, 17 Aug 1808; Thomas Sprott,
bondsman; Isaac Alexander, wit.

Faires, William & Elizabeth Orr, 4 Jan 1813; Joseph Hayes,
bondsman.

Faris, Samuel & Evalina Stinson, 24 Feb 1847; Wm. M. Porter,
bondsman; B. Oates, C. C. C., wit.

Faris, T. P. G. & Margaret R. Stinson, 22 March 1854; John W.
Hayes, bondsman; W. K. Reid, C. C. C., wit.

Faris, Zenas W. & Mary Allen, 9 Feb 1859; D. A. Caldwell, bondsman; W. K. Reid, C. C. C., wit. married __ Feb 1859 by J. B.
Watt, V. D. M.

Farley, P. R. & C. D. Merritt, 15 Sept 1864; H. P. Helper, bondsman. married 4 Oct 1864 by J. L. Kirkpatrick, Pastor College
Ch.

Farr, Ephraim & Easter Latta, 14 July 1801; Joseph Latta, bondsman; Jno Harris, J. P. wit.

Farr, John & Anne Moore, 10 Oct 1803; Daniel Moore, bondsman.

Farra, John & ___ Cox, 25 March 1816; Pressley M. Cox, bondsman.

Farrow, Thomas M. & Mary E. Harrison, 6 May 1848; Alex M. Forster,
bondsman. B. Oates, C. C. C. wit.

Farson, John & Martha Yandell, 8 Sept 1803; Moses Walker, bondsman; Isaac Alexander, wit.

Feezell, Samuel & Lucinda A. Simons, 2 July 1834; David G. Giboney,
bondsman.

Ferrell, Benj. G. & Mary Kincaid, 20 March 1851; William Ferrell,
bondsman; B. Oates, C. C. C. wit. married 20 March by D. L.
Simmons.

Ferell, Matthew R. & Margaret J. Christenbury, 1 March 1859;
John G. Christenbury, bondsman; W. K. Reid, C. C. C., wit.
married 3 March 1859 by R. L. D. Armon, J. P.

Feris, Joseph & Nancy Squicey(?), 5 March 1827; Thomas Hucks,
bondsman; Philemon Morris, wit.

Ferguson, David J. & Permelia Orr, 5 Sept 1832; J. Franklin Orr,
bondsman; W. W. Elms, wit.

Ferguson, F. A. & M. A. Flanigan, 25 Jan 1864; W. H. Hall, bondsman; Wm. Maxwell, bondsman. married 26 Jan 1864 by R. Z.
Johnston.

Ferguson, James R. & Martha E.Williams, 25 Oct 1865; R. W. Sehorn,
bondsman; Wm. Maxwell, wit. married 29 Oct 1865 by E. C.
Williams.

Ferguson, M. W. & Martha E. Galloway, 19 Feb 1856; M. L. Barringer, bondsman; W. K. Reid, C. C. C., wit. married "same
week" by J. R. Pickett, Minister of Gospel.

Ferguson, P. C. & C. C. Hough, 14 Oct 1865; Samuel Blair, bondsman; Wm. Maxwell, wit. married 23 Oct 1865 by E. C. Williams.

Ferguson, Richard & Emeline Arrowood, 22 March 1853; Charles T.
Means, bondsman; B. Oates, C. C. C., wit. married 23 March
1853 by J. P. Ross, J. P.

Ferguson, Seth & Ann Erwin, 7 Aug 1797; Joseph Cooke, bondsman.

Ferrell, John W. & Susan O. Wallace, 14 Aug 1854; George W.
Alexander, Junr., bondsman; W. K. Reid, C. C. C., wit. married 15 Aug 1854 by W. G. Barnett, J. P.

Ferrell, Wm. Jr. & Elvira Brown, 7 Feb 1845; Benj. G. Ferrell,
bondsman; N. B. Taylor, wit.

Ferrell, Edmund R. & Dorcas Erwin, 10 Sept 1828; Abner Hunter,
bondsman; Thomas B. Smart, wit.

Ferrell, James & Mary Sloan, 24 Feb 1821; Gabriel Ferrell, bondsman; Isaac S. Alexander, wit.

Fesperman, Fredrick & Dorins Radish, 6 Jan 1818; Edward Dozier,
bondsman; Isaac Alexander, wit.

Fesperman, Levi & Polly Thompson, 13 March 1824; Frederick Fesperman, bondsman.

Festaman, John & Charity Watts, 3 July 1833; James Melton, bondsman; F. M. Ross, wit.

Festerman, Andrew (free negro) & Julia Cathey (free negro), 17
Dec 1858; Stephen Wilson, bondsman; W. K. Reid, C. C. C., wit.
married 18 Dec 1858 by Stephen Wilson, J. P.

Festerman, Joseph & Miss Nancy Cibbans, 7 Oct 1824; William
Secress, bondsman; R. J. Dinkins, wit.

Festerman, Levi & Frances Tarlton, 2 March 1861; D. S. Rea, bondsman; W. K. Reid, C. C. C., wit. married 4 March 1861 by
William McComb, J. P.

Festerman, Michael & Betsey McKibben, 29 Jan 1821; Matthew Hall,
bondsman; Isaac Alexander, wit.

Fewell, William P. & Agnes Alexander, 5 Nov 1853; Wm. B. Pressley,
bondsman; W. K. Reid, C. C. C., wit. married "Dr. Wm. B.
Fewell & Miss Agness Alexander in the county of Mecklenburg N. C.
on the 22d day of November 1853." by C. K. Caldwell, minister.

Fields, Minos & Mary L. Alexander, 25 Dec 1849; Henry Cruse,
bondsman; Saml A. Davis, J. P., wit.

Fields, Stephen & Susanna McDonald, 24 Aug 1790; Hezekiah Briant,
bondsman; Hansell Hicks, bondsman; Isaac Alexander, wit.

Fifer, David & Poly McCollum, 3 June 1800; John Harkey, bondsman;
Wm. McCall, J. P., wit.

Fight (Fite), George & Jenny Owens, 27 June 1797; William Owens, bondsman; Isaac Alexander, wit.

Fincher, Benjamin & Elisebeth McKaven (McKown?), 29 June 1815; Philemon Morris, bondsman.

Fincher, John & Mary McCay, 12 Sept 1805; Joseph Fincher, bondsman; J. Wallis, wit.

Fincher, Joseph & Mary Horn, 5 Feb 1822; Ezekiel Horn, bondsman; Isaac Alexander, wit.

Fincher, Levi G. & Nancy Morris, 25 Feb 1841; Wm. M. Mathews, bondsman.

Fincher, McKuon & Sarah Phifer, 9 Jan 1845; John Phifer, bondsman; Daniel Wentz, J. P., wit.

Fincher, Silas A. & Margaret Stitt, 6 Jan 1842; Robert Patton, bondsman; C. T. Alexander, wit.

Fincher, William & Nancey Skipper, 28 Nov 1840; William Rourk, bondsman; Philemon Morris, wit.

Fincher, Wm. C. & Mary L. Craig, 8 Oct 1857; M. J. Anderson, bondsman; W. K. Reid, C. C. C., wit.

Finley (Findlay), James & Miss Mary Duffey, 23 April 1824; Daniel Robison, bondsman; R. J. Dinkins, wit.

Finley (Findley), William & Sarah Hamilton, 3 Aug 1796; Charles Finley, bondsman; James Wallis, wit.

Fisher, Adam & Mary Woolf, 8 July 1794; John Wolf, bondsman; Shared Gray, wit.

Fisher, John & Mary Starnes, 11 Dec 1837; Philip Wolfe, bondsman; B. Oates, C. C. C., wit.

Fisher, John & Jane Little, 13 Oct 1865; Wm Dillon, bondsman. married 15 Oct 1865 by Jno. F. Butt.

Fisher, Philip & Miss Margaret Thompson, 16 Jan 1843; James A. McLoud, bondsman.

Fite, Abraham & Jane Abernathy, 12 Nov 1834; Thomas T. Johnston, bondsman; B. Oates, C. C. C., wit.

Fite, Green L. P. & Nancy A. C. McCuie, 12 May 1846; Elam M. Sprott, bondsman; S. J. Lourie, wit.

Fite, James & Mary L. Owens, 5 June 1819; John Fite, bondsman; Isaac Alexander, wit.

Fite, John & Elizabeth Owens, 15 July 1798; William Owens, bondsman; Isaac Alexander, wit.

Fite, Joseph N. & Nancy E. Cashion, 10 June 1844; Peter Fite, bondsman; N. B. Taylor, wit.

Fite, Solomon & Elizabeth Blades, 18 July 1843; Adam C. Anderson, bondsman.

Fite, William J. & Sarah R. Wilson, 20 April 1850; John D. Rankin, bondsman; James Parks, wit.

Fitten, John & Polly Franklin, 27 Feb 1798; James Cunningham, bondsman.

Flanigan, John O. & Jane R.˙ Walker, 6 Sept 1839; Robert W. Reid, bondsman.

Flanigan, Samuel & Margaret H. Brown, 10 Feb 1834; Pearsall Thompson, bondsman.

Flanikan, Samuel & Susannah Hayse, 2 Sept 1812; Joseph Hays, bondsman; Isaac S. Alexander, wit.

Flenaken, Andrew & Miss Jane Wallis, 9 March 1824; Silas Alexander, bondsman; R. J. Dinkins, wit.

Flaniken, David & Louisa Byram, 8 Oct 1835; John F.Orr, bondsman; B. Oates, C. C. C., wit.

Flennagen, Jes. P. & A. A. McEwen, 2 Dec 1864; C. M. Ray, bondsman. married 1 Dec 1864 by Richd. H. Griffith.

Flenniken, James N. & Eliann Hood, 15 Nov 1817; Isaac Flenniken, bondsman; Isaac Alexander, wit.

Flenniken, John & Elizabeth Searcy, 24 March 1828; Isaac Hyams, bondsman; P. Thompson, wit.

Flenniken, Samuel & Martha Flenneken, 15 Dec 1824; William Walker, bondsman; Isaac S. Alexander, wit.

Flenniken, John & Maryann W. Reed, 15 Aug 1849; M. D. L. McLeod, bondsman; Saml J. Lourie, wit.

Flenniken, R. G. & E. R. Kerr, 12 Nov 1860; S. M. Gallant, bondsman; John T. Downs, bondsman; W. K. Reid, C. C. C., wit. married 14 Nov 1860 by J. Rumple.

Flenniken, William & Winny Culpeper, 30 July 1801; John Williamson, bondsman; Isaac Alexander, wit.

Flin, Joseph & Elizabeth Sample, 26 April 1802; Joseph Bowman, bondsman.

Flincher, Elisha & Malinda Paxton, 13 March 1833; Gilbert Paul, bondsman; R. J. Dinkins, wit.

Flinn, Joseph & Hannah Moore, 19 Oct 1812; Josiah Alexander, bondsman; Isaac Alexander, wit.

Flinn, William & Mrs. Mary Irwin, 6 Feb 1804; Robert Irwin, bondsman; Isaac Alexander, wit.

Flinn, Wm. M. & Eliza C. Henderson, 15 Dec 1834; Joseph C. Nicholson, bondsman; B. Oates, C. C. C., wit.

Flow, Ambrose C. & H. J. Gingles, 7 Jan 1857; Jas. C. Flow, bondsman; W. K. Reid, C. C. C., wit.

Flow, David & Mary Miller, 1 Feb 1809; John Flow, bondsman; Isaac Alexander, C. M. C., wit.

Flow, David & Jane McLoud, 6 July 1819; Nehemiah A. Harrison, bondsman; Isaac Alexander, wit.

Flow, Evan A. & Mary E. Houston, 31 Jan 1859; Joseph H. McClain, bondsman; W. K. Reid, C. C. C., wit. married 3 Feb 1859 by J. Rumple, V. D. M.

Flow, James & Mary E. McNeely, 23 March 1836; James T. McKelvy, bondsman.

Flow, John & Peggy Miller(?), 23 Nov 1819; David Flow, bondsman; Isaac S. Alexander, wit.

Flow, John & Miss Jane Russell, 6 Feb 1843; John W. Miller, bondsman.

Flow, John & Sarah Wilson, 23 Feb 1838; McCamey W. Miller, bondsman.

Flow, Jonathan H. & Ann Eliza Walkup, 20 Oct 1840; Robt H. Weddington, bondsman; W. F. Alexander, wit.

Foard, William & Nancy Barr, 6 Oct 1813; Daniel Fox, bondsman; Susan R. Alexander, wit.

Foard, William & Elisebeth Neel, 6 Oct 1814; John Foard, bondsman; Phm. Morris, wit.

Foard, Wm. C. & Matilda Woodall, 9 July 1859; Thomas Woodall, bondsman; J. L. Brown, wit. married 14 July 1859 by William McComb, J. P.

Foard, Zebulon & Ann Millar, 4 Aug 1813; Z. Morris, bondsman.

Forbes, J. C. & Sarah R. Lee, 12 Nov 1860; J. C. Deans, bondsman; W. K. Reid, C. C. C., wit. married 12 Nov 1860 by A. W. Lineberry.

Ford, Charles A. & Susan Hux, 1 Deč 1856; D. W. Hux, bondsman; W. K. Reid, C. C. C., wit.

Ford, Henry & Mary Moore, 19 Dec 1796; Michael Lawrence, bondsman.

Ford, John & Dorcas Flow, 13 Nov 1855; Wilson Wallace, bondsman; W. K. Reid, C. C. C., wit.

Ford, John C. & Mary Ann Osborne, 23 May 1846; George A. Gaskey, bondsman; B. Oates, C. C. C., wit.

Ford, Wm. G. & Matilda S. Clark, 22 Feb 1866; A. W. Alexander, bondsman; Wm. Maxwell, wit. rarried 1 March 1864 by John Douglas.

Fore, Dick & Culdinia Sloan, 11 Jan 1866; Lawson Fore, bondsman; Wm. Maxwell, wit. married 12 Jan 1866 by J. Alexander.

Forsythe, John & Nancy Doulin, 10 Feb 1807; Robert Duffy, bondsman. (not on microfilm)
Forsythe, John & _____, (no date), C. Lafayette Alexander, bondsman.

Forsythe, John & Lilly Butler, 15 Nov 1797(?); James Reid, bondsman; Isaac Alexander, wit.

Foster, Daniel & Jamima Gardner, 7 April 1812; Francis Irwin, bondsman; Isaac S. Alexander, wit.

Foster, Henry & Miss Jane Alexander, 24 Jan 1824; Pinkney Alexander, bondsman.

Foster, J. E. & Ellen Davis, 13 Aug 1856; Samuel W. Harris, bondsman; W. K. Reid, C. C. C., wit. married 13 Aug 1856 by R. H. Lafferty, Pastor of the Congregation of Sugar Creek.

Foster, Joseph & Elizabeth Furr, 22 Dec 1830; William Graham, bondsman; E. Elms, wit.

Foster, William (free) and Anabella Wilson (free), 29 Dec 1857; Isaac Reid (free), bondsman; W. K. Reid, C. C. C., wit. married 29 Dec 1857 by Horatio H. Hewitt, Presbyter.

Fosythe, Hugh & Eliza Kerr, 16 Jan 1824; Joseph Rogers, bondsman; Isaac Alexander, wit.

Fowler, Washington & Sarah Ray, 2 July 1833; Jason Winchester, bondsman; Daniel Harget, wit.

Fox, Daniel & Elizabeth Foard, 3 Feb 1813; Zebulon Morris, bondsman; Isaac Alexander, wit.

Fox, John & Rachel Briant, 22 Nov 1815; John McQuay, bondsman; Isaac Alexander, wit.

Fox, Stephen (Dr.) & Cynthia Irwin, 18 April 1810; William Beaty, bondsman.

Foy, Isaac & Nicey Irwin, 26 Feb 1866; Ed Wheeler, bondsman; Wm. Maxwell, wit. married 26 Feb 1866 by Richd H. Griffith

Franklin, Saml & Dorcas Parker, 6 Aug 1800; Thomas Parker, bondsman; Isaac Alexander, wit.

Frantz, Lorenzo D. & Lucinda E. Rayborne, 3 Oct 1865; John Sheak, bondsman. married 5 Oct 1865 by Jno F. Butt.

Fraser, Isaac & Polly Todd, 11 April 1804; Jas. H. Fraser, bondsman.

Frazer, Isaac A. & Margaret A. Montgomery, 12 Feb 1855; Saml J. Lourie, bondsman; W. K. Reid, C. C. C., wit. married 13 Feb 1855 by G. L. Campbell, J. P.

Frazer, J. N. & Miss M. Marshal, 4 May 1865; Oswald Alexander, bondsman. married 8 May 1865 by G. McDonald, J. P.

Frazer, John T. & Margaret A. Sizer, 17 June 1861; Eli Stephens, bondsman; W. K. Reid, C. C. C., wit. married 17 June 1861 by C. Overmand, J. P.

Frazer, P. J. & Mary J. C. Talley, 7 Oct 1865; John T. Frazer, bondsman; married 12 Oct 1865 by J. D. Carpenter, Preacher in Charlotte Ct.

Frazer, Waren F. & Mary J. Montgomery, 8 Aug 1859; John T. Fraser, bondsman; W. K. Reid, C. C. C., wit. married 11 Aug 1859 by G. L. Campbell, J. P.

Frazier, John D. & Margaret Ewart, 24 March 1853; John W. Rainey, bondsman; B. Oates, C. C. C., wit. married 6 April 1853 by Walter S. Pharr.

Frazier, W. C. & Miss Cornelia R. Beaty, 19 Jan 1843; Moses W. Alexander, bondsman.

Freaser, John C. & Mary Griffith, 10 Feb 1832; Joseph C. Nicholson, bondsman; B. Oates, wit.

Freaser, John L. & Margaret E. Jamison, 24 Dec 1859; Thomas Ledwell, bondsman; W. K. Reid, C. C. C.,wit. married 1 Jan 1860 by C. Overman, J. P.

Freaser, Joseph A. & Flora Calder, 15 April 1837; Robert G. Robison, bondsman; Jno. J. Dunlap, wit.

Freeman, Archd. A. & Jane Byram, 4 March 1816; Willm. Rudisill, bondsman.

Freeman, Charles & Nancy Ballard, 16 July 1811; Nicholas Anderson, bondsman; Isaac Alexander, wit.

Freeman, Charles T. & Margaret Simpson, 24 Jan 1829; Wm. A. Simpson, bondsman; Isaac Alexander, wit.

Freeman, George & Margaret E. McCord, 12 April 1845; Thomas T. McCoard, bondsman; N. B. Taylor, wit.

Freeman, James & Mary Lee Gibson, 21 Dec 1818; Saml Berryhill, bondsman; Isaac S. Alexander, wit.

Freeman, Jas. & Mary Saunders, 6 Aug 1844; James Reid, bondsman; N. B. Taylor, wit.

Freeman, James T. & Isabella Collins, 22 Nov 1852; James S. Collins, bondsman; B. Oates, C. C. C., wit. married 23 Nov 1852 by J. B. Watt, V. D. M.

Freeman, John & Margaret Holmes, 23 Oct 1862; Robert B. Wallace, bondsman; married 24 Oct 1862 by R. McEwen, J. P.

Freeman, John B. & Parmelia Todd, 22 Dec 1824; John Reid, bondsman; Isaac S. Alexander, wit.

Freeman, Michael W. & Harriet M. Henry, 14 Aug 1854; James T. Freeman, bondsman; W. K. Reid, C. C. C., wit. married 15 Aug 1854 by A. M. Watson, minister.

Freeman, Reuben N. & Miss Margt. E. Todd, 3 March 1824; John A. Todd, bondsman; R. J. Dinkins, wit.

Freeman, Reuben N. & Martha Caroline Farris, 22 Dec 1851; Michael W. Freeman, bondsman; B. Oates, C. C. C., wit. married 23 Dec 1851 by A. L. Watts,V. D. M.

Freeman, Reuben N. & Mrs. Mary A. Cathcart, 4 Feb 1856; John W. Moore, bondsman; W. K. Reid, C. C. C., wit. married 11 Feb 1856 by G. C. Cathey, J. P.

Freeman, Riley & Sarah Robison, 2 April 1861; married 2 April 1861 by Wm. S. Norment, J. P. Jones Skinner, bondsman.

Freeman, Robt A. & Elvina F. Clark, 27 Dec 1855; John W. Clark, bondsman; W. K. Reid, C. C. C., wit. married 5 Feb 1856 by G. L. Campbell, J. P.

Freeman, Robert A. & Martha J. Berryhill, 5 Jan 1859; W. W.
Cathcart, bondsman; W. W. Grier, wit. married 6 Jan 1859 by
J. B. Watts (Pastor).

Freeman, Thomas J. & Harriet C. Reed, 16 Dec 1850; George F. Reed,
bondsman; B. Oates, wit.

Freeman, W. A. & Francis A. Cathey, 1 Jan 1866; Alexander Cathey,
bondsman; married 2 Jan 1866 by S. P. Berryhill, J. P.

French, William & Elisabeth Skipper, 3 Oct 1855; Joseph Hartis,
bondsman; W. K. Reid, C. C. C., wit. married 3 Oct 1855 by
J. Walker, J. P.

Freser, James & Katherine Davies, 31 Mar 1791; Alexd Robeson,
bondsman; J. Mc. Alexander, wit.

Freser, Saml & Mary Semple, 31 March 1790; Ezek. Alexander, bondsman; J. Mc. Alexander, wit.

Frew, Archibald & Ann S. Cowen, 5 Feb 1806; David F. Cowan,
bondsman.

Friday, Sidney & Julia Festerman, 10 Jan 1866; Jackson Friday,
bondsman. married 11 Jan 1866 by L. J. Sloan, J. P.

Frizzle, John & Margret Bowan, 20 Feb 1799; James Ramsey, bondsman.

Fuller, Alsey & Margaret Whitesides, 23 Sept 1835; Abel Bollinger,
bondsman; B. Oates, C. C. C., wit.

Fuller, Bartholomew, & Darcus C. Alexander, 8 Aug 1848; Wm Smith,
bondsman; Sam. J. Lourie, wit.

Fullwood, John M. & Elizabeth Howard, 10 Sept 1818; William Howard,
bondsman.

Fullwood, Robert & Margaret R. Blythe, 23 March 1847; Thos. L.
C. W. Moore, bondsman; Sam. J. Lourie, wit.

Fulwood, Saml M. & Ann B. Howard, 17 Oct 1831; Arthur Greer,
bondsman; R. S. Dinkins, wit.

Gage, George W. & Nancy Garris, 1 Sept 1829; Elam Hunter, bondsman;
A. Cooper, wit.

Galbreth, James & Jean Walker, 13 June 1796; John Walker, bondsman.

Gallant, John F. & Mary O. Simril, 27 Oct 1857; John B. Grier,
bondsman; W. K. Reid, C. C. C., wit. married 27 Oct 1857 by
James B. Watt, V. D. M.

Gallant, John F. & E. M. Stowe, 24 Sept 1864; A. C. Williamson,
bondsman; married 29 Sept 1864 by J. C. Chalmers, minister.

Gallant, S. M. & Mrs. Margaret Gary, 20 Feb 1864; D. G. Maxwell,
bondsman; Wm. Maxwell, wit. married 23 Feb 1864 by Jas. C.
Chalmers, minr.

Gallant, Stephen M. & Harriet C. Rudisill, 15 Jan 1834; Matthew
Neagle, bondsman.

Galloway, F. L. & Martha N. Hunter, 15 Dec 1838; Wm. C. Cowan, bondsman.

Galloway, Francis L. & Nancy Galloway, 1 Aug 1836; Thomas H. Galloway, bondsman; B. Oates, wit.

Galloway, Henry H. & Esther E. Walker, 19 Dec 1846; James M. C. Hunter, bondsman; Saml. J. Lourie, wit.

Galloway, Robert H. & Sarah A. Neal, 2 April 1862; Wm. H. Alexander, bondsman; W. W. Grier, wit. married 4 April 1862 by J. G. McLaughlin.

Galloway, Robert W. & Elizabeth W. Galloway, 23 Sept 1845; Hugh Galloway, bondsman; Wm. T. Alexander, wit.

Galloway, Samuel & Deborah Black, 2 Oct 1820; George W. Houston, Junr., bondsman; Isaac Alexander, wit.

Galloway, Thomas H. & Caroline Query, 20 Oct 1840; Jos. C. Ross, bondsman; W. F. Alexander, wit.

Gallway, Hugh & Nancy Querie, 17 Nov 1813; Robert Hunter, bondsman; Isaac S. Alexander, wit.

Gallway, John & Lucy Thompson, 18 Jan 1809; Thomas Hunter, bondsman; Isaac Alexander, wit.

Gallway, Josiah & Esther Walker, 29 Jan 1817; Cyrus Henderson, bondsman.

Gallway, Thomas & Peggy Black, 31 March 1813; Robert Hunter, bondsman.

Gamble, James & Nancy K. Morrow, 19 Aug 1851; Joseph R. Morrow, bondsman.

Gardner, Hezekiah & Margaret E. Archer, 23 Sept 1859; Cyrus A. Archer, bondsman; W. K. Reid, C. C. C., wit. married 26 Sept 1859 by W. G. Barnett, J. P.

Gardner, John R. & Dorcas Baker, 19 July 1835; Isaac Hyams, bondsman; B. Oates, C. C. C., wit.

Gardner, Robert & Jean Meek, 10 March 1796; Thomas Boal, bondsman.

Gardner, Thomas H. & Nancy Irwin, 17 Oct 1832; Thomas A. Mera, bondsman.

Gardner, William & Eleanor Thompson, 13 Jan 1806; Daniel Galloway, bondsman; Isaac Alexander, wit.

Garris, Marquis, & Sarah A. Hunter, 18 April 1857; Samuel Wittowsky, bondsman; W. K. Reid, C. C. C., wit. married 23 April 1857 by R. H. Lafferty, Pastor of the congregation of Sugar Creek.

Garris, Marcus L. & Susan A. Farris, 21 June 1849; Robert W. Farris, bondsman; Saml. J. Lourie, wit.

Garrison, Benjamin & Mary Ann Hunter, 7 Oct 1838; James M. Alexander, bondsman.

Garrison, D. B. & M. H. Hunter, 5 Dec 1859; J. W. Brown, bondsman; W. K. Reid, C. C. C., wit. married 8 Dec 1859 by A. Ranson.

63

Garrison, James T. & Emily Smith, 12 Feb 1857; Wm. K. Bowdon, bondsman; W. K. Reid, C. C. C., wit. married 16 Feb 1857 by P. Nicholson.

Garrison, Manson A. & Margaret Hunter, 16 Oct 1838; J. W. Simmons, bondsman; B. Oates, wit.

Garrison, Samuel & Martha Morrison, 13 March 1811; Thomas Morrison, bondsman.

Garrison, Samuel & Nancy C. Hunter, 9 Sept 1845; James Wallace, bondsman; Wm. F. Alexander, wit.

Garrison, Samuel & Jane E. Hunter, 25 Nov 1850; David Allen, bondsman; B. Oates, C. C. C., wit. married "short after the date of the licence" Walter S. Pharr.

Garrison, William, & Rebecca A. Hunter, 28 Sept 1847; Abner S. Hunter, bondsman; S. J. Lourie, wit.

Garrison, William G. & Nancy E. Bigham, 8 Jan 1855; D. B. Garrison, bondsman; W. K. Reid, C. C. C., wit. married 11 Jan 1855 by Rev. R. F. Taylor, Pastor of Prosperity.

Garriss, Turner & Miss Nancy Holms, 17 March 1825; Humphrey S. Hunter, bondsman; Richd Gillespie, wit.

Garrisson, Thomas & Lucy Jenkins, 10 Nov 1865; Lewis Potts, bondsman; Wm. Maxwell, wit. married 13 Nov 1865 by W. J. Alexander

Gascoigne, Robert & Polly Moore, 7 Jan 1813; Allen Reed, bondsman; Ruthy Alexander, wit.

Gaskey, William & Susanna Hogard(?), 15 Nov 1824; Charles Dennis, bondsman; Jas. Ritch, wit.

Gaston, John B. & Sarah J. Torrence, 11 Nov 1857; James M. Hutchison, bondsman; W. K. Reid, C. C. C., wit. married 11 Nov 1857 by Rev. S. C. Phar, D. D.

Gaston, Larkin B. & Miss H. C. Reid, 2 Jan 1843; Hugh Kirkpatrick, bondsman; C. T. Alexander, C. C. C., wit.

Gean, James & Almina L. Blalock, 21 Sept 1836; John D. Elliott, bondsman; B. Oates, wit.

Gheen, Danl & Amanda Smart, 18 May 1848; W. H. Neel, bondsman.

Gibbins, John & Giney Dunn, 24 June 1800; Francis Gibbens, bondsman; Shared Gray, wit.

Gibbon, Robert & Miss Mary A. Rodgers, 14 Dec 1865; John E. Brown, bondsman. married 20 Dec 1866 by R. Burwell.

Gibbs, John A. & Ellen A. L. Osborne, 27 Sept 1856; W. B. Osborne, bondsman; W. K. Reid, C. C. C., wit. married 3 Oct 1856 by Walter S. Pharr.

Gibbs, Willis & Peggy Wear, 4 Sept 1809; Robert Parks, bondsman; Isaac Alexander, wit.

Gibony, David G. & Sarah Ann Julin, 2 Jan 1837; James S. Patterson bondsman; B. Oates, wit.

Gibony, John & Hannah Maxwell, 1 Feb 1806; Adam M. Raben(?), bondsman.

Gibson, Charles L. & Mary An Graham, 18 Aug 1856; E. C. Elms, bondsman; W. K. Reid, C. C. C., wit. married 18 Aug 1856 by J. R. Pickett, Min. of Gospel.

Gibson, David M. & Mary Almina Glen, 29 Dec 1857; Franklin C. Glenn, bondsman; W. K. Reid, C. C. C., wit. married 31 Dec 1857 by Jos. C. Nicholson, J. P.

Gibson, Henry & Caroline Klutze, 22 Jan 1866; Henry Johnston, bondsman.

Gibson, J. Augustus & Susan Thomas, 17 Dec 1857; J. R. Long, bondsman; John Phelan, wit. married 17 Dec 1857 by Stephen Wilson, J. P.

Gibson, J. P. & Matte M. Kirkpatrick, 13 Jan 1864; D. R. Phifer, bondsman. married 13 Jan 1864 by J. L. Kirkpatrick, Pastor College Church.

Gibson, John & Catharine Johnston, 18 June 1808; R. Johnston, bondsman; Isaac Alexander, wit.

Gibson, John & Rachel Davis, 4 Sept 1824; Daniel Davis, bondsman; Isaac Alexander, wit.

Gibson, John & Jane O. McCaleb, 31 Jan 1855; B. F. Davidson, bondsman; W. K. Reid, C. C. C., wit. married 1 Feb 1855 by John Hunter, Pastor of Back Creek Congn.

Gibson, John A. & Rachel E. Bell, 23 April 1836; Decature Whitley, bondsman; John Nance, wit.

Gibson, Joseph H. & Sally Edwards, 7 Oct 1806; Isaac Edwards, bondsman; Isaac Alexander, wit.

Gibson, Samuel & Mary Davies, 10 Feb 1791; John Gibson, bondsman; J. Mc. Alexander, wit.

Gibson, Thomas & Eliza Houston, 14 Sept 1840; David O. McRaven, bondsman; James Johnston, wit.

Gibson, William & Cornelia A. West, 15 July 1826; Neal A. West, bondsman.

Gibson, William & Jane Huckaby, 21 Dec 1859; James A. Boyles, bondsman; R. F. Blythe, J. P., wit. married 21 Dec 1859 by R. F. Blythe, J. P.

Gibson, William & Matilda Moore, 31 Dec 1861; S. H. Brown, bondsman; W. K. Reid, C. C. C., wit. married 31 Dec 1862 by R. F. Blythe, J. P.

Gilbreath, Hugh & Sally Knighten, 1 Dec 1804; Hugh Walker, bondsman.

Giles, H. A. & Mary E. Houston, 27 Oct 1859; Franklin Horah, bondsman; W. K. Reid, C. C. C., wit. married 26 Oct 1859 by Drury Lacy, Off: Clergyman.

Giles, Miles & Mae W Camer(?), 26 Feb 1822; William A. Canon, bondsman.

65

Giles, Wm. & Hannah Gardner, 2 Aug 1792; Robt Smith, Nat. Giles, bondsmen.

Giles, William Mason & Drucinda Gray, 21 March 1821; Edwin Alexander, bondsman; Isaac S. Alexander, wit.

Gilland, John H. & Nancy C. Godsey, 13 Dec 1854; married 13 Dec 1854 by James Johnston.

Gillespie, A. Monroe & Miss R. M. Sloan, 26 Oct 1863; J. S. Collins, bondsman.

Gillespie, Archibald & Druscilla S. Gray, 9 Jan 1840; William T. Robinson, bondsman; B. Oates, C. C. C. wit.

Gillespie, David A. & Adelia Gray, 20 Dec 1860; Thos E. Washam, bondsman; P. S. Whisnant, wit. "When application was made for this licence the questin was asked by the clerk as to the age of the Girl, and answered by Gilespie that she would be 16 next Febry..." married 20 Dec 1860 by Charles Overman, J. P.

Gillespie, Joseph R. & Catharine E. Douglass, 26 July 1858; Wm. A. Gillespie, bondsman; W. K. Reid, C. C. C., wit.

Gillespie, T. A. & Mary A. Sloan, 20 Feb 1864; Thos. M. Kerns, bondsman; married 23 Feb 1864 by Robt Burrvill(?).

Gillespie, Theophilus A. & Nancy E. Potts, 10 April 1843; William A. Gillespie, bondsman.

Gillespie, Thomas & Margret Allison, 11 Jan 1827; Ezekiel Elms, bondsman; Eli Spring, wit.

Gillespie, Thomas D. & Laura L. Sadler, 31 July 1862; S. P. Alexander, bondsman; married 31 July 1862 by A. Sinclair, Presbyterian Pastor.

Gillespie, Wm. A. & Mary C. Cathey, 13 April 1858; Joseph R. Gillespie, bondsman; Jno Phelan, wit. married 20 April 1858 by L. M. Little.

Gilley, Armead & Matthay Tarlton, 18 Jan 1830; James Tarlton, bondsman; Braly Oates, wit.

Gilliland,Aaron & Ann Alexander, 28 Jan 1793; John Gilleland, bondsman; James Meek, wit.

Gilleland, Aaron & Sarah Saloman, 25 April 1815; David Alexander, bondsman; Isaac Alexander, wit.

Gilliland, Aaron & Nancy Bridges, 16 June 1818; Thomas Kennedy, bondsman.

Gilliland, Thos & Mary Barr, 16 Oct 1815; John Berry, bondsman.

Gillon, John & Eleanor T. Moore, 27 Nov 1835; James F. Houston, bondsman; B. Oates, wit.

Gilmore, Richard & Eliz. Wilson, 28 Oct 1800; John Duckworth, bondsman.

Gilmore, William & Susan Simons, 7 Jan 1822; Josiah Gilmer, bondsman; Isaac S. Alexander, wit.

66

Gilmor, William & Martha Curry, 24 Jan 1797; Robert Slone, bondsman; Isaac Alexander, wit.

Givenes, Allen & Mary Forsythe, 15 Nov 1791; Thomas Reid, bondsman; Isaac Alexander, wit.

Givens, Robert & Susy White, 23 Aug 1787; Robert Phillips, bondsman; Thos Burke, wit.

Givens, Samuel & Mary Pitman, 8 Jan 1818; Chas Cook, bondsman.

Glass, Francis & Miss Sally Varner, 13 March 1822; Francis G. Query, bondsman; Isaac Alexander, wit.

Glenn, Franklin C. & Mary J. Cashon, 29 May 1854; Julius D. Rodgers, bondsman; W. K. Reid, C. C. C., wit. married 1 June 1854 by G. C. Cathy, J. P.

Glen, John & Jane J. Hart, 11 April 1861; J. W. Blair, bondsman; P. S. Whisnant, wit. married 16 April 1861 by W. R. Maxwell, J. P.

Glenn, Benjamin F. & Rachel C. M. Gingles, 18 Jan 1855; John Mcw. Alexander, bondsman; W. K. Reid, C. C. C., wit. married 23 Jan 1855 by Danl A. Penick.

Glenn, D. P. & R. H. E. Rodden, 11 Jan 1865; B. G. Hiney, bondsman.

Glenn, David F. & Mary Simpson, 23 Jan 1830; Benjamin Simpson, bondsman.

Glenn, William J. & Sarah Standly, 29 Dec 1830; Henry B. Williams, bondsman; E. Elms, wit.

Glover, Hartel & Jane Smith, 15 Nov 1809; Daniel Smith, bondsman.

Glover, Hesekiah & Sarah Taylor, 14 Jan 1793; John Glover, bondsman; James Meek, wit.

Glover, Nelson & Eliza Stewart, 5 Jan 1825; George Buchanan, bondsman; Isaac S. Alexander, wit.

Glover, William & Sarah McCloud, 21 Nov 1851; Henry H. Glover, bondsman; James Parks, wit.

Goforth, John & Polly Ferrill, 14 Dec 1813; John Benham(?), bondsman; Isaac Alexander, wit.

Gooden, David & Margra S. Stockton, 5 Aug 1856; Wm. A. Owens, bondsman; W. K. Reid, C. C. C., wit. married 6 Aug 1856 by C. Overman, J. P.

Goodin, Andrew & Mary Johnson, 15 Dec 1828; Robert Cathcart, bondsman; Pearsall Thompson, wit.

Goodin, Jesse C. W. & Sarah E. Warwick, 7 April 1851; Jno A. Young, bondsman; Sam. E. Belk, wit.

Goodrum, William H. & Elizabeth D. Bell, 11 Oct 1844; Wm Johnston, bondsman; N. B. Taylor, wit.

Goodrum, Z. J. & Rebeca B. Alcorn, 17 Dec 1850; Moses P. Alexander, bondsman; Wm. Patterson, wit.

Gordon, Eli & Elizabeth Craig, 8 Dec 1818; Uriah Gordon, bondsman; Isaac Alexander, wit.

Gordon, Isaac & Rebecah Joster(?), 27 Nov 1821; Levi Gorden, bondsman; Jno Ritch, J. P., wit.

Gordon, Uriah & Barbara Redding, 11 Dec 1819; Levi Gordon,bondsman; Isaac Alexander, wit.

Gough, Edward & Madulsy Jenkins (both colored), 19 Oct 1865; S. F. Houston, bondsman; married 19 Oct 1865 by Jno. F. Butt.

Graham, Alexander & Mary Taylor, 28 Jan 1829; Pearsall Thompson, bondsman; Thomas Harris, wit.

Graham, George & Lydia Potts, 30 Nov 1802; Wm. McKee, bondsman; J. Mealas(?), wit.

Graham, George F. & Martha Ann E. Harris, 15 March 1826; Moses W. Alexander, bondsman; Isaac S. Alexander, wit.

Graham, John, a free man of color, & Mary, a free girl of color, 15 Dec 1854; Wm. E. Skinner, bondsman; W. K. Reid, C. C. C., wit.   married 21 Dec 1854 by G. C. Cathey, J. P.

Graham, John D. & Elizebeth E. Connor, 30 May 1815; Richard S. Maclean, bondsman; Isaac S. Alexander, wit.

Graham, Richard & Ruth Massey, 12 Oct 1807; John Graham, bondsman; Isaac Alexander, wit.

Graham, Samuel & Sarah Strawbridge, 20 Jan 1800; John Walker, bondsman.

Graham, William & Nancy Booker, 24 Aug 1812; James Robison, bondsman; Isaac Alexander, wit.

Grant, James & Betheney Prim, 20 Feb 1812; Adam McRaven(?), bondsman; W. Monteith, wit.

Grant, Rufus & Senea A. Taylor, 3 May 1862; Yany Pace, bondsman; W. K. Reid, C. C. C., wit. married by J. G. McLaughlin.

Gray, Admiral N. & Elizabeth A. Mason, 9 Oct 1834; Wm. A. F. Davidson, bondsman;

Gray, Alexander, & Esther Paxton, ___ 179_; Moses Dickey, bondsman; James Wallis, wit.

Gray, Bill, free boy of color, & Nelly Little, free girl of color, 12 Nov 1857; A. P. Gray, bondsman; W. K. Reid, C. C. C., wit. married 12 Nov 1857 by Wm. S. Norment, J. P.

Gray, E. D. & Sarah E. Weathers, 25 Sept 1836; Admiral N. Gray, bondsman.

Gray, George A. & Mary Wallace 10 Sept 1832; Ira A. Orr, bondsman.

Gray, Grief William & Miss Ann Grier Todd, 4 Feb 1823; John McQuay, bondsman; R. J. Dinkins, wit.

Gray, James H. & Margaret H. Hill, 10 March 1840; Richard L. Dearmon, bondsman; B. Oates, wit.

Gray, James W. & Prudence S. Davis, 5 Dec 1834; John Q. R. Campbell, bondsman; B. Oates, wit.

Gray, Joseph G. & Dorcas Shields, 14 Dec 1839; R. L. Dearmon, bondsman; B. Otes, C. C. C., wit.

Gray, N. C. & Jane Henderson, 26 April 1838; L. A. Harris, bondsman.

Gray, Nelson, & Nancy Robison, 9 July 1811; Wm. Cheves, bondsman; Isaac Alexander, wit.

Gray, Ransom & Zelia Barnett, 10 Jan 1826; David Thomason, bondsman; Isaac S. Alexander, wit.

Gray, Ransom A. & Sarah H. Thomason, 5 June 1849; James W. Gray, bondsman.

Gray, Richard H. & Margaret J. Combs, 31 Dec 1841; Wm. R. Harkey, bondsman; C. T. Alexander, wit.

Gray, Thomas & Susey Hill, 3 Feb 1819; David Gray, bondsman; Isaac Alexander, wit.

Gray, William & Martha Dunn, 9 March 1802; William Stuart, bondsman; J. Wallis, wit.

Gray, William & Cherine Rodgers, 17 March 1809; John Hook, bondsman.

Gray, William & Jane Elizabeth Rea, 3 Dec 1834; William Hudson, bondsman; B. Oates, wit.

Gray, William G. & M. A. Jamison, 4 Oct 1865; H. M. Prichard, bondsman. married 5 Oct 1865 by R. Burwell.

Gray, William H. & Miss Fanny E. Lee, 4 May 1864; G. N. Hunter, bondsman; married 4 May 1864 by Richd. H. Griffith, minister of the Gospel.

Gray, Winslow G. & Nancy S. Nipper, 19 May 1860; Ransom A. Gray, bondsman; W. K. Reid, C. C. C., wit.

Green, David H. & Nancy Ross, 30 March 1812; Mathew Bigham, bondsman; Isaac Alexander, wit.

Green, G. A. & Mary E. Howard, 8 Sept 1863; Isaac N. Alexander, bondsman. married 10 Sept 1863 by J. L. Phillips, J. P.

Green, George & Martha Green, 21 June 1865; N. Haight, bondsman; no wit.

Green, Moses & Catharin Kerr, 6 Oct 1807; Wm. Beatey, bondsman; Michl. M Leary, wit.

Green, Nathaniel & S. C. Dinkins, 13 April 1828; Richd. Long, bondsman; Richd. Gillespie, wit.

Greer, Alexander & Mary Sprott, 19 May 1802; Thomas Sprott, bondsman; Isaac Alexander, wit.

Greer, Alexander & Margaret J. Sprott, 12 Aug 1818; Larkin Stowe, bondsman; Isaac Alexander, wit.

Greer, Alexander & Mary Wilson, 4 Jan 1845; Thomas P. Grier,
bondsman; N. B. Taylor, wit.

Greer, James Junr & Dorcas Neely, 27 Dec 1814; James Neely, bondsman; Isaac Alexander, wit.

Greer, James S. & Ann Barry, 19 Nov 1834; Zenas A. Greer, bondsman; B. Oates, C. C. C., wit.

Gregors, Absalom & Rachel Flowers, 6 Dec 1820; Thomas Surry,
bondsman; Isaac Alexander, wit.

Gregory, William W. & Martha N. Carson, 13 Dec 1860; H. B. Williams, bondsman; P. S. Whisnant, wit. married 13 Dec 1860
by A. Sinclair, Pres. Pastor.

Grey, Hugh A. & Jane M. Parks, 23 Oct 1856; Saml. P. Smith,
bondsman; W. K. Reid, C. C. C., wit. married 30 Oct 1856 by
G. D. Parks.

Gribble, James & Cynthia Black, 22 March 1859; J. C. Moore, bondsman: W. K. Reid, C. C. C., wit. married 23 March 1859 by
David Henderson, J. P.

Gribble, James H. & Sarah J. Houston, 5 May 1852; N. B. Taylor,
bondsman; James Parks, wit. married 6 May 1852 by John Hunter,
Pastor of Back Creek Church.

Gribble, Samuel J. & Harriet E. Clark, 7 Jan 1841; Ambrose M.
Rea, bondsman.

Gribble, Thomas & Hanah Shanks, 4 Feb 1801; James Black, bondsman.

Gribble, William & Mary Smith, 19 July 1823; James N. H. Patterson, bondsman; Isaac S. Alexander, wit.

Grier, Arthur & Martha Boys, 23 May 1846; R. H. Maxwell, bondsman; S. J. Lourie, wit.

Grier, Eli C. & Lydia Reed, 11 Jan 1848; M. D. L. McLeod, bondsman; Saml J. Lourie, wit.

Grier, J. M. & Miss A. M. McLaughlin, 27 Feb 1866; M. A. Wilson,
bondsman; Wm. Maxwell, wit.

Grier, James H. & Martha L. Byram, 19 March 1846; F. M. Ross,
bondsman.

Grier, James H. & Mary A. Porter, 7 March 1862; Samuel William
Grier, bondsman; W. K. Reid, C. C. C., wit. married 11 March
1862 by J. C. Chalmers, minister.

Grier, John & Mary McCombs, 28 Feb 1789; Robert McCombs, bondsman; Jno Rogers, wit.

Grier, John & Miss Margaret Cathy (both colored), 24 June 1865;
Peter Porter, bondsman.

Grier, J. C. & Mary R. Fincher, 19 Nov 1864; J. W. Wadsworth,
bondsman; married 22 Nov 1864 by R. Z. Johnston, minister.

Grier, Robert & Elizabeth Reed, 9 Jan 1832; Abram Reed, bondsman;
B. Oates, D. C., wit.

Grier, Robert & Mary Rea, 11 July 1861; J. S. Reid, bondsman; W. K. Reid, C. C. C.,wit. married 16 July 1861 by John Hunter, Pastor of Sardis Congregation.

Grier, R. L. & Martha A. Kirkpatrick, 17 April 1856; Thomas A. Kirkpatrick, bondsman; W. K. Reid, bondsman. married 24 April 1856 by J. B. Watt, V. D. M.

Grier, Thomas H. & Jane K. Richardson, 10 Sept 1853;W. K. Reid, bondsman; N. B. Taylor, wit.

Grier, Thomas J. & Mary Lucky, 7 April 1846; C. L. Alexander, bondsman.

Grier, Z. A. & Sarah L. Davidson, 9 Dec 1862; G. W. Caldwell, bondsman; A. B. Downs, wit. married 9 Dec 1862 by R. Z. Johnston.

Griffin, B. E. & M. J. Craig, 9 July 1856; James A. Campbell, bondsman; W. K. Reid, C. C. C., wit. married 9 July 1856 by J. R. Pickett, Min. of Gospel.

Griffin, Holder & Polly Rogers, 5 Nov 1835; G. W. Crowell, bondsman; _____, J. P. wit.

Griffin, James C. & Eliza Jane Gillet, 18 Dec 1852; Wm. Deaton, bondsman; B. Oates, C. C. C., wit. married 23 Dec 1852 by R. H. Lafferty, Pastor of the congregation of Sugar Creek.

Griffin, Lee & Holly Broom, 29 Feb 182_; Richd. Griffin, bondsman; Isaac Alexander, wit.

Griffin, Solomon & Mary Ann Lowe, 23 Oct 1854; James C. Deaton, bondsman; W. K. Reid, C. C. C., wit. married 26 Oct 1854 by David Henderson, J. P.

Griffith, Aaron H. & Martha J. Cook, 29 Sept 1840; Benjamin F. Brown, bondsman; B. Oates, wit.

Griffith, Charles F. & Amanda Baker, 3 Nov 1859; J. W. Griffith, bondsman; W. K. Reid, C. C. C., wit. married 3 Oct 1859 by Lorenzo Hunter, J. P.

Griffith, Elam & Elizabeth Holden, 26 Nov 1822; Thomas Searcy, bondsman; Isaac Alexander, wit.

Griffith, James B. & Eveline Hodge, 14 May 1855;John H. Barnhill, bondsman; W. K. Reid, C. C. C., wit. married 14 May 1855 by C. Overman, J. P.

Griffith, James C. & Catharine Byram, 28 Jan 1822; Jonathan Griffith, bondsman; Isaac Alexander, wit.

Griffith, James E. & M. E. Baker, 1 Feb 1845; Charles M. Baker, bondsman; N. B. Taylor, wit.

Griffith, John L. & Jane Lenora Baker, 6 March 1851; Eli Griffith, bondsman; John Walker, wit.

Griffith, Jonathan & Sarah Jamison, 7 Oct 1801; Jonathan Baker, bondsman.

Griffith, Jonathan & Jane Henderson, 12 June 1822; James C. Todd, bondsman; Chas T. Alexander, wit.

Griffith, Jonathan W. & Roxana A. Baker, 3 Nov 1853; Samuel B.
Griffith, bondsman; W. K. Reid, C. C. C., wit. married 3 Nov
1853 by James M. Walker, Min.

Griffith, Saml B. & Mary B. Weaver, 17 March 1856; J. W. Griffith,
bondsman; W. K. Reid, C. C. C., wit. married 17 March 1856 by
James M. Walker, Min.

Griffith, Thomas D. & Martha Jane Stewart, 25 Sept 1854; Thomas
N. Alexander, bondsman; W. K. Reid, C. C. C., wit. married
28 Sept 1854 by J. M. Walker, Min.

Griffith, William & Winifred Edwards, 7 Jan 1805; William Rawdon,
bondsman; Isaac Alexander, wit.

Griffith, William F. & Emily M. Read, 28 Jan 1850; George W.
Houston, bondsman; B. Oates, wit.

Griffithe, David & Elizabeth Cook, 5 July 1797; John Mitchell,
bondsman; Ruth A. John, wit.

Griggs, Edmond & Mary Williamson, 5 Dec 1792; Robert Cook, bondsman; Isaac Alexander, wit.

Griggs, Hugh & Mary Porter, 4 Nov 181_; Alexander Porter, bondsman;
Isaac Alexander, wit.

Grissam, James & Mary Martin, 15 Aug 1832; James H. Martin, bondsman.

Groff, E. Drake H. & Margaret King, 22 Oct 1856; Jacob Duls,
bondsman; W. K. Reid, C. C. C., wit. married 22 Oct 1856 by
J. P. Ross, J. P.

Groff, Ephraim J. & Martha Saunders, 29 Aug 1843; George Plum(?),
bondsman. married 31 Aug 1843 by Ira L. Potter.

Groner, Samuel & Jane Coover, 21 Feb 1844; James Jackson Lee,
bondsman; N. B. Taylor, wit.

Groom, Steven & Miss M. H. Harky, 11 July 1865; P. C. Harky,
bondsman. married 11 July 1865 by Jno F. Butt, Local Deacon.

Grover, Samuel & Elsey Rogers, 26 April 1803; John Springs, bondsman; Thos. Harris, wit.

Guarde, Christopher & Matilda Morris, 15 Jan 1864; Joseph Prim,
bondsman.

Gudger, J. W. & Louiza Armour, 8 Aug 1855; R. H. Gudger, bondsman.
married 9 Aug 1855 by E. F. Rockwell, V. D. M.

Gullet, John & Nancy Boyd, 14 Jly 1802; David Griffith, bondsman;
Isaac Alexander, wit.

Gundry, Henry & Jane Phillips, 7 Sept 1864; J. W. McCoy, bondsman. married 7 Sept 1864 by A. Sinclair, Pastor Pres. Ch.,
Charlotte.

Guyer, Alexander & Margaret Manson, 4 Feb 1845; Samuel H. Kirkpatrick, bondsman.

Guyer, Nathanial & Mary Smith, 6 May 1815; John McGill, bondsman.

Guyer, Samuel & Pamelia Alexander, 4 Jan 1822; David V. Wilson, bondsman; Isaac Alexander, wit.

Haas, Abraham & Sarah Auton, 30 Nov 1819; John Anton, bondsman; Isaac Alexander,wit.

Hadley, Joshua & Rachel Flow, 9 April 1824; Thomas Hadley, bondsman; Isaac Alexander, wit.

Hafner, Alfred & Luiza Springs, 22 Oct 1829; Isaac Spencer, bondsman; A. Cooper, wit.

Hagan, John T. & Julia A. Terres, 1 Aug 1864; J. A. Fox, bondsman. married 3 Aug 1864 by F. Milton Kennedy, Chaplain P. A. C. S.

Hagan, Simon & Susannah Alexander, 23 Feb 1829; Peter Evens, bondsman; Pearsall Thompson, wit.

Hagler, Evan & Eliza Davis, 24 May 1837; William Hunter, bondsman; P. E. Launier(?), wit.

Hagler, Adam & Mary Crowell, 29 March 1838; George A. Long, bondsman; Wm. H. Simpson, J. P., wit.

Hagler, John & Margaret Hinson, 14 Feb 1828; John A. Clonts, bondsman.

Hall, Edward & Ann Allen, 23 June 1813; William Yandell Senr., bondsman; Isaac Alexander, wit.

Hall, Henry L. & Hannah McKinny, 11 April 1852; John Kimbrell, bondsman; Saml. A. Davis, J. P., wit. married 11 Aprl 1852 by Saml. A. Davis, J. P.

Hall, Hiram W. & Rachel Ducas, 8 Aug 1843; James D. Price, bondsman; Edwin Potts, J. P., wit.

Hall, James & Surena Dulin, 6 Feb 1851; Francis A. Biggers, bondsman; A. J. Hood, J. P., wit. married 6 Feb 1851 by A. J. Hood, J. P.

Hall, James & Mary E. Clontz, 5 Jan 1865; Andrew S. Crowell, bondsman; Wm. Maxwell, C. C. C., wit. married 12 Jan 1865 by R. McEwen, J. P.

Hall, James H. & Eliza Purviance, 8 April 1826; Wm. M. Kerr, bondsman; Isaac S. Alexander, wit.

Hall, James W. & Elizabeth Orr, 14 Aug 1840; David W. Flow, bondsman; W. F. Alexander, wit.

Hall, John & Hannah Griffith, 4 Nov 1825; Peter E. Ross, bondsman; Richd. Gillespie, Jr., wit.

Hall, John C. & Margaret Patterson, 27 April 1852; John R. Knier, bondsman; Samuel A. Davis, J. P., wit. married 27 April 1852 by Saml. A. Davis, J. P.

Hall, R. B. & Mary Jane Weant, 13 Sept 1855; James L. Phelan, bondsman; W. K. Reid, C. C. C., wit. married 13 Sept 1855 by C.Overman, J. P.

Hall, Robert B. & Caroline Weant, 11 Dec 1851; John L. Watson, bondsman; Saml J. Lourie, wit. married 11 Dec 1851 by J. B. Watt, Pastor of Steel Creek N. C.

Hall, Samuel & Lucretia Rodgers, 21 Aug 1826; Edwin Potts, bondsman; J. Doherty, J. P., wit.

Hall, Samuel B. & Hannah C. Young, 12 Oct 1842; John Blair, bondsman.

Hall, Thomas & Elizabeth Walls, 3 April 1865; John W. Wonsor, bondsman.

Hall, William H. & Jane F. Hayes, 10 Jan 1855; John A. Cooper, bondsman; W. K. Reid, C. C. C., wit.

Halyburton, A. G. & Mary J. Hampton, 7 Nov 1864; J. M. Henderson, bondsman. married 8 Nov 1864 by S. C. Pharr.

Hamilton, Eli & Mary Thomas, 3 July 1822; Samuel Whiteside, bondsman; Isaac Alexander, wit.

Hamilton, John & Mary Skelington, 22 Feb 1791; Jon: McCollugh, bondsman; John Alison, wit.

Hamilton, R. P. & M. J. Maxwell, 6 Nov 1865; E. A. McLeod, bondsman; Wm. Maxwell, C. C. C., wit. married 7 Nov 1865 by Wm. McDonald.

Hamilton, Robert & Eliza McKinley, 6 June 1827; William C. McCormick, bondsman.

Hamlet, Peter A. & Franke Master, 9 Dec 1823; Jane Colley, bondsman.

Hammond, John & Margaret Baydar Gullet, 18 Dec 182-; A. Wallace Alexander, bondsman.

Hammond, Samuel & Martha D. Meacham, 17 Aug 1841; William Boyd, bondsman.

Hamond, John & Sally Pitman, 14 July 1819; Grief W. Gray, bondsman; Chas. T. Alexander, wit.

Hampton, George & Cornelia Henderson, 29 Feb 1804; Isaac S. Henderson, bondsman.

Hanks, Abraham & Judy Rodden, 12 Oct 1825; James Brown, bondsman; ' Isaac Alexander, wit.

Hanna, James H. & Elizabeth J. Hanna, 22 March 1862; Jno. N. Kerr, bondsman; Jno Phelan, wit. married 26 March 1862 by W. M. Kerr.

Hannon, Alexander D. & Jane E. Howard, 1 Sept 1852; Jno. N. Kerr, bondsman; Saml. A. Davis, J. P., wit. married 1 Sept 1852 by Saml. A. Davis, J. P.

Hannon, Jesse & Casiah Stephens, 26 March 1844; James Byram, bondsman.

Hannon, Thomas A. & Martha Stephens, 15 Jan 1842; David Weante, bondsman; C. T. Alexander, wit.

Hannon, W. A. & Nancy Purviance, 2 Jan 1865; F. W. Ahrens, bondsman.

Hannon, William A. & Jane E. Henderson, 16 Aug 1849; John R. Glover, bondsman; S. A. Davis, J. P., wit.

Happoldt, John M. & Evelina W. Foster, 14 Feb 1827; Pearsall Thompson, bondsman; P. Thompson, wit.

Happoldt, John M. Dr. & Dorcas H. Foster, 2 March 1837; Henry C. Owens, bondsman.

Hargett, Casper & Sarah Finny, 18 Dec 1856; N. B. Taylor, bondsman; W. K. Reid, C. C. C., wit. married 18 Dec 1856 by John Walker, J. P.

Hargett, Harris & Mrs. Marthew Hall, 21 Dec 1846; Robert M. McEwen, bondsman; Philemon Morris, wit.

Hargett, James & Dianna Johnson, 23 Dec 1800; James Miller, bondsman; Saml Black, John McCraven, wit.

Hargett, James O. & Ms. Mary Ann McCall, 23 Sept 1851; D. A. Hargett, bondsman; Philemon Morris, wit. married 23 Sept 1851 by Philemon Morris, J. P.

Hargett, Stephen & Barber Wince, 5 June 1823; Andrew Hargett, bondsman; Jno. Ritch, J. P., wit.

Hargett, Stricklen & Clary Helms, 1 Aug 1833; William Harget, bondsman.

Hargett, Morrison & Elizabeth Harkey, 11 Sept 1851; Johnson Harkey, bondsman; Philemon Morris, wit.

Harison, Elam & Elizebeth Gault, 1 Oct 1823; Telemans Alexander, bondsman; Isaac S. Alexander, wit.

Harkey, David & Ceclia Flow, 5 Feb 1856; Washington Harkey, bondsman; W. K. Reid, C. C. C., wit.

Harkey, John & Sarah Baker, 1 Aug 1822; Hosea McCain, bondsman; Philemon Morris, wit.

Harkey, William F. & A. L. Orr, 10 Nov 1865; R. C. Cochran, bondsman; Wm. Maxwell, C. C. C., wit. married 10 Nov 1865 by Jno. F. Butt.

Harky, David & Margaret Thompson, 11 Aug 1818; Isaac Rich, bondsman; Isaac Alexander, wit.

Harky, Joshua & Trisse Hooks, 19 Dec 1826; Cyrus Black, bondsman; Philemon Morris, wit.

Harky, Josiah & Rebecka E. Robison, 18 Dec 1840; Samuel D. White, bondsman; Philemon Morris, wit.

Harky, Matthias & Elizabeth Starnes, 17 Jan 1837; James B.Reid, bondsman.

Harky, Peter & Peggy Drew, 9 Dec 1813; Philemon Morris, bondsman; Isaac Alexander, wit.

MECKLENBURG MARRIAGES 1783-1868

Harky, Solomon & Caroline Knowles, 25 Jan 1859; James M. Stitt (Still?), bondsman; Jno. Phelan, wit. married 27 Jan 1859 by C. Moretz, Clerg.

Harlin, John & Mary Dunn, 5 Dec 1795; John Hipp, bondsman.

Harlon, George & Hannah Lesley, 19 Jan 1803; John Johnston, bondsman.

Harmon, Peter & Rachel Perry, 10 Oct 1818, Francis Perry, bondsman.

Harover, Benjamin & Polly Price, 27 Feb 1826; George Simons, bondsman; Isaac S. Alexander, wit.

Harris, Coleman & Hannah Walls, 25 April 1839; John Sloan, bondsman; B. Oates, C. C. C., wit.

Harris, George & Elisabeth Finney, 3 July 1800; Robert Corlett, bondsman; Wm. McCall, J. P., wit.

Harris, Hugh & Elizabeth T. Stitt, 26 Feb 1825; Neil M. Stitt, bondsman; Isaac S. Alexander, wit.

Harris, Hugh & Jane H. Matthews, 1 Sept 1835; Neil M. Stitt, bondsman.

Harris, James & Margret Davidson, 10 Dec 1813; Robert Davidson, bondsman; Robert Wilson, wit.

Harris, James & Deborah Walker, 18 March 1836; Wm. T. Alexander, bondsman; B. Oates, C. C. C., wit.

Harris, James A. & Elizabeth Stanford, 10 March 1832; Philip Wolf, bondsman; B. Oates, D. C., wit.

Harris, John & Martha Hunter, 31 March 1790; James McRee, bondsman; Isaac Alexander, wit.

Harris, John C. & Martha Smith, 12 Oct 1852; Charles Elms, bondsman; J. W. Morrow, J. P., wit. married 12 Oct 1852 by J. W. Morrow, J. P.

Harris, John H. & Margaret A. Hunter, 13 Aug 1817; Jno M. Harris, bondsman; Isaac Alexander, wit.

Harris, John M. & Evalina Ross, 18 April 1825; Thomas J. Grier, bondsman; Richd. Gillespie Jr., wit.

Harris, Joshua & Ann Allen, 10 Sept 1811; John Allen, bondsman.

Harris, Josiah & Harriet Crisenbury, 25 Dec 1841; Moses Stricker, bondsman; C. T. Alexander, wit.

Harris, Laird H. & Harriet Alexander, 23 June 1840; David Parks, bondsman; B. Oates, C. C. C., wit.

Harris, Moses & Catharine Miller, 17 Jan 1810; Henry Foster, bondsman; Isaac Alexander, wit.

Harris, Moses M. & Martha L. Harris, 30 Jan 1856; Jesse W. Harris, bondsman; W. K. Reid, C. C. C., wit. married 31 Jan 1856 by W. R. Maxwell, J. P.

Harris, Nathaniel A. & Mary Gilmore, 23 July 1831; Jno W. Rodgers, bondsman; B. Oates, wit.

Harris, Robert & Margaret Robb, 16 Jan 1793; George Stafford, bondsman; Isaac Alexander, wit.

Harris, Robert C. & Mary O. Alexander, 1 March 1831; Franklin Harris, bondsman.

Harris, Robert H. & Mary E. Query, 10 July 1856; John L. Brown, bondsman; W. K. Reid, C. C. C., wit.

Harris, Robert W. & Mary Stafford, 9 Aug 1834; John N. Lee, bondsman; B. Oates, C. C. C., wit.

Harris, Salathiel & Harriet Summerville, 6 April 1839; Richard Tredinnick, bondsman.

Harris, Samuel & Elizabeth McClure, 21 March 1796; John Brown, bondsman; Isaac Alexander, wit.

Harris, Samuel A. & C. A. Watson, 9 Nov 1841; James A. Johnston, bondsman.

Harris, Samuel S. & Martha Ann Graham, 5 Dec 1831; Pearsall Thompson, bondsman; B. Oates, wit.

Harris, Samuel W. & Martha E. Davis, 19 April 1856; Mc. A. Harris, bondsman; W. K. Reid, C. C. C., wit. married 22 April 1856 by R. H. Lafferty, pastor of the Congregation of Sugar Creek.

Harris, Thomas (Dr.), & Elizabeth C. Locke, 12 Dec 1831; Washington Morrison, bondsman; B. Oates, D. C., wit.

Harris, William J. & Emaline Wolf, 10 Feb 1843; J. Horten Wolf, bondsman; M. W. Alexander, wit.

Harris, Wylie L. & Evalina Harris, 16 April 1811; Cunningham Harris, bondsman; Isaac Alexander, C. M. C., wit.

Harrison, Daniel & Esther Hutchison, 20 Nov 1820; William Alexander, bondsman; Isaac Alexander, wit.

Harrison, Elam & Ellen C. Flow, 26 Aug 1847; Thomas N. Alexander, bondsman.

Harrison, Griffin & Susan Harrison, 24 July 1820; Thomas Harrison, bondsman; Isaac Alexander, wit.

Harrison, Joseph & Sarah E. Hill, 28 March 1833; Alexander Dobbin, bondsman.

Harrison, Joseph & Fanny D. Christenbury, 21 June 1854; Samuel Garrison, bondsman; W. K. Reid, C. C. C., wit. married 22 June 1854 by R. D. Alexander, J. P.

Harrison, Robert & Catharine Wilson, 16 March 1841; Jackson Wallace, bondsman; B. Oates, wit.

Harrison, William & Mary Burnett, 31 March 1834; Joshua Sikes, bondsman; Wm. H. Simpson, J. P., wit.

Harriss, Edmond & Patsey Smartt, 17 Dec 1800; Robert Saville, bondsman.

Harrisson, Nehemiah Adams & Polly Wilson, 5 July 1815; Samuel
Wilson, bondsman; Isaac Alexander, wit.

Harry, David & Ann A. Berry, 6 Nov 1828; Richd. Gillespie, bondsman; Isaac S. Alexander, wit.

Harry, John F. & Rebecca E. Price, 12 Oct 1857; M. D. L. McLeod,
bondsman; W. K. Reid, C. C. C., wit. married 15 Oct 1857 by
G. D. Parks.

Harry, John T. & Martha J. Alexander, 23 July 1853; Joab P. Smith,
bondsman; B. Oates, C. C. C., wit.

Harry, John T. & Susan D. Shelby, 25 March 1858; Joab P. Smith,
bondsman; W. K. Reid, C. C. C., wit. married 25 March 1858
by Richd. H. Griffith, Minister of the Gospel.

Hart, Andrew & Betsey Clendining, 25 Jan 1800; William Hart
(Hort?), Esqr., bondsman;

Hart, James & Sarah Hamilton, 27 Dec 1788; Patrick Hamilton,
bondsman; J. Mck. Alexander, wit.

Hart, James T. & Mary M. McCall, 3 Dec 1857; John M. Orr, bondsman; W. K. Reid, C. C. C., wit. married 3 Dec 1857 by H. B.
Cunningham.

Hart, James T. & R. R. McCall, 25 Jan 1865; John Gleen, bondsman;
Wm. Maxwell, C. C. C., wit. married 26 Jan 1865 by R. McEwen,
J. P.

Hart, Moses N. & Mrs. E. C. Spratt, 16 Dec 1844; Thos F. Porter,
bondsman; N. B. Taylor, wit.

Hart, Robert S. & Betsey Archer, 5 March 1816; Hiram T. Sloan,
bondsman; Isaac Alexander, wit.

Hart, William & Esther Hamilton, 2 Jan 1788; Andrew Hamilton,
bondsman; J. McK. Alexander, wit.

Hart, William H. & Susanah Woods, 9 Aug 183-; John Brinkley,
bondsman; James Johnston, wit.

Hartgrove, John & Clarrisa H. Alexander, 14 Sept 1812; William
McCleary, bondsman; Isaac S.Alexander, wit.

Hartgrove, John & Polly Rawdon, 15 May 1830: Zekiel Fite, bondsman;
B. Oates, wit.

Hartgrove, R. W. & M. E. CLark, 7 Sept 1865; H. P. McCorkle,
bondsman; Wm. Maxwell, C. C. C., wit. married 7 Sept 1855
by R. R. Rea, J. P.

Hartgrove, William & Mary McKinney, 19 June 1811; Walter Carruth,
bondsman; M. McLeary, wit.

Hartis, A. L. & Matilda L. Thompson, 3 Jan 1857; Joshua Harky,
bondsman; W. K. Reid, C. C. C., wit.

Hartis, Anthony & Betsey Tye, 26 Oct 1810; Martin Harkey, bondsman; Isaac Alexander, wit.

Hartis, John & Sarah Adams, 14 Oct 1812; Nicholas Starnes, bondsman; Isaac S. Alexander, wit.

Hartt, David & Diana McRee, 16 Aug 1797; David Polk McRee, bondsman.

Hartt, James & Hanah Nealy, 19 Dec 1791; Thomas Neely, bondsman.

Hartt, James M. & Margaret C. Taylor, 9 July 1830; Robert C. Neely, bondsman.

Hartt, Joseph & Nancy Neely, 30 Dec 1818; Moses Neely, bondsman; Isaac Alexander, wit.

Hartwich, Conrad & Patsey Stephens, 6 Nov 1816; John Hartwich, bondsman; Isaac Alexander, wit.

Hartwich, John & Susanna Pitman, 20 Oct 1806; Henry Crump, bondsman; Isaac Alexander, wit.

Harvey, Lewis & Eliza Irwin, 26 Oct 1825; William Moore, bondsman; Isaac S. Alexander, wit.

Hatch, John & Keturah Simmons, 24 May 1805; William Simmons, bondsman; Isaac Alexander, wit.

Hauser, John & Amelia Curry, 8 Feb 1837; Robert H. Johnston, bondsman; James Johnston, J. P., wit.

Hawfield, James & Elizabeth Cunningham, 25 July 1832; Robert Cunningham, bondsman.

Hawkins, Jacob L. & Elizabeth Caldwell, 4 July 1853; John Caldwell, bondsman; B. Oates, C. C. C., wit. married 14 July 1853 by W. H. Neal, J. P.

Hawkins, Samuel J. & Hannah M. Gooden, 26 Jan 1855; Henry J. Walker, bondsman; W. K. Reid, C. C. C., wit. married 27 Jan 1855 by Alex. Cooper, J. P.

Hayes, Elijah & Johannah Spears, 30 July 1860; D. C. Sharp, bondsman; W. K. Reid, C. C. C., wit. married 31 July 1860 by Charles Overman, J. P.

Hayes, Jessee & Margaret J. Tradenick, 3 Nov 1860; I. A. Johnson, bondsman; P. S. Whisnant, wit. married 6 Nov 1850 by Lorenzo Hunter, J. P.

Hayes, John L. & Margaret M. Smith, 7 Nov 1833; Braly Oates, bondsman.

Hayes, John W. & Elizabeth C. Stinson, 31 July 1848; William A. Stinson, bondsman; B. Oates, C. C. C., wit.

Hayes, Samuel & Elizabeth Elvira Hawkins, 13 Sept 1856; Matthew Laurance Wallace, bondsman; W. K. Reid, C. C. C., wit. married 18 Sept 1856 by R. B. Jones, M. G.

Hayes, William & Jensey Black, 2 April 1805; Samuel Boyes, bondsman; J. Wallis, wit.

Hayes, William B. & Mary Reed, 7 April 1829; Aaron R. Patton, bondsman; E. Elms, wit.

Hayes, William J. & Izabella L. Alexander, 19 Aug 1847; James A. Sadler, bondsman; Saml. J. Lourie, wit.

Hayes, William S. W. & Violet E. L. Harris, 18 Oct 1831; Braly
Oates, bondsman.

Haynes, Bartholomew & Sarah Carruth, 30 Aug 1793; Moses Beaty,
bondsman; Edw. Waine, wit.

Haynes, David G. & Harriet Cathcart, 10 Nov 1835; William Boyles,
bondsman; B. Oates, C. C. C., wit.

Haynes, Joseph & Levina Beaty, 21 April 1800; John Beaty Jr.,
bondsman.

Hays, John & Elen Sharp, 24 March 1842; P. M. Burnnet, bondsman.

Hays, Joseph & Mary Vanpelt, 15 Aug 1811; William McCormick, bondsman.

Hays, Samuel B. & Mary Robinson, _____; William Comstock,
bondsman; E. Elms, wit.

Hazzard, Cornelious & Cathrine Roan, 31 March 1817; John Black,
bondsman; John Rea, J. P., wit.

Hearm, George & Margaret Biggart, 18 Nov 1858; Henry Gundry,
bondsman; W. K. Reid, C. C. C., married 18 Nov 1858 by
F. M. Ross, J. P.

Heathcock, William & Eliza Jane Colthrap, 17 March 1855; John
Page, bondsman; W. K. Reid, C. C.C., wit. married 24 May
1855 by B. H. Garrison, J. P.

Helmes, Joel & Mary McGuirt, 13 Oct 1833; David McGuirt, bondsman;
Henderson Helmes, wit.

Helmes, John & Holly Chaney, 7 Jan 1834; Jackson Chaney, bondsman;
Joel Helmes, wit.

Helms, Ezekiel T. & Sidney E. Galloway, 10 Nov 1860; Wm. H.
Alexander, bondsman; W. K. Reid, C. C. C., wit. married
15 Nov 1860 by I. S. McLaughlin.

Helms, Gabriel & Rhoda Williams, 23 Feb 1813; Jacob Helmes, bondsman; Isaac Alexander, wit.

Helms, Israel & Sarah Cazar, 16 Jan 1829; Richard S. Dinkins,
bondsman; E. Elms, wit.

Helms, John & Abegel Reden, 31 Dec 1851; Thomas Prestan, bondsman; Casper Hargett, J. P., wit.

Helms, Wiley & Marthew Crowell, 3 Dec 1826; Charles Crowell,
bondsman; Wm. Pyron, wit.

Helper, H. P. & Mattie McGaw, 1 Sept 1863; R. M. White, bondsman;
Wm. Maxwell, C. C. C., wit. married 3 Sept 1863 by J. E.
Pressly, Minister.

Hemby, Eli & Mary Starns, 20 Aug 1835; Andrew Wentz, bondsman;
P. Thompson, wit.

Hemby, John & Betsy Ritch, 23 Aug 1804 (1814?); Edmond Ritch,
bondsman.

Henderson, Andy (colored) & _____; 21 June 1865; John Crun, bondsman (colored): S. A. Harris, wit.

Henderson, Carnes & Lilly Parks, 24 Jan 1792; John Robison, bondsman; Isaac Alexander, wit.

Henderson, Carnes Davidson & Carline Gray, 7 Jan 1823; Green Kendrick, bondsman; Isaac Alexander, wit.

Henderson, David & Minty S. Wallace, 7 Feb 1827; Rufus A. Wallace, bondsman; Pearsall Thompson, wit.

Henderson, David & Harriet C. Henderson, 15 Nov 1836; Francis M. Ross, bondsman.

Henderson, David R. & Peggy Alexander, 3 May 1820; Amzi McGinn, bondsman; Isaac Alexander, wit.

Henderson, Isaac S. & Cynthia McRee, -- Oct 1806; Andw T. Davidson, bondsman.

Henderson, Isaac S. & Rebecca J. Wilson, 28 Sept 1865; F. W. Ahrens, bondsman; Wm. Maxwell, C. C. C., wit. married 5 Oct 1865 by H. B. Pratt.

Henderson, J. Chesley, & Mary J. Alexander, 11 Jan 1866; J. J. McLaughlin, bondsman; Wm. Maxwell, C. C. C., wit. married 12 Jan 1866 by H. B. Pratt.

Henderson, James H. & Cordela A. L. Irwin, 24 May 1858; M. D. McLeod, bondsman; W. K. Reid, C. C. C., wit. married 25 May 1858 by R. H. Lafferty, pastor of the congregation of Sugar Creek.

Henderson, James H. & Jane C. Hannon, 19 Nov 1863; G. H. Rigler, bondsman; Wm. Maxwell, C. C. C., wit. married 19 Nov 1863 by J. P. Ross, J. P.

Henderson, James M. & Elizabeth McFarlin, 16 March 1814; Joseph Blackwood, bondsman; Isaac Alexander, wit.

Henderson, James M. & Mary E. Hunter, 7 Oct 1836; Joseph M. Hunter, bondsman; B. Oates, C. C. C., wit.

Henderson, James P. & Harriett Wallace, 14 Dec 1818; Davidson Henderson, bondsman; Isaac Alexander, wit.

Henderson, James S. & Margaret E. Harry, 10 Aug 1858; David I. Sample, bondsman; W. K. Reid, C. C. C., wit. married 11 Aug 1858 by S. C. Pharr

Henderson, John & Rebekah Henderson, 30 Jan 1798; Robert Wilson, bondsman; Isaac Alexander, wit.

Henderson, John & Ann Sample, 4 April 1804; John Robison, bondsman; Isaac Alexander, wit.

Henderson, John & Nancy Cooper, 20 Dec 1820; Adam Cooper, bondsman; A. M. Alexander, wit.

Henderson, John A.& Precilla Porter, 9 July 1828; Thomas Trotter, bondsman; Pearsall Thompson, wit.

Henderson, John E. & Abagail Bradley, 3 Dec 1834; Amzi A. Moore, bondsman; B. Oates, C. C. C., wit.

Henderson, John W. & Harriet E. Cooper, 5 Aug 1856; John A. Cooper, bondsman; W. K. Reid, C. C. C., wit. married 6 Aug 1856 by G. D. Parks.

Henderson, John W. & L. G. H. Wilson, 25 Feb 1861; William G. Gray, bondsman; W. K. Reid, C. C. C., wit. married by R. Burwell, minister of the Gospel, 26 Feb 1861.

Henderson, John W. & Elizabeth Stevens, 4 Sept 1861; Thomas Ledwell, bondsman; W. K. Reid, C. C. C., wit. married 5 Sept 1861 by J. P. Ross, J. P.

Henderson, Mathew & Margret Harris, 6 March 1798; Saml. Harris, bondsman; John Harris, wit.

Henderson, Matthew & Isabella Henderson, 26 Dec 1810; Robert Henderson, bondsman; Isaac Alexander, wit.

Henderson, McKnit A. & Louisa Herron(?), 25 Feb 1845; Thomas P. Grier, bondsman.

Henderson, Richard & Isabel Jamison, 8 Feb 1798; Andrew Jemison, bondsman; Isaac Alexander, wit.

Henderson, Robert & Zelinda Potts, 11 March 1816; Edwin Potts, bondsman; Isaac Alexander, wit.

Henderson, Robert & Hannah Doherty, 28 Aug 1821; Davisson Henderson, bondsman; Isaac S. Alexander, wit.

Henderson, Robert & Louisa Simmons, 21 Dec 1826; James Clark, bondsman.

Henderson, Robert & Martha C. Sample, 11 Dec 1832; Robert M. Sample, bondsman. R. S. Dinkins, wit.

Henderson, Robert H. & Harriet T. Dickson, 22 Aug 1851; Hugh M. Dickson, bondsman; James Parks, wit. married 26 Aug 1851 by Walter S. Pharr.

Henderson, Robert N. & Isabella N. Henderson, 19 Aug 1840; Robert H. Henderson, bondsman; James Johnston, wit.

Henderson, Robert Z. & Abigal A. Sample, 23 April 1832; Robt. Henderson, bondsman; R. S. Dinkins, wit.

Henderson, Samuel (Dr.) & Peggy Roberts, 10 June 1806; Richard Huson, bondsman; Isaac Alexander, wit.

Henderson, William F. & Nancy S. White, 10 Jan 1856; Edward S. Washam, Wm. Patterson, bondsmen. married 10 Jan 1856 by Wm. Patterson, J. P.

Henderson, Wm. Steel & Elizabeth Baldridge, 18 Sept 1804; Adam Miller, bondsman; Isaac Alexander, wit.

Henderson, William Timothy & Cornelia Foster, 10 Oct 1855; A. N. Gray, bondsman; W. K. Reid, C. C. C., wit.

Hendricks, James M. & Mary A. Martin, 10 Sept 1859; Samuel B. Holdbrooks, bondsman; W. K. Reid, C. C. C., wit.

Hennigan, James & Sarah A. Stewart, 6 Jan 1834; William T. Phifer, bondsman.

Hennigan, James & Margaret H. Orr, 5 Jan 1848; John M. Parks, bondsman.

Hennigan, Robert & Patsy Crowell, 2 Aug 1821; Turner Morgan, bondsman; Wm. Pyron, wit.

Henry, Abner & Jane Howie, 3 Oct 1832; John Penman, bondsman.

Henry Cyrus, & Martha Montgomery, 3 Jan 1810; Isaac S. Alexander, bondsman.

Henry, Frank (colored) & _____, 21 June 1865; R. N. Henry, bondsman; S. A. Harris ,wit.

Henry, George R. & Martha Price, 21 Dec 1809; Isaac Price, bondsman; Isaac Alexander, wit.

Henry, Isaac & Catharine Barnett, 30 May 1800; James McNight, bondsman; Isaac Alexander, wit.

Henry, Joseph & Elizabeth Porter, 2 Jan 1800; Jas. Porter, bondsman; Isaac Alexander, wit.

Henry, Mike & Malinda Miller, 23 Oct 1845; Saml. M. Withers, bondsman.

Henry, T. B. & Molly Saville, 8 Aug 1864; F. M. Ross, bondsman; Wm. Maxwell, C. C. C., wit. married 10 Aug 1864 by J. P. Ross, J. P.

Henry, Thomas & Marjery Cannon, 8 May 1815; Isaac S. Alexander, bondsman.

Henson, William & Margaret Cook, 10 Jan 1824; Daniel Cook, bondsman; Isaac Alexander, wit.

Hepworth, John & Sally Freeman, 9 June 1818; John Todd, bondsman; Isaac S. Alexander, wit.

Herndon, James M. & Virginia C. Cochran, 16 April 1864; T. J. Hunter, bondsman; Wm. Maxwell, C. C. C., wit. married 19 April 1864 by John Hunter, minister.

Heron, J. W. & M. J. Stewart, 21 June 1865; H. S. Barkley, bondsman; S. A. Harris, wit. married 21 June 1865 by Jno. F. Butt.

Heron, William McL. & Sarah Byram, 30 Sept 1818; Samuel Smith, bondsman; Isaac Alexander, wit.

Herran, William S. & Susan Spratt, 1 Dec 1855; Arthur Armstrong, bondsman; W. K. Reid, C. C. C., wit.

Herron, Allen & Isabella Johnston, 31 March 1828; John Graham, bondsman; P. Thompson, wit.

Herron, Isaac & Martha McKee. 25 June 1802; William McKee, bondsman; Isaac Alexander, wit.

Herron, J. W. & A. M. Cooper, 18 June 1856; Joseph Thompson, bondsman; W. K. Reid, C. C. C., wit. married 19 June 1856 by G. D. Parks.

Herron, John & Sarah Jane Todd, 4 June 1856; James M. Herron,
bondsman; W. K. Reid, C. C. C., wit. married 5 June 1856 by
G. L. Campbell, J. P.

Herron, John A. & Sarah M. Stewart, 14 Jan 1851; Arthur Armstrong,
bondsman; Thomas C. Allison, wit.

Herron, John W. & Elizabeth M. Freeman, 22 Feb 1821; John Rudisill,
bondsman; Isaac Alexander, wit.

Herron, Samuel W. & Jane E. Henderson, 7 Oct 1851; W. H. Clark,
bondsman; B. Oates, C. C. C., wit. married 8 Oct 1851 by
H. B. Cunningham.

Herron, William & Esther C. McCloud, 11 Dec 1844; Wm. P. Brown,
bondsman; N. B. Taylor, wit.

Hester, Fransis M. & Mary Taylor, 11 June 1846; Nancy Tanner,
bondsman; Philemon Morris, wit.

Heuston, Daniel & Sophia Bankes, 13 March 1822; Robert T. Plunket,
bondsman; Isaac Alexander, wit.

Hibbets, James & Nancy Crawfor, 23 Dec 1792; Joseph Crawford,
bondsman; Jno Allison, wit.

Hill, Jacob & Mariah Davis, 2 June 1820; Archibald Crockett,
bondsman.

Hill, James R. L. & Harriet B. Sloan, 19 Dec 1857; James N.
Alexander, bondsman; W. K. Reid, C. C. C., wit. married 22
Dec 1857 by Walter S. Pharr.

Hill, James S. & Betsey Beaty, 4 Dec 1821; Thomas Kenedy, bondsman; Isaac Alexander, wit.

Hill, James W. & Violet S. Williamson, 7 Feb 1852; Wm. R. Hill,
bondsman; James Parks, wit. married 10 Feb 1852 by G. C. Cathey,
J. P.

Hill, John S. & Henritta Dewese, 5 Aug 1835; James Doherty,
bondsman; James Johnston, wit.

Hill, Joseph F. & Martha A. Dearmond, 12 Nov 1835; Henry M. Ray,
bondsman.

Hill, Miles & Sarah E. Henderson, 10 July 1823; Edward M. Bronson,
bondsman; Isaac S.Alexander, wit.

Hill, Milton & Sarah Ewing, 21 July 1860; Wm. E. Ewing, bondsman;
W. K. Reid, C. C. C., wit. married 25 July 1860 by W. M.
Kerr.

Hill, Robert & Isabella White, 28 Dec 1815; Wm. Stuart, bondsman.

Hill, Walter & Jennet Henry, 20 Oct 1798; Jno Duckworth, bondsman;
Jno Harris, J. P., wit.

Hill, Walter A. & Mary N. Montgomery, 27 Dec 1830; William B. Sloan,
bondsman.

Hill, Whitmell & Mary Sharp, 21 March 1814; John L. Daniels,
bondsman; Isaac S. Alexander, wit.

Himenes, Lorenso & Mary Porter, 7 Aug 1823; William H. Folger, bondsman; Pearsall Thompson, wit.

Hinson, Charles & Elizabeth M. Russell, 20 May 1840; Joshua Teeter, bondsman; B. Oates, C. C. C., wit.

Hinson, F. M. & Emaline Dulin, 6 Feb 1866; Wm. C. Miller, bondsman; Wm. Maxwell, C. C. C., wit. married 6 Feb 1866 by Jno F. Butt.

Hipp, Andrew & Mabel Perry, 24 Sept 1810; Jacob Hipp, bondsman; Isaac Alexander, wit.

Hipp, Andrew & Martha Lawing, 21 Jan 1840; William Hipp, bondsman; B. Oates, C. C. C., wit.

Hipp, David & Catharine Parish, 22 Aug 1808; Vallentine Hipp, bondsman; Michl. McLeary, wit.

Hipp, James F. & Margaret A. Cathey, 5 Aug 1856; Eli H. McCoy, bondsman; W. K. Reid, C. C. C., wit. married 7 Aug 1856 by H. B. Cunningham.

Hipp, James N. & Lucinda Simmons, 10 March 1845; John M. Hipp, bondsman; N. B. Taylor, wit.

Hipp, John & Judah Hicks, 5 April 1783; John Dun, bondsman; Wm. Polk, wit.

Hipp, John & Polly Rogers, 12 Oct 1799; Joseph Rodgers, bondsman.

Hipp, John & Sylvia Harwell, 7 Oct 1817; Andrew Hipp, bondsman; Isaac Alexander, wit.

Hipp, John M. & Fanny Lawing, 23 Feb 1858; Gray P. Hipp, bondsman; W. K. Reid, C. C. C., wit. married 25 Feb 1858 by Stephen Wilson, J. P.

Hipp, Robert & Ruthy Perry, 7 Oct 1817; Andrew Hipp, bondsman; Isaac Alexander,wit.

Hipp, William & Margaret B. Johnson, 21 Nov 1832; Thomas Hoover, bondsman; W. W. Elms, wit.

Hipp, William B. & Jane Lawing, 3 Sept 1836; William N. Hipp, bondsman.

Hobbs, Alfred L. & Susanh. Brinkly, 11 Jan 1830; Wm. H. Hart, bondsman; A. B. Jetton,wit.

Hobbs, Washington & Sarah Kelly, 16 Feb 1861; Andrew A. Kelly, bondsman; W. K. Reid, C. C. C., wit.

Hockenbery, Jeremiah & Matilda Fox, 6 Nov 1865; Joshua Culver, bondsman; Wm. Maxwell, wit. married 8 Nov 1865 by T. W. Dewey, J. P.

Hodge, James & Rebecca Cumby, 30 April 1798; John McKee, bondsman; J. Wallis, wit.

Hodge, Samuel & Mrs. Sarah Hartis, 23 June 1832; William Howard, bondsman; Philemon Morris, wit.

MECKLENBURG MARRIAGES 1783-1868

Hodge, Thomas & Eddy Parish, 16 Feb 1819; Cyrus McClure, bondsman; Isaac Alexander, wit.

Hodge, William F. & Nancy R. Puckette, 23 April 1841; Milas F.
Puckett, bondsman.

Hodges, C. T. & Mary A. Pharr, 7 Jan 1861; P. A. Hodges,bondsman;
W. K. Reid, C. C. C., wit.

Hodges, Josiah & Jane E. Dixon, 5 Aug 1845; Pleasant B. Hodges,
bondsman; Isaac S. Alexander, wit.

Hodges, P. B. & Sarah E. Cochran, 22 Sept 1856; R. W. Allison Jr.,
bondsman; W. K. Reid, C. C. C., wit. married 23 Sept 1856 by
Isaac S. McLaughlin.

Hodges, Patrick A. & Susan E. Wallace, 9 Feb 1850; W. L. Houston,
bondsman; B. Oates, C. C. C., wit.

Hodges, Patrick A. & Ursula Taylor, 6 Jan 1858; F. H. Maxwell,
bondsman; John Phelan, wit.

Hodges, William G. & M. J. Orr, 7 Sept 1853; R. W. Alexander,
bondsman; W. K. Reid, wit. married 8 Sept 1853 by John Hunter,
M. G.

Holbrooks, Saml. B. & Izabella Johnston, 2 Mav 1846; S. H. Foard,
bondsman; S. J. Lourie, wit.

Holdbrooks, Theophilus & Margaret A. Howell, 7 Feb 1846; S. H.
Foard, bondsman; S. J. Lourie, wit.

Holden, Elisha M. & Jane A. Simpson, 27 Dec 1854; W. K. Reid,
Clk, wit. married 28 Dec 1854 by T. M. Farrow.

Holden, James & Marey Russel, 21 May 1800; James Russel, bondsman;
Jno Hoey, J. P., Robert Lackey, wit.

Holden, Lewis J. & Sara Cox, 8 April 1844; Richard Sercy, bondsman; N. B. Taylor, wit.

Holley, Alexander & Jane Robb, 25 Aug 1812; Joseph Bigger, bondsman; Isaac Alexander, wit.

Holliday, Wm. E. & Mary S. Binton, 30 April 1845; T. N. Pettey,
bondsman.

Hollifield, Joseph & Elizabeth H. Bolton, 1 Feb 1844; Robt Shaw,
bondsman.

Holton, Francis M. & Eliza A. Blount, 11 Oct 1837; David R. Dunlap, bondsman. B. Oates, wit.

Honeycutt, Demsey J. & Tabitha Helms, 3 Sept 1835; Israel Helmes,
bondsman; S. D. Belk, wit.

Hood, A. B. & Laura C. Hunter, 14 Feb 1860; Samuel. A. Boyce,
bondsman; John Phelan, wit. married 23 Feb 1860 John Hunter,
minister.

Hood, James C. & Mary A. Johnston, 5 Oct 1844; James J. Orr,
bondsman. N. B. Taylor, wit.

Hood, James C. & Louiza A. Newell, 21 July 1851; M. W. Robison, bondsman; B. Oates, C. C. C., wit. married 22 July 1851 by G. W. Houston, J. P.

Hood, Jeremiah & Marey McRosky, 16 Jan 1816; William Morris, bondsman; Philemon Morris, wit.

Hood, John H. & Mazy Russell, 10 Dec 1833.

Hood, Reuben & Mary Neal, 15 Dec 1825; Saml. Parks, Richd Gillespie Jr., wit.

Hood, Robert & Elizabeth McRaven, 15 May 1797; John Maxwell, bondsman.

Hood, Robert L. & Mary Ann Wiatt, 8 Jan 1849; George W. McKinney, bondsman; Saml. A. Davis, J. P., wit.

Hood, Thomas O. & Jane Culp, 13 March 1845; John H. Hood, bondsman; N. B. Taylor, wit.

Hood, Tunis & Catherine Starns, 22 Feb 1822; James A. Harris, bondsman; Isaac S. Alexander, wit.

Hood, Tunis H. & Mary McComb, 13 March 1862; John R. Hood, bondsman; W. K. Reid, C. C. C., wit. married 18 March 1862 by W. R. Maxwell, J. P.

Hooks, Berry Groves & Jane Crowell, 16 Sept 1822; Eli McCall, bondsman; Isaac Alexander, wit.

Hooks, John L. & Susannah J. Biggers, 30 March 1858; A. F. Stevens, bondsman; W. K. Reid, C. C. C., wit. married 6 April 1858 by W. R. Maxwell, J. P.

Hoover, Alfred & Elizabeth Dunn, 23 Feb 1831; Isaac J. Thompson, bondsman.

Hoover, C. A. & Margaret A. Faires, 12 July 1842; James L. Martin, bondsman; Jas. A. Johnston, wit.

Hoover, Henry & Jane Collins, 28 Dec 1849; Tho. H. Brem, bondsman; B. Oates, C. C. C., wit.

Hoover, James D. & Emaly Hoover, 19 July 1865; Robert P. Chapman, bondsman; Wm. Maxwell, C. C. C., wit. married 19 July 1865 by T. W. Dewey, J. P.

Hoover, W. L. & Margaret J. McDonald, 16 April 1851; James A. Cathey, bondsman; B. Oates, C. C. C., wit. married 17 April 1851 by Cyrus Johnston.

Hoover, Washington L. & Harriet E. Nicholson, 13 Feb 1865; James H. Henderson, bondsman; WM. Maxwell, C. C. C., wit. married 16 Feb 1865 by C. W. McDonald, J. P.

Hope, Levi & Janie Malissa Harris, 1 Oct 1823; Edward L. Harris, bondsman; Isaac S. Alexander, wit.

Horn, Richard & Sarah McKinney, 28 May 1801; Jesse Horn, bondsman.

Hornbury, Alison & Fanny Shoman, 19 May 1842; James Holobaugh, bondsman; James A. Johnston, wit.

MECKLENBURG MARRIAGES 1783-1868

Hotchkis, Henry & Henrietta Standley, 8 March 1832; Pearsall
Thompson, bondsman.

Hough, J. F. & Nancy S. Hart, 12 March 1853; James Thomas Hart,
bondsman; B. Oates, C. C. C., wit. married 22 March 1853
by P. T. Penick.

Houghland, John & Haly Gadberry, 20 Jan 1834; William Carson,
bondsman; B. Oates, wit.

Houghlin, John & Nancy McBride, 2 Feb 1810; James Dinkins,
bondsman; Isaac Alexander, wit.

House, Samuel & Betsy Foster, 8 May 1845; Isaac F. Jones, bondsman; C. T. Alexander, C. C. C., wit.

Houstin, John M. & Jane D. Robison, 18 March 1834; John P. Houstin,
bondsman.

Houston, Ambrose P. & Eliza B. Lawson, 29 March 1839; William F.
Lawson, bondsman; B. Oates, C. C. C., wit.

Houston, George & Jenny Henderson, 26 March 1816; Arthur Jameson,
bondsman; Isaac S. Alexander, wit.

Houston, George S. & Rachel Johnston, 7 June 1822; John Irwin,
bondsman; R. J. Dinkins, wit.

Houston, George W. & Jane Young, 8 May 1833; J. H. Maxwell, bondsman; F. M. Ross, wit.

Houston, George Weir & Jane Kirk, 7 Feb 1802; William Alexander,
bondsman.

Houston, Henry & Martha Houston, 15 Oct 1791; Thomas Houston,
bondsman.

Houston, James & Casandra Alexander, 1 Jan 1803; Abdon Alexander,
bondsman; Isaac Alexander, wit.

Houston, James A. & Jane A. Moore, 7 Jan 1828; Isaac Wilson, bondsman; P. Thompson, wit.

Houston, James F. & Mary A. Patterson, 29 Oct 1853; Saml. M.
Withers, bondsman; W. K. Reid, C. C. C., wit. married 2 Nov
1853 by Saml. B. O. Wilson, minister.

Houston, James N. & Elizabeth Walker, 4 Jan 1798; James Houston,
bondsman; J. Wallis, wit.

Houston, James T. & Ann J. Henderson, 2 March 1840; James A. G.
Potts, bondsman; James Johnston, wit.

Houston, John & Anne Howie, 21 Dec 1797; James Houston, bondsman;
J. Wallis, wit.

Houston, John H. & Clarinda J. Blair, 2 Feb 1829; Wilson C. Houston,
bondsman; Pearsall Thompson, wit.

Houston, John M. N. & Mary Reid, 14 Oct 1822; Abram Reid, bondsman.

Houston, Levenes & Polly Shields, 27 Jan 1817; John Houston, bondsman.

Houston, Robert B. & Mary Dunn, 18 Nov 1826; Thomas Whiteside, bondsman; Thomas B. Smartt, wit.

Houston, S. F. & Sarah P. McGilvray, 28 Nov 1860; J. Nick Hunter, bondsman; P. S. Whisnant, wit. married 29 Nov 1860 by A. Sinclair, minister.

Houston, Samuel & Mary Kirck, 30 Nov 1795; Robert Parks, bondsman; Ruthe Alexander, wit.

Houston, Thomas & Mary Sample, 6 June 1798; William Alexander, bondsman.

Houston, William & Elisabeth Lingo, 18 Jan 1803; William Alexander, bondsman.

Houston, William L. & Martha A. Alexander, 24 Nov 1858; Wm. Johnston, bondsman; W. K. Reid, C. C. C., wit. married 25 Nov 1858 by R. H. Lafferty, minister.

Houston, William McKee & Mary C. Watson, 12 Oct 1858; Wm. J. Kerr, bondsman; W. K. Reid, C. C. C., wit. married 14 Oct 1858 by J. M. Walker, minister.

Houston, Wilson C.& Abigail A. E. Moore, 28 Jan 1833; Ezekiel Johnson, bondsman.

Houston, Wilson C. & Elizabeth C. Blair, 20 Dec 1841; George W. Houston, bondsman.

Hovis, Franklin & Mary Ann McKnight, 4 Aug 1852; Henry M. Hovis, bondsman; B. Oates, C. C. C. married 12 Aug 1852 by A. L. Watts, V. D. M.

Howard, James & Nancy McCorkle, 2 Nov 1829; Joseph Tagert, bondsman; A. Cooper, wit.

Howard, Robert G. & Mary Phifer, 15 Sept 1838; Andrew J. Ezzell, bondsman; B. Oates, C. C. C.,wit.

Howard, Samuel B. & Margaret Oliver, 14 July 1851; John R. Warwick, bondsman; B. Oates, C. C. C., wit. married 17 July 1851 by S. C. Pharr.

Howel, John & Mrs. Louisa Bridges, 3 Aug 1864; A. Delane, bondsman; Wm. Maxwell, C. C. C., wit. married 3 Aug 1864 by I. S. McLaughlin.

Howel, John W. & Eley Tarlton, 28 Jan 1824; John Harmon, bondsman; Isaac Alexander, wit.

Howel, Stephen & Fanny Festerman, 9 Aug 1829; Lewis Howel, bondsman; E. Elms, wit.

Howel, Sterling P. & Rachael Wyatt, 6 Jan 1822; Mitchel Wiatt, bondsman; R. J. Dinkins, wit.

Howell, Edmund & Fanny Hornbarrier, 14 April 1859; Moses A. Stouffer, bondsman; W. K. Reid, C. C. C., wit. married 14 April 1859 by C. Overman, J. P.

Howell, Jeremiah & Fanny Gibson, 25 Dec 1856; Jordan McCreary, bondsman; W. K. Reid, C. C. C., wit. married 25 Dec 1856 by Thomas M. Farrow

Howell, Kinchen P. & Elizabeth Owensby, 15 Sept 1830; Charles N. Price, bondsman; Isaac S. Alexander, wit.

Howell, Lewis & Polly Festerman, 9 Jan 1826; John Howell, bondsman; Isaac S. Alexander, wit.

Howell, Stephen & Jincy Mitchell, 9 Nov 1843; Saml. Paul, bondsman; C. T. Alexander, wit.

Howell, William J. & Lavina Waisner, 14 July 1851; James N. Todd, bondsman; B. Oates, C. C. C., wit. married 14 July 1851 by David Henderson, J. P.

Howey, Aaron H. & Martha Stitt, 1 June 1835; William Wilson, bondsman.

Howey, John & Frances Baxter, 22 Oct 1788; John McCorkel, bondsman.

Howey, William & Mary Gordon, 14 Aug 1834; H. W. Black, bondsman; W. F. Alexander, wit.

Howie, James & Jane Lee, 30 Dec 1861; W. W. Quinn, bondsman; W. K. Reid, C. C. C., wit. married 2 Jan 1862 by J. C. Chalmers.

Howie, James H. & Mary Strube, 17 Sept 1863; Rufus L. Alexander, bondsman; Wm. Maxwell, C. C. C., wit. married 17 Sept 1863 by Tho. W. Dewey, J. P.

Howie, Monroe & Mima Howie (colored), 17 Aug 1865; Forney Alexander, bondsman; Wm. Maxwell, C. C. C., wit. married 19 Aug 1865 by I. S. McLaughlin.

Howie, William & _____, 17 Oct 1803; Ezekiel Alexander, bondsman.

Howie, William & Polly Polk, 8 May 1823; John Rape, bondsman; Isaac Alexander, wit.

Hoyl, Andrew & Matilda D. McRum, 20 Oct 1852; James H. Davis, bondsman; Saml. A. Davis, J. P., wit. married 21 Oct 1852 by W. C. Patterson, M. G.

Hucks, Benjn. & Elizabeth Hucks, 1 Feb 1825; James Wilson, bondsman; Isaac S. Alexander, wit.

Hucks, David W. & Mary Kenon, 19 May 1849; William C. Beaty, bondsman; B. Oates, C. C. C., wit.

Hucks, Solomon A. & Mary D. Robards, 5 Dec 1842; Hardy C. Lewelen, bondsman; Jas. A. Johnston, wit.

Hudelson, Wm. & Nancy Caps, 28 April 1826; Wm. Nickelson, bondsman; Richd. Gillespie, Jr., wit.

Hudson, John & Nancy Means, 8 March 1823; William Robison, bondsman; Isaac Alexander, wit.

Hudson, Richard & Patty Gray, 25 Jan 1814; William Robison, bondsman; Isaac Alexander, wit.

Hudson, William & Jane Swann, 4 March 1833; W. W. Elms, bondsman; F. M. Ross, wit.

Hudson, William & Permelia A. Winchester, 25 Jan 1842; Jos. H. Irwin, bondsman.

Huey, John & Margret Craige, 9 March 1804; Alexander Craig, bondsman; Jas. Conner, wit.

Huie, William H. & Mary Jane White, 27 Feb 1857; M. Del. McLeod, bondsman; John Phelan, wit. married 3 March 1857 by Danl. A. Penick.

Hull, William & Hannah Sharpe, 24 July 1821; Whit Men Hill, bondsman; Isaac Alexander, wit.

Hunt, Mekim & Elisabeth Love, 12 June 1791; David Ellison, bondsman; Isaac Alexander, wit.

Hunt, William & Mary Duckworth, ---- 1816; George Duckworth, bondsman; Robt. Wilson, wit.

Hunt, William C. & Rosannah B. Potter, 23 Nov 1843; Thomas F. Hampton, bondsman; A. J. York, wit.

Hunt, William Henry & Nancy Capps, 3 April 1851; Tho. B. Maclean, bondsman; B. Oates, C. C. C., wit. married 16 April 1851 by A. L. Watts

Hunter, Elam, & Martha Yourgin, 29 Sept 1830; James N. Hunter, bondsman; B. Oates, wit.

Hunter, George S. & Susan M. Reich, 8 Feb 1859; George N. Faires, bondsman; W. K. Reid, C. C. C., wit. married 10 Feb 1859 by W. R. Maxwell, J. P.

Hunter, H. C. & M. A. Reich, 8 Aug 1861; Abner Hunter, bondsman; P. S. Whisnant, wit.

Hunter Henery & Caroline Black, 29 Aug 1810; Adam Meek, bondsman; Isaac Alexander, wit.

Hunter, Henery & Martha Clark, 6 Oct 1840; William B. Hunter, bondsman; Wm. F. Alexander, wit.

Hunter, Henry & Allice Taylor, 10 Oct 1816; Frederick Ezell, bondsman; John Rea, J. P., wit.

Hunter, Henry & Jane R. Hill, 25 Aug 1841; James McHunter, bondsman; B. Oates, wit.

Hunter, Hugh M. & Martha R. Rodgers, 7 July 1848; David M. Henderson, bondsman.

Hunter, Hugh M. & Mary Jane Montgomery, 21 Aug 1850; Nathan F. Orr, bondsman; B. Oates, C. C. C., wit.

Hunter, Humphrey & Margt. Ross, 20 July 1795; Samuel Houston, bondsman.

Hunter, James & Mary McClure, 7 July 1800; Joseph Hunter, bondsman.

Hunter, James Mc. & Mary E.Houston, 10 Nov 1847; Thos. H. Alexander, bondsman; Saml. J. Lourie, wit.

Hunter, James Mc. & Martha E. McConnel, 13 June 1865; J. W.
   Garrison, bondsman. married 13 June 1865 by R. L. DeArmon, J.
P.

Hunter, John & Hannah Ross, 31 Jan 1828; Abner Hunter, bondsman;
   Eli Springs, wit.

Hunter, John D. & Martha Colthrop, 14 Dec 1844; Mathew Miller,
   bondsman; N. B. Taylor, wit.

Hunter, John W. & Mary E. Parks, 22 Jan 1855; James H. Walker,
   bondsman; W. K. Reid, C. C. C.,wit. married 23 Jan 1855 by
J. M. Walker, minister.

Hunter, Joseph & Rhoda Colthrop, 14 Sept 1806; John Hutchison,
   bondsman.

Hunter, Lorenzo & Matilda R. Alexander, 31 July 1858; Amzi W.
   Blair, bondsman; John Phelan, wit. married 3 Aug 1858 by
I. S. McLaughlin.

Hunter, R. B. & R. W. Jones, 8 Jan 1845; John D. Hunter, bondsman.

Hunter, Robert & Jane Black, 19 April 1818; Elam Hunter, bondsman;
   Almira M. Alexander,wit.

Hunter, Robert & Mary Bigham, 14 Nov 1837; Robert Porter, bondsman;
   P. E. Saunier, wit.

Hunter, Robert H. & Mary N. F. Hall, 24 Feb 1858; Joseph W.
   Bigham, bondsman; W. K. Reid, C. C. C., wit.

Hunter, Silus C. & Caroline Porter, 6 Sept 1851; Joseph N. Hunter,
   bondsman; James Parks, wit.

Hunter, Thomas & Peggy H. Walker, 15 Oct 1810; James Kirk, bondsman.

Hunter, Thomas & Rosanna A. Walker, 22 Feb 1832; Lorenzo Hunter,
   bondsman; Isaac Alexander, wit.

Hunter, Thomas J. & Isabella Hood, 25 Oct 1860; Robert C. Cochran,
   bondsman; Jno. Phelan, wit. married 27 Oct 1860 by John
Hunter, minister.

Hunter, William & Sophia Phillips, 3 Sept 1831; Herman S.Noble,
   bondsman; Thos. Palmer, wit.

Huson, David & Judy Glover, 10 Aug 1792; James Glover, bondsman;
   Isaac Alexander, wit.

Huston, David & Elenor Barkley, 10 March 1788; John Barckly,
   bondsman; Sam Mark, wit.

Huston, George & Margaret T. McCoy, 12 Jan 1825; Thomas Kerns,
   bondsman; Isaac Alexander, wit.

Huston, Hugh L. & Dovey E. Stewart, 30 Jan 1855; Columbus W.
   McCoy, bondsman; W. K. Reid, C. C. C., wit. married 1 Feb
1855 by H. B. Cunningham.

Hutchison, Andrew J. & Elizabeth C. King, 31 Jan 1846; Matthew H.
   Hutchison, bondsman; B. Oates, C. C. C., wit.

Hutchison, Charles F. & Margaret Lawing, 23 July 1850; John T. Todd, bondsman.

Hutchison, Charles H. & Frances K. Lawing, 6 March 1822; James Hutchson, bondsman; Isaac Alexander, wit.

Hutchison, Charles H. & Adeline Thompson, 14 Jan 1840; John H. McCoard, bondsman; B. Oates, wit.

Hutchison, Cyrus, & Mary Cross, 28 Dec 1822; Daniel Harrison, bondsman; Isaac Alexander, wit.

Hutchison, David & Polly McRee, 22 May 1805; Isaac S. Henderson, bondsman; Isaac Alexander, wit.

Hutchison, David S. & Dorcas E. Alexander, 8 June 1852; John G. Cross, bondsman; B. Oates, C. C. C., wit. married 17 June 1852 by R. H. Lafferty, minister.

Hutchison, George & Dicey Emerson, 11 June 1799; Henry Emerson, bondsman; Isaac Alexander, wit.

Hutchison, George W. & Mary G. Abernathey, 1 Jan 1861; A. A. Kanady, bondsman; W. K. Reid, C. C. C., wit. married 3 Jan 1861 by J. P. Ross, J. P.

Hutchison, James & Matilda Hayse, 25 Dec 1815; Jno B. Hutchison, Charles Hutchison, bondsmen.

Hutchison, John M. & Mary T. Kirkpatrick, 27 Dec 1843; Hugh Kirkpatrick, bondsman. C. T. Alexander, wit.

Hutchison, John M. & Jane A. White, 27 Jan 1852; Thomas A. Kirkpatrick, bondsman; James M. Walker, wit. married 27 Jan 1852 by Jas. M. Walker, minister.

Hutchison, Samuel T. & Jane Lawing, 14 Dec 1816; Daniel Harrison, bondsman; Isaac Alexander, wit.

Hutchison, Scott B. & Rachel Scott, 15 Jan 1853; William Johnston, bondsman; B. Oates, C. C. C., wit. married 20 Jan 1853 by George L. Campbell, J. P.

Hutchison, Thomas L. & E. Y. Price, 20 March 1844; J. Montgomery, bondsman; C. T. Alexander, wit.

Hutchison, W. Harvey & Cornelia C. Hipp, 9 Jan 1833; Winslow McKee, bondsman; R. S. Dinkins, wit.

Hutchison, William & Mary Shields, 8 Jan 1829; Thomas L. Hutchison, bondsman; Pearsall Thompson, wit.

Hux, Levix & Dicey Warsham, 22 March 1830; Isaiah Hux, bondsman; Tho. B. Smartt, wit.

Hux, William & Milly Cheristenbury, 15 July 1833; Richard Jordan, bondsman; F. M. Ross, wit.

Hux, William & Sarah Steele. 29 Nov 1853; Stanhope H. Brown, bondsman; W. K. Reid, C. C. C., wit. married 1 Dec 1853 by Isaac Wilson, J. P.

Ince, John & Agniss Campbell, 24 April 1800; James Ross, bondsman; Isaac Alexander, wit.

Ingle, Peter & Amelia Williamson, 31 Aug 1861; M. L. Canslir, bondsman; W. K. Reid, C. C. C., wit. married 1 Sept 1861 by J. P. Ross, J. P.

Ingrim, Hezekiah & Nancy Bibb, 22 April 1819; William Bibb, bondsman; Jno Rea, wit.

Irvin, Isaiah D. & Jane E. Alexander, 25 Aug 1859; Wm. W. Grier, bondsman; W. .K Reid, C. C. C., wit. married 31 Aug 1859 by Alexr. Ranson.

Irwin, Alexander & Margaret L. Alexander, 14 Oct 1833; James Hood, bondsman.

Irwin, Batte & Eleanor R.Barry, 2 Dec 1833; Wm. M. B. Flinn, bondsman.

Irwin, Batte & Eliza C. Flinn, 18 Dec 1841; R. R. Taylor, bondsman.

Irwin, Caleb & Sarah Irwin, 29 Dec 1818; James Irwin, bondsman; Isaac Alexander, wit.

Irwin, Davis & Mary Flangan, 7 Dec 1831; David Parks, bondsman; W. W. Elms, wit.

Irwin, James & Eleanor P. Davis, 12 Dec 1845; J. B. Kerr, bondsman; B. Oates, wit.

Irwin, John & Margaret Witherspoon, 11 Feb 1818; William Walker, bondsman; Isaac Alexander, wit.

Irwin, John & Seeley Black, 5 Oct 1820: Robert McEwen, bondsman; Philemon Morris, wit.

Irwin, John & Delphia Graham (colored), 18 April 1863; Madison Phillips (colored), bondsman; Wm. Maxwell, C. C. C., wit. married 19 April 1863 by J. W. Martin, J. P.

Irwin, Joseph H. & Mary Ann Ray, 21 Feb 1850; F. M. Ross, bondsman; Saml. J. Lourie, wit.

Irwin, Robert (Gen'l.) & Mary Barry, 26 March 1798; Daniel Gallent, bondsman.

Irwin, Robert & Elizabeth Rea, 29 April 1817; John Irwin, bondsman; Isaac Alexander, wit.

Irwin, Robert & Martha Alexander, 6 Aug 1838; Samuel A. Harris, bondsman.

Irwin, Samuel & Martha Parks, 7 May 1825; John Irwin, bondsman; Isaac S. Alexander, wit.

Irwin, Silas & Ginny Sloan, 14 Oct 1812; Robert S. Hart, bondsman.

Irwin, William & Sarah Irwin, 7 Feb 1804; Thomas Irwin, bondsman; Isaac Alexander, wit.

Irwin, William & Rebecca S. Allison, 8 Feb 1826; John Allison, bondsman; Isaac Alexander, wit.

Inyard, John & Ann Young, 1 Dec 1865; Henry Whisler, bondsman;
Wm. Maxwell, C. C. C.,wit. married 1 Dec 1865 by Jno. F.
Butt.

Ivey, Thomas R. & Malinda Scott, 24 Aug 1812; Mathew Wallace,
bondsman; Isaac Alexander, wit.

Jackson, Elias & Mary J. Johnston, 18 March 1841; Wm. A.Todd,
bondsman.

Jackson, Henry & Mary Bell, 18 Jan 1790; Francis Smart, bondsman;
Jn. Rogers, wit.

Jackson, James & Rebekah Weathers, 23 July 1804; Zebulon Jackson,
bondsman.

Jamerson, James & Jane Adaline Berean, 18 April 1828; Eli Springs,
bondsman; E. Elms, wit.

James, Charles M. & Margaret J. Kelly, 5 March 1849; Miles Hill,
bondsman; B. Oates, C. C. C., wit.

Jameson, Isaac & Arlicimase Murphy, 3 March 1828; Eli Springs,
bondsman; E. Elms, wit.

Jameson, Thomas & Mary Sullivan, 16 Sept 1789; Patrick Sullivan,
bondsman; Jno. Rogers, wit.

Jameson, Thomas & Elizabeth McGinn, 7 July 1819; John Cox, bondsman; Isaac Alexander, wit.

Jameson, Thomas & Jane McClure, 18 April 1844; Wm. Sandry,
bondsman; N. B. Taylor, wit.

Jamison, Andrew & Mary Ann Rea, 30 July 1841; William J. Jamison,
bondsman; B. Oates, C. C. C., wit.

Jamison, Arthur & Mary Simeral, 6 Jan 1801; John Johnston, bondsman; Isaac Alexander, wit.

Jamison, James & Melinda Long, 28 June 1849; B. Oates, bondsman.

Jamison, John R. & Hannah J. Todd, 9 Nov 1858; W. K. Reid, C. C.
C., wit; Thomas J. Jamison,bondsman; married 21 Dec 1853 by
G. L. Campbell, J. P.

Jamison, R. J. & Catherine Wilson, 9 Jan 1866; J. L. Osborn,
bondsman; Wm. Maxwell, C. C. C., wit. married 10 Jan 1866
by W. M. Kerr.

Jamison, R. M. & Hannah F. Todd, 25 Jan 1843; Wm. A. Todd, bondsman.

Jamison, Robert & Isobel Johnston, 25 March 1797; John Dunn,
bondsman; Isaac Alexander, wit.

Jamison, Robert & Ann Stinson, 8 Nov 1817; Jonas Clark, bondsman.

Jamison,Robert M. & Sarah L. Todd, 29 Sept 1862; William G.Gray,
bondsman; Wm. Maxwell, wit. married 30 Sept 1862 by J. P.
Ross, J. P.

Jamison, Thomas & Sarah A. Hipworth, 15 March 1848; Joseph C.
Capps, bondsman; Saml. J. Lourie, wit.

Jamison, Thomas J. & Rosanna B. McCord, 9 Dec 1851; John King,
bondsman; B. Oates, C. C. C., wit. married 9 Dec 1851 by
Batte Irvin.

Jamison, William & Polly Johnston, 8 Jan 1811; Hugh Elliotte,
bondsman; Isaac Alexander, wit.

Jamison, William Jr. & Margaret Todd, 6 May 1835; Thompson Walker,
bondsman.

Jamison, William J. & Jane E. Brown, 18 March 1844; Robert Carson,
bondsman; N. B. Taylor, wit.

Jenkins, William & Nelly Parker, 26 Oct 1809; Isaac Parker, bondsman.

Jennings, C. J. & Rachel R. Cook, 9 Sept 1865; R. M. White, bondsman; Wm. Maxwell, C. C. C., wit. married 14 Sept 1865 by
P. Nicholson, minister.

Jennings, George W. & Sarah C. Stanford, 23 Oct 1858; Charles L.
Stanford, bondsman; K. W. Berryhill, wit. married 28 Oct
1858 by William Reid , J. P.

Jennings, J. H. & Margaret Stanford, 3 Jan 1859; Amzi W. Allen,
bondsman; W. K. Reid, C. C. C.,wit. married 4 Jan 1859 by
Lorenzo Hunter, J. P.

Jennings, John, & Lucy Smith, 26 Dec 1818; Green Kendrick, bondsman; Isaac Alexander, wit.

Jennings, Richard & Eliza Carter, 11 Aug 1825; John Varner, bondsman; Isaac S. Alexander, wit.

Jennins, William P. & Mary Cornelia Alexander, 16 July 1836;
Braly Oates, bondsman.

Jetton,Abraham & Jane Oliphant, 29 May 1787; James Gillespy,
bondsman; J. McK. Alexander, wit.

Jetton, Asaph & Elizabeth Johnston, 5 Nov 1812; John Harris,
bondsman.

Jetton, Isaac & Araminta Davis, 24 Sept 1814; Robert Osborn,
bondsman; Isaac Alexander, wit.

Jewell, Stephen & Margret Menteith, 31 July 1792; John Duckworth,
bondsman; James Meek, wit,

Johns, Zephaniah & Margaret Sharp, 22 Dec 1824; James Sharp,
bondsman; Isaac S. Alexander, wit.

Johnson, Andrew & Sarah McCombs, 20 May 1791; Robert McCombs,
bondsman; Isaac Alexander, wit.

Johnson, Benjamin & Martha Hayse, 21 Jan 1824; Thomas L. Hutchison,
bondsman; Isaac Alexander, wit.

Johnson, David M. & Nancy Howard, 5 Aug 1856; Wm. W. Quinn,
bondsman; W. K. Reid, C. C. C.,wit. married 5 Aug 1856 by
C. Overman, J. P.

Johnson, George & Mary Taylor, 3 Jan 1850; John Harty, bondsman;
Saml. J. Lourie, wit.

Johnson, Isaac M. & Eliza Finch, 31 Dec 1844; H. H. Rainey,
bondsman; James Johnston, wit.

Johnson, Isaac M. & Sarah A.Cox, 22 Feb 1854; Hugh W. Elliotte,
bondsman; W. K. Reid, C. C. C., wit. married 25 Feb 1854 by
George L. Campbell, J. P.

Johnson, James & Jane Hodge, 16 Nov 1835; Richard W. Elliott,
bondsman; B. Oates, wit.

Johnson, James & Debora Galloway, 14 April 1846; Joseph P. Black,
bondsman; Philemon Morris, wit.

Johnson, James A. & Sarah Ann Tradenick, 22 March 1858; Henry A.
Love, bondsman; John Phelan, wit. married 23 March 1858 by
John Walker, J. P.

Johnson, James L. & Abigail Dewese, 24 Jan 1838; John M. Alexander, bondsman; P. E. Saunier, wit.

Johnson, Jesse & Margaret Hypp, 8 Nov 1830; James Murphy, bondsman;
B. Oates, wit.

Johnson, Jesse B. & Jane Wallace, 6 Oct 1858; R. H. Maxwell,
bondsman; K. W. Berryhill, wit.

Johnson, John & Jane Robeson, 18 Nov 1829; Nathaniel Johnston,
bondsman; A. Cooper, wit.

Johnson, John & Elizabeth C. Alexander, 18 Dec 1833; Winslow
McRee, bondsman; B. Oates, C. C. C., wit.

Johnson, John C. & Margaret T. Black, 16 April 1833; James M.
Black, bondsman; B. Oates, D. C., wit.

Johnson, John C. & Annis Dewese, 8 Jan 1836; John A. Dewese,
bondsman; B. Oates, C. C. C., wit.

Johnson, John H. & Lydia B. Wallace, 3 Feb 1840; R. L. DeArmon,
bondsman; B. Oates, wit.

Johnson, John M. & Jane Morrison, 7 Jan 1861; M. W. Robison,
bondsman; W. K. Reid, C. C. C., wit.

Johnson, John Mack & Miriam Wallace, 29 April 1863; J. P. McGinnis, bondsman; Wm. Maxwell, C. C. C., wit. married 30 April
1863 by John Walker, J. P.

Johnson, John William & Mary Jane Hoover, 24 Feb 1860; John Phelan,
bondsman; W. K. Reid, C. C. C.,wit. married 28 Feb 1860 by
Stephen Wilson, J. P.

Johnson, Philip & Rachael Johnston, 23 Nov 1813; William Johnson,
bondsman; Isaac S. Alexander, wit.

Johnson, Reuben & Jenny Curry, 17 Sept 1816; Robert Jamison,
bondsman; Isaac Alexander, wit.

Johnson, Robert & Mary Davis, 9 Jan 1806; Thos. Hill, bondsman;
Isaac Alexander, wit.

Johnson, Samuel & Luisa Henderson, 1 March 1813; John Nixon,
bondsman; Isaac Alexander, wit.

Johnson, Samuel E. & Rebecca Caldwell, 29 Oct 1842; Alex. J. Caldwell, bondsman; James Johnston, wit.

Johnson, Thomas A. & J. Cox, 21 June 1865; G. W. Gatlin, bondsman; Wm. Maxwell, C. C. C., wit. married 21 June 1865 by Jno. F. Butt, Local Deacon.

Johnson, Thomas J. & Sarah T. Davidson, 29 Sept 1824; Pinkney C. Caldwell, bondsman; R. J. Dinkins, wit.

Johnson,William & Elizabeth Hipp, 25 Oct 1808; David Love, bondsman; Michl. McLeary, wit.

Johnson, William & Rebeca Allen, 18 Dec 1811; Daniel Harrison, bondsman; Susan R. Alexander, wit.

Johnson, William A. & Mary C. Johnston, 6 March 1849; Elisha Scott, bondsman.

Johnston, Andrew Dunn & Jane Johnston, 20 Jan 1810; John Black, bondsman; Isaac Alexander, wit.

Johnston, Bob & Lucy Boyce, 26 Jan 1866; J. B. Black, bondsman; Wm. Maxwell, wit.

Johnston, David & Harriet C. Hipp, 23 July 1838; Jesse B. Johnston, bondsman; B. Oates, C. C. C., wit.

Johnston, David & Sarah Overbay, 14 May 1849; R. B. Wallace, bondsman; B. Oates, wit.

Johnston, Ezekiel & Eliza Morris, 10 Sept 1833; John K. Harrison, bondsman.

Johnston, J. D. & E. S. Jetton, 3 March 1853; E. Nye Hutchison, bondsman; James Parks, wit. married 16 March 1853 by Saml. B. O. Wilson, V. D. M.

Johnston, J. G. & M. E. Barnett, 15 Nov 1864; Wm. Maxwell, C. C. C., wit. married 24 Nov 1864 by R. Z. Johnston, minister.

Johnston, James S. & Sarah J. Reddock, 26 Feb 1861; B. A. Johnston, bondsman; W. K. Reid, C. C. C., wit. married 14 March 1861 by Wm. W. Pharr.

Johnston, John & Peggy Harris, 10 Jan 1817; Samuel Gingles, bondsman.

Johnston, John R. & Delia R. Torrence, 17 June 1856; James Abernathy, bondsman; W. K. Reid, C. C. C., wit.

Johnston, John T. & Sarah S. Campbell, 10 July 1844; George L. Campbell, bondsman; N. B. Taylor, wit.

Johnston, John T. & Mary Scott, 28 Sept 1859; William A. Scott, bondsman; W. K. Reid, C. C. C.,wit. married 29 Sept 1859 by J. P. Ross, J. P.

Johnston, Joseph C. & Dorcas Orr, 11 Oct 1815; Elias Alexander, bondsman; Isaac Alexander, wit.

Johnston, M. W. & A. H. Bost, 29 Oct 1859; J. W. Young, bondsman; W. K. Reid, C. C. C., wit. married 31 Oct 1859 by Danl. A. Penick Sr., minister.

MECKLENBURG MARRIAGES 1783-1868

Johnston, Patrick & Ann Wallis, 28 June 1794; Bengyman Maxwell,
bondsman; James Meek, wit.

Johnston, Robert & Pamelia Henderson, 11 Spt 1820; James G.
Barnet, bondsman; Isaac Alexander, wit.

Johnston, Robert & Martha Blair (colored), 29 July 1865; Joe
Johnston, bondsman; Wm. Maxwell, wit. married 29 July 1865
by John Alexander, minister.

Johnston, S. E. & Cynthia Brem, 19 Sept 1865; J. M. Potts, bondsman; W. Maxwell, C. C. C., wit. married 19 Sept 1865 by S. C.
Pharr.

Johnston, Samuel & Izabella Neely, 17 Jan 1810; James R. Neely,
bondsman; Isaac Alexander, wit.

Johnston, Samuel & Prudy Moore, 17July 1811; Joseph Johnston,
bondsman; Isaac Alexander, wit.

Johnston, Samuel N. & Margaret Welsh, 13 Nov 1841; C. T. Alexander,
wit.

Johnston, Sandy & Roxannah Pitts (colored), 26 Aug 1865; R. C.
McGinnis, bondsman.

Johnston,Thomas L. (Dr.). & Darcus E. Lucky, 24 May 1852; Tho.
H. Brem, bondsman; B. Oates, wit. married 25 May 1852 by R.
H. Lafferty, minister.

Johnston, Thomas T. & Elizabeth McDonald, 21 July 1814; William
Jamison, bondsman; Isaac S. Alexander, wit.

Johnston, William & Mary Black, 6 Oct 1807; William Beaty, bondsman; Samuel Johnston, wit.

Johnston, William & Rebecca Cunningham, 20 Oct 1814; Jacob F.
Cunningham, bondsmn.

Johnston, William & Ann Eliza Graham, 16 March 1846; C. E. Spratt,
bondsman; B. Oates, C. C. C.,wit.

Johnston, William C. & Margret M. McRee, 1 Nov 1828; Isaac Wilson,
bondsman; Pearsall Thompson, wit.

Jones, Andrew & Rebecca Wilson, 24 Oct 1821; Cyrus A. Alexander,
bondsman; Isaac Alexander, wit.

Jones, Andrew & Abby E. Parks, 3 Nov 1829; James Wilson, bondsman;
A. Cooper, wit.

Jones, Andrew & Jane H. Bain, 5 Aug 1837; Ira Parks, bondsman;
P. E. Saunier, wit.

Jones, Edmund H. & Harriet N. Dunlap, 2 Nov 1843; Braly Oates,
bondsman.

Jones, Edward P. & Octavia E. Irwin, 28 Nov 1849; T. L. Avery,
bondsman; W. M. Shipp, bondsman; Saml. J. Lourie, wit.

Jones, Isaac & Nancy Treese, 13 Dec 1832; William Spenser Grimes,
bondsman; B. Oates, wit.

Jones, John W. & Amanda H. E. Stinson, 3 Oct 1867; Wm. Maxwell, clk, wit. married 3 Oct 1867 by Thomas B. Price, J. P.

Jones, Julius A. & Patsey Walker, 10 July 1821; Sam Black, bondsman; Isaac Alexander, C. M. C.,wit.

Jones, Richard & Susan Seymore, 19 Oct 1835; Swen Johnston, bondsman; B. Oates, wit.

Jones, Sherrod & Margaret Kerr, 23 Feb 1830; William Osborn, bondsman.

Jones, William C. & Margaret Tefaboy, 22 May 1833; William Irwin, bondsman.

Jordan, Ananias & Elizabeth A. Spears, 14 July 1856; Chas. A. Ford, bondsman; W. K. Reid, C. C. C., wit. married 16 July 1856 by G. W. Houston, J. P.

Jordan, Erasmus & Mrs. Sarah Crump, 13 Feb 1845; Ervin Finney, bondsman; Philemon Morris, wit.

Jordan, Henry & Elizabeth L. Furr, 11 Oct 1858; Jeptha J. Spears, bondsman; K. W. Berryhill, wit. married 14 Oct 1858 by C. Overman, J. P.

Jordan, Richard & Martha Cashon, 3 Feb 1836; James J. Williams, bondsman; B. Oates, C. C. C., wit.

Jordan, Richard & Baily Christenbury, 25 Feb 1843; Daniel A. Christenbury, bondsman; N. B. Taylor, wit.

Jordan, Samson H. & Jane E.Steele, 10 Nov 1851; Robert C. Bell, bondsman; B. Oates, C. C. C., wit. married 10 Nov 1851 by R. D. Alexander, J. P.

Jordan, Solomon I. & Delilah D. Ferrell, 1 Jan 1849; Benj. G. Ferl, bondsman.

Jordan, William G. & Elizabeth P. Christenberry, 23 Feb 1828; James Christenburry, bondsman; Isaac Alexander, wit.

Julian, George & Rebekah McKinish, 9 April 1791; Jacob J. Julian, bondsman; Isaac Alexander, wit.

Julian, Jacob C. & Catherine E. Moore, 23 June 1853; John G. Maxwell, bondsman; B. Oates, C. C. C., wit. married 7 July 1853 by R. H. Lafferty, minister.

Kanady, Aron A. & Jane N. Sloan, 8 Nov 1827; David A. Sloan, bondsman.

Karr, Samuel & Nelly Jetton, 4 March 1802; Osborne Roberson, bondsman; J. Wallis, wit.

Karr, Samuel & Elizabeth Lambert, 9 Aug 1822; John F. Morris, bondsman; Isaac S. Alexander, wit.

Keenan, Hugh & Purcilla Wyle, 26 Dec 1832; Edwin Maxwell, bondsman; Phn. Morris, wit.

Keefer, Calvin W. & Agness Hawie, 7 Nov 1865; Philip H. Rosenburg, bondsman; married 8 Nov 1865 by Wm. P. Kontz, Chaplain 128th Ind. Vols.

Keisler, George & Sally Phillips, 16 Dec 1818; Joseph Phillips, bondsman; Isaac Alexander, wit.

Keistler, Moses E. & Jane T. Love, 16 Feb 1857; Thomas H. Hoover, bondsman; W. K. Reid, C. C. C., wit. married 18 Feb 1857 by Stephen Wilson, J. P.

Kelley, Gershom & Mary A. J. Spears, 12 Nov 1852; Wm. F. Davidson, bondsman; B. Oates, C. C. C., wit. married 14 Nov 1852 by Thomas M. Farrow.

Kenan, John & Dorcas Alexander, 9 Jan 1823; James Grehem, bondsman; Isaac Alexander, wit.

Kenan, John & Nancy Hucks, 8 June 1846; Joseph Roberts, bondsman.

Kendrick, Ephrim & Dorcas H. Dinkins, 21 Dec 1818; Lewis Dinkins, bondsman; Isaac Alexander, wit.

Kendrick, Jno. D. & Violet A. Hoover, 18 Dec 1850; T. H. Brem, bondsman; James Parks, wit.

Kendrick, John F. & Elizabeth Daniel, 2 March 1812; Joseph Glover, bondsman; Isaac Alexander, wit.

Kendrick, Joseph & Catharine E. Fairis, 31 Oct 1857; John Phelan, bondsman; W. K. Reid, C. C. C., wit. married 5 Nov 1857 by Wm. C. Owens.

Kendrick, William & Winny Darnell, 9 Sept 1794; Thomas Cole, bondsman.

Kenley, E. W. & Nancy A. Alexander, 7 July 1854; James T. White, bondsman; W. K. Reid, C. C. C.,wit. married 27 July 1854 by H. B. Cunningham.

Kenley, George & Polly Bain, 30 Aug 1832; John Bunker, bondsman; B. Oates, D. C., wit.

Kennedy, David & Dorcas Sample, 14 July 1796; Samuel Kennedy, bondsman.

Kennedy, David & Nancy Dowell, 14 April 1803; William Kennedy, bondsman.

Kennedy, Henry & Missouri Walker (colored), 29 April 1858; James Mitchell, bondsman; Jno Phelan, wit. married 29 April 1858 by Wm. S. Norment, J. P.

Kennedy, James & Nancy Milven, 9 Dec 1805; Thomas McCoard, bondsman; Isaac Alexander, wit.

Kennedy, James H. & Jane Weeks, 3 March 1832; John N. Lees, bondsman.

Kennedy, John & Jane Griffith, 13 May 1816; Eli Griffith, bondsman.

Kennedy, Marcus T. C. & Pamelia Wilson, 18 Nov 1816; Elias Alexander, bondsman; Isaac S. Alexander, wit.

Kennedy, Robert & Cresy Beaty, 9 Feb 1860; Wm. Frank Beaty, bondsman; John Phelan, wit. married 9 Feb 1860 by Chas. Overman, J. P.

Kennedy, Thomas & Rebekah Alexander, 5 Feb 1798; William Kennedy, bondsman.

Kennedy, William & Mary McGinty, 27 Aug 1816; John Flow, bondsman.

Kennedy, Wilson & Eliza Mull, 10 May 1843; Even Hagler, bondsman.

Kennellay, George W. & Cecelia Howell, 23 Jan 1843; David Howell, bondsman; Jas. A. Johnston, wit.

Kenney, E. W. & Elizabeth White, 22 Aug 1859; S. F. Houston, bondsman; John Phelan, wit.

Kenton, William & Mary E. Wicks, 20 Nov 1865; Martin Langley, bondsman; W. K. Reid, C. C. C., wit. married 20 Nov 1865 by Jno. F. Butt.

Kernes, Morris & Violet Alexander, 28 Oct 1865; John Alexander, bondsman; Wm. Maxwell, C. C. C.,wit. married 2 Nov 1865 by R. L. DeArmon, J. P.

Kernes, William C. & Martha V. McKnight, 2 Nov 1852; Tho. A. Stuard, bondsman; B. Oates, C. C. C., wit. married 7 Nov 1852 by H. B. Cunningham.

Kerns, J. D. & Mary L. Alexander, 15 Dec 1858; C. W. McCoy, W. K. Reid, C. C. C., wit. married 16 Dec 1858 by S. C. Pharr.

Kerns, James H. & Clareesa Alexander, 20 Aug 1825; Marsall McCoy, bondsman; Richd. Gillespie, Jr., wit.

Kerns, James H. & Margaret J. McKnight, 22 Jan 1852; Marshal R. McCoy, bondsman; B. Oates, C. C. C., wit. married 27 Jan 1852 by H. B. Cunningham.

Kerns, Thomas M. & Jane McKnight, 19 Dec 1826; William C. Houston, bondsman.

Kerr, Adam & Mary Sharp, 17 Feb 1823; James Sharp, bondsman; R. J. Dinkins, wit.

Kerr, James & Polly Sprott, 1 Dec 1802; Aaron Mathews, bondsman; J. Wallis, wit.

Kerr, James M. & Margaret E. Kerr, 11 March 1852; Jno. N. Kerr, bondsman; B. Oates, C. C. C.   married 11 March 1852 by Wm. M. Kerr.

Kerr, Jerome B. & Jane E. Johnston, 21 Oct 1851; Richard M. Norment, bondsman; B. Oates, C. C. C., wit. married 22 Oct 1851 by Cyrus Johnston, V. D. M.

Kerr, John & Mary Gardner, 10 Feb 1818; John Gardner, bondsman.

Kerr, John & Jane Barnett, 8 Dec 1823; James G. Barnett, bondsman; R. J. Dinkins, wit.

Kerr, John & Jane Bradly, 19 April 1859; William M. Kerr, bondsman; W. K. Reid, C. C. C., wit. married 20 April 1859 by R. H. Lafferty, minister.

Kerr, John N. & Sarah A. Hanna, 6 May 1862; James H. Henderson, bondsman; W. K. Reid, C. C. C., wit. married 6 May 1862 by W. M. Kerr

Kerr, Joseph & Peggy Sample, 22 July 1812; James Woods, bondsman;
Isaac S.Alexander, wit.

Kerr, Moses & Lydia Shaffer, 7 Feb 1799; Tomase Shaffer, bondsman;
Isaac Alexander, wit.

Kerr, Robert M. & Cynthia Byrum, 19 April 1830; Robert Cathcart,
bondsman.

Kerr, Samuel & Lucy Black, 25 Oct 1800; James Martin, bondsman.

Kerr, Samuel & Hannah A.Alexander, 9 April 1855; N. B. Taylor,
bondsman; W. K. Reid, C. C. C., wit. married 12 April 1855
by W. H. Neal, J. P.

Kerr, William & Ann McKnight, 27 Feb 1802; James McNight, bondsman.

Kerr, William Alexr. & Dorcas Shelby, 9 Feb 1807; William Carr,
bondsman; Isaac Alexander, wit.

Kesiah, G. W. & Lucinda White, 18 July 1862; J. W. McCoy, bondsman; W. K. Reid, C. C. C.,wit.

Kesiah, Hiram & Mary Anderson, 22 March 1834; James Squires, bondsman; John Oates, wit.

Kessiah, Wm. & Nancy Fincher, 27 Feb 1864; Jno. N. Kerr, bondsman;
Wm. Maxwell, C. C. C., wit. married 29 Feb 1864 by R. McEwen,
J. P.

Keziah, John & Hesther Harget, 1 Aug 1833; Wm. Hargett, bondsman.

Keziah, John & Mehaly Helmes, 2 April 1834; Stricklen Harget,
bondsman; Daniel Harget,wit.

Kibben, James McN. & Jane Rylie, 6 Dec 1813; Armstrong Rylie,
bondsman.

Kichar, Charles & Milly Minyard, 27 Feb 1815; Thomas Minyard,
bondsman; Isaac Alexander, wit.

Kiker, Benjamin & Sally Howell, 30 Dec 1819; Charles Kichar,
bondsman; Wm. Pyron, wit.

Kiker, Evan & Jane Smith, 15 Dec 1825; Charley Kiker, bondsman;
Wm. Pyron, wit.

Kiker, John & Isabella Crowell, 12 Nov 1833; John Barnett, bondsman.

Kiker, Joshua L. & Cyntha Dulin, 8 Oct 1835; Jacob Long Jr.,
bondsman; Wm. H. Simpson, J. P., wit.

Killough, David & Rachel Newman, 27 Oct 1795; Geor. Alen, bondsman.

Killough, J. W. & Mary C. Solomon, 5 Aug 1851; Wm. C. Earnheart,
bondsman; B. Oates, C. C. C., wit. married 5 Aug 1851 by
B. H. Garrison, J. P.

Killough, J. W. & Elizabeth Sings, 9 Sept 1858; David Solmon,
bondsman; F. M. Ross, wit. married 9 Sept 1858 by David Henderson.

Killough, William & Eleanor Neal, 7 Dec 1792; David Killough,
bondsman; Isaac Alexander, wit.

Killough, William & Mary Dermond, 8 April 1816; James Dearmond, bondsman.

Killough, William J. & Mary Wallace, 25 Oct 1856; Stanhope H. Brown, bondsman; W. K. Reid, C. C. C., wit. married 6 Nov 1856 by R. F. Taylor, minister.

Kilpatrick, James & Anne Parks, 23 May 1803; John McKee, bondsman; J. Wallis, wit.

Kimbal, Robert & Sally Galthorp, 4 Jan 1807; Joseph Hunter, bondsman.

Kimbell, J. A. & Martha Wingate, 24 May 1854; M. L. Wallace, bondsman; J. W. Morrow, J. P., wit. married 23 May 1854 by J. W. Morrow, J. P.

Kimbell, John & Eliza M. Sovell, 1 Feb 1852; William J. Culp, bondsman; Saml. A. Davis, J. P., wit. married 1 Feb 1852 by Saml. A. Davis, J. P.

Kimbell, Spell & Sally Miller, 16 Oct 1810; William Parks, bondsman; Isaac Alexander, wit.

Kimbirl, L. H. & Sarah A. Coldiron, 10 Aug 1848; Tho. F. Porter, bondsman; Saml. J. Lourie, wit.

Kimmons, Andrew & Nancy Beaty, 29 May 1817; Nathan Beaty, bondsman; Isaac S. Alexander, wit.

Kimmons, Samuel & Terza A. Stafford, 16 Jan 1858; Samuel A. Harris, bondsman.

Kimmons, Samuel & _____, --- 184-; Hugh H. Kimmons, bondsman; C. T. Alexander, C. C. C., wit.

Kincaid, William M. & S. E. Irwin, 8 Jan 1856; George A. Locke, bondsman; W. K. Reid, C. C. C., wit. married 10 Jan 1856 by E. F. Rockwell, V. D. M.

Kindley, William & Susannah Skinner, 11 May 1839; Benjamin F. Shaffer, bondsman

Kiney, Benjamin & Mary Ann Simpson, 24 Aug 1847; John C. Abernathy, bondsman; Saml. J. Lourie, wit.

King, A. S. & Margaret H. Hart, 17 Oct 1840; Joab P. Smith, bondsman; Wm. F. Alexander, wit.

King, Colin & Cynthia Hipp, 15 June 1822; Francis Perry, bondsman; Isaac Alexander, wit.

King, Colin C. Jr., & Narcissa Wright, 7 Jan 1858; J. A. Wood, bondsman; John Phelan, wit. married 7 Jan 1858 by Wm. Means, J. P.

King, George & Polly Hipp, 12 June 1821; William H. McLeary, bondsman; Isaac Alexander, wit.

King, George W. & Mary Isabella Todd, 13 June 1860; Wm. M. Porter, bondsman; W. W. Grier, wit. married 14 June 1860 by Alex. Cooper, J. P.

King, James & Elizabeth Smith, 30 June 1798; William Black, bondsman; Isaac Alexander, wit.

King, John & Margaret Rogers, 21 Dec 1818; Jessee Cathy, bondsman; Isaac Alexander, wit.

King, John & Eliz. McCormick, 26 April 1797; William Conner, bondsman.

King, John O. & Rosana E. Alexander, 3 April 1854; M. D. L. McLeod, bondsman; W. K. Reid, C. C. C., wit. married 4 April 1854 by R. H. Lafferty, minister.

King, Julius & Elizabeth Freeman, 2 April 1861; Jerry Skinner, bondsman; Wm. S. Norment, wit. married 2 April 1861 by Wm. S. Norment, J. P.

King, R. R., & Martha E. Morris, 4 Aug 1852; W. S. Alexander, bondsman; B. Oates, C. C. C., wit. married 10 Aug 1852 by P. T. Penick.

King, R. R.,& Sarah J. Parks, 1 Jan 1857; Martin L. Barringer, bondsman; W. K. Reid, C. C. C., wit. married 6 Jan 1857 by R. H. Lafferty, minister.

King, Richard & Matilda Morrison, 25 Nov 1823; Elam J. Morrison, bondsman.

King, William J. A. & Sarah J. Plummer, 3 Oct 1861; James H. Hutchison, bondsman; W. K. Reid, C. C. C., wit. married 3 Oct 1861 by W. M. Kerr.

Kinsel, John F. & Margaret Collins, 31 July 1855; Thomas Anderson, bondsman; W. K. Reid, C. C. C., wit.

Kirk, James & Jenny McGinness, 25 Dec 1811; Robert Hunter, bondsman.

Kirk, John Jr. & Peggy Shields, 9 May 1809; George W. Houston, bondsman; Isaac Alexander, wit.

Kirk, John & Adalade H. Alexander, 16 March 1842; G. W. Houston, bondsman; C. T. Alexander, wit.

Kirk, Tom & Martha Caldwell (colored) 18 Dec 1865; Jack Alexander, bondsman; Wm. Maxwell, C. C. C.,wit. married 18 Dec 1865 by John Alexander, minister.

Kirkpatrick, Francis & Elizabeth Callens, _____; Robert H. Callen, bondsman.

Kirkpatrick, James B. & Isabella Bowie, 23 Feb 1835; Williamson Wallace, bondsman.

Kirkpatrick, John & Caroline H. Wilson, 6 Oct 1832; Williamson Wallace, bondsman; B. Oates, D. C., wit.

Kirkpatrick, John C.& Margaret H. Orr, 31 Jan 1849; John R. Warwick, bondsman; B. Oates, C. C. C., wit.

Kirkpatrick, John C. & Mary E. Brown, 24 Dec 1851; S. A. Kirkpatrick, bondsman; James Parks, wit. married 25 Dec 1851 by Samuel C. Pharr, V. D. M.

Kirkpatrick, Robert & Almira M. Alexander, 2 July 1860; Robert E. Cochrane, bondsman; W. K. Reid, C. C. C., wit. married 9 July by J. W. Miller, Pastor Methodist Church.

Kirkpatrick, Samuel H. & Cynthia D. Grier, 8 March 1842; Thos. B. McKee, bondsman.

Kirkpatrick, Silas A. & Sarah M. Flannagan, 11 March 1858; Samuel C. Wolfe, bondsman; W. K. Reid, C. C. C., wit. married 23 March 1858 by Jethro Rumple.

Kirkpatrick, Thomas & Ann Yandele, 19 March 1794; Wilson Yandell, bondsman; Isaac Alexander, wit.

Kirkpatrick, Thomas A. & A. P. Wolf, 31 Aug 1857; Ulyses C. Alexander, bondsman; W. K. Reid, C. C. C., wit. married 1 Sept 1857, by G. W. M. Creighton.

Kirkpatrick, Thomas A. & Harriet D. Alexander, 5 Dec 1865; J. B. Stewart, bondsman; married 5 Dec 1865 by John Hunter, Pastor Sardis Congregation.

Kirkpatrick, Thomas Mc. & Mary C. Alexander, 15 May 1849; Wm. Johnston, bondsman; Saml. J. Lourie, wit.

Kirkpatrick, W. L. & M. J. Walker, 28 Jan 1863; S. W. Alexander, bondsman; married 29 Jan 1863 by John Hunter, Pastor Sardis Church.

Kistler, David & Miss Margaret Allison, 24 Sept 1829: Richd. Gillespie, bondsman; A. Cooper, wit.

Kistler, George & Fanny Mason, 26 March 1839; Joshua Trotter, bondsman; B. Oates, C. C. C., wit.

Kistler, Peter & Isabella McAulay, 14 Jan 1826; Zebulon Morris, bondsman; Isaac Alexander, wit.

Klutts, William H. A. & Ann Jane Condor, 22 Feb 1862; Nelson Hagler, bondsman; W. K. Reid, C. C. C.,wit. married 27 Feb 1862 by C. Moretz, Clerg.

Knowles, James & Elizabeth Anderson, 7 Feb 1824; Nicholas Anderson, bondsman (German signature); Isaac Alexander, wit.

Knowles, Wiley A. & Christina Black, 29 Aug 1853; Valentine W. Rice, bondsman; N. B. Taylor, wit. married 29 Aug 1853 by W. R. Maxwell, J. P.

Knowles, William & Margaret Thompson, 7 Jan 1846; John Auton, bondsman; B. Oates, C. C. C., wit.

Knox, David & Elizabeth McCowin, 20 Feb 1794; John Guine, bondsman; Wm. Matthews, wit.

Knox, Henry N. & E. A. Whiteside, 28 Oct 1844; John J. Knox, bondsman; C. T. Alexander, wit.

Knox, Isaac & Elisabeth Price, 24 Feb 1784; Thomas Ferguson, bondsman; Rd. Martin, wit.

Knox, James & Hanah McFalls, 31 Jan 1797; Samuel Neel, bondsman.

Knox, James B. & Ann G. Price, 31 Aug 1842; Henry N. Knox, bondsman.

Knox, John & Polly B. Robison, 10 Nov 1813; James A. Todd, bondsman; Isaac Alexander, wit.

Knox, John & Margaret Price, 15 Dec 1820; John Bell, bondsman.

Knox, John & Jane J. Price, 13 Feb 1817; Reece Price, bondsman.

Knox, John & Elizabeth McRumm, 9 March 1830; Henry N. Knox, bondsman; Isaac S. Alexander, wit.

Knox, John & Hannah Neely, 1 May 1826; Thomas B. Neely, bondsman; Isaac S. Alexander, wit.

Knox, Joseph & Eliz. Whiteside, 8 Feb 1797; Samuel Whiteside, bondsman; Isaac Alexander, wit.

Knox, Joseph & Violet B. Simeral, 7 Dec 1838; Henry H. Knox, bondsman; B. Oates, C. C. C., wit.

Knox, Joseph E. & Francis T. Litten, 2 April 1856; E. P. Hall, bondsman; James Johnston, wit. married 3 April 1866 by James Johnston, J. P.

Knox, Joseph E. & Mary L. White, 11 Jan 1859; E. P. Hall, bondsman; James Johnston, wit. married 11 Jan 1859 by James Johnston, J. P.

Knox, Joseph E. & Margaret White, 22 May 1865; David A. Caldwell, bondsman; Wm. Maxwell, C. C. C., wit. married 28 May 1865 by R. F. Blythe, J. P.

Knox, Matthew & Nancy Watson, 2 April 1831; James B. Knox, bondsman; Isaac S. Alexander,wit.

Knox, Robert & Margaret Bain, 6 July 1843; George Cross, bondsman.

Knox, Robert J. W. & Martha N. Jetton, 9 Aug 1845; Sherod Little, bondsman; Isaac S. Alexander, wit.

Knox, Samuel & Jane Neely, 14 June 1824; Ezekiel C. Neely, bondsman; R. J. Dinkins, wit.

Knox, Samuel & Rachel L. Neely, 9 Oct 1850; Samuel M. Whiteside, bondsman; B. Oates, C. C. C., wit.

Knox, Samuel B. & Ann Lowrie, 2 Oct 1835; George S. Sloan, bondsman; B. Oates, C. C. C., wit.

Knox, Samuel W. & Sarah C. Wallace, 24 Oct 1859; E. P. Hall, bondsman; W. K. Reid, C. C. C., wit. married 25 Oct 1859 by A. Ranson.

Knox, William & Margaret E. Wilson, 28 Feb 1834; Saml. J. McRum, bondsman; John Oates, wit.

Knox, William & Martha Smith (colored), 13 Feb 1866; Wm. Smith, bondsman; married 22 Feb 1866 by Thos. P. Grier, J. P.

Koehler, Frank & Esther Michael, 28 Aug 1861; J. C. Deaton, bondsman; W. K. Reid, C. C. C., wit.

Konkright, Isaac & Dorathy Kook, 8 Sept 1788; Henry Goldman, bondsman; J. Mc. Alexander, wit.

Lafferty, R. H. & Miss Cornelia H. Parks, 1 Jan 1850; Charles T. Alexander, bondsman.

Lafferty, Robert H. & Jane T. Chamberlain, 7 Feb 1848; Charles T. Alexander, bondsman; B. Oates, C. C. C., wit.

Lambeth, J. C. & Mary J. Hoover, 4 March 1862; J. M. McCrary, bondsman; John Phelan, wit. married 5 March 1862 by S. C. Alexander.

Lambeth, Samuel & Sophia Hammond, 1 Aug 1831; Ezekiel J. Hammond, bondsman.

Lane, David & Elizabeth A. Reed, 27 Oct 1865; Wm. Warwick, bondsman; Wm. Maxwell, C. C. C.,wit. married 30 Oct 1865 by J. S. Reid, J. P.

Laney, Nelson, & Jane Polk, 19 Feb 1835; Peter Thompson, bondsman; J. Stilwell, wit.

Laney, Nelson & Jane Givens, 12 May 1836; Ambrose Houston, bondsman; John Stilwell, wit.

Langley, John & Sally Blankenshipp, 27 April 1810; John Ritch, bondsman; Isaac Alexander, wit.

Lankford, George & Delina Perry, 2 Feb 1802; David Lawing, bondsman.

Latta, William A. & Camilla C. Torrence, 24 June 1834; Hugh Torrence, bondsman; B. Oates, C. C. C., wit.

Laughlin, Marcus & Isabella Beaty, 6 March 1830; Colin C. King, bondsman; B. Oates, wit.

Lauson,William F. & Emelia Stitt Morrison, 29 Oct 1839; John N. Ormond, bondsman; Ml. Saunier, wit.

Laverty, John & Selina Parks, 15 Aug 1810; Richard Mason,bondsman.

Lawing, A. W. & Mary A. McGee, 7 March 1866; James Harty, bondsman; Wm. Maxwell, C. C. C., wit. married 15 March 1866 by B. G. Jones, minister.

Lawing, David & Elizabeth Prim, 7 Jan 1815; John Barnhill, bondsman; Isaac Alexander, wit.

Lawing, David & Caroline Price, 29 Jan 1830; James W. Baker, bondsman; E. Elms, wit.

Lawing, David & Adaline Fidler, 24 Jan 1857; Moses E. Kistler, bondsman; W. K. Reid, C. C. C., wit. married 29 Jan 1857 by Stephen Wilson, J. P.

Lawing, George A. & Jane P. Cox, 29 Dec 1843; David Cowan, bondsman; N. B. Taylor, wit.

Lawing, James J. & Julia H. Rossick, 26 Dec 1843; Middleton Lawing, bondsman; N. B. Taylor, wit.

Lawing, Jethro & Sarah M. Cox, 25 Feb 1840; William H. Waddell, bondsman.

Lawing, John & Nancy Johnston, 25 Feb 1812; Joseph Blackwood,
bondsman; Isaac Alexander, wit.

Lawing, John M. & Violet J. Dunn, 15 July 1857; John W. McCoy-
bondsman; W. K. Reid, C. C. C.,   married 16 July 1857 by G.
L. Campbell, J. P.

Lawing, Middleton & Peggy Waddell, 3 June 1820; Josiah Cathey,
bondsman; Isaac Alexander, wit.

Lawing, Samuel & Amelia Dow, 19 Dec 1826; Jacob Tipps, bondsman;
Pearsall Thompson, wit.

Lawing, Samuel & Susan Means, 16 Sept 1834; Middleton Lawing,
bondsman; B. Oates, C. C. C., wit.

Lawing, Samuel & Elizabeth Adley Auton, 1 Nov 1849; William Auton,
bondsman; N. B. Taylor, wit.

Lawing, Samuel & Ellen Alexander, 3 Feb 1853; William Gray,
bondsman; B. Oates, C. C. C. married 10 Feb 1853 by R. H.
Lafferty, minister.

Lawing, Samuel & Jane O. Gibson, 20 Sept 1856; M. DeL. McLeod,
bondsman; W. K. Reid, C. C. C., wit. married 23 Sept 1856 by
W. S. Pharr.

Lawing, Thomas & Margaret Lawing, 24 Sept 1836; Robert F. Cathey,
bondsman; B. Oates, C. C. C., wit.

Lawing, William & Susanna Robeson, 8 Sept 1791; Wm. Armstread
Bradshaw, bondsman; Wm. B. Alexander, wit.

Lawing, Wm. P. & Christian E. Dunn, 5 Feb 1852; Robert B. Dunn,
bondsman; B. Oates, C. C. C., wit. married 6 Feb 1852 by
G. L. Campbell, J. P.

Lawson, Thomas & Mary Barnett, 4 April 1791; Thomas Coughran,
bondsman; Isaac Alexander, wit.

Leach, Levi & Elizabeth Lucinda Page, 5 Sept 1857; John Page,
bondsman; W. K. Reid, C. C. C., wit. married 8 Sept 1857 by
B. H. Garrison, J. P.

Leathers, John & Rebecca Rogers, 13 Nov 1829; Robert N. Kerr,
bondsman; A. B. Jetton, wit.

Ledford, Walter & Mary Long, 17 March 1836; Matthew R. McCoard,
bondsman.

Ledwell, David & Sarah J. Auton, 24 July 1860; R. M. Martin, bondsman; W. K. Reid, C. C. C., wit. married 25 July 1860 by Wm.
Means, J. P.

Lee, John N. Jr. & Francis F. Cathey, 21 Dec 1857; Jacob C. Stout,
bondsman; W. K. Reid, C. C. C., wit. married 22 Dec 1859 by H.
B. Cunningham.

Lee, Robert A. & Isabella Hickman, 7 Feb 1849; Wm. W. Dearmon,
bondsman; B. Oates, C. C. C., wit.

Lee, Solomon & Jannett Griffith, 13 March 1792; George Baker,
bondsman.

Lee, William & Maria Jane Rosser, 7 March 1853; Silas Alexander, bondsman; married 8 March 1853 by S. C. Pharr, V. D. M.

Lee, William L. & Jane C. Cathey, 8 April 1837; G. F. Fite, bondsman; B. Oates, C. C. C., wit.

Leeper, John & Sarah Sloan, 23 March 1820; John Sloan, bondsman; Isaac Alexander, wit.

Lees, James & Mary Maxwell, 5 March 1796; James Russel, bondsman; Ruthy Alexander, wit.

Lees, Robert & Margaret Cathey, 21 Jan 1824; Ja. Cathey, bondsman; Isaac Alexander, wit.

Lees, William & Jenit Taylor, 1 April 1795; John Taylor, bondsman; Ruthy Alexander, wit.

Lees, William & Mary Ann McKnight, 6 Nov 1828; Stephen D. Manson, bondsman; Pearsall Thompson, wit.

Leese, Richard & _____, ---- 182-; Asa Stephens, bondsman.

Leetch, James & Amelia Sophia Kennedy, 1 Jan 1810; Isaac S. Alexander, bondsman.

Leggett, Charles S. & Mary Ezel, 6 March 1828; John N. Houston, bondsman; S. Williamson, wit.

Leggett, James & Jean Jorden, 14 May 1796; Wm. Leggett, bondsman; Shared Gray, wit.

Leiser, John & Mary Vogle, 17 Dec 1859; Charles Roediger, bondsman; W. K. Reid, C. C. C., wit. married 17 Dec 1859 by Alex. Phillippi.

Lemmonds, Marcus D. L. & Jane A. Rea, 1 Sept 1853; M. D. L. McLeod, bondsman; N. B. Taylor, wit. married 13 Sept 1853 by Paul F. Kistler, M. P.

Lemmond, Mars & Miss Elizabeth Mason, 12 April 1831; Isaac Mason, bondsman; B. Oates, D. C.,wit.

Lemmond, Robert & Elizabeth Walker, 25 Feb 1817; Alexander McRea, bondsman; Isaac Alexander, wit.

Lemmond, Sandy & Dorcas McCappin, 3 Nov 1865; Spencer Potts, bondsman.

Lemmond, William K. & Betsey M. Todd, 28 March 1821; John Freeman, bondsman; Isaac Alexander, wit.

Lemond, James & Elizabeth Moore, 26 March 1811; James Todd, bondsman; Isaac Alexander, wit.

Lemond, John & Margaret Collins, 27 Feb 1816; Azariah Coburn, bondsman; Isaac Alexander, wit.

Lemond, John Q. & Rebecca Secrist, 2 Jan 1832; Jas. Pyron, bondsman; B. Oates, D. C., wit.

Lemond, John Q. & Margaret Hood, 27 Feb 1845; Ephraim W. Secrest, bondsman; N. B. Taylor, wit.

MECKLENBURG MARRIAGES 1783-1868

Lemond, Robert & Terrissa Neely, 6 March 1816; John Neely, bondsman; Isaac Alexander, wit.

Lemond, William & Peggy Mackoy, 8 Nov 1815; Peter Crowel, bondsman; Isaac Alexander, wit.

Lenier, Robert & Ann Worke, 4 Sept 1830; Robert Westmoreland, bondsman; A. B. Jetton, wit.

Lentele, C. C. M. & Elizabeth Hayes, 22 April 1862; B. E. A. F. Griffin, bondsman; W. K. Reid, C. C. C., wit. married 23 April 1862 by C. Overman, J.P.

Lentile, Henry & Polley Adams, 17 Aug 1824; Reuben Dulen, bondsman; Philemon Morris, wit.

Lentile, Jackson & Jane Hipworth, 19 May 1838; Robert Todd, bondsman; John M. Sharpe, wit.

Lentile, Joe & Rebecky Louis (colored), 21 July 1864; Zedick Dewey (colored), bondsman.

Lentile, Shadrick L. & Mary Todd, 13 April 1836; James S. Patteson, bondsman; B. Oates, C. C. C., wit.

Lentile, Shedrick L. & Polly Long, 28 Sept 1829; Thomas Norton, bondsman; A. Cooper, wit.

Lentile, William & Laura Shuman, 9 Jan 1852; Jos. R. Cathy, bondsman; James Parks, wit.

Leonard, Charles & Mary N. Todd, 7 Aug 1834; Joseph A. Freasure, bondsman; B. Oates, wit.

Leonard, Jacob & Jane Simons, 7 Jan 1818; Wm. Lamm, bondsman; Isaac S. Alexander, wit.

Lewallen, Jesse & Elizabeth Rodgers, 24 Jan 1850; Jesey R. Lewellen, bondsman; B. Oates, C. C. C., wit.

Lewallen, John & Margaret Nowles, 6 April 1846; George Jordan, bondsman; B. Oates, C. C. C., wit.

Lewellen, Hardy & Catherin Secress, 27 Jan 1823; David Parks, bondsman; R. J. Dinkins, wit.

Lewellen, Jesse R.& Laney McLelland, 6 April 1844; James Montgomery, bondsman; N. B. Taylor, wit.

Lewis, Elisha & Mary Laney, 27 Nov 1832; Eli Stewart, bondsman.

Lewis, Francis & Mary Robison, 9 July 1834; Godfrey W. Williamson, bondsman; B. Oates, wit.

Lewis, James M. & Margaret L. Starnes, 21 Aug 1855; James H. Stilwell, bondsman; W. K. Reid, C. C. C., wit. married 23 Aug 1855 by C. B. Cross, J. P.

Lewis, James S. & Esther Holbrooks, 12 Nov 1842; Rowland H. Carter, bondsman.

Lewis, John & Nancy Brown, 13 Oct 1808; James McLeary, bondsman; Michl. McLeary, wit.

111

Lewis, Jonathan & Lucinda Morris, 7 Jan 1850; William Morris, bondsman; Tho. B. Smartt, wit.

Lewis, Jonathan & Mary McLoud, 23 Jan 1849; John P. Morris, bondsman; Saml. J. Lourie, wit.

Lewis, Joseph & Kezia H. Porter, 29 April 1816; James C. Porter, bondsman; Isaac Alexander, wit.

Lewis, Joseph & Eliza Jennings, 25 Dec 1828; John Spears, bondsman; Pearsall Thompson, wit.

Lewis, Robert & Prudence Hudson, 28 Nov 1827; Jonathan Lewis, bondsman; Isaac S. Alexander, wit.

Lewis, Samuel F. & Elisabeth Russ, 11 June 1824; William Hugs, bondsman; Jno Ritch, J. P.,wit.

Lide, Eli H. & Dorcas Jane Alexander, 7 Nov 1827; Charles W. H. Alexander, bondsman; Thomas B. Smartt, wit.

Lide, William W. & Elmina Davis, 23 Jan 1832; Edwin W. Maxwell, bondsman

Lide, William W. & Isabella Kerr, 15 Nov 1836; George W. Kerr, bondsman; B. Oates, C. C. C. wit.

Liebermann, Charles S. & Francis L. Davis, 24 July 1862; Jacob Coldiron, bondsman; W. K. Reid, C. C. C., wit. married 7 Aug 1865 by Jas. C. Chalmer, minister.

Ligon, E. L. & Mrs. R. A. Cofer, 18 March 1865; Charles T. Myers, bondsman; Wm. Maxwell, C. C. C., wit. married 19 March 1865 by Richd. H. Griffith, M. G.

Liles, William & Evaline Rodden, 11 April 1846; R. J. Reid, bondsman; B. Oates, C. C. C., wit.

Lindsay, David & Mary M. McCullough, 15 April 1856; Thomas A. Sharp, bondsman; W. K. Reid, C. C. C., wit. married 15 April 1856 by Lorenzo Hunter, J. P.

Lindsay, Robert & Mary B. McDowell, 25 Sept 1822; Moses Neely, bondsman.

Linear, Reaves & Nancy N. Westmoreland, 6 Sept 1827; Peterson Westmoreland, bondsman; Alexander B. Jetton, wit.

Ling, Ananias & Sarah Hipworth, 23 March 1825; Joseph J. Berryhill, bondsman; Isaac S. Alexander, wit.

Linn, David & Elisabeth Robison, 26 March 1794; Samuel Davidson, bondsman; James Meek, wit.

Little Franklin & Jane Jetun, 7 Dec 1842; Alfred B. Little, bondsman.

Little, George & Keziah Price, 16 Jan 1816; William Little, bondsman.

Little, James & Elizabeth Maxwell, 1 Oct 1805; Jno. Maxwell, bondsman.

Little, R. W. & Mary J. Whitty, 22 July 1865; Wm. P. Little, bondsman; Wm. Maxwell, C. C. C., wit. married 23 July 1865 by W. M. Kerr.

Lock, James R. & Sarah Jackson, 15 Dec 1835; M. R. Cury, bondsman.

Locket, Newton & Elizabeth Ormond, 25 July 1867; Wm. Maxwell, C. C. C., wit. married 25 July 1867 by C. Overman, J. P.

Logan, John W. & Anabella J. Wilson, 30 Oct 1847; P. J. Wilson, bondsman; N. B. Taylor, wit.

Long, Felix & Mary Williams, 4 March 1843; John Brinkley, bondsman; Edwin Potts, J. P., wit.

Long, George A. & Elizabeth Cuthbertson, Jur., 24 Dec 1835; Charles C. Hinson, bondsman; Wm. H. Simpson, J. P., wit.

Long, Jacob & Elizabeth Morris, 5 Feb 1841; John E. Long, bondsman; B. Oates, C. C. C., wit.

Long, John & Mary McClenahan, 12 March 1794; Alexander McClenachan, bondsman; Isaac Alexander, wit.

Long, John & Molley Finey, 2 June 1795; John Finey, bondsman.

Long, John Jr. & Elizabeth Burnett, 5 Aug 1834; Henry Long Jr., bondsman; Wm. H. Simpson, J. P., wit.

Long, John R. & Susan Ann Hope, 30 Dec 1856; Henry Thomas,bondsman; W. K. Reid, C. C. C., wit. married 30 Dec 1856 by Thomas M. Farrow.

Lossen, James & Mary Ann Davis (colored), 16 Sept 1865; Wm. Wirely, bondsman.

Loughary, William & Elizabeth Thomas, 28 April 1821; William Toler, bondsman; Isaac Alexander, wit.

Lourey, Samuel & Mary Johnson, 25 Feb 1830; Alexander Caldwell, bondsman; B. Oates, wit.

Love, David & Jean Thompson, 24 Aug 1802; Joseph Thompson, bondsman.

Love, John S. & Jane Hoover, 13 Feb 1833; David Cowan, bondsman; B. Oates, wit.

Love, Joseph T. & E. J. Auton, 3 Feb 1845; Robert F. Auton, bondsman; N. B. Taylor, wit.

Love, Moses & Mary Hoover, 8 Jan 1842; Wm. Taylor Robison, bondsman; C. T. Alexander, wit.

Love, Samuel & Eliz. Nation, 30 March 1789; William Blackwood, bondsman; Jn. Rogers, wit.

Love, Thomas & Elizabeth Rawdon, 8 March 1836; Andrew B. Dunn, bondsman; B. Oates, C. C. C.,wit.

Lovelace, Dyson & Louisa Cawan Fite, 9 March 1825; Peter Fite, bondsman; Isaac S. Alexander, wit.

Lovell, James & Elizabeth Simmons, 3 March 1809; William Simmons, bondsman.

Lowing, D. F. & Sarah D. Robinson, 4 Oct 1864; W. J. A. King, bondsman; Wm. Maxwell, C. C. C., wit. married 4 Oct 1864 by Wm. S. Norment, J. P.

Lowrance, W. M. & Octavia Hill, 29 Oct 1850; H. H. Holmes, bondsman; James Parks, wit.

Lowrie, James & Elizabeth Bentley, 8 May 1820; William Sharp, Moses Kerr, bondsmen; Isaac Alexander, wit.

Lowrie, Robert J. A. & Mary A. Hargrove, 3 Dec 1821; John McQuav, bondsman; Isaac Alexander,wit.

Lowrie, Robert J. A. & Ann Sloan, 28 July 1827; John B. Cottrell, bondsman; Pearsall Thompson, wit.

Lowwell, John K. & Mary Sample, 25 Feb 1830; Telemacus Alexander, bondsman

Lucas, Hugh & Kitty McCoy, 24 Nov 1812; John Henderson, bondsman; Isaac Alexander, wit.

Lucas, James & Jinny Duglass, 14 Feb 1807; Joseph Hunter, bondsman; Isaac Alexander, wit.

Lucky, William & Matilda Davis, 22 Jan 1812.

Lucky, William & Mary Young Alexander, 18 Dec 1828; Richard S. Dinkins, bondsman; E. Elms, wit.

Lumley, Thomas & Sally Green, 13 Aug 1806; William Griffith, bondsman; Isaac Alexander, wit.

Lynch, J. Henry & Laura McGinn, 18 Sept 1862; I. F. Little, bondsman; W. W. Grier, wit. married 18 Sept 1862 by David Henderson, J. P.

Lyon, John & Mary Margaret Springs, 3 Dec 1855; W. K. Reid, C. C. C., wit. married 4 Dec 1855 by A. W. Miller.

Macoy, William & Sally Cochran, 16 Oct 1816; Robert Parks, bondsman; John Rea, J. P., wit.

McAllister, Cornelius & Sarah McGinniss, 4 Oct 1803; Wm. McCleary, bondsman; Isaac Alexander, wit.

McAllister, H. B. & Lucinda Dixon, 23 July 1860; J. H. McAllister, bondsman; P. S. Whisnant, wit. married 26 July 1860 by James C. Chalmers.

McAllister, H. B. & Mary Ann Williams, 26 Jan 1863; J. W. McAllister, bondsman; married 27 Jan 1863 by A. Sinclair, Pres. Minister.

McAllister, James & Eliza Freeman, 8 Dec 1823; Alexdr. Starret, bondsman.

McAllister, James H. & Sarah Taylor, 6 Sept 1845; Wm. Clark, bondsman.

McAllister, John W. & Dicey Williams, 25 Aug 1849; John G. Cross, bondsman; B. Oates, C. C. C., wit.

McAllister, William C. & Susan J. Emmerson, 17 April 1851; Alexander Taylor, bondsman; B. Oates, C. C. C., wit. married 20 April 1851 by Jos. C. Nicholson.

McAulay, Daniel & Martha Black, 20 Sept 1787; Samuel Black, bondsman; John Rogers, wit.

McAulay, Daniel & Prudence Alexander, 7 Feb 1802; John Black, bondsman.

McAulay, Rodrick, & Margaret Black, 22 March 1803; William Black, bondsman; J. Wallis, wit.

McAuley, Wm. & Amanda E. Rea, 1 May 1847; Thos. M. Black, bondsman; Saml. J. Lourie, wit.

McAun, or McEwen, Duncan & Elizabeth Grier, 5 April 1820; Samuel Black, bondsman; Isaac Alexander, wit.

McBrid, Henry & Clarrissa Byram, 26 Nov 1818; James C. Griffith, bondsman; Isaac S. Alexander, wit.

McBryde, Steven & Louisa Lowrie (colored), 12 Oct 1865; Elam Orr, bondsman; R. M. White, wit. married 12 Oct 1865 by Jno. F. Butt.

McCachern, J. C. & D. P. Stewart, 17 Sept 1859; John O. King, bondsman; W. K. Reid, C. C. C., wit.

McCachren, Hector & Elisabeth Huea, 26 July 1791; Peter Huie, bondsman; Isaac Alexander, wit.

McCain, George & Margaret McCain, 28 Feb 1820; Hugh J. McCain, bondsman; Isaac Alexander, wit.

McCall, A. L. & Margaret E. Harrison, 28 Sept 1859; R. J. Howie, bondsman; W. K. Reid, C. C. C., wit. married 28 Sept 1859 by P. McEwen, J. P.

McCall, Addison G. & Melinda L. Query, 9 May 1850; E. C. Stewart, bondsman; B. Oates, C. C. C., wit.

McCall, Cyrus, L. & Sarah A. McCall, 19 Aug 1852; B. Oates, C. C. C., wit. married 19 Aug 1852 by C. B. Cross, J. P.

McCall, Eli & Mary Hooks, 22 March 1823; Thomas Wilson, bondsman; Isaac Alexander, wit.

McCall, Harris & Rachel Stillwill, 27 Nov 1832; William R. Hook, bondsman; Isaac S. Alexander, wit.

McCall, Harris & Amanda Moore, 16 Feb 1836; Samuel B. Hall, bondsman; B. Oates, C. C. C., wit.

McCall, John & Elizabeth M. Cuthbertson, 22 Oct 1859; John A. McCall, bondsman; W. K. Reid, C. C. C., wit. married 22 Oct 1859 by P. McEwen, J. P.

McCall, John A. & Mary A. Yandle, 7 Sept 1848; Josiah F. McCall, bondsman; Saml. J. Lourie, wit.

McCall, Josiah & Isabel Blair, 12 March 1833; John Hooks, bondsman; B. Oates, D. C., wit.

McCall, Josiah F. & Cecelia Cathey, 30 Aug 1849; D. C. Robison,
bondsman; Saml. J. Lourie, wit.

McCall, Milas W. & Marina C. Gray, 17 Jan 1842; Samuel B. Hall,
bondsman.

McCall, Silvester & Charlotte Yandle, 8 Jan 1840; Samuel Yandle,
bondsman; B. Oates, C. C. C., wit.

McCall, Thomas & Elizabeth Black, 8 April 1812; Hamilton Black,
bondsman;

McCamey, William E. & Hamie E. Kelly, 15 May 1848; Robt M.
Shirley, bondsman; Saml. J. Lourie, wit.

McCan, James & Elender Boyd, 15 Oct 1799; Hance McCain, bondsman;
Shared Gray, wit.

McCarver, Alexander W. & Elizabeth Capps, 25 June 1846; Thos. B.
Capps, bondsman; S. J. Lourie, wit.

McCarver, Eli P. & Clarissa Capps, 19 Nov 1841; Wm. A. Brown,
bondsman; C. T. Alexander, C. C. C., wit.

McCaulay, E. A. & M. /S. Alexander, 19 Dec 1849; John Wallace,
bondsman; James Nance, J. P., wit.

McCaulay, Hugh & Nancy D. Alexander, 13 May 1822; James Doherty,
bondsman; W. S. Davidson, wit.

McCaulo, John & Rachel Kerr, 12 Sept 1795; Joseph Kerr, bondsman.

McCauly, Zachariah & Margret N. Hood, 20 Nov 1827; John Walker,
bondsman.

McClelan, Joseph & Mary Laurens, 25 Jan 1792; Wm. McRee, bondsman; Isaac Alexander, wit.

McClellan, James H. & Sarah E. Davis, 10 Dec 1855; John M. W.
McCachren, bondsman; W. K. Reid, C. C. C.,wit. married 13
Dec 1855 by R. H. Lafferty, minister.

McClery, Wm. & Susannah Campbell, 6 July 1795; James Hutchison,
bondsman.

McClughan, James & Anne Rea, 21 Feb 1797; Andrew Rea, bondsman;
J. Wallis, wit.

McClure, Charles & Sarah Bell, 15 Jan 1793; Isaac Alexander, wit.

McClure, James & Jane Harlin, 15 Dec 1800; George Harlin, bondsman.

McClure, James & Mary Sharp, 4 April 1803; Andrew Olipher,
bondsman; J. Wallis, wit.

McClure, John & Sara Allen, 18 Dec 1792; William Walker, bondsman;
Ruthy Alexander, wit.

McClure, John & Mary Hodge, 10 Feb 1795; Moses McClure, bondsman.

McClure, John & Eleanor Polston, 5 Jan 1799; Alexander Hodge,
bondsman.

McClure, John & Mary Todd, 11 Dec 1799; Hugh Todd, bondsman.

McClure, Moses & _____, 8 Sept 1789; Moses McClure Jr.,
bondsman; Barthw. Thompson, wit.

McClure, Robert & Margaret Wallace, 20 Feb 1793; Mathew Wallace,
bondsman; Isaac Alexander, wit.

McClure, William & Elizabeth Crocket, 13 Feb 1804; Robert Robison,
bondsman.

McCoard, Elam T. & Elizah Baker, 3 Nov 1841; Benjamin F. Brown,
bondsman.

McCoard, John & Betsey Russell, 16 May 1803; Joseph Canon,
bondsman; Isaac Alexander, wit.

McCoard, Robert C. & Martha V. Pelt, 7 March 1827; James R.
Hutchison, bondsman.

McCoard, Thomas & Rebekah Thompson, 26 Jan 1819; James Thompson,
bondsman; Isaac Alexander, wit.

McCoard, Thomas T. & Amelia Baker, 23 Oct 1845; Wm. A. Cooper,
bondsman; C. T. Alexander, wit.

McComb, James & Amy Morris, 21 March 1828; Cyrus Black, bondsman;
Eli Springs, wit.

McComb, James E. & Jane G. Oakes, 22 Aug 1833; Wm. A. Davidson,
bondsman; B. Oates, D. C., wit.

McComb, Joseph & Martha Parks, 29 Feb 1836; James Gingles, bondsman; B. Oates, C. C. C., wit.

McComb, Robert & Sarah Huson, 19 Aug 1817; Joseph McConnaughy,
bondsman.

McComb, Robert W. & Margaret Jane Young, 20 March 1858; Charles
Wilson, bondsman; John Phelan, wit. married 25 March 1858 by
R. H. Lafferty, minister.

McComb, William & Mary Philips, 7 May 1794; John Phillips, bondsman.

McComb, William & Elizabeth Harrison, 25 May 1798; Robert Rankin,
bondsman; Isaac Alexander, wit.

McConnel, James & M. E. Porter, 14 Feb 1857; Wm. A. Bell, bondsman;
W. K. Reid, C. C. C., wit. married 17 Feb 1857 by R. H.
Lafferty, minister.

McConnel, John & Martha Galloway, 15 Dec 1830; William Caldwell,
bondsman; A. B. Jetton, wit.

McConnel, Robt. K. & Nancy D. Ewart, 12 Nov 1855; James McConnel,
bondsman; W. K. Reid, C. C. C., wit. married 15 Oct 1855 by
Walter S. Pharr.

McConnel, William & Mary Ross, 31 Dec 1838; Thomas McConnel, bondsman; J. Doherty, J. P., wit.

McConnell, A. J. & Mary L. McKnight, 18 Dec 1855; Robert V. Kerns,
bondsman; W. K. Reid, C. C. C., wit. married 20 Dec 1855 by
H. B. Cunningham.

McConnell, Andrew & Jane F. Alexander, 26 Feb 1822; Washington Harris, bondsman.

McConnell, Benjamin & Sarah Wilson, 1 Oct 1789; James Courier, bondsman; Mary Alexander, wit.

McConnell, James H. & Margaret N. Montgomery, 27 July 1857; James H. Montgomery, bondsman; W. K. Reid, C. C. C., wit. married 28 July 1857 by Saml. A. Davis, J. P.

McCord, D. L. & Martha E. McCoy, 15 Jan 1856; Robert F. McGinn, bondsman; W. K. Reid, C. C. C., wit. married 15 Jan 1856 by J. P. Ross, J. P.

McCord, John & Mary Means, 10 Jan 1827; John Means, bondsman; Isaac S. Alexander, wit.

McCord, William & Hanah Kennedy, 9 Sept 1794; James Kennedy, bondsman; Isaac Alexander, wit.

McCord, William & Mary Wilson Yandell, 24 March 1801; James Yandell, bondsman.

McCord, William M. & Nancy Summerville, 18 Dec 1851; William Summerville, bondsman; James Parks, wit. married 18 Dec 1851 by Batte Irwin.

McCorkle, Hugh P. & Cynthia C. Beaty, 20 Feb 1843; Thomas F. Porter, bondsman;M. W. Alexander, wit.

McCorkle, James & Margaret Kennedy, 14 Feb 1804; Wm. Givens, bondsman; Shared Gray, wit.

McCorkle, James & Mary Jane Orr, 14 Jan 1840; Green P. Fite, bondsman; B. Oates, wit.

McCorkle, Joseph & Polly Porter, 9 June 1812; Hugh Porter, bondsman; Thomas Greer, bondsman; Isaac Alexander, wit.

McCorkle, Nelson & Matilda Blount, 28 Oct 1839; John McCorkle, bondsman.

McCorkle, Patrick W. & Union Bevins, 15 Sept 1818; Elias Stilwell, bondsman; Jno Teavis, Jr., wit.

McCorkle, Thomas & Eliza Westmoreland, 21 June 1827; Clement Nantz, bondsman; A. B. Jetton, wit.

McCorkle, Thomas J. & Mary Ann Pucket, 6 Oct 1846; T. A. Stuard, bondsman; B. Oates, C. C. C., wit.

McCorkle, William H. & Elvira M. Dixon, 14 Aug 1860; W. K. Reid, C. C. C., wit. married 16 Aug 1860 by J. B. Watt, M. G.

McCormick, Robert & Adaith Singleton, 8 June 1799; John Porter, bondsman; Isaac Alexander, wit.

McCoy, C. W. & M. C. Sample, 16 Feb 1855; Robert D. Whitley, bondsman; R. F. Blythe, J. P., wit. married 20 Feb 1855 by H. B. Cunningham.

McCoy, David & Sarah Caldwell, 22 Dec 1851; John Caldwell, bondsman; James Parks, wit. married 23 Dec 1851 by Jas. B. Watt, M. G.

McCoy, David F. & Mary H. Reid, 28 Feb 1861; R. S. Reid, bondsman; S. P. Alexander, wit. married 28 Feb 1861 by J. P. Ross, J. P.

McCoy, Edwin A. & Cristian Williamson, 27 Dec 1826; Robert C. McCoard, bondsman; Isaac Alexander, wit.

McCoy, Hugh A. & Frances Beaty, 5 Sept 1838; James McAlexander, bondsman.

McCoy, James M. & Jane Beaty, 12 March 1843; John B. Rogers, bondsman.

McCoy, John & Esther Fraser, 16 March 1799; James A. Bradley, bondsman.

McCoy, John H. & Clarrissa C. Beaty, 8 Feb 1826; Hiram C. Braley, bondsman; Isaac S. Alexander, wit.

McCoy, Lawson H. & Dorcas Berryhill, 3 Jan 1820; Samuel Berryhill, bondsman; Isaac Alexander, wit.

McCoy, McKinney & Martha Robinson, 3 Aug 1825; Wallis Robison, bondsman; Eli Springs, wit.

McCracken, Elihu & Esther Kerr, 12 April 1819; Thomas Shelby, bondsman; Isaac Alexander, wit.

McCracken, John & Nancy Jolly, 27 Sept 1824; Samuel Porter, bondsman; R. S. Dinkins, wit.

McCrackene, Robert C. & Jane D. McKelvy, 31 July 1845; Robert F. Auten, bondsman; Isaac S. Alexander, wit.

McCrackene, Robert C. & Martha A. Ross, 6 Feb 1850; Robert S. Price, bondsman; B. Oates, C. C. C., wit.

McCrery, David & Charlotte Read, 4 Sept 1839; Henry Cashon, bondsman; James Johnston, wit.

McCrery, John & Elesebeth Yandel, 27 Aug 1799; Moses Cochran, bondsman; Shared Gray, wit.

McCulloch, James & Jenny Potts, 13 Jan 1801; Jno McCulloh, bondsman; Jas. Wallis, wit.

McCulloch, James & Amanda Taylor (colored), 7 Sept 1865; Alexr. Henderson, bondsman; Wm. Maxwell, C. C. C., wit. married 7 Sept 1865 by Wm. H. Pitts, minister.

McCulloch, John & D. M. Robinson, 5 June 1829; Benedick Alderson, bondsman; Ben Morrow, wit.

McCulloch, Milas J. & Ann Rebecca Elms, 18 Aug 1852; William Ross, bondsman; B. Oates, wit.

McCulloch, Elijah & Jenny Weeks, 10 Nov 1801; Isaac McCulloch, J. Wallis, wit.

McCulloch, John Jr. & Mary Shanks, 7 Dec 1797; James McCulloch, bondsman; James Wallis, wit.

McDonald, David & Elizabeth Hayse, 15 Feb 1810; H. G. Burton, bondsman.

McDonald, George W. & Ann E. Campbell, 6 Aug 1834; Joseph C.
Nicholson, bondsman; B. Oates, C. C. C.,wit.

McDonald, George W. & Mary L. McCord, 5 Oct 1836; Thompson Walker,
bondsman.

McDonald, George W. & Elizabeth A. B. McCord, 19 Jan 1849; William
Harty, bondsman.

McDonald, James & Jane Cathey (colored), 10 Jan 1866; Sidney
Friday, bondsman; Wm. Maxwell, C. C. C., wit. married 11 Jan
1866 by J. J. Sloan, J. P.

McDonald, James R. & Sarah Elwood, 9 March 1855; James Wiley
Gray, bondsman; W. K. Reid, C. C. C., wit.

McDonald, John & Isabella Rogers, 3 Aug 1825; Jno. W. Rodgers,
bondsman; Isaac Alexander, wit.

McDonald, Joseph B. & Martha K. McCoard, 24 Oct 1827; Jno. W.
Rodgers, bondsman; Isaac Alexander, wit.

McDonald, Thomas & Susan M. Alexander, 20 July 1825; Moses J.
B. Hayes, bondsman; Isaac S. Alexander, wit.

McDonald, William & Eliz. Sadler, 16 Sept 1789; Wm. Hutchison,
bondsman; Barthw. Thomson, wit.

McDonald, William & Carrie C. Morris, 9 Sept 1865; W. C. Maxwell,
bondsman; Wm. Maxwell, C. C. C., wit. married 12 Sept 1865
by R. Z. Johnston, M. G.

McDowell, Hugh & Peggy Irwin, 31 March 1802; William Irwin, bondsman.

McDowell, John & Rebekah Davis, 2 Sept 1799; Charles Wright,
bondsman.

McDowell, John D. & Nancy Irwin, 9 May 1832; John H. McDowell,
bondsman.

McDowell, John H. & Martha L. Henderson, 27 Oct 1846; Robert W.
McDowell, bondsman; B. Oates, C. C. C., wit.

McDowell, John H. & Agness R. Watt, 28 Oct 1853; L. S. Williams,
bondsman; W. K. Reid, C. C. C., wit. married 31 Oct 1853 by
A. L. Watts, V. D. M.

McDowell, Robert W. & Nancy H. E. Neel, 24 July 1848; I. H. McDowell, bondsman.

McDowell, William A. & Martha M. Price, 19 April 1841; Jonathan
Reid, bondsman.

McDugald, John & Nancy Stinson, 9 Dec 1794; Hugh Stinson, bondsman;
Isaac Alexander, wit.

McEachren, Peter R. & Elizabeth Jingles, 20 April 1824; Osmund
Alexander, bondsman; Isaac Alexander,wit.

McElroy, James & Sarah Shreybery, 13 Aug 1801; James Litle, bondsman; Andw. Walker, wit.

McElroy, S. J. & Maggie J. Sample, 1 Jan 1866; J. G. McCorkle,
bondsman; Wm. Maxwell, C. C. C., wit. married 19 Jan 1866
by S. C. Pharr.

McElwee, Thomas & Jane McComb, 17 July 1799; William Brown, bondsman; Isaac Alexander, wit.

McEwan, Samuel & Sarah Parks, 1 Dec 1795; James Parks, bondsman; Ruthe Alexander, wit.

McEwen, James M. & Mary F.Hart, 6 Nov 1860; Joseph Orr, bondsman; W. K. Reid, C. C. C., wit. married 8 Nov 1860 by W. R. Maxwell, J. P.

McFaddin, Isaac & Nancy M. Grier, 9 May 1848; Thos. McGee, bondsman; Saml. J. Lourie, wit.

McFarlind, Jacob & Jane Varner, 14 April 1792; John Varner, bondsman.

MaGahey, Thaddeus C. & Mary C. Hutchison, 3 Sept 1865; G. W. Gatlin, bondsman; Wm. Maxwell, C. C. C., wit. married 3 Sept 1865 by Thos. M. Carr, J. P.

McGahey, Thomas A. & Eloisa Potts, 14 March 1824; Milton McGahy, bondsman; W. L. Davidson, wit.

McGee, Daniel & Nancy L. McCord, 2 Oct 1855; J. C. Hand, bondsman; W. K. Reid, C. C. C., wit. married 3 Oct 1855 by H. B. Cunningham.

McGee, John & Agness Walker, 27 Dec 1788; John Walker, bondsman; Jo. Duglass, wit.

McGee, Robert & Sarah Capps, 7 April 1831; James Abernathy, bondsman; Thomas T. Johnston, wit.

McGee, Robert S. & Harriet Capps, 28 Dec 1840; Hampton Penny, bondsman; Wm. A. Lawing, wit.

McGill, John & Rebekah McCormick, 12 May 1796; Robert McCormick, bondsman; Isaac Alexander, wit.

McGilvray, James A. & Caroline Johnston, 15 Dec 1840; John N. Porter, bondsman.

McGin, James & Christiana Todd, 13 Oct 1794; James Todd, bondsman; Isaac Alexander, wit.

McGin, James & Jane C. McCord, 6 Aug 1823; Robert A. Todd, bondsman; Isaac Alexander, wit.

McGin, John & Margaret Boal, 3 Nov 1796; Thomas McLure Jr., bondsman.

McGin, Robert A. & Mary M. Henderson, 4 Feb 1854; James W. McGinn, bondsman; W. K. Reid, C. C. C., wit. married 7 Feb 1854 by H. B. Cunningham

McGin, Thomas & Ann McKinley, 22 July 1795; Thomas Boal, bondsman.

McGin, Thomas & Mary Todd, 16 Dec 1800; George Todd, bondsman.

McGin, William A. & Isabella Dun, 28 Aug 1825; James H. McGinn, bondsman; Jno Hutchison, wit.

McGinn, James W. & Christian A. Henderson, 15 June 1855; John W. Henderson, bondsman; W. K. Reid, C. C. C., wit. married 20 June 1855 by H. B. Cunningham.

McGinn, W. A. & Adelaide C. Alexander, 30 Oct 1865; Abdon Alexander, bondsman. Wm. Maxwell, : . C. C., wit. married 31 Oct 1865 by R. Z. Johnston, M. G.

McGinnes, Charles B. & M. C. Alexander, 21 Aug 1851; James Parks, wit. married 28 Aug 1851 by John Hunter.

McGinnes, John & Permelia A. Parks, 6 Sept 1825; David Parks, bondsman; Richd Gillespie, Jr., wit.

McGinnes, Joseph & Milly Orr, 14 April 1823; John Cheves, bondsman; Isaac Alexander, wit.

McGinnes, William & Z. Cook, 30 March 1865; R. M. White, bondsman; Wm. Maxwell, C. C. C., wit. married 30 March 1865 by F. M. Ross, J. P.

McGinnis, James P. & Jane L. Caldwell, 2 March 1840; R. J. Rankin, bondsman.

McGinnis, Joseph H. & A. J. Kennedy, 30 Oct 1845; Moses B. Taylor, bondsman.

McGinnis, Joseph William & Margaret H. Patterson, 16 Sept 1844; D. H. Robison, bondsman.

McGinty, Abner & Selina McEwen, 5 Aug 1816; Robert Johnston, bondsman.

McGlaughlan, John & Hanna Sconnel, 23 March 1783; Samuel McGlaughlin, bondsman; Samuel Martin, wit.

McIntire, Isaac & Betsey Thompson, 16 Nov 1811; Alexander McClure, bondsman; Isaac Alexander, wit.

McIntosh, John H. & Martha Ann Williams, 20 Oct 1852; A. C. Fulenwider, bondsman; B. Oates, C. C. C., wit. married 21 Oct 1852 by R. F. Morrison

McKee, John & Agness Ramsey, 18 Nov 1797; William Ramsey, bondsman.

McKee, John & Elizabeth Hodge, 23 April 1798; Alex. Hodge, bondsman; J. Wallis, wit.

McKelvey, James T. & Nancy Patterson, 8 Feb 1857; Thompson Walker, bondsman; B. Oates, wit.

McKelvy, John M. & Jane Jamison, 31 March 1825; Jesse H. Clark, bondsman.

McKelvy, William & Martha Brown, 28 Jan 1801; Jnoh. Brown, bondsman.

McKelvy, William & Betsey Plummer, 3 Jan 1831; Alexander Gibney, bondsman; B. Oates, wit.

McKelvy, William & Mary A. McCracken, 22 Dec 1845; John Capps, bondsman; B. Oates, C. C. C., wit.

McKenney, William & Mila Hemm, 18 Sept 1845; Deleny Stuart, bondsman.

McKenney, William & Mrs. Mary Pierce, 3 Dec 1851; George W. McKiny, bondsman; Saml. A. Davis, J. P., B. Oates, C. C. C., wit. married 4 Dec 1851 by Saml A. Davis, J. P.

McKibben, Alick & Agness Wiley, 1 June 1796; James Miller, bondsman; Isaac Alexander, wit.

McKibben, John & Sarah Hannigon, 17 Sept 1827; John A. McCall, bondsman; Isaac S. Alexander, wit.

McKibben, John A. & Mary Duest, 31 Jan 1825; Marcus Alexander McKibben, bondsman;

McKibben, Robert L. & Jane Blount, 13 July 1840; Joseph M. Roberts, bondsman; B. Oates, C. C. C., wit.

McKibben, Thomas & Elizabeth Duffey, 1 March 1825; David S. Kerr, bondsman; Isaac Alexander, wit.

McKimberl, Hugh & Mary E. Faggert, 26 March 1860; Joseph A. Fagert, bondsman; Jno Pheland, wit. married 27 March 1860 by J. P. Ross, J. P.

McKiney, Samuel J. & Manda Craig, 21 Jan 1857; Samuel Kerr, bondsman; Jas. B. Robinson, J. P., wit.

McKiney, T. A. & Mary B. Hood, 9 Jan 1851; J. Thomas Downs, bondsman; J. W. Morrow, J. P., wit.

McKinley, Alexander & Ann A. Hope, 2 March 1831; David Allen, bondsman.

McKinley, Robert & Peggy Neel, 23 Aug 1802; John McCord, bondsman; Isaac Alexander,wit.

McKinley, Stephen & Dovey L. Robinson, 4 Jan 1824; Zenas White, bondsman; R. S. Dinkins, wit.

McKinny, John W. & Sarah J. Erwin, 17 Oct 1865; Wm. Lee Manson, bondsman; Wm. Maxwell, C. C. C., wit. married 19 Oct 1865 by W. M. Mills, J. P.

McKinny, Seth & Jane Merchant, 14 Jan 1800; Jesse McKinney, bondsman; Isaac Alexander, wit.

McKnight, John N. & Sarah J. Todd, 17 Feb 1847; Robt. N. Bigham, bondsman; Saml. J. Lourie, wit.

McKnight, Robert H. & Mary H. Hamilton, 18 Aug 1842; John L. Todd, bondsman.

McKnight, Thomas & Margaret Falls, 30 Dec 1795; John Falls, bondsman; Ruth Alexander, wit.

McKorkle, Thomas & Katharine Evits, 15 Oct 1807; Joel McKorkle, bondsman; Jno. Harris, J. P., wit.

McLarty, Samuel W. & Mary Polk, 16 May 1826; Wm. N. Parks, bondsman; Richd. Gillespie Jr., wit.

McLaughlin, J. J. & M. L. Alexander, 11 Jan 1866; J. Chresbey Henderson, bondsman; Wm. Maxwell, C. C. C.,wit. married 12 Jan 1866 by H. B. Pratt.

McLaughlin, Samuel & Abigail Orr, 5 June 1844; John B. Peoples, bondsman; N. B. Taylor, wit.

McLean, Hugh & Elizabeth Morris, 24 April 1810; Zabulon Morris, bondsman; Isaac S. Alexander,wit.

McLean, John M. & Elizabeth Dickson, 23 March 1831; James A. Dixon, bondsman.

McLean, John W. & Sarah Hall, 11 Nov 1851; Saml. M. Withers, bondsman; Jas. Johnston, J. P., wit. married 12 Nov 1851 by Saml. B. O. Wilson, V. D. M.

McLean, R. G. & Catherine E. Sandifer, 3 Dec 1846; James L. Davidson, bondsman; S. J. Lourie, wit.

McLean, William W. & Margaret Dixon, 23 Dec 1839; Henry H. Galloway, bondsman; B. Oates, C. C. C., wit.

McLeary, James & Elizabeth Boyd, 27 Feb 1822; Joshua P. Smith, bondsman.

McLeary, John & Isabella Dow, 5 Feb 1823; William Dow, bondsman.

McLeary, William H. & Eliza Daw, 23 Jan 1822; John W.McLeary, bondsman.

McLeod, Alexander, & Mary Brown, 9 Dec 1826; John W. Brown, bondsman; Isaac Alexander, wit.

McLeod, Alexander & Sarah Herron, 12 Dec 1831; J. W. W. Faires, bondsman; B. Oates, D. C., wit.

McLeod, Daniel & Peggy McDonald, 8 June 1809; Hugh Stinson, bondsman; Isaac Alexander, wit.

McLeod, James & Matilda Williamson, 15 Jan 1849; M. Del. McLeod, bondsman; Saml. J. Lourie, wit.

McLure, Alexander & Esther McGill, 10 Oct 1798; John McGin, bondsman; Isaac Alexander, wit.

McLure, Cyrus & Mary McGinn, 14 May 1856; C. S. McLure, bondsman; W. K. Reid, C. C. C., wit. married 14 May 1856 by David Henderson, J. P.

McLure, David C. & Nancy Jackson, 24 Feb 1823; Jacob Linsay, bondsman; Isaac S. Alexander, wit.

McLure, James & Jane Lawing, 28 July 1834; Cyrus W. Alexander, bondsman; B. Oates, C. C. C., wit.

McLure, James & Caroline McKelvy, 16 Jan 1843; James W. Plumer, bondsman.

McLure, James & Eliza Prim, 15 Nov 1859; Powell Auten, bondsman; W. K. Reid, C. C. C., wit. married 15 Nov 1859 by G. L. Campbell, J. P.

McLure, James L. & E. C. Jamison, 9 June 1847; Chas. L. Hutchison, bondsman; S. J. Lourie, wit.

McLure, Robert & Eliza Davis, 24 Nov 1826; William McLure, bondsman; Isaac S. Alexander, wit.

McLure, William & Margaret Sloan, 13 Oct 1825; William Bigham, bondsman; Isaac Alexander,wit.

McMicken, Andrew & Mary McKee, 13 April 1792; Richard Brown,
    bondsman; Isaac Alexander, wit.

McMillen, David & Elizabeth Cunningham, 20 Dec 1854; James R.
    Cunningham, bondsman; W. K. Reid, C. C. C., wit. married 28
Dec 1854 by S. C. Pharr, V. D. M.

McMurrey, John & Jennett S. McCoy, 1 Feb 1804; Even L. Wiley,
    bondsman.

McNeel, Thomas & Clarissa Polk, 29 Sept 1803; Thomas Elliott,
    bondsman; Isaac Alexander, wit.

McNeel, William R. & Margaret Porter, 24 Feb 1831; James H. Orr,
    bondsman; B. Oates, D. C., wit.

McNeeley, David & Kiziah Fincher, 15 May 1798; John McNeeley,
    bondsman; Shared Gray, wit.

McNeely, John & Hanah McCorkle, 26 Feb 1798; Samuel McCrery,
    bondsman.

McNeely, Joseph B. & Mary Ann McConnaughey, 8 Jan 1849; John R.
    Davidson, bondsman; B. Oates, wit.

McNeely, Robert A. & Louisa R.Caldwell, 13 Aug 1853; Robert N.
    Caldwell, bondsman; Braly Oats, C. C. C., wit. married 16
Aug 1853 by R. H. Lafferty, minister.

McNeely, T. N. & Isabella E.Henderson, 21 Nov 1855; Jas. M.
    Barnett, bondsman; W. K. Reid, C. C. C., wit.

McNeely, William & Polly Roper, 28 Nov 1820; John McCorkle, bonds-
    man; Isaac Alexander,wit.

McNight, James & Ann Reed, 6 June 1796; William Porter bondsman;
    Isaac Alexander, wit.

McNight, Robert & Margrit Moore, 27 Jan 1803; Wm. Kerr, bondsman;
    Isaac Alexander, wit.

McQuaiston, Thomas & Sally Stephens, 11 Dec 1815; Isaac Alexander,
    wit.

McQuay, Seborn & Martha E. Arwood, 7 Feb 1854; R. Samuel Reid,
    bondsman; W. K. Reid, C. C. C.,wit. married 8 Feb 1854 by J.
P. Ross, J. P.

McQuin, Thomas & Peggy Atchison, 17 Nov 1827; Thomas Gillespie,
    bondsman.

McRacken, William D & Mary R. Riley, 14 Aug 1858; James Page,
    bondsman; Jno Phelan, wit. married 14 Aug 1858 by Wm. S.
Norment.

McRaven, Adam & Minty Doherty, 9 Feb 1811; Andrew T. Davidson,
    bondsman; Isaac Alexander, wit.

McRavin, David & Mary Lowry, 29 Oct 1848; Clement Williams, bonds-
    man; James Nance, J. P., wit.

McRee, A. F. & Margaret E. L. Henderson, 28 March 1846; Moses B.
    Taylor, bondsman.

McRee, Andrew & Martha Elliotte, 28 May 1791; George Graham, bondsman; Isaac Alexander, wit.

McRee, Cruser A. (Dr.) & Margaret R. Sadler, 14 Feb 1852; Robert Gibbon, bondsman; married 24 Feb 1852 by Jas. E. Morrison

McRee, David & Sarah Orr, 4 Nov 1823; John Orr, bondsman; Isaac S. Alexander,wit.

McRee, David H. & Violet A. Hipp, 15 Dec 1830; John W. Rodgers, bondsman; B. Oates, D. C.,wit.

McRee, James & Jamima S. Caruthers,28 March 1825; Joseph Ratchford, bondsman; Isaac S. Alexander, wit.

McRee, William E. & Jane Graham, 23 Dec 1818; James McRee, bondsman; Isaac Alexander, wit.

McRee, Winslow J. & Peggy Patterson, 27 June 1808; Isaac S. Henderson, bondsman; Isaac Alexander, wit.

McRory, William & Thirza Neel, 21 July 1828; David Simpson, bondsman; Wm. Pyron, wit.

McRum, Samuel & Eleanor Hart, 2 June 1800; David Hartt, bondsman.

McRum, Samuel J. & Sarah H. Rodgers, 2 March 1835; S. D. Parton, bondsman; B. Oates, C. C. C.,wit.

McRum, Saml. W. & Mary D. Capps, 9 Aug 1856; Neel Wingate, bondsman; W. K. Reid, C. C. C., wit. married 13 Aug 1856 by G. D. Parks.

McRum, Stephen & Mary Ferguson, 3 Jan 1819; Joseph McRum, bondsman.

McRum, Stephen & Matilda P. Rodgers, 8 April 1826; Joseph McRum, bondsman.

McSwain, Gabriel W.& Elizabeth L. Flow, 18 Dec 1841; Daniel Asbury, bondsman.

McWhirter, G. B. & Benece P. Wilson, 22 May 1841; F. V. Lewis, bondsman; J. M. Stewart, wit.

McWhirter, Martin & Eliza McCorkle, 26 Oct 1816; Michael Polk, bondsman; John Rea, J. P.,wit.

McWhorter, Aaron & Agnis Tenis(?), 28 Aug 1793; John Ozeburn, bondsman; Willm. Mathews, wit. (one place on bond shows Moses McWhorter, but signature is clearly Aaron McWhorter).

McWhorter, James H. & Catharine L. McKnight, 28 Sept 1826; William M. Grier, bondsman; Isaac Alexander, wit.

Madden, Edward & Eliza Nowlan, 4 Jan 1862; D. McGinnis, bondsman; W. K. Reid, C. C. C., wit. married 6 Jan 1862 by J. V. O'Connell, D. D.

Maessy, James & Mrs. Eliza McCall, 25 Nov 1837; Ezekiel W. Polk, bondsman; Philemon Morris, wit.

Main, Bryan & Patsey Cooper, 24 Sept 1810; Joseph Reed, bondsman.

Malor, William & Sally Ferrel, 15 Sept 1817; James Ferrell,
bondsman; Isaac Alexander, wit.

Manning, James & Mary Hendrix, 5 Sept 1864; George Moore, bondsman;
Wm. Maxwell, C. C. C., wit. married 5 Sept 1865 by J. T.
O'Connell, D. D.

Manning, John W. & Mary Ann Smith, 6 Dec 1864; John C. Looker,
bondsman; married 7 Dec 1864 by F. M. Ross, J. P.

Manson,Stephen & Margret Lees, 7 March 1827; Marcus D. Manson,
bondsman; Pearsall Thompson, wit.

Manson, William & Adaline M. Walker, 22 Feb 1825; Marcus D.
Manson, bondsman; Isaac S. Alexander, wit.

Markert, Jacob & Jane A. Gray, 25 Nov 1827; William N. Spears,
bondsman; Pearsall Thompson, wit.

Marks, Henry & Rebecca A. Cheek, 24 July 1823; William H. Smith,
bondsman; R. J. Dinkins, wit.

Marks, Thomas & Marget E. Button, 28 April 1832; Gideon Olmsted,
bondsman; Thomas Harris, wit.

Marks, Thomas E. & Nancy H. Robison, 27 June 1854; Wm. W. Robison,
bondsman; W. K. Reid, C. C. C., wit. married 27 June 1854 by
A. M. Watson.

Marks, William S. & Mary E. Faris, 26 Feb 1855; John W. McCoy,
bondsman; Saml. J. Lourie, wit. married 6 March 1855 by J.
B. Watt, V. D. M.

Mars, John & Susannah Baker, 16 July 1833; Isaac A. Baker, bondsman;
B. Oates, wit.

Marshall, James Henry & Susan Cornelia Shelby, 18 Aug 1840; Wm.
M. Porter, bondsman; B. Oates, C. C. C., wit.

Marshal, William & Margaret A. McCord, 5 Aug 1841; Wm. M. Porter,
bondsman.

Marshal, William & Cynthia P. Todd, 9 Oct 1845; Saml. H. Wilson,
bondsman; C. T. Alexander, wit.

Marshal, William & Margt. J. Shelby, 14 June 1864; Geo. W. Mc-
Donald, bondsman; married 16 June 1864 by Geo. W. McDonald,
J. P.

Marshall, John & Ann Newmon, 21 May 1813.

Martin, Edwin & Mary Westmoreland, 8 Jan 1827; William Nantz,
bondsman; A. B. Jetton, wit.

Martin, Eli & Polly Capps, 13 May 1823; George Graham, bondsman;
Isaac Alexander, wit.

Martin, Ephriem R. & Caroline Dewese, 25 Dec 1839; J. F. Gillespie,
bondsman; James Johnston, wit.

Martin, Henry & Emily Simpson, 13 July 1837; John Reid Jr., bondsman; B. Oates, C. C. C., wit.

Martin, Henry & Eliza Clark, 17 Feb 1841; Wm. C. Neelly, bondsman;
B. Oates, wit.

Martin, Isaac & Nancy Green, 30 Jan 1815; Nathan Green, bondsman; Susan R. Allison, wit.

Martin, James & Peggy Kerr, 27 Feb 1797; Richard Kerr, bondsman; Isaac Alexander, wit.

Martin, James W. & Harriet D. Rea, 21 Nov 1837; James M. Kerr, bondsman; B. Oates, wit.

Martin, Robert & Hannah Kerr, 10 Nov 1806; John Kerr, bondsman; Isaac Alexander, wit.

Martin Robert A. & Sarah S. Bozzle, 4 Dec 1838; Jonathan Downs, bondsman.

Martin, Thomas & Ann Blythe, 17 Oct 1786; Walter Bell, bondsman; J. McK. Alexander, wit.

Martin, William & Eleanor Booker, 2 Nov 1808; Philip McDay, bondsman; Isaac Alexander, wit.

Martin, William & Mary Redding, 26 Jan 1854; Saml Yandle, bondsman; Casper Hargett, J. P., wit. married 26 Jan 1854 by Casper Hargett, J. P.

Mason, Charles & Hannah Clark, 4 Nov 1814; Charles Hutchison, bondsman.

Mason, Charles C. & Margaret Carothers, 2 Oct 1835; James A. Grier, bondsman; B. Oates, C. C. C., wit.

Mason, Isaac & Mary Montgomery, 22 June 1831; Andrew H.Porter, bondsman.

Mason, R. G. & Mary Ann King, 14 May 1849; F. Thomas Alexander, bondsman; Saml. J. Lourie, wit.

Mason, Richard & Margaret Walker, 18 March 1812; Francis Irwin, bondsman; Isaac Alexander, wit.

Mason, Richard C. & Charity Hartwick, 23 Jan 1821; James Hutchison, bondsman; Isaac Alexander, wit.

Mason, Winfield & Priscilla Miller, 4 May 1808; John B. Springs, bondsman; Isaac Alexander, wit.

Mass, Marion & Minerva Wheeler, 25 Jan 1860; Coney Ortis, bondsman; Jno Phelan, wit. married 26 Jan 1860 by Wm. S. Norment, J. P.

Massey, Thomas P & Elizabeth Warsham, 24 Oct 1843; William A. Gillespie, bondsman; James Johnston, wit.

Mathes, Andrew & Easter Haggard, 16 Feb 1819; Charles Dennis, bondsman; Philemon Morris, wit.

Mattheus, Robert & Agnes Henderson, 2 March 1797; John Henderson, bondsman; Isaac Alexander, wit.

Mattheuws, William & Mary Oliver, 28 Dec 1841; William M. Bigham, bondsman; C. T. Alexander, wit.

Matthews, John & Margaret McKibbens, 10 Nov 1794; James Matthews, bondsman; Isaac Alexander, wit.

Matthews, John M. & Margaret E. Hagan, 10 Jan 1854; John S. Porter, bondsman; W. K. Reid, C. C. C., wit. married 10 Jan 1854 by Cyrus Johnston.

Matthews, Robert & Nancy McCubbins, 11 Feb 1802; James Houston, bondsman; J. Wallis, wit.

Matthews, Samuel & Mary Rea, 13 Nov 1809; John Harris, bondsman; Isaac Alexander, wit.

Matthues, James & Jane Stitt Jr., 25 Feb 1834; John Stitt Jr., bondsman; John Oates, wit.

Maxwell, A. L. & Elizabeth Snell, 14 July 1854; Milton Dulin, bondsman; W. K. Reid, C. C. C.,wit.

Maxwell, Andrew Washington & Louisa Rodgers, 26 Sept 1827; William Maxwell, bondsman.

Maxwell, David & M. J. Harrison, 4 June 1841; Samuel A. Harris, bondsman.

Maxwell, Edwin W. R. (Dr.) & Margaret McLarty, 16 June 1832; Ezekil Johnston, bondsman.

Maxwell, Henry K. & Mrs. Mary A. Snead, 6 Feb 1864; C. M. Ray, bondsman; Wm. P. Buell, wit.

Maxwell, James & Jean McClung, 28 March 1788; John Bell, bondsman; James Meek, wit.

Maxwell, James J. & Margaret Wallis, 8 Feb 1823; Hugh Wilson Rodgers, bondsman; R. J. Dinkins, wit.

Maxwell, Jeremiah H. & Elizabeth C. Houston, 28 Aug 1827; James Irwin, bondsman;

Maxwell, John & Caroline Graham (colored), 14 March 1866; Stephen Torrince, bondsman; Wm. Maxwell, wit.

Maxwell, John G. & Sarah H. Baker, 18 Nov 1856; John Phelan, bondsman; W. K. Reid, C. C. C., wit.

Maxwell, John S. & Charlotte E. McGee, 9 Dec 1854; James L. Alexander, bondsman; W. K. Reid, C. C. C., wit. married 14 Dec 1854 by T. M. Farrow, V. D. M.

Maxwell, John T. & Elizabeth Black, 19 Feb 1831; Ezekiel Johnson, bondsman; B. Oates, D. C., wit.

Maxwell, Joseph & Elisabeth Mentieth, 10 Jan 1794; Nathaniel Mentieth, bondsman; James Meek, wit.

Maxwell, Moses & Elizabeth Brown, 1 Dec 1802; Alexr. Wallace, bondsman.

Maxwell, Robert & Elizabeth Hood, 7 May 1795; John Maxwell, bondsman; Isaac Alexander, wit.

Maxwell, Robert H. & Ann Rogers, 31 Dec 1823; Hugh W. Rodgers, bondsman; Isaac Alexander, wit.

Maxwell, Robert H. & Mary R. Rea, 12 May 1856; J. C. Flow, bondsman; W. K. Reid, C. C. C., wit. married 12 May 1856 by J. R. Pickett, minister.

MECKLENBURG MARRIAGES 1783-1868

Maxwell, Sam & Ila Morris (colored), 10 Jan 1866; Abram Tanner, bondsman; Wm. Maxwell, C. C. C., wit. married 11 Jan 1866 by Wm. McDonald.

Maxwell, William & Nancy Simpson, 14 July 1804; Guy Maxwell, bondsman.

Maxwell, William & Martha Hux, 22 Nov 1832; Samuel Hux, bondsman; B. Oates, D. C.,wit.

Maxwell,. William M. & Sarah H. Wilson, 8 June 1824; George Wilson, bondsman; R. J. Dinkins, wit.

Maxwell, William M. & Addeline Wilson, 14 May 1835; Elias N. Alexander, bondsman; B. Oates, C. C. C., wit.

Maxwell, William R. & Mary E. Johnston, 21 July 1832; Ezekiel Johnston, bondsman; B. Oates, D. C., wit.

Maxwell, William R. & Nancy A. Morris, 12 Nov 1836; James M. Black, bondsman; B. Oates, C. C. C., wit.

May, Daniel & Margaret Jane Maxwell, 24 Oct 1853; J. W. Miller, bondsman; W. K. Reid, wit. married 25 Oct 1853 by Paul F. Kistler, M. G.

Mayfield, Stephen & Margaret Cook, 20 May 1797; John (Johannes) Sterns, bondsman.

Mead, Joseph & Mary E. Gribble, 23 June 1851; Tho. N. Alexander, Saml. J. Lourie, bondsmen; B. Oates, C. C. C., wit. married 24 July 1851 by R. H. Lafferty.

Means, C. T. & Susan S. Robinson, 8 Dec 1841; C. T. Alexander, bondsman; C. T. Alexander, wit.

Means, John M. & Mary E. Goodin, 7 April 1851; Jno. A. Young, bondsman; Sam E. Belk, wit.

Means, John W. & Margarett M. Wilson, 27 May 1822; John McClellan, bondsman; Isaac S. Alexander, wit.

Means, William & Caroline Hipp, 18 Dec 1838; Robert H. Braley, bondsman.

Means, William & Esther A. Wilkinson, 18 Oct 1852; Joseph Hudson, bondsman; B. Oates, C. C. C., wit. married 20 Oct 1852 by W. E. Patterson,minister.

Medcalf, Joel & Elisabeth Purser, 19 Jan 1797; John Purser, bondsman; David Cuthbertson, bondsman; Jordan Sellers, Benjamin Wise, wit.

Meguirt, David & Rebecah Winchester, 12 Nov 1833; Joel Helmes, bondsman; Henderson Helmes, wit.

MeHaffey, Joseph & Sarah Pharr, 9 March 1826; John C. Pharr, bondsman; Isaac S. Alexander, wit.

Melton, James & Elizabeth Festerman, 26 Feb 1833; Levi Festerman, bondsman; B. Oates, D. C., wit.

Menteith, Alexander & Elizabeth Walker, 1 Dec 1790; Samuel Davidson, bondsman; J. McK. Alexander, wit.

130

Menteith, John & _____ Hargrove, 10 Sept 1814; John Hartgrove, bondsman.

Menteith, William & Susanna Williams, 13 Nov 1804; William Beaty, bondsman; Isaac Alexander, wit.

Menteith, William & Violet Barry, 4 Sept 1807; Hugh Barry, bondsman; Isaac Alexander, wit.

Miles, Archibald & Patsey Washam, 25 June 1804; Burwell Cashon, bondsman; Isaac Alexander, wit.

Miles, Augustus N. & Elizabeth Connel, 7 Jan 1815; Thomas H. Connell, bondsman; Isaac Alexander, wit.

Miller, Adam & Jane Henderson, 13 April 1804; John Knox, bondsman; Isaac Alexander, wit.

Miller, Andrew & Margaret Miller, 28 July 1795; James Maxwell Junr., bondsman.

Miller, David & Jane Wilson, 22 May 1815; Saml Wilson, bondsman; Isaac S. Alexander, wit.

Miller, David M. & Martha P. Hartt, 22 Nov 1849; Francis A. Biggers, bondsman; B. Oates, C. C. C., wit.

Miller, David W. & Sarena Morrison, 8 Aug 1845; Isaac N. Alexander, bondsman.

Miller, James & Mary Smith, 30 July 1791; James Black, bondsman; Isaac Alexander, wit.

Miller, James & Rebekah McKibbin, 2 May 1796; James Miller, bondsman; Isaac Alexander, wit.

Miller, John & Mary Ann Smith, 10 Jan 1794; William Walker, bondsman; Isaac Alexander, wit.

Miller, John & Mrs. Nancy Tanner, 3 June 1835; Samuel H. Rodgers, bondsman; Philemon Morris, wit.

Miller, John & Jane Viporell, 1 Sept 1843; Richard Treelase, bondsman.

Miller, John W. & Jane C. Johnston, 6 Sept 1843; Samuel. C. Harrison, bondsman; C. T. Alexander, C. C. C, wit.

Miller, Mathew & Harriet C. Simmons, 29 Oct 1844; Jesse W. Harris, bondsman.

Miller, Robert C. & Elizabeth Pucket, 27 Feb 1860; Wm. P. Little, bondsman; W. K. Reid, C. C. C., wit. married 1 March 1860 by S. C. Pharr.

Miller, Robert C. & Mary Stewart, 17 March 1866; Solomon Sifford, bondsman; Wm. Maxwell, C. C. C., wit. married 20 March 1866 by W. M. Kerr.

Miller, Saml. & Martha Crawford, 10 Aug 1792; Alex McGinty, bondsman.

Miller, William & Isabella Lewis, 24 Oct 1797; James Miller, bondsman; J. Wallis, wit.

Miller, William & Catharine Moore, 16 Feb 1803; Isaac Moore, bondsman; Isaac Alexander, wit.

Miller, William C. & Ruthy McKee, 14 Jan 1837; Thos. J.Mills, bondsman.

Miller, William C. & Nancy Dulin, 16 Nov 1849; James Hall, bondsman; B. Oates, C. C. C., wit.

Milwee, William & Catharine Kilpatrick, 30 Oct 1793; Philip Weeks, bondsman; Isaac Alexander, wit.

Mitchel, David & Julia Wilks (colored), 6 Dec 1865; Jno F. Butt, wit; married 6 Dec 1865 by Jno. F. Butt.

Mitchell, D. N. & Mary Jane Sloan, 4 Feb 1865; Wm. A. L. Owen, bondsman.

Mitchell, Daniel & Patsey Wiggins, 19 Dec 1804; John Shurling, bondsman.

Mitchell, Ephraim & Margarett J. N. Matthews, 31 Aug 1825; John Hall, bondsman; Isaac S. Alexander, wit.

Mitchell, James & Virginia Graham (colored), 19 Dec 1859; S. A. Harris, bondsman; W. K. Reid, C. C. C., wit. married 20 Dec 1859 by C. Overman, J. P.

Mitchell, John & Rebekah Baker, 31 Jan 1797; George Baker, bondsman; Isaac Alexander, wit.

Mitchell, John & Rebecca Varnor, 17 July 1804; James Mitchel, bondsman; Isaac Alexander, wit.

Mitchell, John & Esther Jarrett, 14 July 1812; Richard Mason, bondsman.

Mitchell, Nathan & Nancy Shields, 9 Jan 1804; Robert Mitchell, bondsman.

Mitchell, Randol & Tillitha Wiggins, 14 Jan 1805; John Shierling jr., bondsman.

Mitchell, Robert & Isabella Russell, 26 July 1792; James Orr Jr., bondsman; Isaac Alexander, wit.

Mobley, Edward G. & Isla A. Graham, 10 May 1860; John M. Springs, bondsman; W. K. Reid, C. C. C., wit. married 10 May 1860 by Richd. H. Griffith, M. G.

Mock, William A.& Margaret E. Boyles, 1 Nov 1860; Thos E. Potts, bondsman; W. K. Reid, C. C. C., wit. married 19 Dec 1860 by R. F. Blythe, J. P.

Mohon, Curtis & Martha -------, 30 Dec 1826; William Menteith, bondsman; Isaac Alexander, wit.

Monteith--see also Menteith.

Monteith, Nathaniel & Martha Campbell, 1 March 1858; Wm. Cochran, bondsman; W. K. Reid, C. C. C., wit. married 4 March 1858 by I. G. McLaughlin. ·

Monteith, Rufus A. & Sophia J. Black, 5 Feb 1850; B. Oates, C. C. C., wit.

Montgomery, A. F. & E. A. Brown, 12 June 1865; Wm. Maxwell, C. C. C., wit. married 15 June 1865 by J. D. Carpenter, Jun. preacher on the Charlotte Circuit, S. C. Conf.

Montgomery, James & Rebekah Clark, 8 Jan 1800; Robert Montgomery, bondsman; Isaac Alexander, wit.

Montgomery, James & Delila Herron, 16 June 1846; Jesse Lewallen, bondsman; B. Oates, C. C. C., wit.

Montgomery, John & Mary Clarke, 1 Aug 1795; Robert Walker, bondsman; Isaac Alexander, wit.

Montgomery, John & Margarett Bicket, 26 Feb 1802; Robt Davis, Robt. Robinson, bondsmen; Jno Hoey, Wm. Rodgers, wit.

Montgomery, John & Jane Robison, 27 March 1805; John Robison, bondsman.

Montgomery, John & Mary Wiley, 14 July 1827; John Johnston, bondsman; Pearsall Thompson, wit.

Montgomery, John H. & Hannah E. Moore, 27 Dec 1831; Walter A. Hill, bondsman.

Montgomery, R. C. & Margaret B. Wallace, 12 Feb 1855; Saml. J. Lourie, wit. married 13 Feb 1855 by R. F. Taylor, Pastor of Prosperity.

Montgomery, R. C. & Mary C. Hutchison, 8 Dec 1859; Tho. H. Brem, bondsman; W. K. Reid, C. C. C., wit. married 8 Dec 1859 by A. Ranson.

Montgomery, R. F. & Eliza Jane Cathey, 17 Jan 1849; James A. Todd, bondsman; B. Oates, C. C. C., wit.

Montgomery, Robert & Eleanor McCleary, 10 Nov 1804; Thos Henry, bondsman.

Montgomery, Samuel & Rachel Clark, 28 March 1812; John Montgomery, bondsman; Isaac Alexander, wit.

Montgomery, Wilson & Mary A. Alexander, 15 April 1846; Wm. Warwick, bondsman; S. J. Lourie, wit.

Montieth, John & Martha C. Alexander, 29 Jan 1833; William W. Elms, bondsman; R. S. Dinkins, wit.

Montith, Elias & Hanah Wilson, (colored), 8 July 1865; Jordon Wilson, bondsman; Wm. Maxwell, C. C. C., wit. married 8 July 1865 by T. W. Dewey, J. P.

Mooney, Wm. B. & Susan McMullen, 13 March 1865; John McCorell, bondsman.

Moor, David & Agness Helms, 9 May 1816; Martin McWhirter, bondsman; John Rea, J. P.,wit.

Moor, Isaac & Nancy Foard, 5 Nov 1800; Jno Johnston, bondsman.

Moor, John & Aminta Moore, 23 Oct 1800; Joseph Moore, bondsman.

Moor, John A. & Martha E. Goens, 30 Oct 1865; James Fifer, bondsman; Wm. Maxwell, wit. married 31 Oct 1865 by Jno. F. Butt.

Moor, Thomas & Isabella Dunn, 26 Feb 1793; James Todd, bondsman;
Ruthy Alexander, wit.

Moore, Andrew F. & Ariminta B. Christenbury, 20 Aug 1846; Samuel
H. Christenbury, bondsman; B. Oates, C. C. C., wit.

Moore, Charles B. & Catherine Rodden, 19 June 1809; Jacob Rodden,
bondsman.

Moore, David J. & Nancy L. Wilson, 8 Oct 1845; E. C. Stewart,
bondsman; C. T. Alexander, wit.

Moore, Elam & Efrieza Campbell, 18 Jan1826; Ira Parks, bondsman;
Isaac S. Alexander, wit.

Moore, G. R. & Christian E. Todd, 3 Jan 1849; Franklin Riley,
bondsman; Saml. J. Lourie, wit.

Moore Green & Martha Morris (colored), 16 Feb 1866; Peter Laney,
bondsman; Wm. Maxwell, wit.

Moore, Hugh & Helena Alexander, 19 March 1824; Eleazer Alexander,
bondsman; Isaac Alexander, wit.

Moore, J. T. & Susan A. Stewart, 7 Aug 1865; S. Alexander, bondsman; Wm. Maxwell, wit.

Moore, James & Ellen McEwen, 12 June 1793; Samuel McEwen, bondsman;
Isaac Alexander, wit.

Moore, James & Syntha Johnston, 13 Feb 1827; David Parks, bondsman;
Pearsall Thompson, wit.

Moore, James C. & Mary J. McCorcle, 1 May 1855; Edward H. Moss,
bondsman; W. K. Reid, C. C. C., wit.

Moore, James H. & Kiziah Parks, 6 April 1825; Levi Parks, bondsman;
Isaac S. Alexander, wit.

Moore, James W. & Isabella S. G. Davidson, 19 Jan 1835; A. L.
Erwin, bondsman; B. Oates, C. C. C., wit.

Moore, John E. (Capt.) & A. M. Morris, 18 Oct 1864; R. M. White,
bondsman; Wm. Maxwell, C. C. C., wit. married 20 Oct 1864 by
Wm. McDonald.

Moore, John W.& Maggie Gibbon, 4 Sept 1865; T. H. Brem, bondsman.

Moore, Joseph S.& Sarah Emberson, 20 Dec 1826; Stephen Emerson,
bondsman; Pearsall Thompson,wit.

Moore, Joshua T. & Locky D. Abernathey, 6 Jan 1830; Abner Sharpe,
bondsman; E. Elms, wit.

Moore, Phillip & Peggy Simison, 12 March 1801; Allen Reed, bondsman;
J. Wallis, wit.

Moore, Samuel & Eveline C. Wallace, 9 March 1830; Joseph Y. Wallace,
bondsman.

Moore, Samuel A. & Martha Ann Kennedy, 16 April 1851; James
Jamison, bondsman; B. Oates, C. C. C., wit.

Moore, Thomas J. (Col.) & Mary Ann Irwin, 20 Sept 1838; John T.
Irwin, bondsman; A. B. Moore, Jr., wit.

Moore, William & Polly Felton, 19 Feb 1805; Joseph Reid, bondsman;
J. Wallis, wit.

Moore, William & Mrs. Ann Todd, 7 April 1821; Robert Wilson,
bondsman; Isaac Alexander, wit.

Moore, William & Biddy Lewing, -- Aug 1833; John A. Todd, bondsman.

Moore, William & S. G. Yountzs, 16 Sept 1858; Joseph McLure,
bondsman; F. M. Ross, wit. married 21 Sept 1858 by J. W.
Morrow, J. P.

Mooree, William & Hanah Stanford, 11 Nov 1800; Robert Stanford,
bondsman; Isaac Alexander, wit.

Morehead, J. L. & Sarah Smith Phifer, 19 April 1855; T. J. Sumner,
bondsman; W. K. Reid, C. C. C., wit. married 19 April 1855
by J. Jones Smyth.

Morgan, Nicholson Ross & Mary W. Alexander, 29° Nov 1820; Elam
Alexander, bondsman; Isaac S. Alexander, wit.

Morris, Allen & Polly Bond, 30 Oct ---, D. T. Morris, bondsman.

Morris, James & Elizabeth Wilson, 16 April 1804; Jno Morris,
bondsman; Isaac Alexander, wit.

Morris, James J. & Anne Mathews, 6 June 1822; Jno Patterson, Jr.,
bondsman; Philemon Morris, wit.

Morris, James S. & Isabella M. Henderson, 26 Jan 1847; James P.
Henderson, bondsman; B. Oates, C. C. C., wit.

Morris, John & Margret Maxwell, 30 July 1792; James Maxwell,
bondsman; Isaac Alexander, wit.

Morris, John & Mary Mahan, 9 June 1796; Patrick Johnston, bondsman; Jas. Conner, wit.

Morris, John F. & Mrs. Polley C. McLarty, 22 July 1830; George
W. McLarty, bondsman; Phn. Morris, wit.

Morris, John Jarmon & Eliza Young, 12 Aug 1822; John F.Morris,
bondsman; Isaac S. Alexander, wit.

Morris, Josiah & Eveline Canon, 11 Aug 1842; Edward J. Canon,
bondsman.

Morris, Philemon & Mary Shaver, 8 April 1794; Robert Maxwell,
bondsman; Isaac Alexander, wit.

Morris, Reuben & Mrs. Mary Houston, 1 Feb 1816; Jas. J. Morris,
bondsman.

Morris, Robert & Catherine Conner, 21 Dec 1811; Torence Coner,
bondsman; J. McK. Alexander, Susan R. Alexander, wit.

Morris, Robert J. & Mrs. Mintey McCombs, 20 Jan 1825; John F.
Morris, bondsman; Philemon Morris, wit.

Morris, William C. & Mc. Johnston, 4 March 1843; Samuel C. Harrison, bondsman; C. T. Alexander, wit.

Morris, Wm. C. & Elisa P. McComb, 1 Feb 1854; E. C. Alexander,
bondsman; W. K. Reid, C. C. C., wit. married 2 Feb 1854
by Danl. A. Penick.

Morris, Wm. H. & Lucinda Cochran, 25 Jan 1844; Wm. L. Dulin,
bondsman; N. B. Taylor, wit.

Morris, Z. L. & Virginia C. Alexander, 6 Sept 1860; Wm. Harty,
bondsman; W. K. Reid, C. C. C., wit. married 6 Sept 1860 by
A. Sinclair, Pres. Pastor.

Morris, Zebulon L. & Mary A. Parks, 20 July 1847; W. Mc. Houston,
bondsman; B. Oates, C. C. C.,wit.

Morrison, Cyrus & Mary Moore, 21 Jan 1824; Saml. Gingles, bondsman;
Isaac Alexander, wit.

Morrison, Henry D. & Jane Porter, 29 Dec 1823; John N. Houston,
bondsman; Isaac Alexander, wit.

Morrison, James & -------, 13 July 1789; Walter Farr, bondsman;
Bathw. Thompson, wit.

Morrison, James & Margaret Johnston, 10 Spt 1799; William Johnston,
bondsman; I. Alexander, wit.

Morrison, James & Mary Simons, 23 Feb 1819; Laird H. Harris,
bondsman; Isaac S. Alexander, wit.

Morrison, James M. & Mary Johnston, 4 Dec 1830; William Morris,
bondsman; Isaac Alexander, wit.

Morrison, John & Jane Bradshaw, 5 April 1791; John Morrison Jr.,
bondsman; Isaac Alexander, wit.

Morrison, John & Dolly Rogers, 31 July 1804; Thomas Morrison,
bondsman; Isaac Alexander, wit.

Morrison, John H. & Mary J. Morrison, 9 Aug 1856; C. F. Caldwell,
bondsman; W. K. Reid, C. C. C., wit. married 14 Aug 1856 by
Walter W. Pharr.

Morrison, Nathaniel & Ruthy Alexander, 20 Jan 1827; James Gingles,
bondsman.

Morrison, Robert & Margaret McComb, 4 March 1797; James McComb,
bondsman.

Morrison, Samuel F. & Rachel Gingels, 18 April 1818; John Gingles,
bondsman.

Morrison, W. & S. E. McLeary, 30 July 1859; J. H. Wilson Jr.,
bondsman; W. K. Reid, C. C. C., wit. married 1 Aug 1859 by
R. Burwell, Min. of Gospel.

Morrison, Washington & Mary Ann Dinkins, 15 Oct 1825; James M.
Hutchison, bondsman.

Morrison, William & Rosannah Gingles, 9 March 1819; Saml Gingles,
bondsman; Isaac Alexander, wit.

Morrison, William & Margaret Houston, 17 Dec 1821; Andrew W. Porter, bondsman; Isaac Alexander, wit.

Morrison, William S. & Helena Kerr, 11 Dec 1830; William W. Lide, bondsman.

Morrow, Allen & Clarissa A. Pearce, 3 Dec 1835; Robert C. Potts, bondsman; B. Oates, C. C. C., wit.

Morrow, Benjn. & Mary Jane Haukins, 20 April 1847; T. N. Alexander, bondsman.

Morrow, David & Jenny McCulloh, 25 Nov 1802; Andrew Foster, bondsman; J. Wallis, wit.

Morrow, David & Margaret Parks, 20 Aug 1839; James H. Davis, bondsman.

Morrow, Drury & Esther McCulloh, 17 Jan 1820; Amos McCuloch, bondsman; Isaac Alexander, wit.

Morrow, Eli & Mary Cook, 19 Dec 1838; Abdon A. Coffey, bondsman; B. Oates, C. C. C.,wit.

Morrow, George & Elisabeth Powers, 23 Sept 1819; William Busby, bondsman; Jno McLane, wit.

Morrow, Hezekiah T. & Elizabeth Jones, 5 Jan 1815; William Busby, bondsman.

Morrow, Hezikiah T. & Elisabeth Ray, 25 April 1820; Wm. Busby, bondsman; W. L. Davidson, wit.

Morrow, Isaac & Elisabeth Morrow, 14 Nov 1820; William Busby, bondsman.

Morrow, Isac & Sally Powers, 18 July 1811; George Morrow, William Stuard, bondsmen; Archd. Cathey, wit.

Morrow, J. W. & Jerusha A. Elliott, 7 Nov 1854; James S. Porter, bondsman; W. K. Reid, t. C. C., wit. married 7 Nov 1854 by J. B. Watt, V. D. M.

Morrow, John White & Patsey Worley, 10 Dec 1807; George Morrow, bondsman; Wm. Stuard, bondsmen; Archd. Cathey, wit.

Morrow, Robert & Martha Morrow, 5 March 1812; Wm. Busby, bondsman.

Morrow, Robert B. & Louise Bradshaw, 11 March 1852; John Gamble, bondsman; B. Oates, C. C. C., wit. married 11 March 1852 by James Johnston.

Morrow, Robert W. & Sarah Williams, 4 Feb 1840; John Brinkley, bondsman.

Morrow, Stephen W. & Marther Morrow, 27 Sept 1841; Daniel Brinkley, bondsman; James Johnston, wit.

Morros, William & Margaret Crocket, 20 March 1794; Eli Crocket, bondsman; Isaac Alexander,wit.

Morse, John G. & Mary Humble, 8 Jan 1822; Isaac S. Alexander, bondsman.

Morse, R. H. & Mary S. Means, 10 Feb 1866; J. M. Carter, bondsman; Wm. Maxwell, C. C. C., wit. married 12 Feb 1866 by Jno F. Butt.

Morton, Charles S. & Obedience Osborn, 18 Jan 1803; Will. Pettus, bondsman; Isaac Alexander, wit.

Moss, C. E. & J. S. Alexander, 21 April 1845; Joseph M. Davidson, bondsman; N. B. Taylor, wit.

Moss, Edward H. & Virginemus G. Clark, 24 Nov 1851; Miles L. Wriston, bondsman; B. Oates, C. C. C., wit. married 25 Nov 1851 by Cyrus Johnston, V. D. M.

Moss, Wiley & Polly Robison, 24 Jan 1805; John Roberson, bondsman. Isaac Alexander, wit.

Mowry, Henry & Nancy R. Ochler, 9 Jan 1855; John B. Thomasson, bondsman; W. K. Reid, C. C. C., wit. married 11 Jan 1855 by Walter S. Pharr.

Moyle, Henry & Matilda Gardner, 24 Feb 1835; Nicholas Tredinnick, bondsman.

Müllerschoen, Jacob & Catharine Kohler, 9 June 1862; J. G. Leiser, bondsman; W. K. Reid, C. C. C., wit. married 9 June 1862 by G. D. Bernheim, pastor of St. Mark's Ev. Luth. Church.

Mullins, Clem & Betsey Parker, 4 Aug 1807; Isaac Parker, bondsman; Isaac Alexander, wit.

Mullins, Peter & Mary Greer, 19 Oct 1790; Jno. Allison, bondsman; Jno. McNit. Alexander, wit.

Mullis, J. J. & Margaret E. Noles, 20 Sept 1865; C. W. Hagler, bondsman; Wm. Maxwell, C. C. C., wit. married 21 Sept 1865 by Danl. A. Penick Sr.

Mulwee, James & Rachel Cook, 27 Feb 1838; William B. Sharp, bondsman.

Mulwee, Milas & Sarah Allen, 20 July 1836; John N. Allen, bondsman; B. Oates, C. C. C.,wit.

Mulwee, R. E. & Mary J. Lawing, 13 Dec 1859; J. W. Johnston, bondsman; W. K. Reid, C. C. C., wit. married 15 Dec 1859 by Stephen Wilson, J. P.

Murphy, Archy & Mary McKinney, 30 March 1798; Seth McKinny, bondsman.

Myers, Franklin & M. A. Myers, 28 Aug 1856; J. A. Myers, bondsman; W. K. Reid, C. C. C., wit. married 28 Aug 1856 by R. F. Taylor.

Nance, Alexander E. & Catharine Luckey, 28 Jan 1855; E. S. Westmoreland, bondsman; W. K. Reid, C. C. C., wit. married 28 Jan 1855 by James Johnston.

Nance, William & Sarah Alcorn, 18 Dec 1818; John Alcorn, bondsman; Robt. Wilson, wit.

Nantz, Shadrack & Elizabeth Chapman, 6 Aug 1857; John P. Ross, bondsman; W. K. Reid, C. C. C.,wit. married 11 Aug 1857 by J. P. Ross, J. P.

Naylor, J. W. & Christian McLeod, 1 Dec 1863; James McLeod, bondsman; Wm. Maxwell, C. C. C., wit. married 1 Dec 1863 by F. A. T. Harris.

Neagle, Matthew & Ann R. Rudesill, 18 Jan 1834; David Parks, bondsman.

Neel, Alexander G. & Mary A. Price, 9 Oct 1839; James B. Knox, bondsman; T. W. Saunier, wit.

Neel, Andrew F. & Nancy C. Hunter, 19 Dec 1848; Robert E. Bell, bondsman; B. Oates, C. C. C., wit.

Neel, C. C. & Eliza A. Clark, 17 March 1866; Calvin E. Grier, bondsman; Wm. Maxwell, C. C. C., wit. married 22 March 1866 by John Douglas.

Neel, George C. & Cornelia Todd, 24 Sept 1850; H. H. Peoples, bondsman; B. Oates, C. C. C., wit.

Neel, Henry & Esther Price, 8 April 1805; James Price, bondsman; Isaac Alexander, wit.

Neel, James H. & Margaret Hipp, 5 July 1838; William A. Todd, bondsman.

Neel, James H. & Mary A. Downes, 1 Sept 1862; J. L. Cathey, bondsman; Wm. Maxwell, C. C. C., wit. married 4 Sept 1862 by J. P. Ross, J. P.

Neel, Jesse C. & Sarah Stinson, 30 June 1824; David Stinson, bondsman; Isaac Alexander, wit.

Neel, John & Sarah Todd, 16 May 1803; Joseph Huston, bondsman.

Neel, John W. & Margaret M. Byrum, 5 Jan 1863; William A. Hannon, bondsman; Wm. Maxwell, C. C. C., wit. married 6 Jan 1863 by Stephen Wilson, J. P.

Neel, Samuel J. & Louisa Ross, 29 April 1830; Francis M. Ross, bondsman.

Neel, Thomas & Jenny Neel, 19 Aug 1793; James Neel, bondsman; Edw. Wains, wit.

Neel, Thomas G. & Ann L. Spratt, 24 May 1838; William H. Neel, bondsman.

Neel, William & Sarah Calhoon, 13 Sept 1800; Robt. McKinley, bondsman.

Neel, William & Hannah Alexander, 23 Nov 1819; Thomas Greer, bondsman; Isaac S. Alexander, wit.

Neel, William & Martha E. Hunter, 24 Jan 1843; Henry F. Hunter, bondsman.

Neel, William B. & Rosanna E. J. Hunter, 5 Jan 1853; Wm. A. Bell, bondsman; B. Oates, C. C. C., wit. married 6 Jan 1853 by J. M. Walker, minister.

Neely, Alexander, N. & Martha M. Price, 11 Dec 1839; G. C. Marvin, bondsman; B. Oates, C. C. C.,wit.

Neely, James & Elizabeth C. Sprott, 12 Nov 1817; John Hartt, bondsman; Isaac S. Alexander, wit.

Neely, James B. & Mary J. N. Hart, 16 Dec 1828; James M. Hartt, bondsman.

Neely, John & Betsey Carothers, 3 Jan 1811 (12?); Joseph S. Carothers, bondsman; Isaac Alexander, wit.

Neely, John & Anne Lemmonds, 29 Feb 1822; Edwin Alexander, bondsman; Isaac S. Alexander, wit.

Neely, John & Margaret Swann, 11 Dec 1843; Robert H. Swann, bondsman; N. B. Taylor, wit.

Neely, John S. & Jane M. Price, 8 Aug 1851; Isaac J. Price, bondsman; Braly Oates, C. C. C., wit. married 13 Aug 1851 by A. S. Watts.

Neely, Moses & Jane McDowell, 22 March 1825; John Haute, bondsman; Richd. Gillespie Jr., wit.

Neely, Robert C. & Margaret P. Reed, 15 Sept 1830; Thomas B. Neely, bondsman; B. Oates, wit.

Neely, Samuel M. & Rachel L. Whitesides, 11 March 1839; Samuel M. Whiteside, bondsman; B. Oates, wit.

Neely, Thomas & Jane Hartt, 28 March 1793; David Hartt, bondsman; Isaac Alexander, wit.

Neely, Thomas B. & Ann Reed, 2 Oct 1832; William A.Carrothers, bondsman; B. Oates, D. C., wit.

Neely, William M. & Cynthia Hayse, 25 May 1813; James Hartt, bondsman

Neilly, John & Besey Todd, 25 Oct 1804; Nathaniel Menteith, bondsman; Isaac Alexander, wit.

Neilly, John & Elizabeth McLarty, 24 Feb 1806; John McLarty, bondsman; Isaac Alexander, wit.

Neisler, S. J. & Maggie C. Alexander, 28 April 1864; J. D. Winslow, bondsman; Wm. Maxwell, C. C. C., wit. married 28 April 1864 by Richd. H. Griffith, M. G.

Nelson, Hugh & Jane Bigham, 28 Aug 1794; Samuel Bigham, bondsman.

Nelson, James & Francis Cochran, 19 March 1855; Hiram M. Mills, bondsman; W. K. Reid, C. C. C., wit. married 20 March 1855 by P.B. Hodges, J. P.

Nelson, Joshua & Nancy Wily, 8 Oct 1825; Hiram Lasras, bondsman; J. Doherty, J. P., wit.

Nelson, Samuel & Margaret Moore, 14 Sept 1790; Joseph Moore, bondsman; J. McK. Alexander,wit.

Nelson, William & Mary D. Cudy, 29 Sept 1827; Robert M. Stirling, bondsman; Pearsall Thompson, wit.

Nesbet, A. S. & M. A. Walker, 26 Feb 1852; Samuel A. Boyce, bondsman; B. Oates, C. C. C., wit. married 26 Feb 1852 by J. M. Walker, minister.

Nesbet, Hugh C. & Elizabeth Starns, 16 March 1836; Alexander Newbet,bondsman; S. V. Simons, wit.

Nesbitt, A. F. & M. J. Hunter, 15 Feb 1866; S. C. Reid, bondsman;
Wm. Maxwell, C. C. C., wit. married 16 Feb 1866 by John
Hunter, minister.

Newbold, Charles H. & Jane E. Little, 17 Jan 1865; Solomon Sifford,
bondsman; married 19 Jan 1865 by W. M. Kerr.

Newby, John & Permelia Nickleson, 13 Feb 1823; Lunsford A.
Paschall, bondsman; Isaac S. Alexander, wit.

Newel, Boswell & Mary Barker 11 Dec 1845; James L. Hartis, bondsman; Daniel Wentez, J. P., wit.

Newel, John & Polly Secrest, 21 Feb 1818; John Rea (Capt.), bondsman; John Rea, wit.

Newel, Ruben N. & Martha N. Owens, 22 June 1848; James L. Hartis,
bondsman; Daniel Wentez, J. P., wit.

Newel, Samuel W. & Jane Dobson, 5 Dec 1843; Wm. R. McClellan, bondsman; N. B. Taylor, wit.

Newell, David & Melena Harget, 10 Oct 1843; Jason Harget, bondsman;
G. W. Houston, J. P.,wit.

Newell, David S. & Rebecca M. Burns, 12 Aug 1852; Andrew Berryhill,
bondsman; B. Oates, C. C. C., wit. married 12 Aug 1852 by W.
R. Maxwell, J. P.

Newell, Peter & Polly Simson, 11 Sept 1801; Daniel McCollum,
bondsman; Isaac Alexander,wit.

Newman, Jacob & Mary Keliah, 5 Dec 1791; Jno Newman, bondsman;
Isaac Alexander, wit.

Nicholson, John & Rachel Lewis, 4 Feb 1796; John Cathey, bondsman;
Isaac Alexander, wit.

Nicholson, Joseph C. & Margaret J. Brown, 4 Oct 1837; Allen H.
Brown, bondsman.

Nicholson, Joseph C. & Harriet M. Jamison, 13 Aug 1850; T. N.
Alexander, bondsman; James Parks, wit.

Nicholson, William & Mary Huddleston, 26 Aug 1822; Samuel K.
Pettus, bondsman; R. J. Dinkins, wit.

Nicholson, William H. & Martha H. Stone, 9 Dec 1861; Wm. R. Clark,
bondsman; W. K. Reid, C. C. C., wit. married 17 Dec 1861 by
J. C. Chalmers, minister.

Niven, Willis & Elisabeth Glover, 27 March 1834; Wiley Glover,
bondsman.

Noales, Abraham & Milly Anderson, 30 Aug 1822; Nicholas Anderson,
bondsman; Isaac S. Alexander, wit.

Noles, Alexander & Margaret Woodall, 16 Feb 1856; Robert S. McKory,
bondsman; J. M. Graham, wit. married 26 Feb 1856 by G. W.
Houston, J. P.

Noles, James & Nancy Philips, 14 March 1837; Abraham Noales,
bondsman; B. Oates, C. C. C.,wit.

Noles, James S. & Elizabeth L. Alexander, 3 Sept 1851; Hugh G.
Porter, bondsman; B. Oates, C. C. C., wit. married 4 Sept
1851 by J. Walker, J. P.

Noles, John & Helena Griffin, 28 Feb 1863; James J. Dulin, bondsman; Wm. Maxwell, C. C. C., wit. married 5 March 1863 by Jos.
L. Phillips, J. P.

Noles, W. A. & Mary Ann Lancaster, 26 Jan 1856; R. H. Maxwell,
bondsman; W. K. Reid, C. C. C., wit. married 29 Jan 1856 by
W. R. Maxwell, J. P.

Noles, William P. & Sarah H. Ledwell, 19 April 1852; James M.
Lancaster, bondsman; B. Oates, C. C. C., wit. married 20
April 1852 by A. G. Stacy, Pastor of the M. E. Church, South,
in Charlotte, N. C.

Norman, David & Mary G. Hutchison, 14 Sept 1867; Wm. Maxwell,
C. C. C.,wit. married 15 Sept 1867 by Soln. Sifford, J. P.

Norment, Charles T. & Harriet M. Hull, 24 Dec 1845; Thos. L.
Beaty, bondsman; John Walker, wit.

Norment, William S. & Jane E. Todd, 24 Feb 1863; John Kirk, bondsman; Wm. Maxwell, C. C. C., wit. married 24 Feb 1863 by A.
Sinclair, Pres. Pastor.

Norment, William Stokes & Margarett Dow, 12 Sept 1812; John
McQuay, bondsman; Isaac S. Alexander,wit.

Norton, Robert S. & Patsey Sinsing, 14 July 1819; Henry Emerson,
bondsman; Isaac Alexander, wit.

Norwood, L. W. & Martha S. F. Williamson, 31 July 1834; James
Lattimer, bondsman; B. Oates, C. C. C., wit.

Norwood, Rufus F. & Prudence M. Alexander, 3 Jan 1855; Silas W.
Alexander, bondsman; W. K. Reid, C. C. C., wit. married 4
Jan. 1855 by Lorenzo Hunter, J. P.

Oates, Braly & Lydia M. Lowrie, 24 March 1825; Joshua D. Boyd,
bondsman; Richd. Gillespie Jr., wit.

OBrien, John C. & Celia A. Hood, 8 Feb 1846; Isaac S. Guyer,
bondsman; B. Oates, C. C. C., wit.

Odom, John & Agnes Vinson, 4 Sept 1798; Edward Richardson, bondsman; Andw Walker, Jacob Perien, wit.

Oehler, George M. & Elizabeth P. Thomason, 5 Jan 1841; Milas W.
McCall, bondsman; B. Oates, wit.

Oehler, John & Margaret Kirk, 21 Dec 1847; William Kirk, bondsman;
Saml. J. Lourie, wit.

Oehler, John G. & Jane Shields, 26 Aug 1837; James Shields, bondsman; P. E. Saunier, wit.

Oliver, Thomas & Jane Kerr, 19 Feb 1821; Isaac Alexander, wit.

O'Neil, Patrick & Catharine Mitchell, 23 Aug 1790; Nathan Mitchell,
bondsman; Richd. Mason, wit.

Ormand, Andrew & Mary D. McCorkle, 12 Feb 1841; William Grey, bondsman;

Ormond, Hugh & Eliza Pratt, 10 Feb 1813; Absalom Black, bondsman.

Ormand, James & Mary Adaline Leaney, 29 May 1832; Reubin Tomberlin, bondsman; Isaac S. Alexander, wit.

Ormand, John N. & Nancy Howard, 22 Dec 1840; Joseph R. Hudson, bondsman; B. Oates, C. C. C., wit.

Ormond, Matthew & Dicey Emerson, 4 June 1818; William George Washington Cowan, bondsman; Isaac Alexander, wit.

Ormond, Robert & Mary Jane Rea, 12 Feb 1840; Thos. N. Lewis, bondsman; B. Oates, wit.

Ormond, Robert & Mrs. Ann Helton, 10 Sept 1864; Jas. H. Henderson, bondsman; Wm. Maxwell, C. C. C., wit. married 15 Sept 1864 by G. D. Bernheim, Pastor of St. Marks Ev. Lutheran Church, Charlotte, N. C.

Orr, A. J. & H. N. Nowell, 3 Sept 1863; F. Scarr, bondsman; Wm. Maxwell, C. C. C., wit. married 8 Sept 1865 by A. Sinclair, Pres. Minister.

Orr, Allen & Martha Townsend, 22 Nov 1814; Sample Orr, bondsman; Isaac Alexander, wit.

Orr, Allen G. & Martha S.Hunter, 4 Aug 1824; Milton Osborne, bondsman; Isaac S. Alexander, wit.

Orr, Allenson & Susan Pettis, 17 Jan 1829; Ephraim Thorn, bondsman; Isaac S. Alexander, wit.

Orr, Bunyan & Mary Vizie, 5 Jan 1797; William Flin, bondsman; Isaac Alexander, wit.

Orr, David & Jane McCracken, 14 April 1857; S. A. Harris, bondsman; W. K. Reid, C. C. C., wit. married 14 April 1857 by G. W. M. Creighton.

Orr, Ira A. & Mary Ann Gray, 24 Jan 1831; Abner Sharpe, bondsman; E. Elms, wit.

Orr, Isaac & Hannah Snell, 20 Oct 1810; Robert Orr, bondsman; Isaac Alexander, wit.

Orr, James & Margaret Miller,23 Jan 1793; John Robison, bondsman; Isaac Alexander, wit.

Orr, James H. & Jane Eliza Smith, 26 April 1832; Jno. L. Hayes, bondsman.

Orr, James J. & Sophia Alexander, 2 April 1834; John Hooks, bondsman; B. Oates, C. C. C., wit.

Orr, James J. & Jane L. Mina McCall, 1 March 1852; Harris Hargett, bondsman; Braly Oates, wit. married 1 March 1852 by Casper Hargett, J. P.

Orr, James L. V. & Maria A. Monteith, 16 Jan 1861; John B. Starnes, bondsman; W. K. Reid, C. C. C., wit. married 17 Jan 1861 by R. H. Lafferty, Pastor of the Congregation of Sugar Creek.

Orr, James R. & Nancy B. Cochran, 19 Nov 1841; John M. McLean, bondsman; C. T. Alexander,wit.

Orr, James T. J. & Amelia S. Alexander, 26 March 1831; John M. Wilson, bondsman; Joseph H. Wilson, wit.

Orr, Jehu F. & Elizabeth Byram, 8 Oct 1835; David Fleniken, bondsman; B. Oates, C. C. C., wit.

Orr, Joab L. A. & Eliza Cook, 9 July 1839; David Morrow, bondsman; B. Oates, C. C. C.,wit.

Orr, John & Martha Houston, 28 March 1842; A. Alexander, bondsman.

Orr, John & Charity Hartis, 3 Feb 1849; James F. W. Freeman, bondsman.

Orr, John Allen & Jane Mitchell, 14 Jan 1811; Rankin Alexander, bondsman; Isaac Alexander, wit.

Orr, John G. A. & Leah E. Montieth, 28 April 1857; Samuel F. Houston, bondsman; W. K. Reid, C. C. C., wit. married 30 April 1857 by R. H. Lafferty, Pres. Pastor.

Orr, John M. & Dorcas C. Starnes, 3 Dec 1857; James T. Hart, bondsman; W. K. Reid, C. C. C., wit. married 3 Dec 1857 by H. B. Cunningham.

Orr, Jonathan L. & Cinthia Alexander, 18 April 1835; Robert C. Flannagan, bondsman; B. Oates, C. C. C., wit.

Orr, Joseph L. & Mrs. Nancy Morris, 7 Jan 1823; John F. Morris, bondsman; Phn. Morris, wit.

Orr, Nathan & Peggy Julian, 27 Jan 1802; Ozni Alexander, bondsman.

Orr, Nathan F. & Martha A. Montgomery, 17 Sept 1851; Samuel E. Howie, bondsman; B. Oates, C. C. C., wit. married 18 Sept 1851 by R. H. Lafferty, Pres. Pastor.

Orr, Nathan H. & Sarah Young, 21 Jan 1833; James A. Young, bondsman; B. Oates, D. C.,wit.

Orr, Samuel W. & Margaret H. Matthews, 7 Nov 1836; James Peoples, bondsman; B. Oates, C. C. C., wit.

Orr, Thomas & Loueza Orr (colored), 14 Sept 1865; Wm. Pethel, bondsman; Wm. Maxwell, wit.

Orr, William W. & Sarah Rodgers, 18 Dec 1854; John W.Blair, bondsman; W. K. Reid, C. C. C., wit. married 19 Dec 1854 by John Hunter, Pastor of Back Creek Con, N. C.

Orsborn, Jonathan H. & Sarah M. Sharpe, 15 Sept 1848; John T. Mulwee, bondsman; Saml. J. Lourie, wit.

Orsburn, Hyram & Margaret E. McCombs, 30 Dec 1859; J. M. Crowell, bondsman; W. K. Reid, C. C. C., wit.

Osborn, James & Margarett Houston, 15 Oct 1821; Thomas Barnett, bondsman; Isaac S. Alexander, wit.

Osborn, Thomas & Elizabeth Flanigan, 17 Jan 1805; William Hays, bondsman; J. Wallis, wit.

Osborne, E. A. & Fanny S. Moore, 13 March 1865; John A. Young, bondsman; Wm. Maxwell, C. C. C., wit. married 15 March 1865 by William C. Butler.

Osborne, James W. & Mary Ann Moore, 5 April 1842; James A. Johnston, bondsman.

Osborne, L. W. & Darcus Todd, 27 July 1864; Wm. Maxwell, C. C. C., wit. married 27 July 1864 by J. P. Ross, J. P.

Osborne, William B. & Leonora Beard, 21 Sept 1858; J. D. Barnett, bondsman; W. K. Reid, C. C. C., wit. married 7 Oct 1858 by Walter S. Pharr.

Osburn, James & Susan Alexander, 28 Oct 1816; Elias Alexander, bondsman.

Osburn, William & Ann Roggers, 4 Sept 1798; John Foster, bondsman; Shared Gray, wit.

Osgood, James & M. A. Dudley, 16 Oct 1865; Jos. W. Jones, bondsman; Wm. Maxwell, C. C. C., wit. married 16 Oct 1865 by Richd. H. Griffith, minister.

Otten, Anthony & Rachel Christenberry, 19 March 1833; Winfield McVey, bondsman; B. Oates, D. C., wit.

Otters, Cooney & Mary Steuffer, 6 June 1860; E. Howell, bondsman; W. K. Reid, C. C. C., wit. married 6 June 1860 by Charles Overman, J. P.

Outon, Paul & Emily Burns, 15 March 1838; Isaac Spencer, bondsman.

Overby, Owen & Jane Sharp, 11 Nov 1822; John McQuay, bondsman; R. J. Dinkins, wit.

Overine, Green & Nelly Shuman, 2 Oct 1851; F. M. Ross, bondsman; B. Oates, C. C. C., wit.

Overman, Charles & Ann L. Allison, 6 April 1837; James A.Johnston, bondsman.

Owen, James & Sarah H. Gray, 14 Nov 1831; Admiral N. Gray, bondsman.

Owen, William & Esther Beaty, 25 Feb 1799; George Fite, bondsman.

Owen, William W. L. & Jane King, 30 March 1848; Tho. F. Porter, bondsman; Saml. J. Lourie Esqr., wit.

Owens, Henry C. & Jane E. Allison, 18 Dec 1832; Richard S. Dinkins, bondsman; W. W. Elms, wit.

Owens, W. A. & Alice B. Caldwell, 24 Nov 1857; J. W. Caldwell, bondsman; W. K. Reid, wit. married 24 Nov 1857 by Horatio H. Hewitt, Presbyter.

Owins, Milas & Sylva Brown (colored), 28 June 1865; Calvin Brown, bondsman (colored); S. A. Harris, wit.

Ozment, John A. & Mary L. Collier, 18 Dec 1855; J. M. Sanders, bondsman; W. K. Reid, C. C. C.,wit.

Ozment, M. S. & Mary Warren, 11 July 1860; Jacob S. Stout, bondsman; W. K. Reid, C. C. C., wit. married 12 July 1860 by J. W. Miller, Pastor Methodist Church, Charlotte.

Pace, N. & Mary Myers, 3 April 1866; Young Pace, bondsman; Wm. Maxwell, C. C. C.,wit. married 3 April 1866 by Jno. F. Butt.

Pace, Young & Nancy Walls, 22 Jan 1858; William M. Lithcoe, bondsman; W. K. Reid, C. C. C.,wit. married 22 Jan 1858 by Wm. S.Norment, J. P.

Page, James & Martha L. McCracken, 3 Oct 1859; Wm. D. McCracken, bondsman; W. K. Reid, C. C. C.,wit. married 5 Oct 1859 by David Henderson.

Page, Nicholas & Jane Troll, 16 March 1793; James Yendel, bondsman; Ruthy Alexander, wit.

Parish, Benjamin & Peggy Parish, 28 Oct 1814; Valentine Parish, bondsman.

Park, Robert & Isabella Robeson, 26 Jan 1796; John Johnston, bondsman; Isaac Alexander, wit.

Park, Thomas & Mary Morrison, 19 Dec 1796; Robert Park, bondsman.

Park, Thomas & Elizabeth Felts, 8 Feb 1798; John Polk, bondsman; J. Wallis, Wm. Potts, wit.

Parke, R. D. & Mary M. Miller, 20 Oct 1854; E. P. Hare, bondsman; James Johnston, wit. married 20 Oct 1854 by James Johnston, J. P.

Parker, John & Lilly Mullen, 5 Jan 1801; Andrew Wallace, bondsman; Isaac Alexander, wit.

Parker, Thomas & Sally Mullen, 7 Sept 1803; John Mullens, bondsman; Isaac Alexander, wit.

Parks, Alexander C. & Saline Parks, 24 July 1822; Alexander Graham, bondsman; Chas. T. Alexander, Wm. Lucky, wit.

Parks, Andrew D. & Elizabeth D. Price, 18 Dec 1823; James Mc-Knight, bondsman; Isaac S. Alexander, wit.

Parks, Andrew D. & Isabella Wilson, 4 March 1858; John N. D. Wilson, bondsman; W. K. Reid, C. C. C., wit. married 9 March 1858 by S. C. Pharr.

Parks, Cyrus & Isabella Wilson, 19 Sept 1836; E. C. Ross, bondsman; B. Oates, C. C. C., wit.

Parks, Cyrus A. & Nancy Black, 20 Sept 1830; Richard Gillespie, bondsman.

Parks, David & Abegail McCoy, 13 March 1792; Beaty McCoy, bondsman; Wm. B. Alexander, wit.

Parks, David & Ann A. Orr, 31 Jan 1827; Adam Cooper, bondsman.

Parks, George D. & Elizabeth Ross, 28 Oct 1851; H. M. Parks, bondsman; James Parks, wit. married 30 Oct 1851 by Saml. C. Pharr, V. D. M.

Parks, George D. & Amelia A. Stitt, 25 April 1854; James Parks, bondsman; W. K. Reid, C. C. C., wit. married 2 May 1854 by S. C. Pharr, V. D. M.

Parks, Halla B. & Jane Stewart, 9 Feb 1825; Will. Lafayette Gardner, bondsman; Chas. T. Alexander, wit.

Parks, Hugh M. & Ann Oliver, 6 March 1854; John G. Query, bondsman; W. K. Reid, C. C. C., wit. married 7 March 1854 by S. C. Pharr, V. D. M.

Parks, Ira & Louisa Wilson, 21 Jan 1827; Isaac Wilson, bondsman.

Parks, Ira & Susan E. Wallace, 2 Feb 1839; Elam Moore, bondsman; B. Oates, C. C. C.,wit.

Parks, James & Sally Robison, 20 Feb 1804; William Johnston, bondsman; Isaac Alexander, wit.

Parks, James & Mary McCulloh, 26 Nov 1832; William Moore, bondsman; Isaac Alexander, wit.

Parks, James & Martha J. Brown, 22 Jan 1859; Wm. P. Barnette, bondsman; Jno Phelan, wit. married 25 Jan 1859 by J. Rumple, V. D. M.

Parks, John & Rebekah Cairns, 26 Jan 1795; Zenas Alexander, bondsman.

Parks, John & Jennet Crockett, 2 Nov 1797; Isaac Crockett, bondsman.

Parks, John M. & Melissa A. McCulloch, 6 Nov 1837; M. A. Parks, bondsman; B. Oates,wit.

Parks, Joshua & Sarah Dempsey, 8 Oct 1799; Bartlett Meacham, bondsman; J. Wallis, wit.

Parks, Levi & Margaret M. Wilson, 15 Aug 1825; Elam Moore, bondsman; Richd. Gillispie, Jr., wit.

Parks, Levi & Terza Davis, 19 May 1834; James W. Wilson, bondsman; B. Oates, C. C. C., wit.

Parks, Moses A. & Nancy P. Stitt, 11 June 1833; William Gray, bondsman; F. M. Ross, wit.

Parks, Robert & Sarah McEwan, 27 Aug 1798; James Moore, bondsman; Isaac Alexander, wit.

Parks, Uriah & Nancy Smith, 9 Nov 1842; Robert A. Ross, bondsman.

Parks, Uriah & Milly Capps, 23 Aug 1847; Adam Seiler, bondsman; B. Oates, C. C. C., wit.

Parks, William & Mary Beaty, 27 Aug 1795; William Beaty, bondsman; Isaac Alexander,wit.

Parks, William B. & Barbra McGinis, 11 Feb 1817; Samuel Caldwell, bondsman.

Parner, Henry H. & Jane Hall, 9 Sept 1865; Andrew Thomas, bondsman; Wm. Maxwell, C. C. C., wit. married 14 Sept 1865 by S. P. Berryhill, J. P.

Parrish, Andrew M. & Betsey Hogdon, 1 Aug 1812; John Hartgrove, bondsman.

Partlow, Samuel & Mary H. McRum, 11 Sept 1838; Robert C. Partlow, bondsman; John R. Hall, bondsman.

Paschall, John T. & Mary Cook, 22 June 1818; Charles Cook, bondsman; Isaac Alexander, wit.

Patterson, Ambrose & Julia Jennings (colored), 10 Nov 1865; Wm. T. Winn, bondsman; Wm. Maxwell, C. C. C., wit. married 11 Nov. 1865 by Rev. J. Alexander.

Patterson, James Ntl. & Mary Lees, 11 Nov 182-; Charles T. Alexander, bondsman; Chas. T. Alexander, wit.

Patterson, John & Louisa Kerr, 3 Feb 1842; Samuel J. Armond, bondsman.

Patterson, John Jr. & Mary A. Potts, 21 July 1823; Edward M. Bronson, bondsman; R. J. Dinkins, wit.

Patterson, John Jr. & Jemimah Weathers, 30 Jan 1828; Larkin Downs, bondsman; Pearsall Thompson, wit.

Patterson, John H. & Nancy A. Clark, 10 Feb 1866; W. C. McAllister, bondsman.

Patterson, John N. & Margret L. Sloan, 5 Feb 1861; John P. Patterson, bondsman; Wm. Patterson, J. P., wit. married 5 Feb 1861 by S. C. Pharr.

Patterson, Joseph & Nancy Houston, 7 Jan 1823; James H. Kerns, bondsman; R. J. Dinkins, wit.

Patterson, Joseph & Margaret Reed, 27 Sept 1844; John B. Peoples, bondsman; N. B. Taylor, wit.

Patterson, Saml L. & Mary A. Therman, 14 Sept 1848; John Hall, bondsman; Saml. A. Davis, J. P., wit.

Patterson, Saml. L. & N. J. Boles, 19 May 1853; Solomon Harris, bondsman; Saml. A. Davis, J. P., wit.

Patterson, William & Elizabeth C. M. Potts, 9 Jan 1828; Larkin Downs, bondsman.

Patteson, James S. & Elizabeth Gibony, 3 June 1837; David Maxwell, bondsman; B. Oates, C. C. C., wit.

Patteson, Jon H. & Nancy Emmerson, 20 Sept 1837.

Patteson, William & Margt. Sloan, 2 Jan 1792; James Sloan, bondsman; Isaac Alexander, wit.

Patteson, William H. & Mary Walker, 17 July 1823; Robert Sloan, bondsman; Isaac S. Alexander, wit.

Patton, James W. Jr. & Cornelia C. Johnson, 12 May 1857; A. Gaines, bondsman; W. K. Reid, C. C. C., wit. married 12 May 1857 by Danl. A. Penick.

Patton, William L. & Nancy Weeks, 4 Jan 1823; William McCulloch, bondsman; Isaac Alexander, wit.

Patton, William L. & Nancy H. Lees, 10 Dec 1831; John N. Lees, bondsman; B. Oates, D. C., wit.

Paul, Jackson L. & Abigail Houell, 10 April 1856; Benjn. M. White, bondsman; W. K. Reid, C. C. C., wit. married 10 April 1856 by Lorenzo Hunter, J. P.

Paul, Samuel & Polly French, 5 March 1834; Andrew Pierce, bondsman; John Oates, wit.

Paxton, James & Liddy Alexander, 1 July 1845; Joseph Hartise, bondsman; Daniel Wentz, J. P., wit.

Payne, Joseph & Patsey Gardner Todd, 6 Aug 1831; Wm. L. Todd, bondsman; B. Oates, wit.

Peacock, John B. & Caroline Matthews, 19 June 1838; William Alexander, bondsman; P. E. Saunier, wit.

Peel, John & Jean Manteeth, 15 March 1797; James Peel Jr., bondsman; Jas. Conner, wit.

Pegg, Hugh & Serena T. Taylor, 2 May 1865; R. B. Pegg, bondsman.

Pegram, W. W. & Margaret E. Elliotte, 13 Oct 1856; Wm. P. Hill, bondsman; W. K. Reid, C. C. C., wit. married 14 Oct 1856 by A. W. Miller

Pender, John H. & Nancy M. Johnston, 7 Dec 1865; J. R. Wallace, bondsman; R. M. White, wit. married 7 Dec 1865 by I. S. McLaughlin

Penhelzd, Richard & Susan Deaton, 21 Dec 1958; J. R. Tredennick, bondsman; W. K. Reid, C. C. C., wit. married 23 Dec 1858 by J. H. Pyron, J. P.

Peninger, Henry & Jane Becket, 19 Jan 1820; Jacob Peninger, bondsman; Isaac S. Alexander, wit.

Peninger, Phillip & Miss Margaret A. Stenson, 24 July 1856; Wm. J. Stephenson, bondsman.

Peoples, John & Sarah Osborn, 31 Oct 1814; Richard Peoples, bondsman.

Peoples, Hugh H. & M. A. Williamson, 5 Sept 1853; James T. Downs, bondsman; S. A. Davis, wit. married 5 Sept 1853 by Saml. A. Davis, J. P.

Peoples, John B. & Mrs. R. M. Stitt, 24 Aug 1846; John Hunter, bondsman; S. J. Lourie, wit.

Peoples, Matthew H. & Margaret A. Neel, 13 Oct 1852; John L. Watson, bondsman; B. Oates, C. C. C., wit. married 14 Oct 1852 by James B. Watt.

Peoples, R. B. & Edney Orsborne, 13 July 1854; Argyle King, bondsman; W. K. Reid, C. C. C., wit. married 13 Jly 1854 by Alexr. Springs, J. P.

Peoples, Silas N. & Martha Hunter, 24 Oct 1833; James M. Kerr, bondsman; B. Oates, C. C. C., wit.

Peoples, Silas N. & Susan A. Capps. 17 Aug 1848; John W. Clark, bondsman; Saml. J. Lourie, wit.

Perry, Aaron & Mary Kerr, 18 Jan 1823; John S.Barnett, bondsman; Isaac S. Alexander, wit.

Perry, Andrew J. & Jane R. Williams, 13 April 1836; David Parks, bondsman; B. Oates, C. C. C., wit.

Perry, Edmund & Charlotte D. Bonsal, 24 Sept 1862; M. W. Robison, bondsman; J. W. Wadsworth, wit.

Person, Benjamin & Hannah Darnell, 29 Jan 1806; Saml Polk, bondsman.

Pery, Gray & Jane Gray, 19 May 1819; Grief W. Gray, bondsman; Isaac Alexander, wit.

Petrea, William & Elizabeth E. Galloway, 15 Dec 1848; H. S. Hunter, bondsman; Saml. J. Lourie, wit.

Pettus, George S. & Jane Knox, 25 May 1789; Jas. Tagert, bondsman; Sam. Martin, wit.

Pettus, George & Mary Taggert, 28 July 1817; Joseph Tagert, bondsman; Isaac S. Alexander, wit.

Pettus, George & Mary E. Persons, 30 Oct 1832; John C. Smith, bondsman.

Pettus, George Jr. & Jane Glouver, 14 Feb 1842; Wm. Nolen, bondsman; C. T. Alexander, C. C. C., wit.

Pettus, John D. O. K. & Violet Wilson, 25 Aug 1812; John Wilson, bondsman; Isaac Alexander, wit.

Pettus, John F. & Margt. Prim, 9 Sept 1852; P. J. Wilson, bondsman; Wm. Patterson, wit. married 9 Sept 1852 by Wm. Patterson, J. P.

Pettus, John W. & Margaret M. Knox, 30 Oct 1865; J. F. Beard, bondsman; Wm. Maxwell, C. C. C., wit. married 2 Nov 1865 by J. R. Gillespie, J. P.

Pettus, Stephen B. & Susan Reed, 21 Sept 1825; Browning Duncan, bondsman; Isaac S. Alexander, wit.

Pettus, Thomas N. & Addeline Burton, 6 Feb 1837; Thomas J. Campbell, bondsman; B. Oates, wit.

Pettus, William & Mary Knox, 6 March 1790; George Pettus, bondsman; Isaac Alexander, wit.

Pettus, William W. & Eliza Ann Benton, 1 June 1838: Jno D. McLean, bondsman; B. Oates, wit.

Petus, Augusta & Jane L. Bigham, 9 Jan 1844; Henry Hunter, bondsman; N. B. Taylor, wit.

Pharr, Alfred & Susan Alexander (colored), 28 Dec 1865; Charles Stinson, bondsman; Wm. Maxwell, C. C. C., wit. married 29 Dec 1865 by S. C. Pharr.

Pharr, Elias & Martha C. Orr, 26 July 1827; Eli Stafford, bondsman.

Pharr, Hugh H. & Catharine J. Davis, 21 Feb 1843; Thomas W.
Davis, bondsman; M. W. Alexander, wit.

Pharr, John C. & Mary P. Davis, 25 July 1840; Elias A. Morrison,
bondsman; B. Oates, C. C. C.,wit.

Pharr, John C. & Rose M. King, 27 Nov 1860; W. K. Reid, C. C. C.,
wit; Mathias L. Harris, bondsman; married 29 Nov 1860 by Danl.
A. Penick.

Pharr, John E. S. & Elizabeth McConnell, 17 Dec 1859; J. N. Hunter, bondsman; W. K. Reid, C. C. C.,wit.

Pharr, Joseph O. & Louiza Black, 16 March 1840; E. B. Burns,
bondsman; B. Oates, C. C. C.,wit.

Pharr, Lafayette & Adaline Stafford (colored), 1 March 1866; Franklin Stafford, bondsman; Wm. Maxwell, wit. married 3 March 1866
by H. S. Pharr, J. P.

Pharr, Robert & Agness F. Allen, 21 Dec 1825; Robert Allen, bondsman; Isaac Alexander, wit.

Pharr, Samuel C. & Margaret Springs, 16 May 1849; D. T. Caldwell,
bondsman; Saml. J. Lourie, wit.

Pharr, W. R. & Jane King, 18 June 1859; E. M. Harris, bondsman;
W. K. Reid, C. C. C.,wit. married 21 June 1859 by Danl. A.
Penick Sr.

Pharr, Walter F. & Jane R. Stafford, 11 July 1826; Ebenezer B.
Burns, bondsman; Thomas B. Smartt, wit.

Pharr, Walter S. (Rev.) & Jane B. Calewell, 11 Dec 1820; David T.
Caldwell, bondsman; Isaac Alexander, wit.

Pharr, Walter W. & Amanda V. Alexander, 15 Nov 1847; Samuel Pharr,
bondsman; B. Oates, C. C. C., wit.

Pharr, Walter W. & Emily S. Neel, 25 Sept 1860; John M. Pharr,
bondsman; W. K. Reid, C. C. C., wit. married 25 Sept 1860 by
J. Monroe Anderson.

Pheby, John & Mary Ann Henry, 23 Feb 1854; Frederick William Ahrens,
bondsman; W. K. Reid, C. C. C., wit. married 25 Feb 1854 by
G. L. Campbell, J. P.

Phestermon, Joseph & Elizabeth Reed, 18 Feb 1836; James B. Morris,
bondsman.

Phifer, David N. & Mary C. Scott, 18 March 1841; Martin J. Harris,
bondsman.

Phifer, Elijah & Mary Perrine, 21 Dec 1847; Miles R. Fincher,
bondsman; Saml. J. Lourie, wit.

Phifer, Elisha & Kissander Fincher, 9 March 1839; Philip Wolf,
bondsman.

Phifer, Ezra & Jane S. Ezzell, 27 March 1837; John L. Robinson,
bondsman; B. Oates, wit.

Phifer, Hezekiah & Mary Gribble, 19 March 1836; Lewis M. Tye,
bondsman; J. Stilwell, wit.

Phifer, John & Sarah Barker, 4 Dec 1844; McCuen Fincher, bondsman; Daniel Wentz, J. P., wit.

Phifer, John F. & Louisa A. Morrison, 6 March 1823; Isaac S. Alexander, bondsman; H. F. Owens, wit.

Phifer, McCollom & Harriet C. Howard, 12 Dec 1838; James Houston, bondsman; B. Oates, wit.

Phifer, Mathew & Leah Wiley, 20 Nov 1790; Paul Phifer, bondsman; Isaac Alexander, wit.

Phifer, Matthew & Drusilla Houston, 15 June 1829; Jno Stilwell, bondsman; B. Oates, wit.

Phifer, Paul & Jane Alexander, 9 Jan 1792; Nathaniel Alexander, bondsman; John Allison, wit.

Phifer, Peter & Mary Skinner, 2 Sept 1850; J. D. Boyte, bondsman; James Parks, wit.

Philips, Johnathan & Betsey Ritchison, 12 Feb 1799; Edward Richardson, bondsman; Andw. Walker, wit.

Philips, Jonas & Mary Miller, 25 Sept 1830; Nathaniel Thomasson, bondsman; B. Oates, wit.

Philips, Junius A. & Dianah Josey, 29 Jan 1857; Jordan B. Phillips, bondsman; W. K. Reid, C. C. C., wit. married 29 Jan 1857 by J. P. Ross, J. P.

Philips, Westley G. & Lucinda Elms, 21 Aug 1839; Alex. H. Dinkins, bondsman; B. Oates, C. C. C., wit.

Phillips, Alexander & Catharine Long, 29 Aug 1826; Daniel Dulin, bondsman; Isaac Alexander, wit.

Phillips, Jordan B. & Henretta Stanly, 30 Sept 1850; James M. Beaty, bondsman; B. Oates, C. C. C., wit.

Phillips, Julius & Caroline Holmes, 8 Feb 1849; John M. Earnheartt, bondsman; Saml. J. Lourie, wit.

Phillips, William & ---- Buchanan, 17 Jan 1801; Robert Lowther, bondsman.

Phillips, William & Franky Taylor, 2 Sept 1802; Willis Phillips, bondsman; Isaac Alexander, wit.

Phillips, William & Amy Dulin, 28 July 1802; Thomas Dulin, bondsman.

Pickell, J. H. & Mary Honysuckle, 11 Sept 1862; W. W. Woodel, bondsman; Wm. Maxwell, C. C. C., wit. married 16 Sept 1862 by F. M. Ross, J. P.

Pierce, Andrew & Elizabeth Paul, 5 Dec 1833; Samuel Pall, bondsman.

Pierce, James & Mary Houston, 20 Dec 1833; Richard Brown, bondsman.

Pierce, John L. & Mary Harrison, 12 Nov 1850; Andrew Stevenson, bondsman; James Parks, wit.

Pippen, Nelson & Esther Worley, 6 Jan 1804; Henry Conner, bondsman; Jas. Conner, wit.

Piront, Samuel & Clarinda Helmes, 4 Dec 1837; Emanuel Helmes, bondsman; A. Broom, J. P., wit.

Pitman, Matthew & Kezia Rodden, 30 Sept 1805; Godfrey Williams, bondsman.

Plaster, John & Catharine Goforth, 12 Dec 1810; Zenos Bunker, bondsman; Isaac Alexander, wit.

Platt, William & Elizabeth Howie, 8 Nov 1863; D. C. Bobo, bondsman; W. W. Grier, wit. married 8 Nov 1863 by Richd. H. Griffith, minister.

Plunket, James & Agness Houston, 3 Jan 1783; John McCacharn, bondsman; Sam. Martin, wit.

Plunket, Robert T. & Mary Gilmer, 24 July 1817; Richd. D. G. Plunket, bondsman; Isaac S. Alexander, wit.

Plumer, William J. & Mary Smith, 11 Feb 1841; James S. Lewis, bondsman; B. Oates, C. C. C., wit.

Plumer, Zephaniah & Nancy Orr, 10 March 1803; Nathan Mitchel, bondsman; Isaac Alexander, wit.

Plummer, James Washington & Susan Alexander, 18 Feb 1829; Rufus L. Alexander, bondsman.

Plummer, Robert A. & Laura E. Stewart, 19 Feb 1861; James H. Montgomery, bondsman; W. K. Reid, C. C. C., wit. married 21 Feb 1861 by B. H. Garrison, J. P.

Plylor, Martin L. & Sarah S. Stinson, 25 April 1859; George M. Stinson, bondsman; Jno. Phelan, wit. married 28 April 1859 by C. Moretz, Min.

Poer, Franklin M. & Manerva C. Thompson, 23 Dec 1865; S. W. Newel, bondsman; Wm. Maxwell, C. C. C., wit. married 2 Jan 1866 by J. S. Reid, J. P.

Polk, John & Mrs. Martha Harris, 22 Oct 1803; Francis B. Smartt, bondsman; Isaac Alexander, wit.

Pope, James & Cynthia Frazer, 30 Dec 1813; Jno. McCoy, bondsman; Robt. Wilson, wit.

Pope, James & Mary C. Spencer, 7 March 1821; Jno. H. Davidson, bondsman; Isaac Alexander, wit.

Pope, Kirby & Aseneth Sloan, 27 Feb 1829; John H. Caldwell, bondsman; Pearsall Thompson, wit.

Porter, Alexander & Jane Welch, 17 Jan 1810; Joseph Smith, bondsman; Isaac Alexander, wit.

Porter, Alexander J. & Sarah Orr, 7 Nov 1832; John Franklin Orr, bondsman; W. W. Elms, wit.

Porter, Andrew H. & Jane C. McKnight, 30 July 1832; John W. Rodgers, bondsman.

Porter, Andrew W. & Mary Morrison, 10 Feb 1823; John N. Houston, bondsman; Isaac Alexander, wit.

Porter, Archable & Nancy Huie, 12 Feb 1840; Tobias Wolf, bondsman; B. Oates, C. C. C., wit.

Porter, Ezekiel & Mary McComb, 17 April 1799; Robert Shields, bondsman; Isaac Alexander, wit.

Porter, Hugh & Elizabeth Walker, 10 Nov 1807; Andw. Walker, bondsman; Isaac Alexander, wit.

Porter, Hugh G. & Mary Elizabeth Query, 8 March 1854; Milas J. Anderson, bondsman; W. K. Reid, C. C. C., wit. married 9 March 1854 by S. C. Pharr, V. D. M.

Porter, James & Nancy Neely, 5 March 1811; John Neely, bondsman; Isaac Alexander, wit.

Porter, John & Martha S. Hunter, 5 July 1831; John H. McDowell, bondsman; B. Oates, D. C., wit.

Porter, John A. & Caroline E. Hartgrove, 1 Dec 1852; William O. Moss, bondsman; B. Oates, C. C. C., wit.

Porter, John M. & Mary C. Hunter, 10 Jan 1840; Wm. M. Bigham, bondsman; B. Oates, C. C. C., wit.

Porter, John M. & Sarah V. V. Prather, 16 Nov 1847; James McHunter, bondsman; B. Oates, C. C. C., wit.

Porter, John M. & Margaret L.Harris, 13 April 1857; John W. Blair, bondsman; W. K. Reid, C. C. C., wit. married 14 April 1857 by E. F. Rockwell.

Porter, John S. & A. W. Cureton, 30 Nov 1847; Wm. T. Stitt, bondsman; Saml. J. Lourie, wit.

Porter, Joseph & Catherine Byram, 28 Oct 1820; Robert Lindsay, bondsman; Isaac Alexander, wit.

Porter, Joseph & Margaret Gordon, 2 Dec 1840; John B. Peoples, bondsman.

Porter, Lorenzo D. & Isabella E. Henderson, 19 Dec 1837; Andrew M. Barry, bondsman.

Porter, Samuel & Jane Dowdle, 18 Feb 1793; John Montgomery, bondsman; Isaac Alexander, wit.

Porter, Saml. A. & Ruth B. Sloan, 20 Feb 1866; J. W. Sloan, bondsman; Wm. Maxwell, C. C. C., wit. married 22 Feb 1866 by John Douglas.

Porter, Samuel L. & Nancy E. Brown, 18 Dec 1854; John M. Porter, bondsman; W. K. Reid, C. C. C., wit. married 19 Dec 1854 by A. M. Watson.

Porter, William & Jean Montgomery, 24 Feb 1808; Thomas Spratt, bondsman; Isaac Alexander, wit.

Porter, William & Mary Ross, 24 Oct 1832; William Hipp, bondsman; B. Oates, wit.

Porter, William B. & Jane M. Barnett, 1 Sept 1818; Thomas J. Grier, bondsman; Isaac Alexander, wit.

Porter, William M. & Nancy C. Hartt, 29 Dec 1848; N. B. Taylor, bondsman; B. Oates, C. C. C., wit.

Porter, Zenas & Margaret C. Walker,19 Dec 1857; Samuel L. Porter, bondsman; W. K. Reid, C. C. C., wit. married 20 Dec 1857 by G. C. Parks, minister.

Potter, David & Peggy Dunn, 4 Jan 1802; Gordan Potter, bondsman; J. Wallis, wit.

Potter, James & Martha McLellan, 31 Jan 1797; Alexr. Stewart, bondsman.

Potter, James D. & Jane Gibbons, 18 Dec 1833; Pearsall Thompson, bondsman; B. Oates, C. C. C., wit.

Potts, J. M. & N. C. Torrence, 25 Aug 1862; J. R. Gillespie, bondsman; W. R. Maxwell, C. C. C., wit. married 27 Aug 1862 by A. Ranson

Potts, James A. G. & Margaret C. McCulloch, 22 Dec 1840; Samuel C. Harrison, bondsman; B. Oates, wit.

Potts, John G. & M. R. Ardrey, 5 Jan 1864; J. R. Williamson, bondsman.

Potts, John M. & Martha J. Grier, 23 Oct 1835; James A. Grier, bondsman.

Potts, John W. & Recinda Robertson, 13 March 1832; Joseph Patterson, bondsman; R. S. Dinkins, wit.

Potts, Jonathan & Cynthia Preson, 29 Dec 1804; Robert Bryson, bondsman; Archd. Cathey, wit.

Potts, Joseph M. & Susanah Washam, 14 Jan 1844; Charles S. Potts, bondsman; James Johnston, wit.

Potts, L. A. & Emma A. Johnston, 18 Dec 1865; J. G. Price, bondsman.

Potts, London & Rachel Baxter (colored), 29 Dec 1865; Alfred Smith, bondsman; R. M. White, wit. married 1 Jan 1866 by Thomas Gluyas, J. P.

Potts, Robert & Nancy R. Gillespie, 20 Aug 1811; Alexr. Gillespie, bondsman; Isaac Alexander, wit.

Potts, Robert C. & Ann R. Potts, 19 July 1836; John M. Potts, bondsman; B. Oates, wit.

Potts, William & Nelly Dunn, 9 April 1829; Jacob Hill, bondsman.

Potts, William & Mrs. Rebecca Daniels, 28 June 1847; Cyrus Johnston, bondsman.

Powers, Daniel & Cynthia Taylor, 18 Aug 1846; Burwell Shepherd, bondsman; Saml. A. Davis, J. P., wit.

Powers, David & Jane Riley, 29 Oct 1800; Andrew Riley, bondsman.

Prather, John S. & Caroline Hedly, 16 June 1855; Silas F. Prather, bondsman; W. K. Reid, C. C. C., wit. married 17 June 1855 by Alex. Cooper, J. P.

Prather, William S. & Margaret J. Kirkpatrick, 11 Jan 1858; Saml.
C. Wolfe, bondsman; W. K. Reid, C. C. C., wit. married 12
Jan 1858 by J. B. Watt, V. D. M.

Presley, Andrew & Elizabeth C. Yandle, 5 Oct 1841; Samuel Yandle,
bondsman; Angus Johnson, wit.

Presley, Asa & Anna Fite, 2 Feb 1836; Charles Overman, bondsman;
B. Oates, wit.

Pressley, Casswell & Antinett Rheimds, 25 Sept 1865; J. L.
Phillips, bondsman; married 25 Sept 1865 by P. T. Penick.

Pressly, William B. & L. B. Harris, 24 May 1858; J. B. Kerr,
bondsman; W. K. Reid, C. C. C., wit.

Prester, Thomas & Jane Agnes Helms, 31 Jan 1851; John Helms,
bondsman; Casper Hargett, J. P., wit. married 31 Jan 1851
by Casper Hargett, J. P.

Prestly, Andrew & Mary Ann McDowell (colored), 21 Oct 1865;
Thomas Davis, bondsman; Wm. Maxwell, C. C. C., wit. married
2 Nov 1865 by Jas. C. Chalmers, minister.

Price, Isaac & Patsey McCoard, 14 Oct 1807; John Price, bondsman;
Isaac Alexander, wit.

Price, Isaac J. & Cynthia H. Knox, 24 Oct 1854; M. B. Swann, bondsman; W. K. Reid, C. C. C., wit. married 31 Oct 1865 by A. M.
Watson,.

Price, James & Sarah Dellipoe,28 Oct 1800; John Bell, bondsman.

Price, James D. & Nelly Ducworth, 16 Aug 1832; John M. Alexander,
bondsman; John Nance, wit.

Price, John & Agness McLean, 13 July 1801; Samuel Knox, bondsman.

Price, John & Polly Robison, 17 Jan 1807; Thomas Henry, bondsman;
Isaac Alexander, wit.

Price, Julius G. & Elizabeth C. Watts, 4 Aug 1856; Thos. B. Price,
bondsman; W. K. Reid, C. C. C., wit. married 12 Aug 1856 by
G. D. Parks.

Price, Reece & Esther Y. McDowell, 30 Aug 1831; David McKnight,
bondsman.

Price, Robert & Delila A. Deaton, 27 Dec 1855; Solomon Griffin,
bondsman; W. K. Reid, C. C. C., wit. married 27 Dec 1855 by
R. H. Lafferty, minister.

Price, Thomas B. & Mary E. Parks, 24 April 1846; A. R. Briard,
bondsman; B. Oates, C. C. C., wit.

Price, William & Margaret Talton, 12 Feb 1824; Theodore Merrell,
bondsman; R. J. Dinkins, wit.

Price, William A. & Mary Potts, 8 April 1802; Jont. Potts, bondsman; Jas. Conner, J. P., wit.

Price, William J. & Elizabeth Black, 14 July 1849; John W. Howel,
bondsman; Saml. J. Lourie, wit.

Prim, James & Margret Tanner, ---- 1833; Jesse Westmorland,
bondsman; John Nance, wit.

Prim, Joe & Lucinda Baker, 30 Jan 1866; A. H. Creswell, bondsman;
Wm. Maxwell, C. C. C., wit. married 30 Jan 1866 by Jno. F.
Butt.

Pritchard, H. M. (Dr.) & Amanda E. Shaw, 14 Feb 1860; Lewis S.
Williams, bondsman; Jno Phelan, wit. married 14 Feb 1860 by
A. Sinclair, minister.

Propest, C. M. & Mary Hickman, 15 Sept 1856; Robert N. Ross,
bondsman; W. K. Reid, C. C. C., wit. married 16 Sept 1856 by
C. Overman, J. P.

Pucket, Pinckney & Celia Moore, 2 Dec 1832; Robert P. Wiley,
bondsman; B. Oates, wit.

Pucket, Robert E. & Rosannah McKnight, 1 Jan 1858; Edward S.
Washam, bondsman; W. K. Reid, C. C. C., wit. married 5 Jan
1858 by S. C. Pharr, M. G.

Pucket, Sydney & Elizabeth Cashon, 7 Jan 1835; Archibald Cashon,
bondsman; B. Oates, wit.

Pucket, William & Louiza Downs, 29 April 1861; Thos. J. McCorkle,
bondsman; P. S. Whisnant, wit. married 30 April 1861 by Samuel
C. Pharr, minister.

Puckett, Abernathy & Caroline M. Worsham, 21 March 1822; Peter
Cashin, bondsman.

Puckett, James & Violet D. Alexander, 15 July 1847; Wm. H.
Alexander, bondsman; Saml. J. Lourie, wit.

Puckett, John & Terissa Alexander, 19 Aug 1846; James H. Kerns,
bondsman; B. Oates, C. C. C., wit.

Puckett, Milas F. & Elizabeth Stewart, 15 Dec 1841; Sidney Puckett,
bondsman; C. T. Alexander, wit.

Puckett, Thomas J. & Martha C. McCord, 16 May 1859; James C.
Terres, bondsman; W. K. Reid, C. C. C., wit. married 18 May
1859 by Wm. Means, J. P.

Purvines, Joseph J. & Catherine Rice, 24 Sept 1832; James Flow,
bondsman.

Pyron, John M. & Harriet H. Flow, 27 Nov 1833; Columbus Hooks,
bondsman.

Pyron, Thomas R. & Mrs. Margaret C. McCall, 22 Feb 1843; Thomas
A.Crowell, bondsman; T. C. Wilson, wit.

Pyron, William M. & Urrisa Williams, 25 July 1841; Green L.
Crowell, bondsma; T. C. Wilson, J. P., wit.

Quarl, Joseph & Prissilla Johnston, 1 Jan 1800; Edward Sharp,
bondsman; Isaac Alexander, wit.

Query, Calvin M. & Pauline Pfeil, 23 Sept 1862; Isaac Eigenbrum,
bondsman; A. B. Downs, wit. married 23 Sept 1862 by A.
Sinclair, minister.

Query, Elam M. & Josephine E. Wilson, 11 Aug 1858; Jno. R. Wilson, bondsman; W. K. Reid, C. C. C., wit. married 12 Aug 1858 by R. H. Lafferty, minister.

Query, F. E. & Sarah M. Cochran, 26 Dec 1857; M. L. Barringer, bondsman; W. K. Reid, C. C. C., wit. married 29 Dec 1857 by R. H. Lafferty, minister.

Query, Francis M. & Anna A. Alexander, 2 Feb 1861; Calvin M. Query, bondsman; W. K. Reid, C. C. C.,wit. married 6 Feb 1861 by S. C. Pharr.

Query, Francis W. & Rosanah E. Black, 23 Jan 1843; Eli C. Grier, bondsman.

Query, James H. & Isabella C. Reed, 27 March 1850; Isaac M. Reid, bondsman; B. Oates, C. C. C.,wit.

Query, James H.& Miriam Lewis, 12 Sept 1856; William Rice, bondsman; W. K. Reid, C. C. C., wit. married 18 Sept 1856 by W. R. Maxwell, J. P.

Query, James P. & Mary M. Alexander, 13 Jan 1862; J. Elam Caldwell, bondsman; W. K. Reid, C. C. C., wit. married 16 Jan 1862 by R. Z. Johnston.

Query, John G. & Elisabeth A. Parks, 14 Dec 1853; Elias A. McKee, bondsman; W. K. Reid, C. C. C., wit. ma-ried 15 Dec 1853 by Samuel C. Pharr, V. D. M.

Query, John Mc. & Margaret D. Alexander, 1 Feb 1836; Alexander H. Cochran, bondsman.

Query, John M. & Sarah Cochran, 29 April 1846; James F. Gilmer, bondsman; B. Oates, wit.

Query, Robert & Jane E.McGinnis, 16 Dec 1839; Joseph L. Cochran, bondsman; B. Oates, C. C. C.,wit.

Query, Robert & Rebecca Parks, 22 Feb 1842; J. W. McGinnis, bondsman.

Query, Robert S. & Elizabeth E. McGinnis, 13 Dec 1845; Charles H. Erwin, bondsman; B. Oates, C. C. C., wit.

Raborn, M. B. & Amanda Hoover, 14 June 1865; M. D. L. Moody, bondsman; W. W. Grier, wit.

Ramsey, Francis Alexander & Margaret Alexander, 7 April 1789; Wm. B. Alexander, bondsman; J. McK. Alexander, wit.

Ramsey, James & Isabella Hall, 8 Feb 1792; David Rodgers, bondsman.

Ramsey, Matthew & Margaret Neilly, 29 Jan 1795; Andw Walker, bondsman; Edw. Waine, wit.

Ramsey, Thomas & Susannah Henderson, 1 Oct 1804; Richard Henderson, bondsman; Isaac Alexander, wit.

Randle, C. T. & M. Cole, 23 June 1865; J. B. Eberly, bondsman.

Randles, William & Jane Johnston, 27 March 1818; Samuel Johnson, bondsman; Isaac Alexander, C. C., wit.

Randolph, John B. & Margaret Kendrick, 8 March 1815; Ephraim Kendrick, bondsman; Isaac Alexander, wit.

Rankin, John & Sarah Farror, 21 Sept 1814; John Farror, bondsman.

Rankin, John S. & Elmira Alexander, 28 Aug 183-; Eli Denny, bondsman; R. M. Ross, wit.

Rankin, Richard & Susanna Doherty, 3 June 1793; Ezekiel Alexander, bondsman; J. McK. Alexander, wit.

Rankin, Richard & Ann Hargrove, 18 May 1825; Robert Wilson, bondsman; Isaac S. Alexander, wit.

Rankin, Samuel & Mary Doherty, 16 Nov 1791; Richard Rankin, bondsman; Wm. B. Alexander, wit.

Rankin, Watson W. & Sarah E. Rankin, 22 May 1847; Joseph A. Cannon, bondsman.

Rape, Augustus S. & Fanny Hancock, 12 Jan 1833; Peter Thompson, bondsman; Isaac Alexander, wit.

Rape, Peter & Elizabeth Polk, 8 Sept 1818; Thos. Jo. Dillon, bondsman; Jno Rea, J. P., wit.

Rape, William H. & Susan Polk, 22 Oct 1832; Peter Thompson, bondsman; B. Oates, D. C., wit.

Ratchford, Joseph & Easther Carathers, 14 Feb 1825; Ezekiel Carrothers, bondsman; Richd. Gillespie Jr., wit.

Ratchford, William & Mary B. Glover, 19 Sept 1832; John D. Smith, bondsman.

Rawdon, John & Dicey Rodden, 3 Oct 1827; Benjamin Rodden, bondsman.

Rawdon, John & Milly Beaty, 1 March 1842; Wm. Boyles, bondsman; C. T. Alexander, wit.

Rawdon, Lewis & Hannah Robinson, 20 Feb 1850; Thomas Love, John Rawdon, bondsmen; James Parks, wit.

Ray, George W. & -----, 23 Jan 1850; Squire Stilwell, bondsman.

Rea, Ambrose M. & -----, 12 April 1842; Wm. L. McLaughlin, bondsman; C. T. Alexander, wit.

Rea, Andrew & Ellenor Hennagen, 14 June 1797; Jno Rea, bondsman; J. Wallis, wit.

Rea, David & ------, --- 1814; William Rea, bondsman

Rea, David H. & Charlotte Sheppard, 14 Nov 1836; Burrel Shepherd, bondsman; B. Oates, C. C. C., wit.

Rea, David L. & Helen M. Clark, 12 Dec 1848; M. W. Robison, bondsman; Saml. J. Lourie, wit.

Rea, David Neel, & Elsy Spears, 26 Nov 1802; Thomas Rea, bondsman.

Rea, Every S. & Mrs. Margaret McSparn, 5 March 1823; Robert J. Morris, bondsman; Philemon Morris, wit.

Rea, James & Polly Bozzell, 13 March 1809; James C. Davis, bonds-man; Isaac Alexander , wit.

Rea, James & Mary Walker, 10 March 1814; Isaac Secrets, bondsman.

Rea, James & Leanah J. McEwen, 28 July 1857; John R. Morris, bondsman; W. K. Reid, C. C. C., wit. married 30 July 1857 by J. M. Walker, minister.

Rea, James M. & Mary Parks, 21 April 1842; Hugh A. Matthews, bondsman.

Rea, John & Jean Smith, 25 April 1801; William Hayes, bondsman.

Rea, John K. & Martha Jane Brown, 18 Jan 1848; Barnes W. Brown, bondsman; Saml. J. Lourie, wit.

Rea, John K. & Mary L. Alexander, 10 March 1860; Amzi L. William-son, bondsman; W. K. Reid, C. C. C., wit. married 15 March 1860 by J. Rumple, V. D. M.

Rea, John L. & Sarah Smith, 29 Aug 1846; William McAuley, bonds-man; N. B. Taylor, wit.

Rea, John M. & Polly Ritch, 13 March 1821; Charles S. Liggett, bondsman; Phn. Morris, wit.

Rea, Jonathan & Polly Glass, 4 June 1816; John Black, bondsman; John Rea, J. P., wit.

Rea, Joseph & Jemima Harkness, 15 July 1809; James C. Davis, bondsman; Isaac Alexander, wit.

Rea, Joseph & Sarah Reid, 1 Feb 1816; John Reid, bondsman.

Rea, Leroy & Hannah McCorkle, 8 Jan 1839; Elias Harkness, bondsman.

Rea, R. R. & Jane R. Fleniken, 18 Aug 1851; J. M. Rea, bondsman; James Parks, wit.

Rea, Robert R. & Mary A. Turner, 22 June 1864; B. C. Glover, bondsman; Wm. Maxwell, C. C. C., wit. married 23 June 1864 by G. D. Bernheim, Pastor of St. Marks Ev. Lutheran Church, Charlotte.

Rea, Samuel & Martha Rea, 5 Sept 1798; David Rea, bondsman; Isaac Alexander, wit.

Rea, Silas & Elizabeth Kerr, 10 Dec 1827; James Pierce, bondsman.

Rea, Silas Sr. & Mrs. M. A. Parks, 28 Feb 1856; Silas H. Rea, bondsman; W. K. Reid, C. C. C., wit. married 28 Feb 1856 by J. M. Walker, minister.

Rea, Thomas S. & Mrs. Sarah Kesiah, 19 March 1829; Squire Stilwell, bondsman.

Rea, William & Hannah Berryhill, 23 March 1814; William Morris, bondsman; Philemon Morris, wit.

Rea, William A. & Nancy Orr, 12 July 1854; James Willson, bondsman; W. K. Reid, C. C. C., wit. married 13 July 1854 by C. B. Cross, J. P.

Rea, William W. & Elizabeth P. Sharpe, 28 Aug 1854; Robert H. Maxwell, bondsman; W. K. Reid, C. C. C., wit.

Ready, William & Emily McGee, 6 Feb 1860; Robert B. Dun, bondsman; W. K. Reid, C. C. C., wit. married 6 Feb 1850 by G. L. Campbell, J. P.

Reding, Robert & Sarah Howard, 19 June 1816; Joel Long, bondsman; Isaac Alexander, wit.

Reed, Allen & Frances Moore, 2 Nov 1797; Jno Fittin, bondsman.

Reed, Jeremiah W. & Eliza Miller, 22 Oct 1836; Joseph Foster, bondsman; B. Oates, wit.

Reed, Samuel & Jane Walker, 5 April 1821; Charles Hutchison, bondsman; Isaac Alexander, wit.

Reed, Samuel & Mary Todd, 4 April 1836; John Reid, bondsman; B. Oates, C. C. C., wit.

Reed, Silas & Nancy Miller, 16 Feb 1842; John W. Woodard, bondsman; C. T. Alexander, wit.

Reeves, Franklin A. & Sarah L. Murphy, 7 Feb 1866; Dallas M. Rigler, bondsman; Wm. Maxwell, C. C. C., wit. married 7 Feb 1866 by Richd. H. Griffith, minister.

Reeves, William & Rachel Parks, 12 Feb 1811; John Bennitt, bondsman; Isaac Alexander, wit.

Reid, Andrew Jackson & Nancy C. Taylor, 20 Sept 1836; Wm. R. Berryhill, bondsman.

Reid, David & Jane Alexander, 7 April 1795; Ezekiel Alexander, bondsman; Isaac Alexander, wit.

Reid, David & Ann Kerr, 11 May 1801; Wm. Kerr, bondsman; Isaac Alexander, wit.

Reid, George F. & Margaret N. Auton, 16 July 1856; R. Samuel Reid, bondsman; married 17 July 1856 by Jas. C. Nicholson, J. P.

Reid, H. C. & M. L. Caldwell, 7 May 1859; Jno. M. White, bondsman; W. K. Reid, C. C. C., wit. married 10 May 1859 by R. H. Lafferty, minister.

Reid, H. C. & M. J. Kirkpatrick, 9 April 1862; John M. White, bondsman; W. K. Reid, C. C. C., wit. married 10 April 1862 by John Hunter, minister.

Reid, H. R. & Eliza Alexander, 18 Nov 1865; H. C. Reid, bondsman; Wm. Maxwell, C. C. C., wit. married 21 Nov 1865 by R. Z. Johnston, minister.

Reid, Hugh & Ann Walker, -- March 1809; William Walker, bondsman; Susan R. Alexander, wit.

Reid, Isaac & Henrietta Tevapaugh, 25 June 1853; Admiral N. Gray, bondsman; B. Oates, C. C. C., wit. married 25 June 1853 by J. W. Miller, minister.

Reid, James & Mary Freeman, 3 June 1818; Abraham M. Fox, Samuel
B. Hill (or Berryhill), bondsmen.

Reid, James & Margaret Dewése, 7 Jan 1841; Joseph F. Gillespie,
bondsman; Jas. Johnston, wit.

Reid, James Jr. & Polly King, 13 April 1802; Joseph Reid, bondsman; J. Wallis, wit.

Reid, James B. & Mary B. Greer, 14 March 1837; John G. Query,
bondsman.

Reid, Jeremiah S. & Mary J. Grier, 29 Oct 1855; William W. Grier,
bondsman; W. K. Reid, C. C. C., wit. married 6 Nov 1855 by
S. C. Pharr.

Reid, John & Margaret E. Bigham, 6 March 1844; W. C. Bigham,
bondsman; N. B. Taylor, wit.

Reid, John & Martha M. Burns, 4 Feb 1846; S. H. Boyce, bondsman;
B. Oates, C. C. C., wit.

Reid, John H. & Elizabeth Williams, 9 March 1835; Elisabeth
Williams, bondsman; B. Oates, C. C. C., wit.

Reid, John Y. & Harriet T. Hipworth, 6 March 1839; Robert W.
Reid, bondsman; B. Oates, wit.

Reid, Jonathan & Jane P. McDowell, 2 Jan 1822; Robert Lindsay,
bondsman; Isaac Alexander, wit.

Reid, Jonathan & Nancy C. Cooper, 19 Jan 1850; R. W. McDowell,
bondsman.

Reid, Jonathan & Esther M. Robison, 4 Nov 1854; A. B. Sloan,
bondsman; W. K. Reid, C. C. C., wit. married 8 Nov 1854 by
J. B. Watt, V. D. M.

Reid, Joseph & Margaret Franklin, 12 March 1810.

Reid, Madison & Matilda Philips (colored), 4 Jan 1861; Pinckny
Berryhill, John H. Hunter, bondsmen; W. K. Reid, C. C. C.,
wit. married 4 Jan 1861 by B. H. Garrison, J. P.

Reid, R. J. & Jane A. Reed, 22 March 1847; James T. Wearn,
bondsman; Saml. J. Lourie, wit.

Reid, Reuben & Nancy Hainy, 11 Aug 1839; Joseph Foster, bondsman;
P. E. Saunier, wit.

Reid, Robert W. & Mary A. Flannagan, 27 Nov 1844; James C. Rea,
bondsman; N. B. Taylor, wit.

Reid, Rufus & Nancy A. Latta, 6 Dec 182-; Tho. B. Smartt, bondsman;
Isaac Alexander, wit.

Reid, Rufus & Elizabeth L. Davidson, 24 Jan 1835; James A. Johnston,
bondsman.

Reid, Samuel C. & Caroline Boyes, 9 Dec 1847; S. A. Boyce, bondsman;
Saml. J. Lourie, wit.

Reid, Thomas & Louisa Blackburn, 5 Feb 1830; Thomas Boyd, bondsman.

Reid, William B. W. & Terza Alexander, 22 Jan 1839; William R.
Harkey, bondsman; B. Oates, C. C. C., wit.

Reid, William & Christian McGin, 29 Sept 1806; John McGin, bondsman; Isaac Alexander, wit.

Reid, William & Eliza McAlister, 18 Feb 1829; James McAllister,
bondsman; Isaac Alexander, wit.

Reid, William & Isabella Kirkpatrick, 1 March 1847; Samuell H.
Kirkpatrick, bondsman; B. Oates, C. C. C., wit.

Reid, William H. & Sophina Todd, 9 Feb 1860; Wm. Todd, bondsman;
Jno. Phelan, wit. married 9 Feb 1860 by G. L. Campbell, J.
P.

Reid, William K. & Margaret Berryhill, 3 Feb 1830; James M. Mc-
Knight, bondsman; B. Oates, wit.

Reid, William K. & A. H. Alexander, 5 Jan 1841; C. T. Alexander,
bondsman.

Reid, William M. & Sarah Berryhill, 6 March 1854; Eli H. McCoy,
bondsman; W. K. Reid, C. C. C., wit. married 7 March 1854 by
Jas. C. Nicholson, J. P.

Reinhardt, Charles E. & Mary E. Rudisill, 28 Dec 1814; William
Rudisill, bondsman; Isaac Alexander, wit.

Renshaw, N. F. & Mrs. E. Sloan, 28 July 1865; S. A. Harris,
bondsman; Wm. Maxwell, C. C. C., wit. married 1 Aug 1865 by
James D. Hall.

Revels, Eli B. & Mary Bird, 8 Feb 1837; Brister Mc. Worrick,
bondsman; B. Oates, wit.

Reynoles, John & Hannah McKee, 17 Oct 1803; William McKee, bondsman.

Rhone, Mobly & Mary Prater, 20 May 1820; Nathan Prather, bondsman;
Isaac S. Alexander, wit.

Rhyne, A. M. & Sallie A. Colvard, 4 Sept 1865; J. J. Sims, bondsman; Wm. Maxwell, C. C. C., wit. married 4 Sept 1865 by Jas.
Stacy.

Rhyne, Hugh T. & N. M. Lawing, 30 Oct 1859; Ephraim L. Rankin,
bondsman; W. K. Reid, C. C. C., wit.

Rhyne, Joseph N. & Mary S. Todd, 26 May 1847; J. A. Todd, bondsman;
Saml. J. Lourie, wit.

Rhyne, Moses H. & Mary C. Springs, 23 Feb 1864; H. G. Springs,
bondsman; Wm. Maxwell, C. C. C., wit. married 2 March 1864
by J. P. Ross, J. P.

Rice, A. B. & Esther Herron, 2 Feb 1865; James Solomon, bondsman;
Wm. Maxwell, C. C. C.,wit. married 2 Feb 1865 by B. H. Garrison, J. P.

Rice, Daniel & Margaret McLure, 19 Feb 1852; Moses Stricklan,
bondsman; Saml. J. Lourie, wit. married 19 Feb 1852 by David
Henderson, J. P.

Rice, John & Catherine Cook, 30 Jan 1818; Jeremiah Adams, bondsman.
John Rea, wit.

Rice, M. W. & Esther Starns, 6 Nov 1865; E. H. Hinson, bondsman;
Wm. Maxwell, C. C. C., wit. married 7 Nov 1865 by Jno. F.
Butt.

Rice, Stewart & Sophia Wentz, 2 Dec 1839; Cyrus D. Alexander,
bondsman; B. Oates, wit.

Rice, Stewart & Jane C. Harison, 31 Dec 1847; James C. McCall,
bondsman; Dn: Wentez, J. P., wit.

Rice, V. W. & Elizabeth Yandle, 24 March 1856; Wm. S. Smith,
bondsman; W. K. Reid, C. C. C., wit.

Rice, Valentine W. & Matilda Baker, 15 Oct 1853; Joseph W. Starns,
bondsman; B. Oates, C. C. C., wit.

Rice, William & Elizabeth Barnes, 14 July 1803; William Burton,
bondsman; Isaac Alexander, wit.

Rice, William & Clarinda Harkey, 13 Dec 1859; S. B. Harkey,
bondsman; W. K. Reid, C. C. C., wit. married 13 Dec 1859 by
C. Moretz, C. C.

Richardson, James & Sally Beard, 11 Dec 1817; Jacob Fox Cuningham,
bondsman.

Richardson, James H. & Esther H. Hunter, 1 Sept 1851; James L.
Grier, bondsman; James Parks, wit. married 3 Sept 1851 by
John H. Grier, J. P.

Richardson, John K. & Adaline Hoover, 23 April 1849; William Moss,
bondsman; Saml. J. Lourie, wit.

Richardson, Mason & Sarah Philips, 2 Feb 1795; Edward Richardson,
bondsman; Shared Gray, wit.

Riddle, T. S. & Sarah L. Marks, 11 June 1856; Thomas Ledwill,
bondsman.

Riley, Jessee & Sally Worke, 22 June 1825; Jno. M. Rily, bondsman;
Jno. Hutchison, wit.

Riley, John & Mary R. Russ, 2 Aug 1849; James C. Johnston, bondsman; B. Oates, C. C. C., wit.

Riley, Michel & Margt. Kelly, 17 Nov 1823; John Sloan, bondsman;
R. J. Dinkins, wit.

Rimer, John L. & Mary Jane Weant, 24 Dec 1864; W. A. Hannon,
bondsman; Wm. Maxwell, wit. married 27 Dec 1864 by James C.
Chalmers, minister.

Riner, Samuel & Martha A. McLean, 14 Feb 1835; Georg W. Ritch,
bondsman; J. Stilwell, wit.

Ritch, Demps & Mary N. Morris, 7 Oct 1834; Philemon W. Morris,
bondsman; B. Oates, C. C. C., wit.

Ritch, Elijah & Elizabeth Morris, 15 Aug 1834; Philemon W. Morris,
bondsman; B. Oates, C. C. C., wit.

Ritch, Isaac M. & Eliza Philips, 26 Feb 1833; John Blount, bondsman; B. Oates, D. C., wit.

Ritch, James S. & Eliza Price, 4 May 1842; L. M. Tye, bondsman.

Ritch, Thomas & Pamelia Harris, 26 May 1840; Abner H. Stevens, bondsman; B. Oates, C. C. C., wit.

Ritchie, Edmon & Rachel Cochron, 28 Nov 1799; Thomas Couchrane, bondsman; Wm. McCall, J. P., wit.

Rives, William & Hanah Smith, 14 Dec 1820; William Walker, bondsman; Isaac Alexander, wit.

Rives, William & Jane H. Cunningham, 20 July 1824; Joshua P. Smith, bondsman; R. J. Dinkins, wit.

Roach, Allen & Patsey McLean, 27 Aug 1824; Richard Jennings, bondsman; Isaac S. Alexander, wit.

Roach, John & Elizabeth H. Acock, 1 March 1823; Thomas H. Acock, bondsman; Isaac S. Alexander, wit.

Roan, Harbert & Elizabeth Martin, 30 July 1818; Jonathan Reed, bondsman.

Roan, Hugh & Hanah Calhoun, 26 May 1792; Thomas Neely Jr., bondsman; Isaac Alexander, wit.

Roan, Solomon & Fanny Parish, 21 March 1818; Herbert Roan, bondsman; Isaac Alexander, wit.

Roark, Joseph M. & Mary Ann Curlee, 24 Jan 1856; E. A. McLeod, bondsman; W. K. Reid, C. C. C.,wit. married 24 Jan 1856 by A. W. Miller.

Robarts, William & Jane Montgomery, 26 Sept 1832; John Robarts, bondsman.

Robb, James & Elizabeth Houston, 1 March 1811; Richard Mason, bondsman; Isaac S. Alexander, wit.

Roberson, Aaron & Jane Dermond, 6 June 1803; Mils Castillo, bondsman; Isaac Alexander, wit.

Roberson, Mathew A. & Adalin Rodin, 13 April 1842; Wm. A. Brown, bondsman; C. T. Alexander, wit.

Roberson, Mathew A. & Margaret Hipp, 2 Dec 1847; R. F. Clark, bondsman; G. C. Cathy, wit.

Roberts, James & Margaret Denkins, 3 June 1799; Wm. Reeves, bondsman; Isaac Alexander, wit.

Roberts, John & Jane Davis, 10 March 1802; Jno Smith, bondsman.

Roberts, Joseph M. & Elizabeth King, 19 May 1841; David Rucks, bondsman; Jas. M. Stewart, wit.

Roberts, Robert R. & Elizabeth L. Montgomery, 18 May 1840; James R. Rily, bondsman.

Roberts, Wiley & Polly Blankenship, 27 Jan 1808; Allen Sims, bondsman; Isaac Alexander, wit.

Roberts, William A. & Nancy V. Orr, 30 March 1858; Lee A. Montgomery, bondsman; W. K. Reid, C. C. C., wit. married 30 March 1858 by I. S. McLaughlin.

Robertson, Alexander & Jannett Cunningham, 15 Oct 1791; William
Corum, bondsman; Isaac Alexander, wit.

Robertson, Allen & Susan Boyd, 26 Aug 1830; Benjamin Smith,
bondsman.

Robeson, Isaac H. & Sally Harket, 6 Feb 1821; John Robison, bondsman; Isaac Alexander, wit.

Robeson, Josiah A. & Jane L. Henderson, 18 May 1843; William
A. Henderson, bondsman.

Robinson, Archibald & Abigal Barnett, 16 Feb 1820; David R.
Henderson, bondsman; Isaac S. Alexander, wit.

Robinson, Carnes H. & Mary A. Alexander, 11 March 1844; N. B.
Taylor, bondsman; C. T. Alexander, wit.

Robinson, Henry & Elizabeth Cunningham, 15 Aug 1809; McGill
Matthews, bondsman; Isaac Alexander, wit.

Robinson, James B. & Mary Stitt, 13 Dec 1836; John N. Lee,
bondsman; B. Oates, C. C. C., wit.

Robinson, John (Revd.) & Mary C. Baldwin, 9 April 1795; Thomas
Henderson, bondsman; Ruthy Alexander, wit.

Robinson, John L. & Amelia E. Howard, 24 Oct 1837; Andrew J.
Ezell, bondsman.

Robinson, M. W. & Kate J. Williams, 7 Oct 1861; Wm. P. Burch,
bondsman; P. S. Whisnant, wit. married 23 Oct 1861 by G. W.
Ivy.

Robinson,R. C. & Martha Johnston, 28 July 1847; David D. Taylor,
bondsman; Saml. J. Lourie, wit.

Robinson, Robert M. & Eliza Jane Taylor, 22 Dec 1840; Peter
Johnson, bondsman; B. Oates, wit.

Robinson, W. W. & L. C. Cooper, 17 July 1865; Thomas S. Cooper,
bondsman; Wm. Maxwell, C. C. C., wit. married 18 July 1865
by Jas. C. Chalmers, minister.

Robinson, William P. & Margaret M. Wiley, 11 May 1833; John M.
Potts, bondsman.

Robinson, William P. & Martha A. Rea, 21 Jan 1854; Thomas J.
Ezell, bondsman; W. K. Reid, C. C. C., wit. married 2 Feb
1854 by S. C. Pharr, V. D. M.

Robison, Alexander & Clarissa Alexander, 16 Aug 1815; James A.
Todd, bondsman.

Robison, Alexander & Martha Robison, 23 July 1818; Reece Price,
bondsman; A. M. Fox, wit.

Robison, Alexander & Elizabeth Robison, 3 Dec 1831; William M.
Grier, bondsman.

Robison, Andrew J. & Sarah N. Lawing, 27 Sept 1855; James J.
Rawdon, bondsman; W. K. Reid, C. C. C., wit. married 27
Sept 1855 by Wm. Boyles.

Robison, Daniel C. & Mary C. Bigger, 27 June 1849; Milds M.
Yandle, bondsman; B. Oates, C. C. C., wit.

Robison, David & Eleanor Bowman, 12 Jan 1803; John Henderson,
bondsman; Isaac Alexander, wit.

Robison, Ezekiel & Eleanor Harris,23 March 1812; Thomas Alexander,
bondsman; Isaac Alexander, wit.

Robison, Haris & Agness Kirk, 11 May 1795; James Henderson,
bondsman; Isaac Alexander, wit.

Robison, John & Esther Wiley, 2 June 1795; William Alexander,
bondsman; Isaac Alexander, wit.

Robison, John & Betsey Sample, 18 April 1804; Robert Montgomery,
bondsman.

Robison, John & Amy Fisher, 9 Dec 1820; Jacob Wolf, bondsman;
Isaac Alexander, wit.

Robison, John K. & Harriet A. Henderson, 2 Dec 1843; William A.
Cooper, bondsman; N. B. Taylor, wit.

Robison, John M. & Peggy Wallace, 27 May 1813; William Robison,
bondsman; Isaac Alexander, wit.

Robison, John P. & Susan E. Rodden, 27 Feb 1856; Wm. G. Rodden,
bondsman; W. K. Reid, C. C. C., wit. married 27 Feb 1856 by
A. Cooper, J. P.

Robison, Joseph M. & Fanny King, 31 July 1856; Wm. A. L. Owen,
bondsman; W. K. Reid, C. C. C., wit. married 31 July 1856 by
A. Cooper, J. P.

Robison, Mathew & Mary Hicks, 21 Jan 1794; William Lawing,
bondsman; Isaac Alexander, wit.

Robison, Matthew R. & Caroline Byrum, 19 Jan 1848; Jas. B. Spratt,
bondsman; Saml. J. Lourie, wit.

Robison, Michael & Esther Brown, 5 Jan 1828; James S. Greer,
bondsman; Pearsall Thompson, wit.

Robison, Moses W. & Virginia Q. Clark, 12 April 1849; Thomas H.
Brom, bondsman; B. Oates, wit.

Robison, Richard & Martha McLeary, 14 June 1790; Michael McCleary,
bondsman; Isaac Alexander, wit.

Robison, Robert & Margaret Henderson, 30 March 1790; Jno Robinson,
bondsman; Isaac Alexander, wit.

Robison, Robert G. & Margaret Calder, 25 April 1837; Joseph M.
Alexander, bondsman; P. E. Saunier, wit.

Robison, Wallis & Mary Brown, 5 March 1831; Robert Cathcart,
bondsman.

Robison, Watson & Margaret Eagle, 25 June 1850; Andrew M. Beaty,
bondsman; James Parks, wit.

Robison, William & Agness Hargrove, 9 Oct 1804; Walter Carruth,
bondsman; Isaac Alexander, wit.

Robison, William & Keziah Lewis, 16 Jan 1812; Alexander Robison, bondsman; Isaac Alexander, wit.

Robison, William & Sally Steward, 23 Feb 1819; Wm. Lucky, bondsman; Isaac S.Alexander, wit.

Robison, William H. & Sarah A. Mathew, 1 Feb 1842; Saml. P. Alexander, bondsman; C. T. Alexander, wit.

Robison, William L. & Martha Reid, 17 Oct 1850; Wm. A. Brown, bondsman; H. B. Williams, wit.

Roch, Abraham & Betsey Pressley, 18 July 1799; George Wolf, bondsman; Andw. Walker, J. P., wit.

Rodden, Andrew & Harriet Judith Rawdon, 26 Jan 1835; William Boyles, bondsman.

Rodden, Benjamin & Betsey Williams, 30 Dec 1807; William Rodden, bondsman; Isaac Alexander, wit.

Rodden, Benjamin & Elizabeth Baker, 22 Sept 1829; A. A. Berryhill, bondsman; E. Elms, wit.

Rodden, Gabriel & Caroline Cook, 18 Oct 1842; Robert W. Reid, bondsman.

Rodden, Jacob & Jane Griffin, 25 Jan 1795; Upton Byram, bondsman; Isaac Alexander, wit.

Rodden, James & Margaret E. Berryhill, 28 Jan 1847; Mathew A. Robberson, bondsman; B. Oates, C. C. 'C., wit.

Rodden, Lewis & Hannah Williams, 7 Sept 1802; William Rodden, bondsman; Isaac Alexander, wit.

Rodden, Matthew & Hannah Warwick, 26 May 1847; Wm. A. Brown, bondsman; Saml. J. Lourie, wit.

Rodden, N. B. & Martha M. Headly, 14 Aug 1865; J. L. Orr, bondsman; Wm. Maxwell, C. C. C., wit. married 15 Aug 1865 by S. J. Berryhill, J. P.

Rodden, Thomas W. & Celina Beaty, 8 April 1834; Allen H. Brown, bondsman; B. Oates, C. C. C., wit.

Rodden, Upton & Rachel Pitman, 14 May 1806; Jonathan Baker, bondsman; Isaac Alexander, wit.

Rodden, William & Polly Williams, 6 Nov 1805; Godphrey Williams, bondsman.

Rodden, William & Hannah R. Rodden, 18 March 1847; Matthew A. Robison, bondsman; Saml. J. Lourie, wit.

Rodden, William R. & Elva Jane Hoover, 20 Sept 1860; Jno. P. Robison, bondsman; Jno Phelan, wit. married 20 Sept 1860 by Jas. C. Nicholson, J. P.

Roddin, James J. & Jane Roddin, 10 June 1847; Pinkney Berryhill, bondsman; Saml. J. Lourie, wit.

Roden, Jackson & Polly Corum, 17 Feb 1810; Bengmin Roden, bondsman.

Rodgers, Andrew Niel & Jenny Miller, 21 Sept 1811; Abraham Miller, bondsman; Isaac Alexander, wit.

Rodgers, E. P. & Sarah Jane McCall, 25 Sept 1865; J. H. Torrence, bondsman; Wm. Maxwell, C. C. C., wit. married 28 Sept 1865 by J. R. Gillespie, J. P.

Rodgers, Edward H. & Elisabeth M. Henderson, 8 Sept 1835; Clement Nantz, bondsman; Edwin Potts, J. P., wit.

Rodgers, James & Hannah Rogers, 4 Dec 1819; Alexander White, bondsman.

Rodgers, James H. & Elizabeth C. Kelly, 25 March 1839; Samuel P. Alexander, bondsman; B. Oates, C. C. C., wit.

Rodgers, James W. & Catharine Maxwell, 5 Feb 1856; William M. Maxwell, bondsman; W. K. Reid, C. C. C.,wit. married 7 Feb 1856 by C. B. Cross, J. P.

Rodgers, Jessee & Ellen Maxwell, 24 Feb 18--; James Rodgers, bondsman; Isaac S. Alexander, wit.

Rodgers, John & Jenny Neely, 27 April 1809; Thomas Rodgers, bondsman; Isaac Alexander, wit.

Rodgers, John & Rachel M. McRum, 17 Sept 1825; Jas. McAmey Morrison, bondsman; Isaac Alexander, wit.

Rodgers, John & Martha Irwin, 7 April 1827; James McMorrison, bondsman; Isaac Alexander, wit.

Rodgers, John R. & Elizabeth Alexander, 11 Feb 1859; Thomas P. Rodgers, bondsman; John Phelan, wit. married 17 Feb 1859 by R. H. Lafferty, minister.

Rodgers, Joseph & Jane Sadler, 6 April 1825; John L. Hayes, bondsman; Isaac Alexander, wit.

Rodgers, Julius D. & Mary Jane Flannagan, 29 May 1854; Franklin C. Glen, bondsman; W. K. Reid, C. C. C., wit. married 1 June 1854 by C. C. Cathy, J. P.

Rodgers, Samuel W. & Jane M. Kirkpatrick, 25 Feb 1823; John Rodgers, bondsman; Isaac S. Alexander, wit.

Rodgers, Thomas P. &·Emily Alexander, 26 Sept 1848; Wilson Wallace, bondsman; B. Oates, C. C. C., wit.

Rogers, Ambrose N. & Sarah Kerr, 9 Feb 1835; John Miller, bondsman; B. Oates, C. C. C., wit.

Rogers, Hugh W. & Jane Parks, 1 May 1824; Samuel W. McLarty, bondsman; Isaac Alexander, wit.

Rogers, J. M. L. & S. E. Knox, 28 Sept 1861;: E. P. Hall, bondsman; W. K. Reid, C. C. C., wit. married 20 Nov 1861 by R.F. Blythe, J. P.

Rogers, J. M. Lafayette & Harriet C. Miller, 28 Sept 1854; E. P. Hall, bondsman; James Johnston, wit. married 28 Sept 1854 by James Johnston, J. P.

Rogers, John & Margaret Russell, 12 May 1789; David Russell, bondsman; Jn. Rogers, wit.

Rogers, Jonas & Mary Julan, 1 Jan 1798; Willis Weathers, bondsman; Isaac Alexander, wit.

Rogers, Joseph & Margarett McEwen, 9 Aug 1822; Robert McEwen, bondsman; Isaac S. Alexander, wit.

Rogers, Robert & Sarah Parks, 23 Sept 1822; Samuel Parks, bondsman; Isaac Alexander, wit.

Rogers, Thomas P. & Tibitha M. Secrest, 31 Jan 1834; Shepherd Rogers, bondsman; Daniel Harget, wit.

Rogers, William & Mary Rhodes, 15 Dec 1806; William Weathers, bondsman.

Rone, William & Elizabeth Bigham, 25 April 1822; Nathan Prather, bondsman; R. J. Dinkins, wit.

Rooker, Jenings, & Mary Wagstaff, 25 Oct 1841; George Washington Wagstaff, bondsman; C. T. Alexander, wit.

Roper, James W.& Biddy Roper, 14 Aug 1821; David Roper, bondsman; Isaac S. Alexander, wit.

Roper, John & Sarah Fincher, 16 Nov 1797; Jonathen Fincher, bondsman; Isaac Alexander, C. C., wit.

Rosich, George W. & Nancy P. Johnson, 28 Aug 1857; Thomas A. Johnson, bondsman; W. K. Reid, C. C. C., wit. married 3 Sept 1857 by J. P. Ross, J. P.

Ross, Francis Madison & Dorcas N. Gilmore, 24 Dec 1839; James A. Johnston, bondsman; B. Oates, C. C. C., wit.

Ross, James & Deborah Ross, 15 Dec 1809; Alexander Owens, bondsman; Isaac Alexander, wit.

Ross, James & Anne Montgomery, 5 Oct 1815; Dr. Robt McKenzie, bondsman.

Ross, James Colman & --- Rogers, 16 Jan 1822; John Henderson, bondsman; Isaac Alexander, wit.

Ross, James N. & Mary L. Wilson, 19 Nov 1845; F. H. Maxwell, bondsman; B. Oates, C. C. C., wit.

Ross, John & Hannah Harris, 16 June 1798; Saml. Harris, bondsman; Jno. Harris, wit.

Ross, John & Susana Porter, 16 May 1799; Isaac Alexander, C. C. C., wit.

Ross, John & Hannah Montgomery, 12 June 1816; William Allison, bondsman; Isaac Alexander, wit.

Ross, John P. & Sarah A. Matthews, 19 Nov 1839; J. H. Sample, bondsman; B. Oates, C. C. C., wit.

Ross, John P. & Sarah Oliver, 8 Jan 1858; Robt. M. Oates, bondsman; W. K. Reid, C. C. C., wit. married 11 Jan 1859 by J. Rumple, minister.

Ross, Joseph C. & Jane Oliver, 15 Dec 1842; Franklin Edmonds, bondsman.

Ross, Joseph W. (Dr.) & Sophia C. Springs, 19 Feb 1822; Robert H. Morrison, bondsman; Isaac Alexander, wit.

Ross, Joseph W. & Elizabeth T. A. Price, 10 July 1850; John L. Watson, bondsman; B. Oates, C. C. C., wit.

Ross, Peter E. & Sarah C. McIntire, 11 March 1830; Ezekiel Elms, bondsman; B. Oates, wit.

Ross, Reuben E. & Mary Hipp, 3 Dec 1823; John Hall, bondsman; Isaac S. Alexander, wit.

Ross, Robt. A.& Mary Jane Grier, 30 Oct 1848; Francis M. Ross, bondsman; Saml. J. Lourie, wit.

Ross, William & Nancy H. Patton, 27 May 1841; John Walker, bondsman;

Ross, William J. & Margaret N. Harrison, 18 Dec 1850; Thos. A. Sales, bondsman; Saml. J. Lourie, J. P., wit.

Ross, Wm. M. & Margaret T. Pool, 24 July 1855; James McConnel, bondsman; W. K. Reid, C. C. C., wit. married 24 July 1855 by R. H. Lafferty, minister.

Rowan, William & Margaret Franklin, 6 April 1809; James Taylor, bondsman; Isaac Alexander, wit.

Rowe, Peter & Betsey Festerman, 17 June 1852; A. H. Martin, bondsman; B. Oates, wit.

Rowland, James & Cynthia Miller, 25 July 1836; John Pascoe, bondsman.

Rozzell, Thomas & Hannah M. A. Pettus, 23 Sept 1835; Patrick J. Wilson, bondsman.

Rudesill, Jonas C. & Mary C. Kerr, 26 Nov 1825; James McKee, bondsman; Isaac S.Alexander, wit.

Rudisill, John & Milissa McLeary, 27 July 1821; James McKnight, bondsman; Isaac Alexander, wit.

Rudisill, Jonas & Susanah Clarke, 19 Sept 1793; Jonas Clark, bondsman.

Run, Andrew & Cynthia Beatey, 2 June 1841; Wm. Boyles, bondsman; J. M. Stewart, wit.

Russ, Levi & Sally Riley, 27 Sept 1821; Jos. Rogers, bondsman; Isaac Alexander, wit.

Russ, William & Amanda Benfield, 30 Sept 1856; Ananias Jordan, bondsman; W. K. Reid, C. C. C., wit. married 2 Oct 1856 by B. H. Garrison, J. P.

Russel, Andrew & Linda Perry (colored), 30 Nov 1865; Edom Watt, bondsman; R. M. White, wit. married 30 Nov 1865 by J. C. Russell.

Russel, James S. & Peggy Gingles,8 Feb 1809; John Gingles, bondsman.

Russel, Robert W. & Sarah Flow, 19 Jan 1853; W. L. Gingles, bondsman; B. Oates, C. C. C., wit. married 27 Jan 1853 by Walter W. Pharr.

Russel, Thomas & Sarah Irwin, 22 May 1792; Philip Weeks, bondsman; Isaac Alexander, wit.

Russell, David M. & Nancy Jane Hunter, 25 Feb 1854; John M. W. Flow, bondsman; W. K. Reid, C. C. C.,wit. married 2 March 1854 by John Hunter, minister.

Russell, Harrey T. & J. E. Baker, 19 July 1860; George F. Baker, bondsman; W. K. Reid, C. C. C., wit. married 19 July 1860 by F. M. Ross, J. P.

Russell, James & Catherine Wolf, 10 Dec 1824; John E. Walker, bondsman; Isaac Alexander,wit.

Russell, Lewis H. & Martha M. Morrow, 23 Dec 1847; Wm. B. Hawkins, bondsman; B. Oates, C. C. C.,wit.

Rutherford, Thomas & Margaret A. Lemmond, 27 Feb 1832; Joseph Walker, bondsman.

Rutledge, Elijah & Frances Urie, 6 Aug 1801; Samuel Bighim, bondsman.

Rutledge, George & Rachel McComb, 18 May 1799; Andrew Johnson, bondsman; Isaac Alexander, wit.

Rylie, Ezekiel A. & Sarah B. Gibson, 28 Dec 1835; Rufus L. Alexander, bondsman; B. Oates, wit.

Rylie, John & Temperence Holton, 19 May 1832; Samuel T. Hutchison, bondsman; B. Oates, wit.

Rylie, Lee C. & Eliza C. Wily, 6 Feb 1831; Ira A. Orr, bondsman; E. Elms, wit.

Rylie, William & Amy Roberts, 2 Dec 1805; Philip Roberts, bondsman; Isaac Alexander, wit.

Sadler, A. F. & Nancy C. Sloan, 31 Jan 1842; G. C. Cathy, bondsman; C. T. Alexander, wit.

Sadler, Anderson & Rebecca Blythe, 20 April 1809; Charles Paten, bondsman; Archd. Cathey, wit.

Sadler, Anderson & Nancy Walker, 4 Feb 1819; Samuel Blyth, bondsman; Isaac Alexander, wit.

Sadler, Henry & Elizth. Carpenter, 14 June 1791; Alexander Cathey, bondsman; Ruthy Alexander, wit.

Sadler, James & Lucy Searcy, 2 May 1827; William Hutchison, bondsman.

Sadler, John & Sabrina Lentile, 30 July 1827; Shadrick Lentile, bondsman.

Sainsing, Littleton C. & Eliza Lancaster, 18 April 1823; Jacob Sainsing, bondsman; Eli Springs, wit.

Saint, John & Flora Brownfield, 27 Jan 1802; Jonas Rudisil, bondsman.

Sammons, William O. & Martha W. Kirkpatrick, 17 Oct 1823; Allen Reid, bondsman; Isaac Alexander, wit.

Samonds, Thomas K. & Mary M. Brown, 1 June 1854; Thomas A. Kirkpatrick, bondsman; W. K. Reid, C. C. C.,wit. married 1 June 1854 by S. C. Pharr.

Sample, Caldwell & Martha Houston, 4 Jan 1791; Samuel Sample, William Huston, bondsmen; Isaac Alexander, wit.

Sample, J. Elam & Margaret C. McKee, 25 Aug 1840; John Weeks, bondsman; B. Oates, C. C. C., wit.

Sample, James & Martha Robinson, 14 June 1802; John Robison, bondsman; Tho. Henderson, wit.

Sample, James & Martha Alexander, 8 Feb 1853; William N. Alexander, bondsman; B. Oates, C. C. C., wit. married 10 Feb 1853 by J. Walker, J. P.

Sample, Joseph & Elizabeth Robison, 4 Feb 1801; Joel Alexander, bondsman.

Sample, Robert A. & Sarah N. Alexander, 30 Aug 1826; William A. Sample, bondsman; Isaac Alexander, wit.

Sample, William & Sally Smith, 17 Jan 1804; William Hayes, bondsman; Isaac Alexander, wit.

Sample, William & Leah Bolick, 3 Feb 1857; Noah Bolick, bondsman; John Phelan, wit. married 5 Feb 1857 by William Reid, J. P.

Sample, William A. & Jane L. Barry, 22 Dec 1829;Robert F. Barnett, bondsman; Isaac S. Alexander, wit.

Sanders, Garner & Rebecca T. Osborn, 25 Jan 1814; Ephraim Kendrick, bondsman; Isaac Alexander, wit.

Sanders, Peter Franklin & Sarah Adeline Jamison, 11 April 1850; Thomas Jefferson Freeman, bondsman; B. Oates, C. C. C., wit.

Sanders, Tillman & Polly Roberts, 9 Jan 1807; Ezra Alexander, bondsman; Isaac Alexander, wit.

Sanders, William Jacob & Eliza Lancaster, 14 Mav 1858; J. B. Kerr, bondsman; W. K. Reid, C. C. C., wit.

Sandifer, John & Ellen Greer (colored), 12 Aug 1865; Simon Houston (colored), bondsman.

Sandifer, T. T. (Dr.) & Elizabeth S. Graham, 23 Jan 1866; G. M. Norment, bondsman; Wm. Maxwell, C. C. C., wit. married 1 Feb 1866 by William W. Power.

Sandifer, Tho. T. & Ann M. Wilson, 21 April 1840; Jno. M. Wilson, bondsman.

Sandres, Isaac C. & Mary S. Harris, 5 July 1838; Richard Searcey, bondsman; B. Oates, C. C. C., wit.

Saunier, Peter E. & Harriet L. Williams, 21 Sept 1837.

Saville, Austin & Martha Wilson, 2 Jan 1837; James Stewart, bondsman; B. Oates, wit.

Sawyer, Willis & Mary King, 3 Feb 1795; Philip King, bondsman; Shared Gray, wit.

Saxon, Seth & Mary Barnhill, 22 May 1820; John Auton, bondsman.

Scarlett, George & Margaret Smith, 16 Dec 1835; William A. Todd, bondsman; B. Oates, C. C. C., wit.

Scarr, Francis & Lydia Tiddy, 14 Dec 1857; Jno Phelan, bondsman; W. K. Reid, C. C. C., wit. married 16 Dec 1857 by Alex. _____.

Scott, Abraham & Mrs. Nancy Lewing, 9 April 1825; William Scott, bondsman; Isaac Alexander, wit.

Scott, Alexander & Martha Simpson, 24 May 1819; David Simpson, William Simpson, bondsmen; Isaac S.Alexander, wit.

Scott, James M. & Ellen Sharpe, 4 April 1848; Wm. W. Quinn, bondsman; S. J. Lourie, wit.

Scott, William & Lucy Johnston, 1 Jan 1800; Andrew Lawing, bondsman.

Scott, Wm. B. & Minerva Jones, 9 Jan 1847; Isaac F. Jones, bondsman; Saml. J. Lourie, wit.

Searcy, Richard & Sally Holton, 28 March 1838; John Sercy, bondsman; B. Oates, C. C. C., wit.

Searsey, John & Elizabeth Wallis, 29 Jan 1828; John Flaniken, bondsman; Tho. B. Smartt, wit.

Secres, Thomas & Susannah Richardson, 2 Sept 1819; Jacob Secrest, bondsman; John Rea, wit.

Secrest, Abram & Milly Pyron, 15 Sept 1825; Michel Crowell, bondsman; Isaac Alexander, wit.

Secrest, Jacob & Patsey Barnett, 13 June 1811; John Secrest, bondsman; Isaac Alexander, wit.

Secrest, Leroy & Malinda Barnett, 26 Feb 1816; Jacob Secrest, bondsman.

Secrest, Wiley & Millecy Jane Lany, 21 April 1827; Jacob Secrest, bondsman; Wm. Pyron, wit.

Secrest, William M. & Jane Wiley, 25 Oct 1820: Robert McEwen, bondsman.

Segars, Hyram, & Elizabeth Wylie, 4 Feb 1818; Robert Johnston, bondsman; Isaac S. Alexander, wit.

Segraves, J. A. & Margaret Ballard, 3 Aug 1865; Wm. Cross, bondsman; Wm. Maxwell, C. C. C.,wit. married 4 Aug 1865 by Jno. F. Butt.

Self, Malchizedeck, & Catharine Moore, 17 March 1801; Henry Ford, bondsman.

Sellars, John C. & Elizabeth Householder, 24 Aug 1830; Charles
N. Price, bondsman; Isaac S. Alexander, wit.

Sercy, Thomas C. & Caroline King, 7 March 1866; R. R. Sercy,
bondsman; Wm. Maxwell, wit.

Sersy, Thomas B. & Martha Ann Howell, 23 July 1849; Robert S.
Price, bondsman; B. Oates, C. C. C., wit.

Shaffer, Frederick & Margaret Brown, 17 Aug 1803; John H. Hood,
bondsman.

Shaffer, James S. & Sarah J. Morris, 5 Jan 1861; David O. Maxwell,
bondsman; W. K. Reid, C. C. C., wit. married 8 Jan 1861 by
W. R. Maxwell, J. P.

Shaffer, Tunas & Margaret Pharis, 29 March 1793; Philemon Morris,
bondsman; Isaac Alexander, wit.

Shaffer, William & Hannah Sloan, 13 March 1833; William Morris,
bondsman; B. Oates, D. C., wit.

Shannon, Andrew J. & Elizabeth J. Walker, 7 Feb 1860; James M.
Warwick, bondsman; W. R. Maxwell, wit. married 7 Feb 1860 by
W. R. Maxwell, J. P.

Shanon, James & Hannah Hamilton, 21 Sept 1821; William Hamilton,
bondsman; Isaac Alexander, wit.

Sharp, John & Jane Scott, 20 Feb 1837; Azriah Sharp, bondsman.

Sharp, John M. & Caroline Reed, 22 Jan 1840; John Reid, bondsman;
B. Oates, C. C. C., wit.

Sharp, Richard Sr. & Ann Vanpelt, 18 Nov 1807; Samuel Flanigan,
bondsman; Isaac Alexander, wit.

Sharp, Thomas Allen & Emily Patterson, 13 Nov 1849; Mark Alexander,
bondsman; Saml. J. Lourie, wit.

Sharp, William & Mary Mulwee, 3 May 1818; Whitme Hill, bondsman.

Sharpe, John & Sarah Jane Taylor, 18 Sept 1854; R. James Reid,
bondsman; W. K. Reid, C. C. C., wit. married 9 Dec 1854 by
J. B. McLaughlin, J. P.

Sharpley, William & Betsey Bibb, 9 Oct 1816; William Allison,
bondsman; Isaac Alexander, wit.

Shaver, Jacob & Margaret Brown, 15 June 1796; John Brown, bondsman.

Shaver, Monroe & Sarah A. K. Deaton, 16 Jan 1860; James R. Deaton,
bondsman; W. K. Reid, C. C. C., wit. married 18 Jan 1859 by
W. S. Barnett, J.P.

Shaw, A. C. & Julia Wade, 6 Nov 1860; William Durden, bondsman;
P. S. Whisnant, wit.

Shaw, Alexander & Amelia De Armond, 5 Dec 1860; D. C. Shaw,
bondsman; P. S. Whisnant, wit. married 6 Dec 1860 by John
Hunter, minister.

Shaw, D. C. & Mary M. Reid, 16 July 1864; J. W. Ross, bondsman;
Wm. Maxwell, C. C. C., wit. married 17 July 1865 by R. Z.
Johnston, minister.

Shelby, David H. & Mary Berryhill, 20 Oct 1858; John M. Shelby,
   bondsman; K. W. Berryhill, wit. married 21 Oct 1858 by
W. H. Neal, J. P.

Shelby, James L. & Henrietta T.Warren, 30 April 1856; William J.
   Brittain, bondsman; W. K. Reid, C. C. C.,wit. married 1 May
1856 by H. B. Cunningham.

Shelby, John M. & Martha J. McDonald, 8 Aug 1859; D. W. McDonald,
   bondsman; W. K. Reid, C. C. C., wit. married 9 Aug 1859 by
J. B. Watt, V. D. M.

Shelby, Smith & Eliza Bodkin, 15 Oct 1831; Charles B. Wilson,
   bondsman; A. B. Jetton, wit.

Shelby, Thomas & Matilda McDonald, 2 Sept 1820; Robert Kerns,
   bondsman; Isaac Alexander, wit.

Shelby, William W. & Margaret J. Kerr, 22 Jan 1859; Wm. J. Kerr,
   bondsman; Jno. Phelan, wit. married 25 Jan 1859 by G. L.
Campbell, J. P.

Shelby, Winfield & Melisa Alexander, 7 Dec 1830; Charles B.
   Wilson, bondsman; A. B. Jetton, wit.

Shell, Henry & Mary Ann Byram, 28 Oct 1834; Thomas Boyd, bondsman;
   B. Oates, wit.

Shepherd, George F. & Mary L. Irwin, 29 Dec 1856; George A. Locke,
   bondsman; W. K. Reid, C. C. C., wit. married 31 Dec 1856 by
E. F. Rockwell, V. D. M.

Shepherd, Thomas & Mary Cashon, 1 Feb 1803; Henry Conner, bondsman; Jas. Conner, wit.

Sheppard, Docter & Judy McNeely (colored), 31 Aug 1865; Saml.
   McNeely, bondsman; Wm. Maxwell, C. C. C., wit. married 31
Aug 1865 by Wm. H. Pitts, Elder.

Shields, David & Jane Moffett, 5 Feb 1803; Robert Shields, bondsman

Shields, James & Nancy Thomilson, 20 March 1833; William Shields,
   bondsman; W. W. Elms, wit.

Shields, James & Cynthia Michal, 26 March 1865; J. D. Boyt, bondsman; W. W. Grier, wit. married 26 March 1865 by W. G. Barnett,
J. P.

Shields, Robert & Martha Alexander, 16 Feb 1801; Isaac Alexander,
   bondsman; Isaac Alexander, wit.

Shields, Thomas & Margaret C. Alexander, 5 Dec 1833; Robert M.
   Clark, bondsman; B. Oates, C. C. C., wit.

Shipley, George & Elizabeth McCord, 5 May 1783; Michael McCleary,
   bondsman; Sam. Martin, wit.

Shiply, Robert & Mary McCracken, 30 Sept 1790; Moses McClure,
   bondsman; Isaac Alexander, wit.

Shive, C. C. & Mary D. Harris, 9 Aug 1853; E. Nye Hutchison,
   bondsman; Braly Oates, C. C. C., wit. married 9 Aug 1853.

Shof, John & Elizabeth Warsham, 10 March 1838; John Brinkley,
   bondsman; James Johnston, wit.

Showalter, Alexander & Rebecca Kezziah, 22 Feb 1866; E. L. Bowdon, bondsman; Wm. Maxwell, C. C. C., wit. married 22 Feb 1866 by Jno. F. Butt.

Shuman, James & Martha Beaty, 11 April 1850; A. N. Gray, bondsman; B. Oates, C. C. C., wit.

Shuman, James & Margaret Steoof, 1 Jan 1857; G. W. Williamson, bondsman; W. K. Reid, C. C. C., wit. married 1 Jan 1857 by J. P. Ross, J. P.

Shuman, James & Jane Steuffer, 13 May 1863; A. N. Gray, bondsman; married 13 May 1863 by J. P. Ross, J. P.

Sibley, William & Sarah Carlock, 2 Oct 1832; Jerh. Wentz, bondsman.

Sikes, D. W. & Miss Roze Alley, 16 Sept 1865; R. M. White, bondsman; Wm. Maxwell, wit. married 21 Sept 1865 by A. L. Stough, M. G.

Sikes, Joshua & Peggy Russle, 15 Jan 1818; Wm Downs(?), bondsman; John Rea, wit.

Simeson, James & Martha Stevenson, 25 Feb 1796; John Simeson, bondsman.

Simeson, John & Mrs. Ann Martin, 16 May 1799; William McKee, bondsman.

Simeson, John & ---- Hall, 29 April 1816; Samuel B. Martin, bondsman; A. M. Alexander, wit.

Simmons, James & Lucy Clark, 19 March 1808; Thomas Simons, bondsman; Isaac Alexander, wt.

Simmons, Jesse & Mary Clifton, 5 Nov 1818; John Cagle (Eagle?), bondsman.

Simmons, John & Sarah Gallway, 25 Dec 1815; Josiah Gallway, bondsman.

Simmons, Jno. W. & Sarah A. Jamison, 9 Sept 1840; Archibald Frew, bondsman.

Simmons, Peter & Sylva White (colored), 28 Dec 1865; Thomas Ferguson, bondsman; Wm. Maxwell, C. C. C., wit. married 28 Dec 1865 by Richd. H. Griffith.

Simmons, Thomas & Charity Orr, 17 Aug 1865; George King, bondsman; married 29 July 1865 by John Alexander, M. G.

Simmons, William C. & Sarah A. Sloan, 26 Nov 1838; Andrew J. Kimbrell, bondsman; B. Oates, C. C. C., wit.

Simons, John & Eliz. Maxwell, 26 Jan 1796; Thomas Simons, bondsman; Isaac Alexander, wit.

Simons, Solomon & Cloey Doster, 18 June 1798; Shared Gray, bondsman; James Ligett, wit.

Simonton, John & Jane Falls, 22 Oct 1792; John Falls, bondsman; Geo. Graham, wit.

Simpson, Benjamin & Matilda Prim, 9 Jan 1832; John C. Freasure, bondsman.

Simpson, D. J. & Mary Taylor, 11 July 1863; John R. Morris, bondsman; Wm. Maxwell, C. C. C., wit. married 11 July 1863 by
Jos. L. Phillips, J. P.

Simpson, D. Jerrod & Martha Taylor, 7 Aug 1852; James C. Flow,
bondsman; C. B. Cross, J. P., wit. married 27 Aug 1852 by
C. B. Cross, J. P.

Simpson, David Jr., & Mary M. Rice, 3 Jan 1840; Jarrod Rice,
bondsman; W. H. Simpson, J. P., wit.

Simpson, George & Sarah Griffeth, 1 Sept 1796; Givens White,
bondsman; Jas. Conner, wit.

Simpson, George & Nancy Law, 20 May 1813; James McLaughlin, bondsman; Robt. Wilson, wit.

Simpson, James & Hannah Waddington, 6 April 1805; John Simpson,
bondsman; Isaac Alexander, wit.

Simpson, James & Nancy Waggoner, 7 Dec 1826; Edmond Caldwell,
bondsman; A. B. Jetton, wit.

Simpson, John & Mary Moore, 9 Feb 1816; Thomas Simpson, bondsman.

Simpson, John & Jane Barnett, 14 Oct 1828; John McQuay, bondsman;
Pearsall Thompson, wit.

Simpson, John Jr. & Malinda Hooks, 14 Nov 1833; John M. Pyron,
bondsman.

Simpson, John Sr. & Polly Eastridge, 14 Feb 1835; Wm. H. Simpson,
J. P., wit.

Simpson, John H. & Elizabeth Tomberlin, 20 April 1842; Wm. Q.
Lemmond, bondsman.

Simpson, John H. & Elizabeth M. Cochron, 9 Aug 1845; Wm. Q.
Lemmonds, bondsman; Isaac S. Alexander, wit.

Simpson, Pearson & Martha Simpson, 29 Sept 1836; John M. Simpson,
bondsman; W. H. Simpson, wit.

Simpson, Thomas & Jean Simpson, 8 March 1831; John Simpson, bondsman; B. Oates, D. C., wit.

Simril, Francis H. & Eliza R. McDowal, 4 Jan 1827; H. J. Cathcart,
bondsman; Pearsall Thompson, wit.

Simril, Franklin G. & Martha Taylor, 15 Sept 1834; Robert Sloan,
bondsman; B. Oates, C. C. C., wit.

Simrill, F. G. & Elizabeth Cathey, 15 Jan 1845; Alexander Springs,
bondsman.

Sims, James J. & Rachel S. Berryhill, 27 Dec 1860; J. H. Potts,
bondsman; W. W. Grier, wit. married 27 Dec 1860 by Richd.
H. Griffith, M. G.

Sims, Nathaniel & Mary A. Morrison, 23 March 1846; James M.
Black, bondsman; B. Oates, C. C. C., wit.

Sing, Ananias & Margaret A. Kerr, 7 Feb 1838; W. K. Reid, bondsman.

Sizer, William & Anne E. McGinn, 23 Dec 1861; T. F. McGinn, bondsman; W. K. Reid, C. C. C.,wit. married 24 Dec 1861 by J. P. Ross, J. P.

Skillenton, John Brown & Martha Caldwell, 27 June 1791; John Hamilton, bondsman; Wm. B. Alexander, wit.

Skiner, Jamiah & Nancey Freeman, 19 Feb 1840; William Roark, bondsman; Philemon Morris, wit.

Skinner, Charles E. & Mary M. Haynes, 9 April 1864; J. B. Boyt, bondsman; Wm. Maxwell, wit. married 10 April 1864 by Wm. S. Norment, J. P.

Skinner, Loranzo D. & Delila Phifer, 24 Nov 1835; Joel Coble, bondsman.

Skinner, Wm. E. & Caroline Barnhill, 2 March 1842; Moses Carter, bondsman; C. T. Alexander, wit.

Slaughter, Lewis G. & Lucinda Dinkins, 20 June 1833; Thomas Mull, bondsman.

Slaughter, Peter & Christian Graham, 20 March 1832; Nathaniel Pabworth, bondsman.

Sloan, A. B. & Sarah Jane Cooper, 27 Feb 1854; Richard B. Harry, bondsman; W. K. Reid, C. C. C.,wit. married 28 Feb 1854 by J. B. Watt, V. D. M.

Sloan, Benjamin & Rachel Wallis, 9 April 1827; Robert D. Alexander, bondsman; Jno. Hutchison, wit.

Sloan, David & Patsey Cashon, 5 Nov 1823; James Doherty, bondsman.

Sloan, Edward & Sarah Slone, 13 Sept 1824; William M. Stinson, bondsman.

Sloan, Edward B. D. & Rebecca C. Sloan, 8 March 1837; Henry D. W. Alexander, bondsman; B. Oates, C. C. C., wit.

Sloan, Edwin R. & Sarah E. Kerns, 2 July 1855; Hugh W. Stinson, bondsman; W. K. Reid, C. C. C.,wit.

Sloan, George F. & Elizabeth Terrence, 24 Oct 1825; William Wynens, bondsman; J. Doherty, wit.

Sloan, H. Thompson & Josephine E. Kerr, 1 Jan 1851; S. Nye Hutchison, bondsman; B. Oates, wit.

Sloan, Henery & Elizabeth Shaffer, 4 Aug 1835; Henry Hunter, bondsman; B. Oates, C. C. C., wit.

Sloan, Henry A. & Harriett C. Stinson, 30 Nov 1831; Edward B. O. Sloan, bondsman; Isaac S. Alexander, wit.

Sloan, I. John & Hannah P. McDonald, 10 Feb 1858; Saml. J. Lourie, bondsman; John Phelan, wit. married 11 Feb 1858 by G. D. Parks, M. G.

Sloan, James & Jenny Alexander, 31 May 1800; James Curry, bondsman.

Sloan, James & Elizabeth Shields, 6 Dec 1806; William Gardner, bondsman; Isaac Alexander, wit.

Sloan, James D. & Mary E. Hill, 23 March 1830; Walter A. Hill, bondsman; B. Oates, wit.

Sloan, James H. & Sarah Steele, 21 April 1859; James F. Ferrell, bondsman; John Phelan, wit.

Sloan, James L. & Harriet M. Sloan, 16 Dec 1854; S. N. Weddington, bondsman; W. K. Reid, C. C. C., wit. married 19 Dec 1854 by Walter S. Pharr.

Sloan, James M. & Martha Marshall, 28 July 1827; James H. Brown, bondsman.

Sloan, James M. & Sarah E. Wiley, 4 Dec 1852; William L. Henderson, bondsman; Braly Oates, C. C. C., wit. married 7 Dec 1852 by Walter S. Pharr.

Sloan, John & Elizabeth Elliott, 8 Oct 1821; Robert McCombs, bondsman; Isaac Alexander, wit.

Sloan, John & Dovy Barry, 27 May 1829; John McKinley, bondsman; Isaac S. Alexander, wit.

Sloan, John & Eliza P. Graham, 12 May 1852; James W. Dick, bondsman; Braly Oates, C. C. C., wit. married 13 May 1852 by C. Johnston, V. D. M.

Sloan, John F. & Nancy R. Kennedy, 25 Oct 1855; Hugh W. Stinson, bondsman; W. K. Reid, C. C. C., wit. married 30 Oct 1855 by R. H. Lafferty, minister.

Sloan, John G.& Mary S. Clampet, 7 March 1860; A. H. Cheshire, bondsman; W. K. Reid, C. C. C., wit.

Sloan, Robert & Ruth Beaty, 14 Feb 1800; William Beaty, bondsman.

Sloan, Robert & Sarah Robison, 22 Jan 1811; Ezekiel Robison, bondsman; Isaac S. Alexander, wit.

Sloan, Robert & Margaret Gilmor, 28 Sept 1825; David Parks, bondsman; Isaac Alexander, wit.

Sloan, Robert J. & Sarah C. Stewart, 6 May 1852; Thos. H. Brem, bondsman; B. Oates, C. C. C., wit. married 6 May 1852 by John Hunter, Minister.

Sloan, Samuel & Celia Shaffer, 30 Sept 1833; William C. Corum, bondsman.

Sloan, Thomas & Deborah McAulay, 13 April 1816; Reuben M. Irwin, bondsman.

Sloan, Thomas A. & Eliza J. Warsham, 5 Jan 1853; James L. Sloan, bondsman; B. Oates, C. C. C., wit. married 11 Jan 1853 by Walter S. Pharr.

Sloan, William B. & Rocinda W. Hill, 26 Dec 1832; Joseph Harrison, bondsman; B. Oates, D. C.,wit.

Sloan, William B. & Ruth B. Wallace, 21 Sept 1844; Calvin M. Ray, bondsman; N. B. Taylor, wit.

Sloan, William L. & Rachel H. Berryhill, 12 Jan 1858; K. W. Berryhill, bondsman; Wallace Berryhill, wit. married 14 Jan 1858 by Jas. C. Nicholson, J. P.

MECKLENBURG MARRIAGES 1783-1868

Smart, Denton & Rosey McWhorter, 26 Feb 1800; Robert Locky, bondsman; Andw. Walker, J. P., wit.

Smartt, Francis B. & Elizabeth Henderson, 3 March 1802; Isaac S.
Henderson, bondsman.

Smartt, George White & Susanna Barnett, 10 Oct 1796; Wm. McRee,
bondsman; Isaac Alexander, wit.

Smartt, Little Bery & Mida Page, 20 Sept 1791; Geo. Smartt, bondsman; Isaac Alexander, wit.

Smith, Abraham & Sally Pervines, 15 Dec 1827; Robert Wilson,
bondsman; Pearsall Thompson, wit.

Smith, Albert J. & Martha E. Elms, 9 June 1865; W. M. Matthews,
bondsman; W. W. Grier, wit.

Smith, Alexander & Peggy Freeman, 30 Jan 1811; Drury Smith, bondsman.

Smith, Ambrus & Sarah Reed, 12 Oct 1812; Edmond Smith, bondsman;
Isaac S. Alexander,wit.

Smith, Bassel & Catharine Byrum, 27 April 1820; James Walker,
bondsman; Isaac Alexander, wit.

Smith, Benjamin B. & Mary B. Knox, 2 Jan 1838; A. M. Rankin,
bondsman; Hugh McAulay, J. P., wit.

Smith, Benjamin R. & Nancy S. Rea, 7 Feb 1832; James W. Spratt,
bondsman; B. Oates, wit.

Smith, Bob & Martha H. Steele (colored), 25 Oct 1858; John
Phelan, wit. married 25 Oct 1858 by Wm. S. Norment, J. P.

Smith, Burton Jr. & Sarah Stewart, 11 Oct 1850; John R. Daniel,
bondsman; B. Oates, C. C. C., wit.

Smith, Cheek & Rebekah Smartt, 31 Jan 1803; Cylass Cheek, bondsman; Isaac Alexander, wit.

Smith, D. H. & M. L. Elliottt, 21 Aug 1860; L. H. Smith, bondsman;
P. S. Whisnant, wit. married 21 Aug 1860 by James C. Chalmers.

Smith, Daniel & Sarah E. Mason, 27 Feb 1816; Thomas Boyd, bondsman;
Isaac S. Alexander, wit.

Smith, Daniel K. & Nancy A. Alexander, 21 Dec 1846; James M. Thorne,
bondsman; Saml. J. Lourie, wit.

Smith, Drury & Rebeca Glover, 4 Jan 1809; Hartill Glover, bondsman.

Smith, Edmond & Nancy Porter, 13 Oct 1831; John Miller, bondsman.

Smith, Edmond & Sarah C. Jamison, 22 July 1840; E. G. Walker,
bondsman; B. Oates, wit.

Smith, Edmond & Josephine Pinion, 17 Oct 1864; William Mccombs,
bondsman; Wm. Maxwell, C. C. C., wit.

Smith, Eliphus & Abigail Garrison, 25 Jan 181-; John C. Garrison,
bondsman; Chas. T. Alexander, wit.

Smith, Franklin & Rebecca Jane Kennedy, 7 March 1861; Junius
  Philips, bondsman; W. K. Reid, C. C. C., wit. married 7 March
1861 by C. Overman, J. P.

Smith, Franklin L. & Isabella Torrance, 9 Sept 1835; Green W.
  Caldwell, bondsman; B. Oates, C. C. C., wit.

Smith, Howel & Martha Kennedy, 30 April 1794; Thomas Kenedy,
  bondsman.

Smith, James B. & Nancy Gilleland, 24 Sept 1822; James Dearmond,
  bondsman.

Smith, James D. & Isabella Calder, 26 Sept 1827; John Graham,
  bondsman.

Smith, James H. & Abigail Johnston, 10 April 1857; John R.
  Smith, bondsman; W. K. Reid, C. C. C., wit; married 14 April
1857 by John E. Pressly, minister of Coddle Creek, Cabarrus
County, N. C.

Smith, James W. & Margaret L. Porter, 16 July 1860; Stephen D.
  Smith, bondsman; W. K. Reid, C. C. C.,wit. married 19 July
1860 by J. C. Chalmers.

 Smith, Joab P. & Mrs. J. S. Moss, 9 Oct 1848; E. N. Hutchison,
  M. D., bondsman; Saml. J. Lourie, wit.

Smith, John & Martha Osborn, 25 Feb 1800.

Smith, John & Deborah P. Campbell, 16 Dec 1818; Thomas Coal,
  bondsman; Isaac Alexander, wit.

Smith, John & Ann Rowlands, 6 Nov 1820; David Termmire, bondsman;
  Isaac Alexander, wit.

Smith, John S. & Hannah J. Davis, 19 April 1859; Daniel W. Smith,
  bondsman; W. K. Reid, wit. married 20 April 1859 by O. A.
Darby.

Smith, Jonothen D. & Margaret E. Caldwell, 31 July 1846; Saml.
  W. Caldwell, bondsman; A. B. Taylor, wit.

Smith, Joseph & Martha T. Johnston, 3 Sept 1864; B. W. Alexander,
  bondsman; Wm. Maxwell, C. C. C., wit. married 24 Nov 1864 by
Walter S. Pharr.

Smith, Joseph N. & Nancy Martin, 9 Oct 1824; Samuel Martin, bondsman; Isaac Alexander, wit.

Smith, Miller & Mary Miller, 15 April 1816; Jno Campbell, bondsman;
  Isaac Alexander, wit.

Smith, Neil & Margaret Foster, 17 Feb 1818; Robert Duffey, bondsman;
  Isaac Alexander, wit.

Smith, Robert & Mary Young, 19 Dec 1795; John Brown, bondsman;
  Ruth Alexander, wit.

Smith, S. B. & Mary C. Wilson, 9 Sept 1851; E. A. McLeod, bondsman;
  James Parks, wit. married 10 Sept 1851 by P. Tinsley Penick.

Smith, Samuel & Agness McRaven, 16 Nov 1790; William Bean, bondsman; Isaac Alexander, wit.

Smith, Samuel B. & Nancy E. Hall, 3 Feb 1859; S. M. McCall, bondsman; W. K. Reid, C. C. C., wit. married 3 Feb 1859 by J. M. Pyron, J. P.

Smith, Samuel H. & Mary Flanagan, 27 Jan 1835; Wm. S. W. Hayes, bondsman; B. Oates, C. C. C., wit.

Smith, Samuel R. & Chesy Bagget, 13 Sept 1821; Burton Smith, bondsman; Wm. Pyron, J. P., wit.

Smith, Stephen H. & Martha Cowan, 9 Aug 1834; Robert R. Taylor, bondsman.

Smith, Sumner J. & Nancy Neil Todd, 6 July 1844; N. B. Taylor, bondsman.

Smith, Thomas & Margaret Miller, 19 Nov 1827; Abraham O. Miller, bondsman; Tho. B. Smartt, wit.

Smith, Thomas & Sarah Ann Black, 13 Feb 1829; Thomas McCall, bondsman; Pearsall Thompson, wit.

Smith, Thomas McGhee & Julia S. Alexander, 30 March 1858; S. P. Alexander, bondsman; W. K. Reid, C. C. C., wit. married 30 March 1858 by Alexander Sinclair, Presbyterian pastor.

Smith, W. M. & Alice O. Davis, 4 April 1866; F. S. DeWolfe, bondsman; Wm. Maxwell, C. C. C., wit. married 12 April 1866 by William C. Power, M. G.

Smith, William & Catharine Miller, 21 Aug 1790; Samuel Monteith, bondsman; Isaac Alexander, wit.

Smith, William & Sabina Armond, 20 April 1814; Hezekiah Alexander, bondsman.

Smith, William & Dorcus Purser, 10 March 1825; Robert Simpson, bondsman; Wm. Pyron, wit.

Smith, William & Nancy McGuyer, 25 Jan 1837; M. A. Edwards, bondsman; B. Oates, C. C. C., wit.

Smith, William & Dorcus S. Campbell, 9 Feb 1846; Cyrus F. Campbell, bondsman; S. J. Lourie, wit.

Smith, William & Caroline McGinnis, 13 Jan 1866; Thos. H. Brem, bondsman; Wm. Maxwell, wit. married 16 Jan 1866 by I. S. McLaughlin.

Smith, William A. & Frances Cathey, 4 Nov 1865; R. D. R. Fite, bondsman; Wm. Maxwell, C. C. C., wit. married 7 Nov 1865 by S. C. Pharr

Smith, William D. & Ann R.Rives, 5 Dec 1848; William Moss, bondsman; P. S. Whisnant, wit.

Smith, William H. & Elizabeth Henderson, 6 Aug 1823; William J. Campbell, bondsman; Isaac Alexander, wit.

Smith, William O. & Jane Miller, 7 May 1822; John Black, bondsman; Isaac Alexander, wit.

Smith, Wm. S. & Margaret D. Pyron, 29 Feb 1864; S. B. Smith, bondsman; Wm. Maxwell, c. C. C., wit. married 29 Feb 1864 by Wm. McDonald.

Snell, Isaac H. & Jane M. Towle, 15 Aug 1848; Thos. M. Alexander, bondsman; Saml. J. Lourie, wit.

Snell, James & Mary Rogers, 10 May 1819; Andrew McCredie, bondsman.

Snell, John & Elizabeth Griffith, 1 March 1825; Milton Blear, bondsman; Isaac S. Alexander, wit.

Snyder, Wm. F. & Mary C. Rowark, 16 June 1859; David Barnett, bondsman; John Phelan, wit. married 61 June 1859 by Alex. Phillippe.

Solomon, James & Polly Cook, 31 Aug 1853; Caleb Erwin, bondsman; B. Oates, C. C. C., wit. married 1 Sept 1853 by ___ Garrison, J. P.

Solomon, W. R. & Nancy C. Nelson, 1 June 1863; John Allen, bondsman; Wm. Maxwell, C. C. C., wit. married 1 June 1863 by I. S. McLaughlin.

Sossmon, John & Mary Hodge, 23 Sept 1826; William S. Alexander, bondsman.

Sossman, John & Margaret Reddish, 11 Jan 1833; William J. Black, bondsman.

Spain, David & Betsey McClure, 2 Oct 1806; Turner Pullen, bondsman.

Spears, Daniel & Matilda Johnston, 2 March 1866; Wade H. Spears, bondsman; R. M. White, wit. married 3 March 1866 by Danl. A. Penick Sr.

Spears, James G. & Mrs. Abigail Vail, 28 Dec 1824; Abel Cowan, bondsman; Isaac Alexander, wit.

Spears, Jason & Jane Davis, 16 June 1851; James H. Spears, bondsman; Braly Oates, C. C. C., wit. married 17 June 1851 by G. W. Houston, J. P.

Spears, Jeptha & Mary N. Montgomery, 14 March 1854; John W. Moore, bondsman; W. K. Reid, C. C. C.,wit. married 15 March 1854 by Thomas M. Farrow.

Spears, William Nelson, & Jane Perry, 6 Aug 1825; John K. Houston, bondsman; Isaac Alexander, wit.

Spearse, Henry James & Mary L. Roberts, 10 April 1851; George W. Houston, bondsman; Braly Oates, C. C. C., wit. married 10 April 1851 by G. W. Houston, J. P.

Speck, William H. & Delitha C. Murrow, 1 Jan 1835; Alfred R. Wolfington, bondsman; B. Oates, wit.

Spencer, Isaac & Elizabeth J. Cowan, 11 Feb 1835; Alfred R. Wolfington, bondsman; B. Oates, C. C. C., wit.

Spencer, Jesse & Polley Dougherty, 12 April 1819; James Doherty, bondsman.

Spencer, John & Elizabeth Bigham, 13 Aug 1802; Robert Bigham, bondsman.

Spirvey, Elisha & Tebitha King, 5 Feb 1800; Julias King, bondsman; Andw. Walker, wit.

MECKLENBURG MARRIAGES 1783-1868

Spratt, Charles E. & Margaret L. Oates, 5 Feb 1850; E. C.
Davidson, bondsman; B. Oates, C. C. C., wit.

Spratt, Charles E. & Mary A. Dunn, 27 Feb 1854; Wm. O. Moss,
bondsman; W. K. Reid, C. C. C., wit. married 28 Feb 1854 by
Samuel C. Pharr, V. D. M.

Spratt, Elam & Ann R. Cathcart, 11 March 1847; Lauson H.
Kimbirl, bondsman.

Spratt, Hugh & Catharine Sprott, 27 Dec 1794; James McNight,
bondsman; Isaac Alexander, wit.

Spratt, James B. & Mary A. Coffey, 28 Jan 1854; A. B. Sloan,
bondsman; W. K. Reid, C. C. C., wit. married 31 Jan 1854 by
J. B. Watt, V. D. M.

Spratt, James W. & Elizabeth C. Lees, 14 April 1832; Jno D.
McDowell Jr., bondsman.

Spratt, Thos. N. & M. E. Robinson, 22 Aug 1851; D. L. Todd,
bondsman; James Parks, wit. married 24 Aug 1851 by A. L.
Watts.

Spratt, Thomas N. & Margaret M. Coffey, 14 Oct 1854; Wm. S.
Prather, bondsman; W. K. Reid, C. C. C., wit. married 18
Oct 1854 by A. M. Watson

Sprinkle, Hiram & Jemima Searcy, 19 July 1837; Wm. A. Todd,
bondsman; P. E. Saunier, wit.

Sprinkle, William J. & Mary S. Holton, 24 Dec 1860; John L.
Deaton, bondsman; F. A. Mood, wit. married 24 Dec 1860
by F. A. Mood

Sproat, Andrew & Elizabeth Haynes, 18 Oct 1791; David Hayns,
bondsman; Isaac Alexander, wit.

Sprott, Allston & Elizabeth Dunn, 10 Feb 1824; Thomas Dunn,
bondsman; Isaac S. Alexander, wit.

Sprott, James & Elizabeth Barnett, 11 Dec 1793; Hugh Sprott,
bondsman; Isaac Alexander, wit.

Sprott, James & Peggy McRee, 31 Jan 1804; Hugh White, bondsman;
Isaac Alexander, wit.

Sprott, John & Rebecca Ellams, 10 April 1818; Saml. Bigham,
bondsman; Isaac S. Alexander, wit.

Sprott, Thomas & Elizabeth Dunn, 16 Dec 1799; Andrew Dunn Jr.,
bondsman.

Squires, James & Polly Flow, 17 June 1830; Osbourne Stansill,
bondsman; B. Oates, D. C., wit.

Squires, James W. & Louisa Stancil, 20 Jan 1858; T. W. Squires,
bondsman; W. K. Reid, C. C. C., wit. married 28 Jan 1858
by Lewis M. Little.

Squires, John B. & M. A. Stevans, 29 Dec 1862; M. J. Anderson,
bondsman; Wm. Maxwell, C. C. C., wit. married 30 Dec 1862
by J. W. Abernathy, minister.

Squires, Robert & Agness Williams, 21 Sept 1808; Mathew Wallace, bondsman; Isaac Alexander, wit.

Squires, Thomas & Jane Anderson, 31 Aug 1833; Hyram Kesiah, bondsman.

Stacy, A. G. (Rev.) & Cornelia F. Gillespie, 24 March 1852; N. B. Taylor, bondsman; Braly Oates, C. C. C., wit. married 25 March 1852 by H. H. Durant.

Stafford, Arthur & Cecilia C. Harris, 13 Oct 1827; Livingston Harris, bondsman.

Stafford, Eli & Elizabeth McComb, 2 Jan 1832; Nehemiah H. McComb, bondsman.

Stafford, Eli & Terressa Jane Cochran, 10 May 1844; Saml. Kimmers, bondsman; N. B. Taylor, wit.

Stafford, Franklin & Mary Farr, 24 Feb 1829; Joseph McComb, bondsman; P. Thompson, wit.

Stafford, George & Jane Robb, 16 Jan 1793; Robert Harris, bondsman; Isaac Alexander, wit.

Stafford, George & Tirza Alexander, 19 May 1797; Cyrus Alexander, bondsman.

Stanford, C. L. & Martha Russell, 31 Dec 1861; J. H. Griffith, bondsman; W. K. Reid, C. C. C., wit. married 31 Dec 1861 by William Reid, J. P.

Stanford, Charles L. & Mary J. Clark, 23 Oct 1858; George W. Jennings, bondsman; K. W. Berryhill, wit. married 27 Oct 1858 by W. H. Neal, J. P.

Stanford, Lyman & Ann Cole, 15 May 1857; Robert Stanford, bondsman; W. K. Reid, C. C. C., wit. married 19 May 1857 by Stephen Wilson, J. P.

Stanford, Taylor & Margaret Sharp, 9 April 1849; John T. Mulwe, bondsman; B. Oates, C. C. C., wit.

Stanley, William H. & Adaline Johnston, 25 Dec 1856; Jordan B. Phillips, bondsman; W. K. Reid, C. C. C., wit. married 25 Dec 1856 by Wm. S. Norment, J. P.

Stansill, Elisha & Sally Williams, 4 April 1816; Wm. H. Stilwell, bondsman; John Rea, J. P., wit.

Stansill, John Sr. & Peggy Kiker (date obliterated; an early handwritten bond); Georg Kiser, bondsman; Wm. Pyron, wit.

Stansill, Milas P. & Nancy Hartis, 10 July 1837; William T. Phifer, bondsman; W. H. Simpson, J. P., wit.

Stansill, Osburn, & Mrs. Elizabeth McCown, 14 Feb 1832; James Brown, bondsman; Philemon Morris, wit.

Stansill, Samuel & Sarah Walker, 12 Jan 1805; Little Bery Smartt, bondsman.

Starne, John R. & Elizabeth Ewing, 24 Feb 1851; Mason Richardson, bondsman; David D. Oates, wit.

Starnes, Reuben & Mary Hood, 8 Feb 1823; Jacob Starnes, bondsman; Isaac Alexander, wit.

Starns, Adam & Elizabeth Skinner, 7 July 1847; Peter Phifer, bondsman; Daniel Wentz, J. P., wit.

Starns, Ambros & Martha Hooks, 10 Dec 1832; Thomas W. Williams, bondsman; Isaac Alexander, wit.

Starns, Andrew & Eliza Hambey, 11 Aug 1840; William Roark, bondsman; Philemon Morris, wit.

Starns, H. M. & Lucinda Sloan, 24 June 1861; C. T. Dewese, bondsman; married 27 June 1861 by Walter S. Pharr.

Starns, Jacob & Esther Vince, 20 April 1798; Feltte Vence, bondsman.

Starns, Jacob & Jane Russell, 31 May 1821; Tunis Hood, bondsman; Isaac S. Alexander, wit.

Starns, John & Mary Starnes, 14 Aug 1851; Joseph W. Starns, bondsman; James Parks, wit. married 14 Aug 1851 by Philemon Morris, J. P.

Starns, John W. & Margaret Barnhardt, 30 July 1858; John S. Black, bondsman; W. K. Reid, C. C. C., wit. married 5 Aug 1858 by W. G. Barnett, J. P.

Starns, Joseph & Rachel Rice, 16 Aug 1796; Falintine Wentz, bondsman; Shared Gray, wit.

Starns, Joseph & Elizabeth Fisher, 28 Oct 1831; Philip Wolf, bondsman; B. Oates, D. C., wit.

Starns, Tobias & Elizabeth McKee, 15 April 1820; William Roper, bondsman; Philemon Morris, wit.

Starns, Valintine & Olleary Ritch, 17 Aug 1824; James Brown, bondsman; Philemon Morris, wit.

Starns, William R. & Ann Darnall, 15 June 1854; Robert Cuningham, bondsman; W. K. Reid, C. C. C., wit. married 4 June 1854 by J. W. Morrow, J. P.

Starr, Obadiah & Harriet Rodgers, 7 Sept 1854; Wesley E. Caudle, bondsman; W. K. Reid, C. C. C., wit.

Steel, James & Betsey Woodsides, 24 Feb 1802; Jacob Moore, bondsman.

Steel, John & Ruth McEwen, (not dated, in the term of Gov. Richd. D. Spaight); Isaiah Spear, bondsman; Isaac Alexander, wit.

Steel, John S. & Peggy Nail, 7 Dec 1812; John Steel, bondsman; Isaac S. Alexander, wit.

Steel, Martin & Sarah Hunter, 22 Jan 1789; John Steel, bondsman.

Steel, Martin & Polly Garris, 7 Jan 1828; Archibald W. Steel, bondsman; P. Thompson, wit.

Steel, Robert & Polly Gelliand, 4 July 1815; David Dougherty, bondsman; Ja. Douglass, J. P., wit.

Steele, A. W. & Sarah E. Cox, 21 Feb 1863; John P. Ross, bondsman; Wm. Maxwell, C. C. C., wit. married 22 Feb 1863 by J. P. Ross, J. P.

Steele, Alexander & Caroline Conner, 19 Feb 1839; Archibald McLarty, bondsman.

Steele, John H. & Emaline Christenbury, 31 Aug 1865; G. W. Alexander, bondsman; Wm. Maxwell, wit. married 31 Aug 1865 by Thos. W. Dewey, J. P.

Steele, Jonathan J. & Eliza A. Orr, 5 Oct 1838; David Parks, bondsman; B. Oates, C. C. C., wit.

Steely, Isaih, & Isabella Price, 13 Dec 1794; Robert Price, bondsman; James Meek, wit.

Stegall, William & Elsey Elms, 12 Jan 1833; Daniel Whaley, bondsman; Isaac Alexander, wit.

Stegall, William & L. M. Staples, 4 Aug 1855; Robert H.Maxwell, bondsman; married 5 Aug 1855 by W. R. Maxwell, J. P.

Stephens, Asa & Violet Dunn, 7 July 1829; Thomas Norton, bondsman; E. Elms, wit.

Stephens, Edward L. & Ann McCracken, 18 April 1838; Thomas Goodlocke, bondsman.

Stephens, G. K. & Margaret Purvines, 1 June 1854; Thomas A. Hannon, bondsman; W. K. Reid, C. C. C., wit. married 1 June 1854 by John Walker, J. P.

Stephens, J.L.& Jane Smith, 1 Jan 1856; J. G. Griffin, bondsman; W. K. Reid, C. C. C., wit. married 2 Jan 1856 by C. Overman, J. P.

Stephens, J.L.& Leah E. Harget, 29 March 1866; J. M. Maning, bondsman; Wm. Maxwell, C. C. C., wit. married 29 March 1866 by Jno. F. Butt.

Stephens, James & Elizabeth Smith, 21 Dec 1818; Ephraim Kendrick, bondsman; Isaac Alexander, wit.

Stephens, James & Catharine Harmon, 13 March 1842; David Weante, bondsman.

Stephens, James L. & Susan E. Harrison, 11 Oct 1848; James Cunningham, bondsman.

Stephens, John & Joanna N. Turner, 9 April 1822; William L. Clark, bondsman; Isaac Alexander, wit.

Stephens, John & Mrs. Nancy Byram, 12 April 1824; John Kirkpatrick, bondsman; Isaac S. Alexander,wit.

Stephens, John S. & Mary H. Todd, 20 Dec 1854; Thomas W. Ledwell, bondsman; W. K. Reid, C. C. C., wit. married 20 Dec 1854 by R. M. Ross, J. P.

Stephenson, John & Mary Arnold, 14 Feb 1826; Samuel Kerr, bondsman; Isaac S. Alexander,wit.

Stephenson, Samuel & Esther Bradley, 23 April 1800; James A. Bradley, bondsman; Isaac Alexander, wit.

Stephenson, William S. & Jone Howie, 4 June 1835; Henry B.
Williams, bondsman; B. Oates, C. C. C., wit.

Sterling, Robt. M. & Margaret Moore, 4 Sept 1829; Benjamin Bowie,
bondsman; E. Elms, wit.

Sternes, E. Alexander, & Mary Jane Searcy, 29 Sept 1858; James
C. Deaton, bondsman; W. K. Reid, C. C. C., wit. married 29
Sept 1858 by David Henderson.

Sterns, Ambrose Lee & Cornelia Gray, 31 Oct 1859; E. R. Sloan,
bondsman; W. K. Reid, C. C. C., wit. married 1 Nov 1859 by
W. G. Barnett, J. P.

Steuart, Kindred & Sarah E. Thomas, 9 Nov 1842; H. P. Turner,
bondsman; C. T. Alexander, C. C. C., wit.

Steurt, Robert & Jane Knox, 23 Feb 1835; James Steurt, bondsman;
B. Oates, C. C. C., wit.

Stevens, Abner H. & Dorcas McEwin, 30 Nov 1840; James S. Ritch,
bondsman.

Stevens, Amos & Genny Howard, 26 Sept 1820; Greenlee M. ----,
bondsman; Jno Rea, wit.

Stevens, Martin & Jane Tonkin, 9 Aug 1836; Nicholas Tredinnick,
bondsman; B. Oates, C. C. C., wit.

Stevens, Moses & Elizebeth Conder, 6 Dec 1838; William Roark,
bondsman; Philemon Morris, wit.

Stevens, Squire & Lydia Harris, 26 Feb 1828; Silas Brown, bondsman;
P. Thompson, wit.

Stevens, Squire & Ellen Lany, 14 Aug 1840; James S. Ritch, bondsman; W. F. Alexander, wit.

Steward, A. J. & Mary Sloan, 16 Dec 1857; Henry M. Starnes, bondsman; W. K. Reid, C. C. C., wit. married 17 Dec 1857 by Walter
S. Pharr.

Steward, John & Rebecca Smith, 15 Jan 1851; R. G. Mason, bondsman;
B. Oates, C. C. C., wit.

Stewart, Berry & Isabella Beaty, 1 Aug 1829; Calvin G. Alexander,
bondsman.

Stewart, Eli & Patsey Lewis, 18 Jan 1820; Jno Rea, bondsman; John
Rea, wit.

Stewart, Hugh & Corina Moore, 2 June 1825; Ellis Caraway, bondsman.

Stewart, Joseph B. & Nancy P. Kirkpatrick, 5 Oct 1847; John O.
Flanigan, bondsman; B. Oates, C. C. C., wit.

Stewart, Joseph B. & Mrs. A. J. Hutchinson, 7 Sept 1858; B. R.
Smith, bondsman; F. M. Ross, wit. married 7 Sept 1858 by
J. Rumple.

Stewart, Josiah H. & Rebecca L. Parks, 21 Sept 1832; David Parks,
bondsman.

Stewart, Mordecai & Milly Kizier, 19 July 1825; John Keziah,
bondsman; Wm. Pyron, wit.

Stewart, N. J. & Margaret M. Rea, 13 Dec 1865; C. G. Erwin,
bondsman; Wm. Maxwell, C. C. C., wit. married 14 Dec 1865
by Wm. McDonald.

Stewart, R. C. & Mrs. M. C. Hunter, 18 Dec 1865; Charles DeCamp,
bondsman; Wm. Maxwell, C. C. C., wit. married 19 Dec 1865 by
I. S. McLaughlin.

Stewart, Robert C. & Mary Thorn, 4 Sept 1848; Wm. Kerr, bondsman.

Stewart, Samuel A. & Minerva C. Stewart, 22 Feb 1858; Z. S.
Morris, bondsman; W. K. Reid, C. C. C.,wit. married 24 Feb
1858 by I. S. McLaughlin.

Stewart, Samuel A. & Jane A. Houston, 6 Nov 1861; S. F. Houston,
J. N. Hunter, bondsmen; W. K. Reid, C. C. C., wit. married
6 Nov 1861 by I. S. McLaughlin.

Stewart, Silas P. & Martha C. Lemmond, 14 Oct 1835; John W.
Davis, bondsman.

Stewart, Thomas A. & Isabella F. Houston, 7 Dec 1854; H. L.
Houston, bondsman; W. K. Reid, C. C. C., wit. married 14 Dec
1854 by H. B. Cunningham.

Stewart, Wm. & Harriet Hartgrave, 15 Sept 1842; Wm. H. McLeary,
bondsman.

Stilwell, E. C. & Harriet E. Condor, 25 Dec 1860; William Secrest,
bondsman; P. S. Whisnant, wit. married 27 Dec 1860 by W. R.
Maxwell, J. P.

Stilwell, Eleazer, & Dorcas Paxton, 20 May 1825; Saml. J. Thomas,
bondsman; Isaac Alexander, wit.

Stilwell, Elias & Elisabeth Osburn, 25 Sept 1818; John M. Rea,
bondsman; Jno Rea, wit.

Stilwell, Elijah & Rebeckah Osbourn, 7 April 1814; William Morris,
bondsman; Philemon Morris, wit.

Stilwell, Elisha & Catharine Morris, 20 July 1795; John Stilwell,
bondsman.

Stilwell, Jesse & Polly Parten, 4 Nov 1818; A. Simpson Rea, bondsman; Jno Rea, wit.

Stilwell, Jesse & Edey Ritch, 10 Feb 1825; Green L. Read, bondsman;
Philemon Morris, wit.

Stilwell, John F. & Ellen Yandel, 20 March 1855; William A.McGin,
bondsman; J. W. J. Harris, wit. married by J. W. J. Harris,
minister, (date obliterated)

Stilwell, Silas N. & Jane White, 8 Dec 1862; James McLeod, bondsman; Wm. Maxwell, C. C. C., wit. married 18 Dec 1862 by John
Walker, J. P.

Stilwell, William H. & Sally Rape, 27 Dec 1814; Elias Stilwell,
bondsman; Isaac Alexander, wit.

Stinson, Alexander & Elizabeth Bradley, 20 Aug 1800; James Alexander Bradley, bondsman; Isaac Alexander,wit.

Stinson, Andrew & Sarah Howie, 15 Dec 1834; Jesse Potter, bondsman;
B. Oates, C. C. C., wit.

Stinson, Hugh & Agness McKinley, 29 July 1799; Michael Stinson,
bondsman.

Stinson, James & Sarah A. Hall, 1 Jan 1816; Andrew Stinson, bondsman; Isaac S.Alexander, wit.

Stinson, John B. & Mary A. E. Hays, 1 Jan 1849; T. P. G. Haris,
bondsman.

Stinson, Michael & Elizabeth McKinley, 20 Oct 1790; Michael
McCleary, bondsman; Isaac Alexander, wit.

Stinson, Robert H. & Jane R. Wilson, 2 May 1837; John Sloan,
bondsman; B. Oates, C. C. C., wit.

Stitt, Amzi & Lina Stitt (colored), 26 Aug 1865; Jack Wallace,
bondsman.

Stitt, J. M. & M. E. Stitt, 2 Nov 1859; P. C. Harkey, bondsman;
W. K. Reid, C. C. C., wit. married 3 Nov 1859 by J. C.
Chalmers.

Stitt, James & Jane McCibbins, 24 Jan 1799; William Stitt, bondsman.

Stitt, James & Mary McKee, 16 Oct 1834; William A. Stitt, bondsman;
B. Oates, C. C. C., wit.

Stitt, John & Amelia Morrison, 26 March 1798; William Stitt,
bondsman; B. Oates, wit.

Stitt, Neil M. & Susannah Hudson, 10 Dec 1828; John E. Stitt,
bondsman; Pearsall Thompson, wit.

Stitt, Neil M. & Mrs. Jane Oliver, 28 July 1846; John R. Warwick,
bondsman; N. B. Taylor, wit.

Stitt, W. M. & M. E. Ross, 13 Sept 1859; W. W. Grier, bondsman;
W. K. Reid, C. C. C., wit. married 15 Sept 1859 by J. Rumple,
V. D. M.

Stitt, William & Martha Walkup,23 July 1831; John W. Potts, bondsman; R. S. Dinkins, wit.

Stitt, William A. & Rebecca M. Orr, 11 Aug 1836; David Parks,
bondsman; B. Oates, C. C. C., wit.

Stitt, William M. & Lucinda C. Ezzell, 10 Sept 1834; John Stitt,
bondsman; B. Oates, C. C. C.,wit.

Stitt, William T. & Nancy C. McKee, 10 Nov 1834; William A. Stitt,
bondsman; B. Oates, C. C. C., wit.

Stitt, William T. & H. R. Young, 21 Dec 1844; J. B. Peoples,
bondsman; N. B. Taylor, wit.

Stitt, William T. & R. M. Allison, 28 May 1862; John W. Wadsworth,
bondsman; W. K. Reid, C. C. C.,wit. married 29 May 1862 by
Walter S. Pharr.

Stockinger, John C. & Meriah Alexander, 26 June 1818; Jacob F.
Cuningham, bondsman; Isaac S. Alexander, wit.

Story, David W. & Betsey T. Fincher, 27 Aug 1816; Joseph Fincher, David Crenshaw, bondsmen; Isaac S. Alexander, wit.

Story, James & Prudence Gammil, 19 Sept 1797; John Polk, bondsman; J. Wallis, wit.

Story, James & Bethia Roper, 25 Feb 1817; Joseph Fincher, bondsman.

Stowe, Abram & Jemima P. Auton, 5 Feb 1853; Joseph L. Wolf, bondsman; B. Oates, C. C. C., wit. married 9 Feb 1853 by J. P. Ross, J. P.

Stowe, Herbert & Martha Robinson, 10 Aug 1838; Wm. H. Neel, bondsman.

Stowe, Larkin & Susan S. Neel, 25 April 1820; John S. Grier, bondsman; Isaac Alexander, wit.

Stricker, Moses & Lucinda Walls, 23 April 1839; Minsegey Wall, bondsman; T. W. Saunier, wit.

Stricklan, Moses & Elizabeth Johnston, 17 Sept 1855; M. W. Reid, bondsman; W. K. Reid, C. C. C., wit. married 20 Sept 1855 by P. B. Hodges, J. P.

Strickland, Ozy & Jeenath Alexander, 7 Jan 1828; Moses Stricklan, Washington Plummer, bondsmen; Tho. B. Smartt, wit.

Stricklan, Samuel G. & O. A. Prime, 27 July 1865; Wm. H. Turrentin, bondsman; Wm. Maxwell, C. C. C., wit. married 27 July 1865 by Richd. H. Griffith, minister.

Stricklin, Thomas & Unity Williams, 15 March 1808; Thomas Kenedy, bondsman.

Stringfellow, William A. & Frances Ashley, 19 July 1851; Wm. K. Reid, bondsman; James Parks, wit. married 27 July 1851 by John H. Grier, J. P.

Strube, John & Sarah Taylor, 8 June 1865; E. S. Teeter, bondsman; Wm. Maxwell, C. C. C.,wit. married 8 June 1865 by Jno. F. Butt, J. P.

Struebe, Wm. & Elizabeth Woodal, 17 Aug 1865; William C. C. Wilson, bondsman; married 17 Aug 1865 by Thos. M. Alexander, J. P.

Stuard, Kindred & Mrs. Elizabeth Phostermon, 25 Feb 1836; John N. Wilson, bondsman; Philemon Morris, wit.

Stuart, James & Marthew Falls, 27 Sept 1798; William Falls, bondsman; Jas. Conner, wit.

Stuart, James M. & Margaret Stinson, 9 Feb 1831; Jonathan Stinson, bondsman; B. Oates, D. C., wit.

Stuart, Othneal & Agness McSpannim, 4 Jan 1820; Misel Hudson, bondsman; Jno Rea, wit.

Stuart, William & Betsey Finch, 15 Jan 1798; James White, bondsman; Jas. Conner, wit.

Stuart, William L. & Mary Ann Brown, 18 Oct 1858; McCamy Puckett, bondsman; John Phelan, wit. married 19 Oct 1858 by Isaac Wilson, J. P.

Stubbs, Benjamin C. & Dorcas Swann, 12 Sept 1812; John Chambers, bondsman; Isaac Alexander, wit.

Stuffer, Moses A. & Margaret Shuman, 25 Jan 1854; Joseph R. Cathy, bondsman; W. K. Reid, C. C. C., wit. married 26 Jan 1854 by Alexr. Springs, J. P.

Sturd, William & Susanah Smith, 8 Jan 1835; Jno. W. Morrow, bondsman; James Johnston, wit.

Sturd, William Jr. & Fanney M. Warsham, 29 Dec 1835; R. J. Curey, bondsman; James Johnston, wit.

Sturgeon, Cooper, & Betsey Hearttess, 8 Jan 1805; John Sturgeon, Robert Campbell, bondsmen; J. Wallis, wit.

Sturgeon, Cyrus S. & Sarah S. Kirkpatrick, 19 Jan 1855; John C. Brown, bondsman; W. K. Reid, C. C. C., wit. married 25 Jan 1855 by William Reid, J. P.

Sturgeon, Henry & Mary Beaty, 14 July 1794; John Beaty, bondsman; Isaac Alexander, wit.

Suggs, George & Margaret C. Rodden, 24 May 1836; Darias Folsom, bondsman; B. Oates, C. C. C., wit.

Suggs, Wiley & Angeline Williams, 22 Jan 1844; Alfred A. Norment, bondsman; N. B. Taylor, wit.

Suggs, William & Fanny Bigham, 30 Oct 1839; Jas. Walker, bondsman; T. W. Saunier, wit.

Suggs, William L. & Margaret J. Bigham, 31 Oct 1844; John Reid, bondsman; N. B. Taylor, wit.

Suliphen, William & Ruhama Robison, 3 March 1807; Thomas Robertson, bondsman.

Sumerrell, John J. & Christain A. Todd, 29 Sept 1818; William A. Todd, bondsman.

Sumers, George & Cynthia Cathey (colored), 4 Jan 1848; Wm. Jamison, bondsman; Saml. J. Lourie, wit.

Sumervill, William & Christrin Dunn, 25 Dec 1813; Thomas F. Johnston, bondsman; Isaac Alexander, wit.

Sumerville, James T. & Rachel A. McCord, 17 Dec 1850; William Sumerville, bondsman; B. Oates, C. C. C., wit.

Sumerville, John W. & Sarah Jane Jamison, 18 Dec 1855; John W. Todd, bondsman; W. .K Reid, C. C. C., wit.

Sumerville, Robert & Christiana A. Todd, 31 Jan 1844; George L. Campbell, bondsman; N. B. Taylor, wit.

Sumerville, William & Martha McCord, 7 Jan 1845; John McCord, bondsman; N. B. Taylor, wit.

Sumerville, William & Ann Elizabeth McDonald, 10 Aug 1852; William H. Todd, bondsman; Braly Oates, C. C. C., wit. married 10 Aug 1852 by G. L. Campbell, J. P.

Summers, George & Betsy Grimes, 30 June 1864; J. H. McGinn, bondsman; Wm. Maxwell, C. C. C., wit; married 30 June 1864 by Wm. S. Norment, J. P.

Summerville, Robert J. & Jane S. Johnston, 25 May 1841; George
L. Elliotte, bondsman.

Suther, Caleb A. & Amanda Å. Berryhill, 29 April 1852; Samuel Murr,
bondsman; B. Oates, C. C. C., wit. married 29 April 1852 by
W. S. Haltom.

Suther, J. H. & Margaret A. Blalock, 7 Sept 1865; Wm. S. Bryan,
bondsman; Wm. Maxwell, C. C. C., wit. married 7 Sept 1865
by I. J. Sloan, J. P.

Swan, John M. & Mary Starns, 18 Oct 1842; Williamson Wallace,
bondsman.

Swan, Joseph & Elizabeth Allen, 12 Jan 1803; Andrew Wilson,
bondsman; J. Wallis, wit.

Swann, Isaac & Ann Robison, 8 Feb 1812; James Parks, bondsman;
Isaac Alexander, wit.

Swann, Moses & Peggy Bigham, 26 July 1803; Samuel Bigham, bondsman.

Syter, Adam & Salina Parks, 17 June 1845; Isaac S. Alexander,
bondsman; C. T. Alexander, C. C. C., wit.

Tagert, J. A. & Susannah Hobbs, 28 Oct 1861; J. G. McCoy, bondsman;
W. K. Reid, C. C. C., wit. married 29 Oct 1861 by Jos. C.
Nicholson, J. P.

Tagert, James & Agness Brown, 17 Dec 1792; James Brown, bondsman;
Ruth J. Alexander, wit.

Tagert, James W. & Amelia S. McKee, 26 Jan 1841; Elias A. McKee,
bondsman.

Tagert, James W. & Mary Cunningham, 31 Jan 1849; T. N. Alexander,
bondsman; Saml. J. Lourie, wit.

Talley, John & Susan Montgomery, 30 Nov 1837; Hardy Lewallen,
bondsman; B. Oates, wit.

Tally, Tise & Polly Barr, 28 May 1816; William Pyron, bondsman;
Isaac Alexander, wit.

Talton, James D. & Mary Jane Blakely, 11 Sept 1863; D. G. Maxwell,
bondsman; Wm. Maxwell, C. C. C., wit. married 11 Sept 1863 by
J. P. Ross, J. P.

Tanner, John & Mary Nickson, 8 March 1790; Joseph Moore, bondsman;
J. McK. Alexander, wit.

Tarlton, Sampson & Frances Lawing, 13 Aug 1839; Cyrus W. Alexander,
bondsman; B. Oates, C. C. C., wit.

Tarlton, William C. & Mary Long, 23 Sept 1836; Evan Alexander,
bondsman; B. Oates, C. C. C., wit.

Tate, A. H. & Eliza Overman, 16 Feb 1863; J. A. Paschall, bondsman; Wm. Maxwell, C. C. C., wit. married 17 Feb 1863 by A.
Sinclair, minister.

Tate, Hugh & Margaret Sloan, 5 Oct 1865; J. D. Currence, bondsman;
Wm. Maxwell, C. C. C., wit. married 5 Oct 1865 by Saml. L.
Watson, V. D. M.

Tate, Thomas R. & M. C. Overman, 20 March 1866; James Harty,
bondsman; Wm. Maxwell, C. C. C., wit. married 20 March 1866
by A. W. Miller.

Tate, William C. & Mrs. Laura T. Polk, 25 Sept 1836; Pinckney C.
Caldwell, bondsman; B. Oates, C. C. C., wit.

Taylor, A. A. N. M. & Julia A. Spratt, 16 Sept 1856; S. W. Davis,
bondsman; F. M. Ross, wit.

Taylor, A. R. & Margaret Garrison, 31 Jan 1860; John H. Tevepaugh,
bondsman; W. K. Reid, C. C. C.; married 2 Feb 1860 by J. B.
Watt.

Taylor, Abraham & Jenny Neely, 5 May 1807; Jonathan Neely, bondsman; Isaac Alexander, wit.

Taylor, Alexander & Sarah J. McAlister, 28 July 1846; E. H.
Bissell, bondsman.

Taylor, Alfred D. & Mary S. Ritch, 1 Oct 1864; John P. Ritch,
bondsman; Wm. Maxwell, C. C. C., wit.

Taylor, Charles & Nancy Dulin, 9 Dec 1848; Wilson Wallace, bondsman; B. Oates, C. C. C., wit.

Taylor, Charles & Elizabeth Strube, 31 Dec 1852; Orsborn Taylor,
Rice Dulin, bondsmen; Braley Oates, C. C. C., wit. married
31 Dec 1852 by C. B. Cross, J. P.

Taylor, Fredrick & Mary Ann Crocket, 13 Dec 1796; John Crockett,
bondsman; J. Wallis, wit.

Taylor, Harvey S. & Mary Ann Jordan, 20 Feb 1861; W. W. Allen,
bondsman; S. P. Alexander, wit. married 21 Feb 1861 by J.
Sample Davis, J. P.

Taylor, James & Peggy Gillam, 9 April 1813; Joseph Love, bondsman;
Isaac Alexander, wit.

Taylor, John & Polly Neely, 18 Sept 1806; Robert Campbell, bondsman; Isaac Alexander, wit.

Taylor, John M. & Sarah Ann Carter (aged 17 years, Wm & Jane C.
Carter gave consent, 30 June 1860), 30 June 1860; William J.
Taylor, bondsman; W. K. Reid, C. C. C., wit. married 2 July 1860
by W. R. Maxwell, J. P.

Taylor, Joshua W. & Salina C. Hyatt, 13 Jan 1846; William D.
Taylor, bondsman; B. Oates, C. C. C.,wit.

Taylor, Joshua W. & Mary Ann Hunter, 28 Dec 1857; Jno Phelan,
bondsman; W. K. Reid, C. C. C., wit. married 31 Dec 1857 by
P. Nicholson.

Taylor, Robert C. C. & Cecelia C. Noles, 4 Sept 1865; H. S. Taylor,
bondsman; Wm. Maxwell, C. C. C., wit. married 5 Sept 1865
by Thos. M. Alexander, J. P.

Taylor, Robert R. & Mary E. Watson, 12 Nov 1839; F. Madison Ross,
bondsman.

Taylor, Stephen & Polly Hartgrove, 23 March 1826; Henry Hoover,
bondsman; Richd. Gillespie Jr., wit.

MECKLENBURG MARRIAGES 1783-1868

Taylor, William T. & Elizabeth Reeves, -- July 1847; Daniel
Ledwell, bondsman; Saml. J. Lourie, wit.

Taylor, Wilson & Mary Shepherd, 21 Nov 1820; Frederick Ezell,
bondsman; Isaac S. Alexander, wit.

Teeter, Joshua & Margaret Caldwell, 6 May 1839; Isaac Harris,
bondsman.

Teeter, Joshua & Mary Hunter, 6 Feb 1863; Hugh M. Dixon, bondsman;
Wm. Maxwell, C. C. C., wit. married 10 Feb 1863 by A. Ranson.

Temples, Joseph C. & Mary T. Reives, 11 April 1845; William W.
Darnall, bondsman; C. T. Alexander, wit.

Templeton, Edwin & Jane Dewese, 22 April 1830; John Sloan, bondsman; Isaac Alexander, wit.

Templeton, Elam & Nancy Amelia Sloan, 28 Oct 1826; Hiram F. Sloan,
bondsman.

Teter, Elam J. & Mary N. Simmons, 30 Aug 1837; John C. Pharr,
bondsman.

Tevepaugh, John & Sarah R. Wingate, 7 Oct 1863; Phillip Tevepaugh,
bondsman; Wm. Maxwell, wit.

Tevepaugh, Philip & Dolly Herron, 18 Jan 1837; Joseph C. Nicholson,
bondsman; B. Oates, wit.

Thomas, George Westley & Harriet Matilda Cox, 17 Sept 1860; John
F. Bloom, bondsman; W. K. Reid, C. C. C., wit. married 17
Sept 1860 by Charles Overman, J. P.

Thomas, Henry & Margaret Hickman, 18 Sept 1856; Wm. W. Quinn,
bondsman; W. K. Reid, C. C. C., wit. married 18 Sept 1856 by
Wm. S. Norment, J. P.

Thomas, James M. & Ann P. Morrow, 16 Aug 1838; Benjamin P. Boyd,
bondsman.

Thomas, John F. & Rachele Kilgrow, 19 Dec 1820; William Loughrey,
bondsman; Isaac Alexander, wit.

Thomas, John M. & Martha Irwin, 26 Oct 1819; Joseph B. Thomas,
bondsman; Isaac Alexander, wit.

Thomasson, David & Mary Barnett, -- April ----; Vincent Barnett,
bondsman.

Thomasson, Needham, & Mary Monteeth, 7 Aug 1841; W. S. Perry,
bondsman; J. M. Stewart, wit.

Thompson, Aron & Elizabeth McWhirter, 26 Feb 1798; Alexander
Orsburn, bondsman; Shared Gray, wit.

Thompson, Azerehab & Sarah Hudson, 25 April 1822; John Williamson,
bondsman.

Thompson, Henry & Polly Hudson, 17 March 1805; John Williamson,
bondsman.

Thompson, Isaac J. & Nancy S. Todd, 16 Aug 1831; John A. Todd,
bondsman; B.Oates, wit.

Thompson, Isaac J. & Anna Summerville, 17 Jan 1838; George A. Todd, bondsman; B. Oates, C. C. C., wit.

Thompson, J. W. & Margaret Dulin, 19 Dec 1865; William Dulin, bondsman; W. W. Grier, wit. married 21 Dec 1865 by E. C. Williams.

Thompson, James & Dorcas McCord, 23 Dec 1812; Cyrus Henderson, bondsman.

Thompson, James & Ann Warrack, 8 Nov 1819; Eli Cochran, bondsman; John Rea, wit.

Thompson, James & Margaret Carter, 28 Sept 1837; Alexander Hood, bondsman; B. Oates, C. C. C., wit.

Thompson, James N. & Margaret Hutchison, 19 Aug 1833; John Mason, bondsman; B. Oates, D. C., wit.

Thompson, John & Polly Steel, 18 Aug 1812; Richard Graham, bondsman; Isaac S. Alexander, wit.

Thompson, John & Ann McLeary, 3 Aug 1813; James Flow, bondsman.

Thompson, John & Nancy Mack, 19 Nov 1813; John Williamson, bondsman; Isaac Alexander, wit.

Thompson, John & Elizabeth D. Jamison, 23 July 1832; Thomas Hoover, bondsman.

Thompson, John & Rachel Lemmond, 21 Aug 1838; Thomas Dulin Jr., bondsman; B. Oates, wit.

Thompson, John N. & Louiza Orr, 7 Dec 1847; Thomas A. Wilson, bondsman.

Thompson, Joseph & Eliz. Johnston, 16 March 1801; John Johnston, bondsman.

Thompson, Moses & Rachel Foard, 30 Aug 1796; Benjamin Thompson, bondsman.

Thompson, Pearsall & Margaret Jane Henderson, 20 Nov 1834; William W. Elms, bondsman; B. Oates, C. C. C., wit.

Thompson, Peter & Mahaly Laney, 22 Oct 1832; Braly Oates, bondsman.

Thompson, R. G. & Mary Ann Anderson, 25 July 1860; Thos. W. Squires, bondsman; P. S. Whisnant, wit. married 26 July 1860 by Charles Overman, J. P.

Thompson, Robert & Ann Thompson, 5 Sept 1801; James Dunn, bondsman; Isaac Alexander, wit.

Thompson, Samuel T. & Mrs. Elizabeth L. Karter, 20 Feb 1845; Martin J. Hartis, bondsman; Philemon Morris, wit.

Thompson, Thomas & M. C. C. K. F. V. Gray, 15 Sept 1830; Admiral N. Gray, bondsman; B. Oates, wit.

Thompson, William J. & Harriet C. Montgomery, 4 March 1861; William R. Berryhill, bondsman; W. W. Grier, wit. married 5 March 1861 by Alex. Cooper, J. P.

Thomson, Gedion & Janie Vance, 8 Jan 1793; John Vance, bondsman; Isaac Alexander, wit.

Thomson, Thomas & Mary Lawin, 9 Jan 1796; Andrew Lawin, bondsman; R. Alexander, wit.

Thomson, William & Martha Lucas, 23 Nov 1814; Hugh Lucas, bondsman.

Thorn, James M. & Elizabeth Alexander, -- Jan 1846; Wm. N. Faires, bondsman; Saml. J. Lourie, wit.

Thornburg, F. B. & Eleanor Jamison, 10 Nov 1846; R. G. McLean, bondsman; B. Oates, C. C. C., wit.

Thornburg, Jonathan & Elizabeth Blackwelder, 10 Feb 1851; John Blackwelder, bondsman; B. Oates, C. C. C., wit.

Thornburg, Samuel & Mary Ann Blackwelder, 19 Dec 1849; Thos. L. Lowe, bondsman; Saml. J. Lourie, wit.

Threadgill, George R. (Dr.) & Celina Harris, 20 Feb 1838; John M. Ingram, bondsman.

Threatt, J. S. & M. A. Garland, 25 Oct 1865; W. P. Williams, bondsman; Wm. Maxwell, C. C. C., wit. married 29 Oct 1865 by E. C. Williams.

Thrower, William & Sarah A. Orr, 30 Nov 1832; Saml. A. Davis, bondsman; Isaac S. Alexander, wit.

Ticor, Samuel & Allany Rea, 28 Nov 1831; Will G. Coxe, bondsman.

Tiede, Charles F. W. & Eliza Bouers, 9 Oct 1861; John F. Bloom, bondsman; W. K. Reid, C. C. C., wit. married 9 Oct 1861 by G. D. Bernheim, pastor of St. Marks Ev. Lutheran Church, Charlotte, N. C.

Todd, Adam & Clementine Alexander, 29 April 1820; James N. Todd, bondsman; Isaac Alexander, wit.

Todd, Adam H. & Mary Todd, 5 Oct 1836; George W. McDonald, bondsman; B. Oates, C. C. C., wit.

Todd, David L. & Christine L. McGinn, 26 July 1852; Geo. L. Campbell, bondsman; Braly Oates, C. C. C.,wit. married 28 July 1852 by G. L. Campbell, J. P.

Todd, George & Hanah Neal, 18 Dec 1793; William Neil, bondsman; Isaac Alexander, wit.

Todd, George A. & Jane Baker, 8 Nov 1843; Elam T. McCoart, bondsman.

Todd, George A. & Sarah V. McCoy, 15 Jan 1856; Robert F. McGinn, bondsman; W. K. Reid, C. C. C., wit. married 15 Jan 1856 by J. P. Ross, J. P.

Todd, Green V. B. & Esther Cathey, 22 Dec 1859; Robert Sumerville, bondsman; W. K. Reid, C. C. C.,wit. married 22 Dec 1859 by G. L. Campbell, J. P.

Todd, James & Agness Neal, 20 Oct 1795; William Neil, bondsman; Isaac Alexander, wit.

Todd, James & Hanah Todd, 28 April 1797; Hugh Todd, bondsman.

Todd, James A. & Elizabeth Hutchison, 17 March 1819; Thomas L. Hutchison, bondsman.

Todd, James A. & Jane E. Wearn, 1 Oct 1851; R. H. Todd, bondsman; B. Oates, C. C. C., wit. married 2 Oct 1851 by H. B. Cunningham.

Todd, James A. & Mary A. Euing, 15 July 1858; Joseph A. McLure, bondsman; W. K. Reid, C. C. C.,wit.

Todd, James C. & Betsy C. McGinn, 24 March 1823; Robert Dunn, bondsman; R. J. Dinkins, wit.

Todd, James C. & Hannah L. Todd, 30 Dec 1863; G. N. Todd, bondsman; Wm. Maxwell, C. C. C., wit. married 31 Dec 1863 by J. P. Ross, J. P.

Todd, James L. & Polly McGinn, 15 Jan 1824; James M. McLure, bondsman; R. J. Dinkins, wit.

Todd, James N. & Mary Y. Todd, 28 Oct 1818; Hugh M. Henderson, bondsman; Isaac S. Alexander, wit.

Todd, James N. & Mary Sadler, 17 March 1821; John T. Sumervill, bondsman; Isaac S. Alexander, wit.

Todd, James N. & Susannah Haffner, 28 Sept 1831; Thomas Hoover, bondsman; B. Oates, wit.

Todd, John & Mary Berryhill, 29 Nov 1800; Samuel Berryhill, bondsman.

Todd, John & Mrs. Rachael Trout, 12 March 1817; John Stinson, bondsman; Isaac S. Alexander, wit.

Todd, John & Nancy Henderson, 8 March 1820; John Henderson, bondsman; Isaac Alexander, wit.

Todd, John & Martha Hamilton, 8 Dec 1840; Silas Todd, bondsman; B. Oates, wit.

Todd, John A. & Jane Henderson, 4 Nov 1817; H. M. Henderson, bondsman; Isaac S. Alexander, wit.

Todd, John A. & Isabella Jemison, 23 April 1834; William Jamison, bondsman; John Oates, wit.

Todd, John L. & Elizabeth Garmon, 18 Jan 1843; Joseph J. Berryhill, bondsman.

Todd, John L. & Jane B. Todd, 14 July 1846; James A. Todd, bondsman; B. Oates, C. C. C., wit.

Todd, John W. & Sarah A. McCord, 28 Sept 1847; James M. McCracken, bondsman; Saml. J. Lourie, wit.

Todd, R. H. & Margaret E. Neel, 25 Oct 1853; Andrew Neil, bondsman; W. K. Reid, C. C. C., wit. married 27 Oct 1853 by John Hunter, minister.

Todd, Robert A. & Polly S. Love, 6 Aug 1823; James McGuin, bondsman; Isaac Alexander, wit.

Todd, Robert S. & Margaret Taylor, 21 July 1848; Robt. M. Sterling, bondsman.

Todd, Samuel H. & Harriett˙Todd, 11 Jan 1826; John A.Todd, bondsman; Isaac S. Alexander, wit.

Todd, Samuel H. & Sarah C. Cathcart, 9 Sept 1857; A. H. Martin, bondsman; W. K. Reid, C. C. C., wit. married 14 Sept 1857 by G. L. Campbell, J. P.

Todd, Silas & Hannah McDonald, 29 May 1818; William N. Todd, bondsman; Isaac Alexander, wit.

Todd, William & Mary Sharpely, 21 Oct 1799; Samuel Berryhill, bondsman; Isaac Alexander, wit.

Todd, William & Isabella Henderson, 13 Aug 1802; Joseph Todd, bondsman.

Todd, William A. & Polly Taylor Gray, 23 Nov 1819; Grief N. Gray, bondsman; Isaac S.Alexander, wit.

Todd, William A. & Sarah E. Henderson, 10 June 1845; J. B. Kerr, bondsman; Isaac S.Alexander, wit.

Todd, William N. & Anne Wilson, 9 Sept 1818; James N. Todd, bondsman; Isaac Alexander, wit.

Todd, William W. & Sophia R. Todd, 15 April 1841; James Jamison, bondsman; B. Oates, C. C. C., wit.

Tomberlin, Moses & Jinsy Wilson, 11 Oct ⁄1822; Edmond Ritch, bondsman; Jos. Ritch, J. P., wit.

Tomberlin, Rheubin & Elisabeth Ormond, 27 March 1817; Amos Stevens, bondsman; John Rea, J. P.,wit.

Tomerlin, William & Liddy Boyet, 7 Sept 1835; Valentin Price, bondsman; Daniel Harget, wit.

Torrence, Adam & Grizell Matthews, 25 Feb 1817; John B. Hutchison, bondsman.

Torrence, Alexander H. & Nancy C. Caldwell, 11 April 1839; Thomas J. Caldwell, bondsman; James Johnston, wit.

Torrence, Charles L. & Margaret P. Fox, -- Oct 1847; Edwin R. Harris, bondsman; Saml. J. Lourie, wit.

Torrence, J. A. & N. V. White, 16 June 1865; J. A. Hall, bondsman; W. W. Grier, wit. married 22 June 1865 by R. F. Blythe, J. P.

Torrence, James G. & Mary Latta , 14 April 1821; Benjamin N. Davidson, bondsman; Isaac S. Alexander, wit.

Torrence, James H. & Martha C.Pippin, 21 Dec 1865; W. Henry Montieth, bondsman; A. McIver, wit. married 28 Dec 1865 by John L. Jetton, J. P.

Torrence, Julius A. & Sarah Jane White, 15 Aug 1849; Thomas E. Potts, bondsman; Saml. J. Lourie, D. C., wit.

Torrence, Levi H. & Margret B. Walker, 21 Jan 1829; Marshel H. Douglass, bondsman; Pearsall Thompson, wit.

Torrence, Oni W. & Mary A. Johnston, 28 March 1850; Jonas Rudisill, bondsman; B. Oates, C. C. C., wit.

Torrence, Stevon & Dovey Maxwell, 18 Sept 1865; Isaac Baaton, bondsman; R. M. White, wit.

Towle, Daniel & Mary Vary, 15 Aug 1826; William C. Houston, bondsman; Isaac S. Alexander, wit.

Towle, Daniel & Sarah Snell, 4 Dec 1835; E. D. Gray, bondsman; Isaac S. Alexander, wit.

Towns, Drury & Elis. Towns, 29 April 1789; Elisha Towns, bondsman; Jn. Rogers, wit.

Townsend, H. P. & Mary B. King, 14 March 1855; M. L. Barringer, bondsman; W. K. Reid, C. C. C., wit. married 22 March 1855 by Danl. A. Penick.

Townsend, William G.& Sarah Baine, 29 Oct 1833; James H. Townsend, bondsman.

Trailor, L. & Susan Trexler, 8 Feb 1863; M. W. Robison, bondsman; W. W. Grier, wit. married 8 Feb 1863 by D. J. Simmons.

Tredinnick, Nicholas & Margaret Wallace, 5 Jan 1833; John Wallace, bondsman; B. Oates, D. C., wit.

Tredinnick, Nicholas & Catharine Smith, (date obliterated), Andrew Smith, bondsman.

Treloar, John & Margaret L. Riglar, 19 March 1861; Jno. Phelan, bondsman; W. K. Reid, C. C. C., wit. married 19 March 1861 by Richd. H. Griffith, minister.

Trent, William & Johanah Pierson, 26 June 1800; David Kennedy, bondsman.

Trotter, Joshua & Nancy G. Wilkinson, 15 Nov 1842; Henry C. Owens, bondsman; James A. Johnston, wit.

Trotter, Thomas & Margret Graham, 18 Nov 1828; Pearsall Thompson, bondsman; P. Thompson, wit.

Trotter, Thomas & Jane Brown, 31 Dec 1850; A. H. Martin, bondsman.

Trout, James M. & Rebecca Archer, 3 Aug 1836; Francis Archer, bondsman; B. Oates, wit.

Tucker, Reubin Rev. & Jane I. Canon, 16 March 1818; Robert J. A. Lowrie, bondsman; Isaac Alexander, wit.

Tucker, Robert & Margaret Martin, 20 May 1819; Jno. Kerr, bondsman.

Tunes, Labon & Elizabeth S. Massey, 22 Sept 1865; John Howell, bondsman; Wm. Maxwell, C. C. C., wit. married 24 Sept 1865 by Jno. F. Butt.

Turner, George & Anne Goodrich, 29 Sept 1864; James D. Craig, bondsman; Wm. Maxwell, C. C. C., wit. married 29 Sept 1864 by J. P. Ross, J. P.

Tye, J. A. & Mary Shaffer, 24 April 1854; P. J. Lourie, bondsman; James Parks, wit. married 25 April 1854 by Thomas M. Farrow

Tye, John & Elizabeth Conder, 13 Nov 1818; John Cagle, bondsman.

Tye, William A. & Cornelia H. Shaver, 14 Feb 1825; Lewis Conder, bondsman; Isaac Alexander, wit.

Underwood, Jedon R. & Mary E. Price, 4 Sept 1865; G. W. Gatlin, bondsman; Wm. Maxwell, C. C. C.,wit. married 7 Sept 1865 by James D. Carpenter, Jun. Preacher on Charlotte circuit 1865.

Underwood, John & Lucinda Osborne, 15 June 1850; Solomon A. Hucks, bondsman; B. Oates, C. C. C.,wit.

Vaden, U. P. & Elizabeth A. Gibson, 11 Sept 1855; George Bargman, bondsman; W. K. Reid, C. C. C., wit. married 17 Sept by Jas. M. Garrison, minister.

Vance, John H. & Arathusus P. McNeely, 22 March 1832; Reubin Tomberlin, bondsman.

Vance, William & Rachel McRee, 18 Dec 1805; Thomas McRee, bondsman.

Vanderburg, Carson & Jane Tally, 9 April 1858; Mike Tally, bondsman; W. K. Reid, C. C. C.,wit.

Vann, Demsey & Ruth Reed, 29 Sept 1807

Van Pelt, Isaac & Ann Quiery, 11 March 1816; Joseph Hays, bondsman; Isaac Alexander, wit.

Van Pelt, Simon & Margaret McCoard, 26 Dec 1804; Thomas McCoard, bondsman; Isaac Alexander,wit.

Van Pelt, Simon & Susan Channels, 9 Oct 1823; Abel Baker, bondsman; Tho. W. P. Springs, wit.

Varner, David J. & Elizabeth Varner, 23 July 1860; A. Woodside Steele, bondsman; P. S. Whisnant, wit. married 23 July 1860 by J. S. Means, J. P.

Varner, John L. & Martha A. Fullum, 14 Aug 1856; William Warsham, bondsman; James Johnston, wit. married 14 Aug 1856 by A. Monroe Gillespie, J. P.

Vawter, James M. & S. E. Underwood, 30 Nov 1865; Robert Blythe, bondsman; Wm. Maxwell, C. C. C., wit. married 30 Nov 1865 by Jno. F. Butt.

Veich, William & Sarah Smith, 3 Sept 1790; John Miller, bondsman.

Vogel, John Frederick & Mary Page, 9 June 1864; Wm. Roediger, bondsman.

Voss, John & Susana Porter, 16 May 1799; William Miller, bondsman; Shared Gray, wit.

Voss, William & Elisabeth Orr, 4 April 1799; David Orr, bondsman; Shared Gray, wit.

Waddel, John Smith & Peggy Potts, 4 Feb 1806; Ezekiel Alexander, bondsman; Isaac Alexander, wit.

Waddell, David F. & Harriet A. Wilson, 16 Nov 1847; Robert A. Ross, bondsman; Saml. J. Lourie, wit.

MECKLENBURG MARRIAGES 1783-1868

Waddel, Georg or Joseph & Esther Cathey, 18 Jan 1804; Walter
Carruth, bondsman; Isaac Alexander, wit.

Waddington, Alexander G. & Hannah Polk, 15 Dec 1828; George W.
McLarty, bondsman; P. Thompson, wit.

Waddington, Robert & Charity Parimore, 3 Aug 1790; Francis Lock,
bondsman; Isaac Alexander, wit.

Waddington, Samuel & Elizabeth Bradshaw, 23 Nov 1787; Robert
Waddington, bondsman; Jno. Eppes Scott, wit.

Waine, Edward B. & Mary Ray, 28 July 1795; Isaac Alexander, bondsman.

Waisner, Curtis R. & Mary A. Walls, 22 Aug 1848; John C. Obrien,
bondsman; Saml. J. Lourie, wit.

Waisner, David & Betsey Moore, 8 Aug 1848; James J. Lee, bondsman.

Waisner, David & Betsey Moore, 13 Dec 1849; Samuel Taylor, bondsman;
B. Oates, C. C. C., wit.

Wait, William E. R. & Sarah Boles, 20 March 1851; S. L. Patterson,
bondsman; Saml. A. Davis, J. P., wit. married 20 March 1851
by Saml. A. Davis, J. P.

Walker, Abraham & Sarah McDugald, 21 July 1814; John Matthews,
bondsman; Isaac Alexander, wit.

Walker, Andrew & Margery Campbell, 20 March 1799; Joseph Haynes,
bondsman.

Walker, Cyrus A. & Ellen Robeson (colored), 21 Dec 1865; Amzi
Miller, bondsman; Wm. Maxwell, C. C. C., wit. married 25 ---
1866 by Jno. F. Butt.

Walker, Daniel & Mrs. Rachel Ritche, 21 Feb 1833; Elijah Ritch,
bondsman; Philemon Morris, wit.

Walker, Euseberus G. & Mary K. Swann, 1 Dec 1831; Joseph H.
Swann, bondsman; B. Oates, D. C., wit.

Walker, H. J. & C. E. Berryhill, 20 June 1864; W. D. Clanton,
bondsman; Wm. Maxwell, C. C. C., wit. married 23 June 1864 by
G. C. Cathey, J. P.

Walker, Hall & Esther Black, 12 Sept 1822; John Snell, bondsman;
Isaac Alexander, wit.

Walker, Henry & Elizabeth Milwee, 5 May 1800; William Walker,
bondsman; Isaac Alexander, wit.

Walker, Henry A. & Sarah Ann Tevepaugh, 30 Dec 1857; Neely J.
Winget, bondsman; W. K. Reid, C. C. C., wit. married 30 Dec
1857 by G. C. Parks, minister.

Walker, Hugh & Peggy Caryl, 12 Jan 1803; John Carson, bondsman;
Isaac Alexander, wit.

Walker, James & Esther Black, 26 May 1796; John Walker, bondsman;
Isaac Alexander, wit.

Walker, James & Elizabeth Morrow, 28 Dec 1815; James D. Wilson,
bondsman; Isaac Alexander, wit.

203

Walker, James & Jane Barkley, 12 Sept 1820; Saml. Blyth, bondsman; Isaac S. Alexander, wit.

Walker, James & Deborah Walker, 1 Feb 1831; Godfrey W. Williamson, bondsman; B. Oates, D. C., wit.

Walker, James & Margaret M. Alexander, 22 Jan 1840; James M. Alexander, bondsman; B. Oates, wit.

Walker, James & Allice Gaston (colored), 27 Sept 1865; Frank Parks, bondsman; R. M. White, wit. married 30 Sept 1865 by Thos. M. Alexander, J. P.

Walker, James D. & Hariet Clark, 19 Nov 1816; John Barnett, bondsman.

Walker, James H. & Margaret J. Rea, 12 Jan 1857; Ulysses L. Alexander, bondsman; W. K. Reid, C. C. C., wit. married 13 Jan 1857 by J. Walker, J. P.

Walker, James M. & Elizabeth J. Harris, 13 May 1851; Jno Walker, bondsman; B. Oates, C. C. C., wit. married 13 Jan 1851 by Jno. Hunter.

Walker, James S. & Mary E. Walker, 16 May 1849; Ephraim A. Walker, bondsman; Saml. J. Lourie, wit.

Walker, John & Rosanna Black, 5 Sept 1791; Robert Hays, bondsman; Isaac Alexander, wit.

Walker, John & Martha Galbraith, 29 June 1793; David Allison, bondsman; Isaac Alexander, wit.

Walker, John & Jane Harris, 23 Nov 1841; Thomas Hunter, bondsman; C. T. Alexander, wit.

Walker, John & Martha A. Hunter, 3 Feb 1845; James McHunter, bondsman; N. B. Taylor, wit.

Walker, John & Martha S. Porter, 7 Dec 1854; Robert C. Hunter, bondsman; W. K. Reid, C. C. C., wit. married 12 Dec 1854 by R. F. Taylor, minister.

Walker, John Jr. & Jane S. McCulloch, 18 Nov 1828; William Black, bondsman; Pearsall Thompson, wit.

Walker, John B. & Nancy E. J. Walker, 27 Aug 1856; Elam B. Wolf, bondsman; W. K. Reid, C. C. C., wit. married 28 Aug 1856 by J. M. Walker, minister.

Walker, John B. & Mary J. C. Cochran, 10 July 1861; Wm. W. Kirk, bondsman; W. K. Reid, C. C. C., wit.

Walker, John E. & Frances Flenniken, 29 March 1825; Charles Brown, bondsman; Isaac Alexander, wit.

Walker, John J. & Sarah Henderson, 14 Feb 1830; Alexander Cathy, bondsman.

Walker, Joseph & Jane Lemmond, 28 May 1831; Joseph McKnitt Alexander, bondsman.

Walker, Joseph C. & Olivia M. Hunter, 23 Aug 1854; James Mc-
Hunter, Jr., bondsman; W.K.Reid, C. C. C., wit. married
24 Aug 1854 by Walter S. Pharr

Walker, L. A. & Mary L. Ray, 24 July 1860; David Stinson, bondsman; W. K. Reid, C. C. C., wit. married 26 July 1860 by
Alex. Phillippe.

Walker, Moses & Mary Walker, 12 Jan 1791; James Irwin, bondsman;
Isaac Alexander, wit.

Walker, Richard & Ann Flennikin, 18 Sept 1810; Allen Curry,
bondsman; Isaac Alexander, wit.

Walker, Robert & Margaret T. Campbell, 2 Jan 1822; William
Walker, bondsman; Isaac Alexander, wit.

Walker, Robert L. & Martha L. Rea, 19 Feb 1848; Robert C. Bell,
bondsman; B. Oates, C. C. C., wit.

Walker, Robert N. & Elizabeth Tefabough, 19 Oct 1835; Philip
Tefabough, bondsman; B. Oates, C. C. C., wit.

Walker, Robert N. & Margaret Clark, 9 Jan 1844; James McAllister,
bondsman; N. B. Taylor, wit.

Walker, Samuel & Susannah Conger, 25 Nov 1807; Julius A. Jones,
bondsman; Isaac S. Alexander, wit.

Walker, Silvanus & Susanah Weathers, 12 March 1799; John
Weathers, bondsman.

Walker, Thomas & Mary Blythe, 1 Oct 1783; Thos Polk, Jas. White,
bondsmen.

Walker, Thomas J. & Jane Beaty, 27 Nov 1834; Alexander L. Porter,
bondsman.

Walker, Thompson & Jane Porter, 18 Oct 1809; David McDonald,
bondsman; Isaac Alexander, wit.

Walker, William & Jean Sharpe, 1 June 1801; John Brown, bondsman.

Walker, William & Mary Walker, 24 March 1827; Joseph Hays, bondsman.

Walker, Wm. & Louisa McPherson (colored), 1 Jan1866; Robt Johnston, bondsman; R. M. White, wit. married 1 Jan 1866 by
Jno. F. Butt.

Walker, William E. & Margaret L. Davis, 7 May 1860; James T.
Freeman, bondsman; W. K. Reid, C. C. C., wit. married 10 May
1860 by J. C. Chalmers, minister.

Walker, William H. & Caroline Walker, 8 March 1839; Calvin S.
Hunter, bondsman; B. Oates, C. C. C., wit.

Walkup, Israel & Peggy Morrow, --- --179-; James Baker, bondsman;
James Wallis, wit.

Walkup, James & Nancy H. Potts, 13 Jan 1827; Benjamin Morrow,
bondsman.

Walkup, Robert & Dorcas Montgomery, 19 June 1827; Alexander H. Ingram, bondsman.

Walkup, Samuel H. & Pamelia R. Price, 28 Sept 1860; Saml. J. Lourie, bondsman; P. S. Whisnant, wit. married 4 Oct 1860 by J. Rumple.

Wallace, Albert & Caroline Reed, 1 Dec 1845; James C. Flow, bondsman.

Wallace, Albert & Cornelia L. Cross, 21 Jan 1861; Saml. P. Caldwell, bondsman; W. K. Reid, C. C. C., wit. married 22 Jan 1861 by I. S. McLaughlin.

Wallace, Alexander & Prudence Smith, 12 July 1817; Telemacus Alexander, bondsman; Isaac Alexander, wit.

Wallace, Alexander & Elizabeth Biggers, 17 Nov 1838; James Wallis, bondsman; B. Oates, C. C. C., wit.

Wallace, Allen W. & Rocinda E. Christenbury, 28 Aug 1851; Samuel H. Christenbury, bondsman; James Parks, wit. married 29 Aug 1851 by R. D. Alexander, J. P.

Wallace, Andrew & Sarah Alexander, 14 Jan 1801; William Alexander, bondsman.

Wallace, Ezekiel & Lidia Knox, 19 April 1797; Ruthy Alexander, wit.

Wallace, George & Sarah Rogers, 28 Aug 1792; Samuel Willson, bondsman; Isaac Alexander, wit.

Wallace, James & Peggy Curry Barnett, 21 July 1810; Thomas Barnett, bondsman; Isaac Alexander, wit.

Wallace, James & Edetha Hunter, 1 Feb 1842; Wm. B. Sloan, bondsman; C. T. Alexander, wit.

Wallace, James & Sarah E. D. Montgomery, 30 Sept 1845; William G. Garrison, bondsman; C. T. Alexander, wit.

Wallace, John & Elizabeth Wallace, 2 April 1831; Matthew Wallis, bondsman; William Brown, wit.

Wallace, John & Sarah Johnson, 13 Feb 1833; Williamson Wallace, bondsman.

Wallace, John W. & S. E. Wallace, 10 Nov 1859; Robert Luckey, bondsman; W. K. Reid, C. C. C., wit. married 10 Nov 1859 by A. Ranson.

Wallace, Joseph & Margarett Houston, 7 Jan 1823; Thomas G. Barnett, bondsman; Isaac S. Alexander, wit.

Wallace, Joseph R. & Alice J. Morris, 9 Oct 1865; A. N. Johnston, bondsman; Wm. Maxwell, C. C. C., wit. married 9 Oct 1865 by Jno. F. Butt.

Wallace, London & Ellen Criffith (colored),27 Sept 1867; Wm. Maxwell, Clk., wit. married 13 Oct 1867 by J. Walker, J. P.

Wallace, M. Lawrence & Nancy S. Smith, 1 Jan 1861; Allison H. Bigger, bondsman; W. K. Reid, C. C. C., wit. married 3 Jan 1861 by Lorenzo Hunter, J. P.

Wallace, Marquis L. & Elisabeth M. Williamson, 31 Oct 1848;
Nathan Orr, bondsman; Saml. A. Davis, J. P., wit.

Wallace, Matthew & Peggy Barnhill, 5 Oct 1811; John Barnhill,
bondsman; Isaac S. Alexander, wit.

Wallace, Mathew B. & Mary Caroline Black, 15 Feb 1822; Alexander
McLarty, bondsman; Isaac Alexander, wit.

Wallace, Robt. B. & Mary Ann Bighers, 11 Jan 1843; John W. Wilson,
bondsman.

Wallace, Robert B. & Jane Ann Morrison, 16 Oct 1865; R. M. White,
bondsman; Wm. Maxwell, C. C. C., wit. married 17 Oct 1865
by Wm. McDonald.

Wallace, Robert L. & Margaret M. Johnston, 21 July 1851; R. M.
Norment, bondsman; Braly Oates, C. C.C., wit. married 22
July 1851 by John Walker, J. P.

Wallace, William & Jean Moffet, 1 Dec 1792; Samuel Meek, bondsman;
John Allison, wit.

Wallace, William & Catharine McLarty, 14 Jan 1800; Robert Wallace,
bondsman; Isaac Alexander, wit.

Wallace, William & Sarah Gilliland, 2 Dec 1806; John Gilliland,
bondsman; Isaac Alexander, wit.

Wallace, William & Jane A. Kerns, 23 Feb 1850; R. V. Kerns,
bondsman; James Parks, wit.

Wallace, William S. & Lucy B. Johnston, 22 Jan 1846; John Phelan,
bondsman; B. Oates, C. C. C., wit.

Wallace, Williamson & Mary Morris, 21 Aug 1848; Jno. T. Reid,
bondsman; Saml. J. Lourie, wit.

Wallis, Ezekiel & Elizabeth Robison, 23 Dec 1806; John Park Jr.,
bondsman; Isaac Alexander, wit.

Wallis, Ezekiel C. & Mary Parks, 17 Dec 1839; Cyrus L. Alexander,
bondsman; B. Oates, C. C. C., wit.

Wallis, William & Rebekah Alexander, 29 Feb 1804; William Beaty,
bondsman.

Wallis, William & Hannah Julian, 14 March 1809; Nathan Orr,
bondsman.

Walls, Janes H. & Violet Buchannon, 29 Jan 1842; David F. Glenn,
bondsman.

Walls, Wm. R. & Matilda A. Page, 31 Dec 1855; Andrew Jackson
Williams, bondsman; W. K. Reid, C. C. C., wit. married 31
Dec 1855 by C. Overman, J. P.

Walsh, Andrew & Mary Blanchart, 26 March 1820; Thomas Blanchard,
bondsman; Isaac Alexander, wit.

Warner, Frederick A. & Mary Robinson, 5 Dec 1864; Gustaf Schneider,
bondsman; Wm. Maxwell, C. C. C., wit. married 5 Dec 1864 by
F. Milton Kennedy, Chap. P. A. C. S.

Warren, Isaac & Sarah Furr, 12 Aug 1856; Ananias Jordan, bondsman;
W. K. Reid, C. C. C., wit. married 14 Aug 1856 by G. W.
Houston, J. P.

Warren, James S. & Elizabeth Haddleston, 2 April 1821; Thomas H.
Acock, bondsman; Isaac S. Alexander, wit.

Warrick, B. A. & Lucinda Simpson, 28 Sept 1847; Henry Gatlin,
bondsman; Saml. J. Lourie, wit.

Warsham, B. E. & Sarah Sims, 13 Jan 1846; R. P. Wiley, bondsman;
E. B. D. Sloan, wit.

Warsham, Bennet & Nancy Warsham, 2 Feb 1820; Branch Warsham,
bondsman; Jno. McLane, wit.

Warsham, Branch A. & Nancy A. E. Johnston, 23 Dec 1861; Calvin
T. Dewese, bondsman; W. K. Reid, C. C. C., wit. married
31 Dec 1861 by Walter S. Pharr.

Warsham, R. R. & R. C. Beard, 23 Dec 1864; J. J. Brown, bondsman;
R. M. White, D. C., wit. married 25 Dec 1864 by R. F. Blythe,
J. P.

Warsham, Thomas & Sarah Rodgers, 7 Feb 1822; Samuel Johnson,
bondsman; W. L. Davidson, wit.

Warsham, William & E. J. Cashion, 15 Dec 1853; James Johnston,
J. P., wit. married -- Dec 1853 by Jas. M. Garrison.

Warwick, John R. & Elizabeth J. Weeks,10 Dec 1851; John S. Porter,
bondsman; B. Oates, C. C. C., wit. married 18 Dec 1851 by
Samuel C. Pharr, V. D. M.

Warwick, William & Elizabeth Baker, 2 June 1862; William D.
Taylor, bondsman; W. R. Maxwell, wit.

Washam, Alfred & Harriet Riley, 12 Nov 1858; Alexander Warsham,
bondsman; K. W. Berryhill, wit. married 16 Nov 1858 by
Walter S. Pharr.

Washington, John & Betsey Rodgers, 9 March 1790; John Rogers,
bondsman; Isaac Alexander, wit.

Wasiner, John D. & Mary Jane Clark, 30 Aug 1848; William W.
Quinn, bondsman; Saml. J. Lourie, wit.

Watson, Nathl. & Sarah Strain, 4 Oct 1792; James Yendel, bondsman;
Isaac Alexander, wit.

Watson, Robert & Abigail Brown, 6 Sept 1792; James Brown, Jno.
Allison, bondsmen.

Watson, Robert & Betsey Blackwood, 21 Feb 1804; James Watson,
bondsman; Isaac Alexander, wit.

Watson, S. B. (Dr.) & Mary E. Taylor, 13 Feb 1865; R. M. White,
bondsman; Wm. Maxwell, C. C. C., wit. married 14 Feb 1865
by John Hunter, minister.

Watson, Samuel B. & Emily C. Dinkins, 8 Sept 1835; R. A. Springs,
bondsman; B. Oates, C. C. C., wit.

Watson, Samuel L. & Nancy H. Neil, 12 Nov 1830; Hugh McDowell, bondsman; B. Oates, wit.

Watson, William & Sarah Rogers, 31 July 1790; James Todd, bondsman; Isaac Alexander, wit.

Watts, Joel J. & Mary J. Morris, 22 Aug 1865; G. C. Morris, bondsman; Wm. Maxwell, C. C. C., wit. married 24 Aug 1865 by Wm. McDonald.

Watts, John & Cynthia Kirkpatrick, 29 Jan 1840; Thos. S. Alexander, bondsman; B. Oates, C. C. C., wit.

Watts, Ruffus F. & Jane E. Otton, 19 March 1856; Samuel B. Christenbury, bondsman; W. K. Reid, C. C. C., wit. married 20 March 1856 by R. D. Alexander.

Watts, W. B. & M. E. Alexander, 21 Nov 1861; E. Nye Hutchison, bondsman; W. K. Reid, C. C. C., wit. married 25 Nov 1861 by A. Sinclair, minister.

Watts, W. G. & Margaret Auton, 18 April 1861; W. G. Christenbury, bondsman; W. K. Reid, C. C. C.,wit. married 25 April 1861 by Walter S. Pharr.

Watts, Wm. T.& Margaret E. Berryhill, 31 Aug 1865; J. Roeseler, bondsman; Wm. Maxwell, C. C. C., wit. married 31 Aug 1865 by I. J. Sloan, J. P.

Wearn, James T. & Mary Collins, 30 Jan 1849; Robert D. Collins, bondsman; B. Oates, C. C. C., wit.

Wearn, W. S. & C. A. Moore, 11 Feb 1863; M. W. Robison, bondsman; Wm. Maxwell, C. C. C., wit. married 11 Feb 1863 by D. J. Simmons, M. M. E. C.

Weathers, Edmund & Betsey Gutridge, 12 Nov 1803; James Denton, bondsman; Isaac Alexander, wit.

Weathers, Henry & Patsey Keeker, 18 Nov 1808; William Wilson, bondsman; Isaac Alexander, wit.

Weathers, John & Patsey Drury, 13 April 1802; Jno. Dinkins, bondsman; Isaac Alexander, wit.

Weathers, Randolph & Sally Bailey, 4 Jan 1803; John Weathers, bondsman; Isaac Alexander, wit.

Weaver, David & Mary A. Headly, 1 May 1851; James A. McCoy, bondsman; B. Oates, C. C. C., wit.

Weaver, Julius A. & Margaret A. Griffith, 24 March 1858; Samuel B. Griffith, bondsman; W. K. Reid, C. C. C.,wit. married 24 March 1858 by Lorenzo Hunter, J. P.

Webb, Lewis & Suckey Walker, 15 July 1806; John Cook, bondsman; Isaac Alexander, wit.

Webb, Thomas & Jane Davis, 12 May 1860; Ezekiel Elms, bondsman.

Weddington, John & Agness Snell, 12 Feb 1817; William Biggers, bondsman; Isaac Alexander, wit.

Weddington, John C. & Elizabeth Hartt, 24 April 1849; F. A. Biggers, bondsman.

Weddington, John R. & Narcissa Black, 25 Aug 1842; J. Y. Weddington, bondsman; C. T. Alexander, wit.

Weddington, Robert H. & Margaret P. Hartt, 23 Oct 1849; David M. Miller, bondsman.

Weddington, Samuel N. & Jane C. M. Lucas, 19 Dec 1840; William Parks, bondsman; B. Oates, wit.

Wedlock, William & Mary E. Morrow, 25 Nov 1859; Henry Gundry, bondsman; W. K. Reid, C. C. C., wit. married 25 Nov 1859 by C. Overman, J. P.

Weeks, J. L. & Maggie R. Robinson, 14 Aug 1865; R. M. White, bondsman; Wm. Maxwell, C. C. C., wit. married 17 Aug 1865 by R. Z. Johnston, M. G.

Weeks, John & Peggy Mulwee, 19 Jan 1796; William Morrison, bondsman; J. Wallis, wit.

Weeks, John & Mary E. Mathews, 14 Jan 1841; Zachariah Hodges, bondsman.

Weir, Calvin S. & Isabella Alexander, 15 March 1839; William C. Corum, bondsman; B. Oates, C. C. C., wit.

Weir, Thomas & Ginnet Haw, 24 Nov 1795; Samuel Houston, bondsman; Ruthe Alexander, wit.

Wells, Anderson, & Cynthia Waddle, 23 Nov 1830; Middleton Lawing, bondsman; Isaac S. Alexander, wit.

Wells, William & Jane Kennedy, 8 Feb 1788; Andrew Kennedy, bondsman; J. McK. Alexander, wit.

Wells, William & Martha Moffit, 31 Jan 1792; Alexander Kennedy, bondsman.

Wels, Burrel & Nancy Owens, 25 Aug 1805; William Owens, bondsman; Isaac Alexander, wit.

Wents, Moses & Jane Goodin, 5 Oct 1855; Jno. A. Young, bondsman; W. K. Reid, C. C. C., wit. married 17 Oct 1855 by W. H. Neell, J. P.

Wents, Moses S. & Rhoda Norment, 9 Dec 1857; David Gooden, bondsman; W. K. Reid, C. C. C., wit. married 10 Dec 1857 by Alex. Cooper, J. P.

Wents, Valentine & Nancy E. Hawkins, 24 Sept 1852; Jacob L. Hawkins, bondsman; B. Oates, C. C. C., wit. married 30 Sept 1852 by Jas. M. Garrison, minister.

Wentz, Aaron & Mrs. Easter Rise, 29 March 1842; Jared Rice, bondsman; Philemon Morris, wit.

Wentz, Andrew & Margaret S. Wilson, 11 Feb 1840; James McLeod, bondsman; B. Oates, C. C. C., wit.

Wentz, Daniel & Polly Stilwell, 23 Dec 1813; Elijah Stilwell, bondsman; Phn. Morris, wit.

Wentz, Jeremiah & Nancy Sibley, 24 May 1824; Samuel McComb, bondsman; Isaac Alexander, wit.

MECKLENBURG MARRIAGES 1783-1868

Wentz, Jeremiah & Margaret Stilwell, 30 March 1854; Nelson
  Stilwell, bondsman; Casper Hargett, J. P., wit. married 30
March 1854 by Casper Hargett, J. P.

Wentze, Andrew & Mrs. Suffiah Stanford, 23 Oct 1827; Stephen
  Harget, bondsman; Philemon Morris, wit.

West, Benjamin S. & Sophia Sloan, 28 Aug 1821; David Sloan, bondsman.

West, Benjmon & Esther Stinson, 9 Jan 1805; Alexander Stinson,
  bondsman; Isaac Alexander, wit.

West, Joseph & Christiania Chapman, 12 June 1860; S. J. Badger,
  bondsman; W. W. Grier, wit. married 12 June 1860 by J. P.
Ross, J. P.

Westmoreland, Jackson & Nancy Hipp, 16 July 1808; John Hipp,
  bondsman; Michl. McLeary, wit.

Westmoreland, Robert & Dorcas Kerr, 19 Aug 1828; Alexander C.
  Worke, bondsman; A. B. Jetton, wit.

Westmorland, Joseph Q. & Mulvina Westmorland, 15 April 1840;
  Merrel Brown, bondsman.

Westmorland, Rhodee & Anne Hipp, 1 Sept 1808; John Hipp, bondsman;
  Michl. McLeary, wit.

Westmorland, Sterling C. & Hannah Gilmore, 24 Oct 1809; Jese
  Cathy, bondsman; Isaac Alexander, wit.

Westmorland, William L. & Mary Black, 31 Dec 1842; Alexander H.
  Torrence, bondsman; James Johnston, wit.

White, Alexander & Betsey Rogers, 4 Dec 1819; James Rodgers,
  bondsman.

White, Alexander & Hellan Dewease, 28 Feb 1852; Braley Oates,
  C. C. C., wit. married 11 March 1852 by Saml. B. O. Wilson,
V. D. M. P. C.

White, Benjamin M. & Jane Flow, 17 Feb 1853; John Stilwell,
  bondsman; B. Oates, C. C. C., wit. married 17 Feb 1853 by
Casper Hargett, J. P.

White, James & Mary Dickson, 28 Jan 1814; John R. Dixon, bondsman;
  Isaac Alexander, wit.

White, James & Nancy Knox, 8 Oct 1859; Alexander Kelly, bondsman;
  W. W. Grier, wit. married 12 Oct 1859 by R. F. Blythe, J. P.

White, James Mc & Mary Morrison, 19 Jan 1825; James M. Morrison,
  bondsman; Isaac S.Alexander, wit.

White, James T. & Sarah Pucket, 31 July 1852; E. W. Kennerley,
  bondsman; James Parks, wit. married 19 Aug 1852 by Isaac
Wilson, J. P.

White, James T. & Dorcas E. Gambel, 18 Oct 1859; Jas. P. Henderson,
  bondsman; W. K. Reid, C. C. C., wit. married 20 Oct 1859 by
R. F. Blythe, J. P.

White, John Mc & M. F. Reid, 20 Dec 1859; Oswald Alexander, bondsman; W. K. Reid, C. C. C., wit. married 22 Dec 1859 by Jethro Rumple, V. D. M.

White, R. M. & Mrs. Elizabeth J. Walker, 11 Dec 1865; M. D. L. McLeod, bondsman; Wm. Maxwell, C. C. C., wit. married 14 Dec 1865 by Wm. McDonald.

White, Robert & Jane Dixon, 23 July 1799; John Houston, bondsman.

White, Robert S. & Martha A. Alexander, 23 Oct 1852; Reuben F. Christenbury, bondsman; B. Oates, C. C. C., wit. married 27 Oct 1852 by S. C. Pharr, V. D. M.

White, Thomas & Elizabeth Shepperd, 28 May 1799; James White, bondsman; Jas. Conner, J. P., wit.

White, W. E. Jr. & S. D. Caldwell, 15 Oct 1860; John C. Burroughs, bondsman; W. K. Reid, C. C. C., wit. married 16 Oct 1860 by E. D. Jenkins, Minister of the Gospel.

White, William & Mary McLarty, 27 Oct 1795; John McLarty, bondsman.

White, William E. & Sarah A. R. Wilson, 23 Feb 1824; Abram F. Alexander, bondsman; Isaac S. Alexander, wit.

White, William F.& Elizabeth C. Dunn, 17 Feb 1845; Thos. H. Brem, bondsman.

Whitesid, James & Mary McFall, 18 July 1801; Robert McKinley, bondsman; Isaac Alexander, wit.

Whitesid, James & Sally Lewis, 24 May 1803; Samuel Whiteside, bondsman; Isaac Alexander, wit.

Whitesid, Joseph & Mary Vann Carothers, 31 Jan 1812; James L. Carothers, bondsman.

Whiteside, Andrew J. & Caroline Blanchard, 4 Sept 1839; William T. Taylor, bondsman.

Whiteside, John N. & Eleanor Rea, 17 Aug 1836; Samuel M. Neely, bondsman; B. Oates, C. C. C., wit.

Whiteside, Samuel & Margaret McKinley, 28 Sept 1799; Robert McKinley, bondsman.

Whiteside, Samuel M. & Esther C. Carothers, 9 March 1850; Ezekiel Carothers, bondsman; B. Oates, C. C. C., wit.

Whiteside, Samuel M. & Sarah M. Brown, 18 March 1852; J. D. Carothers, bondsman; David D. Oates, wit. married 23 March 1852 by A. L. Watts, V. D. M.

Whiteside, William & Rebekah Lensing, 11 Nov 1808; John Taylor, bondsman; Isaac Alexander, wit.

Whitesides, John & Judith Monroe, 2 July 1823; James Neely, bondsman.

Whitley, Adason & Somera Medlen, 25 Feb 1841; Jesse Gilbert, bondsman; Wm. Butt, J. P., wit.

Whitley, Jonathan R. & Jane Price, 23 Aug 1813; B. Wilson Davidson, bondsman.

Whitley, Robert D. & Esther S. McCoy, 16 Feb 1855; R. F. Blythe,
bondsman; W. K. Reid, C. C. C., wit. married 21 Feb 1855 by
H. B. Cunningham.

Whitly, Albert & Cressey Gluyas (colored), 5 Aug 1865; Buck Blythe,
bondsman; Wm. Maxwell, C. C. C., wit. married 5 Aug 1865 by
Thomas Gluyas, J. P.

Whitlow, E. W. & Ruth B. Sloan, 15 June 1857; J. H. Sloane, bondsman; W. K. Reid, C. C. C., wit. married 16 June 1857 by
R. L. DeArmon, J. P.

Whitlow, M. C. & Martha N. Nance, 22 Dec 1849; David F. Davis,
bondsman.

Whyte, Archibald & Susan N. Greer, 14 April 1831; Wil M. Grier,
bondsman.

Wiggens, Dosson & Nancy Michel, 26 March 1805; Henry Crenshaw,
bondsman; Shared Gray, wit.

Wiggens, Elie & Salley Sherlin, 21 March 1805; Jerimiah Cureton,
bondsman.

Wiley, John & Margaret McCulloh, 8 July 1823; William Milwee,
bondsman; Isaac Alexander, wit.

Wiley, Moses & Sarah Simons, 8 Jan 1820; Robert Simons, bondsman;
Isaac Alexander, wit.

Wiley, Oliver & Peggy Morrison, 27 Oct 1801; Saml. McCurdy, bondsman.

Wiley, Robert P. & Betsy Chason, 11 Feb 1829; Thomas S. McKibbon,
bondsman; Tho. B. Smartt, wit.

Wiley, Robert P. & Fanny Washarm, 9 Feb 1843; Alexander Davis,
bondsman; M. W. Alexander, wit.

Wilkerson, T. J. & L. H. Wilson, 2 May 1863; W. J. Collier, bondsman; Wm. Maxwell, C. C. C., wit. married 3 May 1863 by D. J.
Simmons.

Wilkinson, Archibald G. & Nancy Graham, 21 April 1824; Thomas
Gillespie, bondsman; Isaac Alexander, wit.

Wilkinson, Joseph H. & Nancy E. Reed, 22 Dec 1852; William Wilkinson, bondsman; B. Oates, C. C. C., wit. married 22 Dec 1852
by Jos. C. Nicholson, J. P.

Wilkinson, Neill & Emma Trotter, 9 May 1855; Wm. Ps. Hill, bondsman;
W. K. Reid, C. C. C., wit.

Wilkinson, William & Amanda Dewese, 10 June 1841; John W. Rainy,
bondsman; James Johnston, wit.

Wilkinson, William & Nancy A. Dewese, 7 Jan 1852; Dr. Jos. M.
Davidson, bondsman; James Parks, Dpt., wit. married 7 Jan
1852 by J. P. Ross, J. P.

Williams, Andrew J. & Elizabeth Walls, 12 June 1837; David E.
Barnett, bondsman; P. E. Saunier, wit.

Williams, Edmond & Francis Johnston (colored), 23 Sept 1865;
Stevon D. McBride, bondsman; R. M. White, wit. married 23
Sept 1865 by Wm. H. Pitts, Elder.

Williams, Henry B. & Susan E. Boyd, 22 Jan 1845; B. Oates, bondsman; C. T. Alexander, C. C.C., wit.

Williams, Jacob & Sarah Wood, 8 Feb 1820; William Stuard, bondsman;
Jno. McLane, wit.

Williams, James J. & Elizabeth Hartis, 15 Feb 1837; Mathew Miller,
bondsman; B. Oates, wit.

Williams, John J. & Clementine A. Biggart, 8 Dec 1864; James
Biggart, bondsman; Wm. Maxwell, C. C. C., wit. married 8
Dec 1864 by E. Nye Hutchison, J. P.

Williams, John R. & Mary McComb, 7 Nov 1815; Jonas Clark, bondsman;
Isaac Alexander, wit.

Williams, Rufus & Cornelia Allen, 20 March 1855; C. N. Blyth,
bondsman; James Johnston, wit. married 5 April 1855 by H.
B. Cunningham.

Williams, T. F. & Mary Ferguson, 6 Feb 1865; J. M. W. Flow,
bondsman; Wm. Maxwell, C. C. C., wit. married 7 Dec 1865 by
E. C. Williams.

Williams, Thomas & Eliza Brem, 11 Nov 1861; Jos. C. Nicholson,
bondsman; W. K. Reid, C. C. C., wit. married 27 Nov 1861 by
R. F. Blythe, J. P.

Williams,Thomas B.& Catharine Hatch, 26 July 1815; Ransom Gray,
bondsman.

Williams, Thomas W. & Mary Wallace, 5 Aug 1835; James Clark,
bondsman; B. Oates, C. C. C., wit.

Williams, William P. & Mary Muse, 15 July 1841; John M. Muse,
bondsman.

Williamson, Albert C. & Mary A. Fox, 11 June 1851; Robert B.
Boyle, bondsman; married 11 June 1851 at the residence of
Mrs. Cynthia Fox, Charlotte, by Thomas S. W. Motte.

Williamson, Amzi L. & Susan Hayes, 9 Sept 1856; S. W. Alexander,
bondsman; W. K. Reid, C. C. C., wit. married 9 Sept 1856 by
J. Walker, J. P.

Williamson, Cyrus & Hannah Alexander, 12 July 1828; Washington
Morrison, bondsman.

Williamson, David A. & Margaret Walker, 11 June 1832; James
Walker, bondsman.

Williamson, Dauson & Mary Freeman, 24 Nov 1804; Michael Freeman,
bondsman; Isaac Alexander, wit.

Williamson, E. D. & Martha D. Wallis, 31 Dec 1844; Will Johnston,
bondsman; N. B. Taylor, wit.

Williamson, Frederick & Caroline Alexander, 16 Sept 1830; Batte
Irwin, bondsman; Benj. Morrow, wit.

Williamson, G. W. & Angeline P. Reed, 11 April 1836; Robert R. Taylor, bondsman; B. Oates, C. C. C., wit.

Williamson, G. W. & Mrs. Martha D. McCulloch, 9 Oct 1865; Wm. H. Neal, bondsman; Wm. Maxwell, C. C. C., wit. married 10 Oct 1865 by J. C. Chalmers, minister.

Williamson, George W. & J. L. Wilson, 12 Dec 1865; J. C. McCoy, bondsman; Wm. Maxwell, C. C. C., wit. married 19 Dec 1865 by S. C. Pharr.

Williamson, J. B. & Malissa Noles, 7 Aug 1865; William C. Clark, bondsman; Wm. Maxwell, C. C. C., wit. married 7 Aug 1865 by J. S. Reid, J. P.

Williamson, J. R. & Nancy E. Cooper, 10 April 1849; Edward H. Moss, bondsman; Saml. J. Lourie, wit.

Williamson, James B. & Mary S.Noles, 12 June 1851; Hugh G. Porter, bondsman; C. B. Cross, J. P., wit. married 12 June 1851 by C. B. Cross, J. P.

Williamson, James G. & Catherine Knox, 24 March 1849; James A. McCoy, bondsman.

Williamson, James G. & Catharine N. Nicholson, 12 Sept 1859; G. W. Williamson, bondsman; W. K. Reid, C. C. C., wit.

Williamson, John & Peggy Hutson, 6 Aug 1806; Joseph Reed, bondsman; Isaac Alexander,wit.

Williamson, John & Polly Denkins, 2 March 1807; Bevly Byram, bondsman; Isaac Alexander, C. M. C.,wit.

Williamson, John F. & Martha Lewis, 5 Dec 1823; Thos. P. Berryhill, bondsman.

Williamson, John M. & Saline Tye, 1 July 1839; Marquis D. L. McLoud, bondsman; B. Oates, wit.

Williamson, Leander Z. & Sarah C. Harris, 8 April 1830; David A. Pressly, bondsman.

Williamson, Ruben & Agness Campbell, 12 Feb 1800; Armistead Campbell, bondsman; Isaac Alexander, wit.

Williamson, Thomas J. & Elizabeth Black, 14 June 1831; Robert Grier, bondsman; Isaac S. Alexander, wit.

Williamson, Vincent Young & Mary P. McCoy, 1 May 1824; Jno. H. McCoy, bondsman; Isaac Alexander, wit.

Williamson, W. L. & Amanda Knox, 7 Feb 1853; David Williamson, bondsman; B. Oates, C. C. C., wit. married 8 Feb 1853 by A. L. Watts, V. D. M.

Williamson, William & Violet L. McCoy, 14 Feb 1825; Jno. H. McCoy, bondsman; Isaac Alexander, C. M. C., wit.

Williamson, William H. & Elmina Wentz, 12 April 1836; Silas N. Stilwell, bondsman; B. Oates, C. C. C., wit.

Willeford, William A. & Margaret L. Flanagan, 2 Sept 1852; J. A. Patterson, bondsman; B. Oates, C. C. C.,wit.

Willson, James & Margaret Beaty, 2 March 1792; David Stinson, bondsman; Isaac Alexander, C. C., wit.

Willson, James & Eliza Carrigan, 10 Sept 1819; James Carrigin, bondsman.

Wilson, Benjamin & Mary Wilson, 20 Sept 1817; John L. McConnell, bondsman.

Wilson, Bob & Mary Conder (colored), 7 Feb 1866; F. A. Biggers, bondsman; Wm. Maxwell, C. C. C., wit. married 8 Feb 1866 by A. J. Hood, J. P.

Wilson, Charles & Matilda McComb, 20 May 1841; David Maxwell, bondsman; B. Oates, C. C. C., wit.

Wilson, Cyrus J. & Mary J. Patton, 3 Dec 1851; J. W. Barnett, bondsman; B. Oates, C. C. C., wit. married 4 Dec 1851 by Cyrus Johnston, V. D. M.

Wilson, George & Elizabeth Hall, 26 Aug 1805; Mathew Wallace, bondsman.

Wilson, Gorden & Olivia Alexander, 1 April 1839; Sinai Alexander, bondsman; B. Oates, wit.

Wilson, H. H. & M. E. Williamson, 16 May 1849; S. Nye Hutchison, bondsman; Saml. J. Lourie, wit.

Wilson, Isaac & Violet E. L. Alexander, 24 Dec 1831; Wm. M. B. Flinn, bondsman; B. Oates, wit.

Wilson, Isaac & Lucinda M. Wallace, 2 Dec 1834; Samuel McKee, bondsman; B. Oates, C. C. C.,wit.

Wilson, Jackson & Elizabeth Forsythe, 24 Nov 1855; A. L. Maxwell, bondsman; W. K. Reid, C. C. C., wit.

Wilson, James & Martha Orr, 17 Feb 1794; David Stewart, bondsman

Wilson, James & Martha Osborne, 6 Dec 1804; Cunningham Felton, bondsman; J. Wallis, wit.

Wilson, James & Isabella Smith, 28 Sept 1809; Hezekiah Alexander, bondsman.

Wilson, James & Elizabeth Maxwell, 6 April 1819; James Maxwell, bondsman; Isaac Alexander, wit.

Wilson, James & Elizabeth Lewis, 15 Nov 1854; James M. Lewis, bondsman; W. K. Reid, C. C. C., wit. married 16 Nov 1854 by W. R. Maxwell, J. P.

Wilson, James & Mary Todd, 10 Sept 1867; Wm. Maxwell, Clk., wit. married 12 Sept 1867 by John W. Moore, J. P.

Wilson, James M. & Mary J. Allen, 4 July 1848; Albert Wilson, bondsman.

Wilson, James W. & Eleanor C. Cook, 23 Jan1836; Robert W. Parks, bondsman; B. Oates, C. C. C., wit.

Wilson, Jethro & Laura Wood, 23 May 1818; Joseph Wilson, bondsman; Isaac Alexander, wit.

MECKLENBURG MARRIAGES 1783-1868

Wilson, John & Margarett Wallace, 18 Sept 1789; William Wallace,
bondsman; Jn. Rogers, wit.

Wilson, John & Eliz. McCrum, 18 March 1808; John Young, bondsman;

Wilson, John & Mary Brown, 15 Oct 1810; William Brown, bondsman;
Isaac Alexander, wit.

Wilson, John & Nancy Bun, 9 Aug 1811; James Morris, bondsman;
Isaac Alexander, C. M. C.,wit.

Wilson, John & Isabella Thompson, 20 Feb 1817; William Morris,
bondsman.

Wilson, John & Margaret Boyd, 4 May 1838; William Sandry,
bondsman; B. Oates, wit.

Wilson, John B. & Catherine Kimbell, 16 June 1845; Alexander
Beaty, bondsman; Isaac S. Alexander, wit.

Wilson, John J. & Catharine L. Henderson, 3 Jan 1853; John R.
Daniel, bondsman; B. Oates, C. C. C., wit. married 4 Jan
1853 by Cyrus Johnston, minister.

Wilson, John M. & Philadelphia H. Fox, 26 Oct 1831; Samuel McKee,
bondsman.

Wilson, John M. & Martha C. Parks, 9 June 1835; Samuel C. Caldwell, bondsman; B. Oates, C. C. C., wit.

Wilson, John M. & Harriet A. Taylor, 21 April 1840; Tho. T.
Sandifer, bondsman;

Wilson, John M. & Catharine M. Walker, 19 Feb 1856; James T.
Hart, bondsman; W. K. Reid, C. C. C., wit. married 20 Feb
1856 by Walter S. Pharr.

Wilson, John N. & Mrs. Margret A. Wallace, 21 June 1842; James
T. Morris, bondsman; Philemon Morris, wit.

Wilson, John P. & Emily E. Davis, 2 May 1861; John M. Wilson,
bondsman; W. K. Reid, C. C. C., wit. married 2 May 1861 by
W. H. Neal, J. P.

Wilson, John W.& Jane C. Gammel, 28 Dec 1840; Robert G. Kirkpatrick, bondsman.

Wilson, Joseph & Jane Mitchell, 10 Aug 1798; Robert Mishell,
bondsman.

Wilson, Joseph M. & Leonora L. Patterson, 5 April 1856; T. H.
Brem, bondsman; W. K. Reid, C. C. C., wit. married 8 April
1856 by E. D. Jenkins.

Wilson, Marcus K. & E. J. Wilkinson, 25 March 1845; Milas W.
Johnson, bondsman; N. B. Taylor, wit.

Wilson, Matthew N. & Prudence C.Wallace, 11 May 1853; Jonathan
Stinson, bondsman; Braly Oates, C. C. C., wit. married 12
May 1853 by Lorenzo Hunter, J. P.

Wilson, Moses Winslow & An B. Torrence,16 Feb 1815; John Wilson,
bondsman; Jas. G. Torrence, J. P., wit.

Wilson, P. J. & Mary Ann Prim, 30 May 1855; Jas. C. Wilson, bondsman; W. K. Reid, C. C. C.,wit. married 30 May 1855 by James Johnston.

Wilson, Robert & Eleanor Hargroves, 28 April 1813; John Hartgrove, bondsman; Isaac Alexander, wit.

Wilson, Robert & Margaret Alexander, 3 Dec 1816; Henry W. M. Conner, bondsman.

Wilson, Robert & Lucv Stephens, 19 July 1819; Lewis Denkins, bondsman; Isaac S. Alexander, wit.

Wilson, Robert & Elizabeth M. Flow, 16 Feb 1829; Thomas Smith, bondsman; Pearsall Thompson, wit.

Wilson, Samuel & Isabella Stinson, 14 Jan 1807; Samuel Vance, bondsman.

Wilson, Samuel & Sinthy Davis, 11 May 1819; Alexander McLarty, bondsman; Chas. T. Alexander, wit.

Wilson, Samuel & Elizabeth Wilson, 5 Dec 1850; Addam Syler, bondsman; John R. Daniel, wit.

Wilson, Sam C. & H. A. Sandifer, 21 Dec 1864; Jno. W. Faxon, bondsman.

Wilson, Samuel H. & Ann Marshall, 5 Aug 1841; Alexander P. Marshall, bondsman.

Wilson, Samuel W. & Ann C. Alexander, 17 Aug 1833; Benjamin F. Shaffer, bondsman.

Wilson, Stephen & Eliza Hoover, 9 Dec 1833; David Cowan, bondsman; B. Oates, C. C. C., wit.

Wilson, Stephen N. & Mary E. J. Flow, 7 April 1848; Thos. N. Alexander, bondsman.

Wilson, Theodore F. & Anna Trotter, 19 May 1851; Neill Wilkinson, bondsman; B. Oates, C. C. C., wit. married 21 May 1851 by Cyrus Johnston, V. D. M.

Wilson, Thomas & Ann Millar, 11 March 1796; Andrew Miller, bondsman; James Maxwell Jr., Robert Maxwell, wit.

Wilson, Thomas & Jane Black, 6 Dec 1823; William Smith, bondsman; Isaac S. Alexander, wit.

Wilson, Thomas & Nancy Smith, 21 Jan 1824; Cyrus Queery, bondsman; Isaac Alexander, wit.

Wilson, Thomas A. & Mrs. E. Aramentta Wentz, 16 March 1843; Zebulon T. Morris, wit.

Wilson, Thomas A. & Sarah R. Jones, 3 April 1855; John R. Daniel, bondsman; W. K. Reid, C. C. C., wit. married 10 April 1855 by R. H. Lafferty, M. G.

Wilson, Thomas C. & Clarinda Pyron, 19 Oct 1833; Thomas N. Lewis, bondsman; B. Oates, C. C. C., wit.

MECKLENBURG MARRIAGES 1783-1868

Wilson, Thomas C. & Elisa L. Smith, 2 Nov 1853; James Thomas
Hart, bondsman; W. K. Reid, C. C. C.,wit. married 3 Nov 1853
by John Walker, J. P.

Wilson, Thomas C. & M. E. Johnston, 19 Jan 1866; N. P. Tredenick,
bondsman; Wm. Maxwell, C. C. C., wit. married 20 Jan 1866 by
John Hunter, minister.

Wilson, Thomas J. & Celia Black, 3 Sept 1834; John P. Morris,
bondsman; B. Oates, C. C. C.,wit.

Wilson, William & Polly Alexander, 20 Jan 1821; James A. Alexander, bondsman; Chas. T. Alexander, wit.

Wilson, William & Polly Duckworth, 23 July 1821; Andrew Wilson,
bondsman; Isaac Alexander,wit.

Wilson, Wm. A. & Martha M. Davis, 21 Aug 1856; L. A. Walker,
bondsman; W. K. Reid, C. C. C., wit. married 28 Aug 1856 by
W. S. Pharr.

Wilson, William C. C. & Eliza Rodgers, 14 Dec 1863; James H.
Howie, bondsman; Wm. Maxwell, C. C. C., wit. married 21 Dec
1863 by G. W. Houston, J. P.

Wilson, Williamson A. & Mary Semeral, 14 Feb 1833; Wm. H. Neel,
bondsman.

Winchester, John R. & Julia Wolfe, 8 Nov 1856; S. W. Moody,
bondsman; W. K. Reid, C. C. C., wit. married -- Nov 1856 by
G. D. Parks.

Winchester, Thomas & Rachel Finny, 8 Aug 1800; John Finney,
bondsman; Geo. Ford, wit.

Winchester, Thomas D. & Nancy Houston, --- 1830; William D.
Winchester, bondsman.

Winchester, Thomas D. & Elizabeth J. Stitt, 4 Nov 1846; Leroy
Springs, bondsman; B. Oates, C. C. C.,wit.

Winchester, William & Polly Winchester, 2 March 1820; John Lawson,
bondsman; S. B. Howard, J. M. Fullwood, wit.

Winchester, William & Marey Woolf, 5 Feb 1821; John M. Rea, bondsman; Philemon Morris, wit.

Wingat, Moses H. & Susy Hull, 4 Sept 1819; William Bartlett, bondsman; Isaac Alexander, wit.

Wingat, Neel & Elizabeth Bigham, 5 Aug 1856; Thomas Winget, bondsman; W. K. Reid, C. C. C., wit. married 5 Aug 1856 by G. D.
Parks.

Wingate, J. P. & C. A. Taylor, 12 July 1855; E. E. Alexander,
bondsman; J. W. Morrow, J. P., wit. married 12 July 1855
by J. W. Morrow, J. P.

Wingate, William H. & Martha Bailes, 16 March 1853; Thomas Winget,
bondsman; B. Oates, C. C. C., wit. married 17 March 1853 by
Saml. A. Davis, J. P.

Winget, Thomas & Elizabeth E. Richardson, 15 March 1838; William
H. Winget, bondsman; B. Oates, C. C. C., wit.

Winneford, James & Peggy Reed, 11 March 1851; Samuel A. Harris, bondsman; B. Oates, C. C. C., wit.

Winterle, Joseph & Charlotte Balthasar, 1 Sept 1858; James M. Sanders, bondsman; W. K. Reid, C. C. C., wit. married 2 Sept 1858 by E. J. Meynardie, Pastor, M. E. Church.

Wise, Benjamin & Sarah Cuthbertson, 29 July 1794; William Cuthbertson, bondsman; Isaac Alexander, wit.

Witherspoon, John & Jean Black, 13 April 1799; John Walker, bondsman.

Witherspoon, Robert S. (Dr.) & Mary A. Bratton, 20 June 1853; Dr. Jos. M. Davidson, bondsman; Braly Oates, C. C. C.,wit. married 22 June 1853 by H. B. Cunningham.

Wolf, Elam B. & Maria J. Lee, 24 Feb 1858; R. M. White, bondsman; W. K. Reid, C. C. C., wit. married 25 Feb 1858 by Jethro Rumple.

Wolf, Henry & Nancy Fincher, 8 July 1841; Philemon Morris, wit.

Wolf, Ivey H. & Nancy D. Cunningham, 29 Oct 1849; D. C. Wolf, bondsman; B. Oates, C. C. C., wit.

Wolf, James D. & Adaline Crowell, 8 Dec 1836; Ambrose P. Houston, bondsman.

Wolf, John & Mary Rape, 5 Aug 1818; Jacob Wolf, bondsman; Isaac Alexander, wit.

Wolf, John W. & Satirah H. Alexander, 15 Oct 1853; T. A. Kirkpatrick, bondsman; W. K. Reid, C. C. C., wit. married 16 Oct 1853 by S. C. Pharr.

Wolf, Joseph & Hannah Doster, 29 Nov 1825; Jacob Wolf, bondsman; Isaac Alexander, wit.

Wolf, Sampson, & Mary Cristenberry, 9 Oct 1821; John Wolf, bondsman; Isaac Alexander, wit.

Wolf, Tobias & Clarissa Dunn, 2 Feb 1841; Wm. R. Harkey, bondsman.

Wolf, Tobias & Mary S. Cunningham, 27 June 1846; Thos. H. Brem, bondsman; S. J. Lourie, wit.

Wolfe, Daniel C. & Sarah C. White, 19 Dec 1849; T. A. Kirkpatrick, bondsman; Saml. J. Lourie, wit.

Wolfe, James L. & Jane C.Dunn, 25 Oct 1854; P. S. Whisnant, bondsman; W. K. Reid, C. C. C., wit. married 26 Oct 1854 by E. F. Rockwell.

Wonsor, John W. & Sarah E. Taylor, 3 Feb 1865; Jas McCallester, bondsman; Wm. Maxwell, C. C. C., wit. married 3 Feb 1865 by G. F. H. McDonald.

Wood, David J. & Betsy Baily, 13 Jan 1843; Thomas Capps, bondsman.

Wood, William & Sarah Worshan, 11 Feb 1811; John Cashon, bondsman; Isaac Alexander, wit.

Woodall, Samuel & Nancy Dulin, 17 March 1834; William M. Stillwell, bondsman; John Oates, wit.

Woodall, Thomas & Martha A. Solomon, 21 Oct 1859; David Allen, bondsman; W. K. Reid, C. C. C., wit. married 27 Oct 1859 by Wm. McComb, J. P.

Woodall, William & Elizabeth Johnston, 27 July 1858; William Foard, bondsman; John Phelan, wit. married 4 Aug 1858 by William McComb, J. P.

Woodruff, Noah & Mary Grigs, 15 Oct 1800; Godfrey Williams, bondsman; Isaac Alexander, wit.

Woodruff, Noah & Nancy Cook, 29 June 1802; William Menteith, bondsman; Isaac Alexander, wit.

Woods, James Br. & Peggy Alexander, 31 Dec 1811; Thomas Henry, bondsman; Isaac Alexander, wit.

Woodside, Archd. M. & Cornelia H. Curry, 26 May 1828; James Coleman, bondsman; Isaac S. Alexander, wit.

Woodsides, Joseph & Mary J. Alexander, 14 July 1847; William Kernes, bondsman.

Woodwarth, William & Agness Chambers, 25 April 1811; Hugh Kirkpatrick, bondsman; Isaac Alexander, wit.

Woolf, Henery & Milley Doster, 6 Nov 1796; Philip Wolf, bondsman.

Woolf, Philip & ------, 17 July 1794; Joseph Starns, bondsman; Shared Gray, wit.

Workman, Jacob & Mary Martin, 9 July 1791; William Penney, bondsman; Wm. B. Alexander, wit.

Worsham, Archerbald & Rose Cashon, 10 July 1838; Thomas Warsham, bondsman; James Johnston, wit.

Worsham, Branch & Frankey Sloan, 7 Sept 1815; James Sloan, bondsman; Ja. Douglass, wit.

Worsham, Miles & Mary Ann Sterns, 7 Dec 1824; William Sterns, bondsman; J. Doherty, wit.

Wray, Britain & Hannah Cashon, 7 Oct 1802; Olive Cashon, bondsman; Chs. Harris, Ezekiel Mayhew, wit.

Wright, James & Mary Connelly, 2 Aug 1820; John Connelly, bondsman; W. L. Davidson, wit.

Wright, James L. & Martha C. Spratt, 12 March 1832; James D. Gibson, bondsman.

Wright, Perry & Hannah Nivens, 6 Aug 1851; Harvy Nivens, bondsman; J. W. Morrow, J. P., wit. married 6 Aug 1851 by J. W. Morrow, J. P.

Wriston, William J. & Mary Ann Erwin, 26 May 1840; William Overman, bondsman; B. Oates, C. C. C., wit.

Wyatt, A. J. & J. M. Knox, 20 May 1863; R. W. Hartgrove, bondsman; Wm. Maxwell, C. C. C., wit. married 21 May 1863 by S. C. Alexander.

Wylie, James & Sarah Shanks, 20 July 1790; James Shanks, bondsman; Isaac Alexander, wit.

Wylie, Joseph & Margaret Smith, 21 Jan 1792; James Wilson, bondsman; Isaac Alexander, wit.

Wylie, Robert & Elizabeth Haire, 28 Aug 1799; John Riley, bondsman; Isaac Alexander, wit.

Wylie, William & Polly Riley, 12 Feb 1812; Armstrong Rylie, bondsman; Isaac Alexander, wit.

Wymens, John & Peggy Smartt, 16 March 1812; William P. Springs, bondsman; Isaac Alexander, wit.

Wymens, Peter & Elizabeth Allen, daughter of George Allen, 23 Sept 1789 (from abstract only); Abraham Roach, bondsman; Barthw. Thompson, wit.

Yandel, Robert W. & Sarah Hartis, 3 Jan 1816; Hugh Wilson, bondsman; Isaac Alexander, wit.

Yandel, Samuel & Delilah Massey, 3 Jan 1816; John McCall, bondsman.

Yandil, Samuel & Elizabeth Barnett, 26 March 1792; Allen Reed, bondsman; Isaac Alexander, wit.

Yandle, James B. & Delilah Crump, 14 March 1860; Ervin Finny, bondsman; W. K. Reid, C. C. C.,wit.

Yandle, John & Eve Robison, 2 Aug 1828; John Fisher, bondsman; Pearsall Thompson, wit.

Yandle, John M. & Mary A. Pyrant, 8 Aug 1845; James H. McCall, bondsman; Isaac S. Alexander, wit.

Yandle, Samuel & Mary Irwin, 29 May 1832; John Tye, bondsman; Isaac S. Alexander, wit.

Yandle, Samuel & Sarah McCall, 11 March 1839; Thomas McCall, bondsman; B. Oates, C. C. C., wit.

Yandle, Sherrod & Nancy Simpson, 14 Jan 1840; George W. Ritch, bondsman.

Yandle, William A. & Sarah M. Crenshaw, 13 Jan 1860; V. W. Rice, bondsman; John Phelan, wit. married 13 Jan 1860 by R. McEwen, J. P.

Yarbrough, Benjamin & ---- Hartgrove,, 4 Oct 1797; Saml. Kuykendal, bondsman; Ruth Alexander, wit.

Yates, Westin, & Harriet B. Campbell, 27 Jan 1832; James D. Gibson, bondsman.

Yeargain, Jarratt & Martha Sloan, 29 Nov 1826; Adison P. Boules, bondsman.

Young, Adolphis & Martha Lourie (colored), 21 Sept 1865; Wm. B. Neil, bondsman; Wm. Maxwell, C. C. C.,wit. married 21 Sept 1865 by Wm. H. Pitts, Elder.

Young, Alfred & Jane Thompson, 10 Jan 1839; John H. McCoart, bondsman; B. Oates, C. C. C., wit.

Young, Elias & Dorcas E. Orr, 7 Feb 1832; James Hood, bondsman; B. Oates, D. C., wit.

Young, George & Martha McClure, 19 Oct 1793; Moses McClure, bondsman; Isaac Alexander.

Young, James & Jane Parks, 22 June 1795; William Parks, bondsman; Isaac Alexander, wit.

Young, James A. & Cecelia H. Johnston, 26 Oct 1840; David Maxwell, bondsman; B. Oates, C. C. C.,wit.

Young, John & Esther Wilson, 13 Nov 1798; George Wilson, bondsman; Isaac Alexander, wit.

Young, Robert H. & Amelia Wallace, 9 Dec 1835; James A. Johnson, bondsman; B. Oates, C. C. C., wit.

Young, Wallace & Rachel Young, 7 April 1866; Wm. M. Young, bondsman; Wm. Maxwell, C. C. C., wit. married 12 April 1866 by E. Davidson.

Young, William & Nancy Orr, 15 Oct 1802; Jonnathan Orr, bondsman; Isaac Alexander, wit.

Younts, M. G. & E. R. Elms, 7 May 1853; W. W. Morrow, bondsman; J. W. Morrow, J. P., wit. married 7 May 1853 by J. W. Morrow, J. P.

Youst, Nicholes & Sarah Duckworth, 24 Oct 1807; Ezekiel Duckworth, bondsman.

Zimmerman, P. P. & R. J. Elms, 29 Sept 1863; Geo. E. Denby, bondsman; Wm. Maxwell, C. C. C., wit. married 1 Oct 1863 by A. Sinclair, Pres. Minister.

The following are marriages from the manuscript marriage register in the Register of Deeds Office, Mecklenburg County Court House, Charlotte, North Carolina (microfilm N. C. Archives C. 065.63001), for which no bonds have been found.

Hugh Harris to Mary Walker, 30 Jan 1851, married by Rev. John Hunter.

James C. Davis to Mary M. Weeks, 25 Feb 1851, married by Samuel A. Davis, J. P.

D. F. Davis to Fanny E. Sloan, 15 April 1851, married by R. D. Alexander, J. P.

Henry W. Biham to Elizabeth Stephens, 6 May 1851.

R. C. Carson to Martha H. Stewart, 23 Sept 1851, married by Rev. Cyrus Johnston.

Hall M. Harget to Elizabeth Harkey, 11 Sept 1851, married by Philemon Morris, J. P.

John B. McLaughlin to Jane C. Wallace, 25 Sept 1851, married by Rev. James M. Walker.

Hugh M. Dixon to Margaret Howie, 6 Oct 1851, married by Rev. R. H. Lafferty.

Wm. S. Daniels to Mary P. Cooper, 14 Oct. 1851.

Jordan McCreary to Eliza Moore, 22 Nov. 1851, married by John H. Grier, J. P.

Wm. McKinney to Mary Pierce(?), 4 Dec 1851, married by S. A. Davis, J. P.

John N. Hux to H. A. Peoples, 10 Dec. 1851, married by W. G. Barnett, J. P.

Wilson Wallace to Caroline C. Harrison, 2 Dec 1851, married by Rev. R. T. Penick.

Ambrose Dulin to Rachel Smith, 20 Oct 1851, married by A. J. Hood, J. P.

Marcus E. Caldwell to Nancy A. Sloan, 3 April 1852.

Arthur Armstrong to Mary A. Hoover, 3 April 1852; Rev. A. L. Watts, minister.

John Dorrier to Joanna M. Nolan, 19 April 1852; married by Rev. J. T. O'Connell.

Dr. S. N. Hutchison to Mary Adeline Parks, 17 May 1852; married by Rev. Cyrus Johnston.

Nathaniel Alexander to Sarah G. Simonds, 23 August 1852, married by Rev. S. C. Pharr.

E. C. Alexander to Sarah A. Stewart, 23 Oct 1855, married by A. W. Miller.

George W. Alexander to Jane O. Fenell, 8 Jan 1855, married by Wm. G. Barnet, J. P.

John Auton to Martha Kerr, 11 Dec 1855, married by J. L. Campbell, J. P.

R. H. Abernathey to Mary Jane Scehorn, 24 July 1856, married by Rev. J. R. Picket.

A. W. Alexander to Martha A. Wilson, 14 May 1856.

Dan Alexander to Annabella Alexander, 4 June 1856, married by R. H. Lafferty, minister.

Julius P. Alexander to Margaret Alexander, 8 April 1856, married by R. H. Lafferty, minister

S. C. Alexander to Mary Brown, 13 May 1857, married by Drury Lacy.

Lourie Adams to Sarah Baker, 30 Dec 1858, married by C. Overman, J. P.

Benj. P. Alexander to Harriet E. Todd, 7 April 1858, married by G. S. Campbell, J. P.

Cyunius Alexander to Martha A. Kirk, 29 Dec 1858, married by Rev. R. H. Lafferty.

J. B. Alexander to A. W. Souni, 17 May 1858, married by S. C. Alexander.

Powell S. Auton to Harriet R. Prim, 26 June 1858.

M. J. Aydlott to Sarah P. Flannagan, 4 Feb 1858, married by E. J. Maynardie, minister.

Wm. S. D. Alexander to Catharine J. G. Johnston, 14 April 1859, married by Walter S. Pharr.

Thomas Alcorn to Sarah Rodgers, 6 Sept 1860, married by R. F. Blythe, J. P.

James L. Allen to Martha L. Harris, 23 Nov 1860.

Cyrus A. Alexander to Margaret C. Houston, 19 Jan 1861, married by Rev. R. H. Lafferty.

R. D. Alexander to Sarah J. Dewese, 1 March 1861.

R. K. Adylotte to Annie Rich, 30 May 1865, married by Rev. J.D. Carpenter.

Geo. W. Alexander to J. A. Cochran, 7 Dec 1865, married by R. L. Dearmon, J. P.

J. B. Allen to H. M. Norment, 21 Sept 1865, married by Rev. John Hunter.

W. C. Ardry to May M. Robinson, 27 Jan 1865, married by R. B. Johnston, minister.

C. L. Adams to H. S. Henderson, 9 Jan 1866, married by W. M. Kerr.

F. C. Alexander to M. J. Kennedy, 28 March 1866.

J. Lee Alexander to C. C. Smith, 27 Nov 1866.

R. B. Alexander to J. P. Wilson, 1 Oct 1866, married by F. M. Ross, J. P.

Wm. G. Allen to Mary McCarty, 6 March 1866, married by Rev. W. C. Power.

W. J. Anderson to L. R. Henderson, 13 Feb 1866, married by Rev. J. C. Chalmers.

John W. Auton to H. R. Auton, 14 Dec 1866, married by Rev. W. M. Kerr.

R. H. Alexander to M. G. Beaty, 14 March 1867, married by Rev. R. H. Griffith.

T. P. Alexander to H. E. Alexander, 22 Jan 1867.

H. W. Allen to A. E. Thrower, 25 Feb 1867.

Wm. Blakely to Martha Pippins, 17 Dec 1852, married by James Johnston.

Charles E. Bell to Isabella J. Witherspoon, 19 March 1852, married by Cyrus Johnston, minister.

Jas. W. Berryhill to Martha J. D. Collins, 10 Aug 1853, married by James C. Nicholson.

James M. Black to Elizabeth Cook, 14 Sept 1853, married by
B. H. Garrison, J. P.

John Black to Mary T. Downs, 21 Sept 1852, married by Rev. S. C.
Pharr.

J. M. Blount to Kezziah J. Graham, 18 Aug 1853, married by S. A.
Davis, J. P.

Will A. Boatright to Catherine Tally, 13 Jan 1853, married by
J. H. Grier, J. P.

John L. Brown to Nancy J. Kerr, 22 Aug 1853, married by Rev.
Henry J. Sloan.

Moses L. Beatey to Laura Sentile (Lentile?), 27 Aprl 1854,
married by J. P. Ross, J. P.

Jas. S. Berryhill to Mary M. Armor (no date, 1854)

S. A. Blankenship to Adaline Hoover, 8 Aug 1854, married by
Rev. A. M. Watson.

Archibald Bonds to Rebecca Stewart, 17 April 1854, married by
Rev. R. H. Lafferty.

John N. Blythe to D. W. McCoy, 14 Oct 1858, married by Rev.
S. C. Pharr.

Tho. H. Brem to Harriet N. Jones, 15 Sept 1858, married by Rev.
E. J. Meynardie.

Samuel Blythe to Sarah Adams, 14 Jan 1859.

James Bartlett to M. C. Griffith, 16 Oct 1860, married by
Charles Overman.

D. H. Byerly to Jane E. Wriston, 4 Nov 1861, married by Rev.
F. Milton Kenedy.

M. S. Barringer to A. E. Alexander, 23 June 1862, married by A.
Sinclair.

Joseph Brubaum(?) to Theresa Anatham, 20 Oct 1862.

John C. M. Beam to Margt. E. White, 14 Jan 1862, married by
Rev. H. N. Pharr

John A. Biggers to Sarah A. Wilson, 10 Dec 1862, married by
Rev. C. Morritze.

Tho. H. Blakely to Jane Gilden, 31 March 1862, married by B. H.
Garrison, J. P.

C. C. Brigman to Mary Black, 23 Dec 1862, married by T. W. Davey,
J. P.

J. T. Baller to Mary E. Cruse, 8 June 1863, married by Rev. D. L.
O'Connel.

T. L. Barnett to Martha C. Barnett, 4 May 1863, married by R. L.
Dearmon, J. P.

Rich. B. Blackledge to Pinkie Russel, 10 July 1863, married by Rev. A. Sinclair.

John W. Barnhill to Mary Ann Hipp, 14 March 1864, married by G. W. McDonald, J. P.

John D. Brown to Mary C.Johnston, 12 Nov 1864.

W. R. Berryhill to E. E. Arnes, 30 Oct 1865, married by Rev. J. C. Chalmers.

John M. Baker to M. A. Griffith, 6 June 1866, married by Rev. John Hunter.

H. S. Barkley to Martha V. Kernes, 1 Sept 1866.

John D. Barnett to Margt. E. Beard, 20 Nov 1866, married by A. Ransom, minister.

J. S. Barnett to J. E. Saserman, 27 Oct 1866, married by C. Overman, J. P.

J. H. Bartlett to Lizzie Henry, 26 Dec 1866, married by Rev. J. C. Chalmers.

John C. Beard to M. E. Brown, 20 Nov 1866, married by Rev. A. Ransom.

Robert Beard to R. J. Ewart, 16 Oct 1866, married by Rev. W. S. Pharr.

Wm. F. Beatty to Elizabeth Haynes, 12 Nov 1866, married by Rev. J. F. Butt.

Wm. S. Biggert, to T. J. Sellers, 17 Dec 1866, married by Rev. J. F. Butt.

T. J. Black to M. A. Hutchison, 14 Dec 1865, married by Rev. W. D. Kerr.

W. A. Black to J. C. Wedington, 24 Dec 1866, married by Rev. B. C. Jones.

W. J. Blakely to Mary J. Cook, 8 Jan 1866, married by Rev. Jno. F. Butt.

Wm. Blythe to Susan Adams, 23 June 1866, married by D. G. Maxwell, J. P.

E. O. Bostick to Juny Rice, 24 July 1866, married by Rev. John F. Butt.

Hugh Boyce to Mary A. Thompson, 20 Aug 1866, married by Rev. John Hunter.

J. A. Boyles to M. C. Warsham, 31 July 1866.

W. B. Brigman to Elizabeth Walls, 30 July 1866, married by Rev. W. S. Pharr.

W. S. Brown to Ann E. Clanton, 26 Dec 1866, married by Rev. C. C. Land.

John W. Barnett to Zela C. Gray, 30 Jan 1867, married by Rev. A. Ransom.

James M. Beaty to Fanny E. Smith, 12 Feb 1867.

Wm. H. Clark and Ann H. Todd, 12 Oct 1852, married by G. C. Cathey, J. P.

E. D. Cross to Margaret King, 22 Oct 1856; married by J. P. Ross, J. P.

Jas. B. Christenbury to Abigail Simpson, 1 Dec 1857; married by G. M. Creighton.

A. J. D. Cochran to Margaret J. Wallace, 16 April 1861.

Logan Cathey to Adaline Blair, 20 Jan 1862; married by Rev. J. C. Chalmers.

Henry Clark to Alice Hilyard, 27 Feb 1866; married by Rev. J. C. Chalmers.

Bannister Collie to Violet Cathcart, 24 Oct 1866; married by F. M. Ross, J. P.

Jas. Crammond to Laura E. Hendly, 12 Sept 1866; married by Rev. J. F. Butt.

W. H. Crowe to Ann R.Burwell, 27 Sept 1866; married by Rev. R. Burwell.

James Crump to Sarah Crump, 3 Dec 1866, married by R. McEwen, J. P.

James L. Crumpt to R. E. Norket, 8 Oct 1866.

Henry Cathy to M. E. Freeman, 1 Jan 1867, married by Rev. Jno Douglas.

George Cline to Sarah A. Ferril, 6 Feb 1867, married by R. L. Dearmon, J. P.

W. H. Coleman to Jane A. Holden, 5 Jan 1867; married by Solomon Sifford.

James B. Dearmond to Dorcas M. Sturgeon, 17 Oct 1853; married by James M. Walker, minister.

Dillard, John R. to Margt. C. Brown, 7 Dec 1853; married by Rev. Cyrus Johnston.

John Dixon to Elvira M. Grier, 12 April 1853; married by Rev. A. L. Watts.

Samuel A. Douglas to Charlotte E. Sloan, 15 July 1853;married by Rev. Walter S. Pharr.

J. W. Davenport to Mary C. McDonald, 24 Jan 1854; married by Rev. A. L. Watts

Joseph M. Davidson to Mary M. Caldwell, 21 Dec 1854.

A. L. Dearmond to Nancy J. Edwards, 20 Sept 1854; married by Rev. J. M. Walker.

David E. Dixon to Mary E. Jones, 2 Nov 1854; married by Rev. R. H. Lafferty.

George D. Dixon to Malinda J. Ward, 28 Dec 1854; married by Alex. Cooper, J. P.

Martin P. Doby to Sallie H. Grier, 21 Aug 1854; married by Rev. A. L. Watts

Jefferson Dunham to Amelia Davis, 1 Jan 1854; married by John W. Morrow, J. P.

J. Edward A. Davidson to Mary Elms, 5 Nov 1855; married by A. W. Miller.

W. C. Doby to Atona E. Grier (no date, 1855).

J. S. M. Davidson to H. Josephine Blake, 22 Oct 1856; married by A. W. Miller.

C. H. Davis to M. E. Alexander, 6 June 1857, married by Walter S. Pharr.

J. L. Deaton to S. R. Hotton, 16 Feb 1857; married by Jas. Stacy.

William Doubt to Emma Weeks, 31 Oct 1857; married by Rev. Horatio H. Hewitt.

E. C. Davidson to V. J. Henderson, 24 Feb 1858; married by Rev. D. V. Pharr.

E. H. Dearmond to Sarah Tolbert, 6 Feb 1858; married by Lorenzo Hunter, J. P.

Jacob Duls to Wilhelmina Regina Eits, 20 Sept 1858; married by J. R. Peterson.

George Deberry to Catharine Vance, 21 Sept 1859; married by Lorenzo Hunter, J. P.

John C. Dennis to Cynthia M. Hant, 24 Oct 1859; married by Wm. Maxwell, J. P.

Thomas Douglass to Mary A. Hoover, 12 Jan 1859; married by Rev. J. B. Watt.

James T. Dennis to Mary G. Festerman, 31 Aug 1860; married by William Maxwell, J. P.

M. P. Doby to Sarah R. Sadler, 24 Oct 1860; married by Rev. A. Sinclair.

George Donnell to Sarah J. Caldwell, 1 May 1860; married by Rev. R. H. Lafferty.

Milton Dulin to Sophia Weddington, 16 Feb 1860.

S. W. Davis to Margt. H. Cashon, 30 Dec 1861, married by Walter S. Pharr.

James W. Dixon to Laura Brown, 19 Oct 1860; married by Rev. James C. Chalmers.

John Z. Deaton to E. J. Jamison, 13 Dec 1862; married by Walter S. Pharr.

C. T. Dewese to Martha A. Barnett, 21 Jan 1862; married by Walter S. Pharr.

T. L. Dulin to Sarah C. Pharr, 17 Nov 1862; married by J. L.
Phillips, J. P.

J. F. Davidson to Mary C. Galloway, 29 Sept 1863; married by
Rev. R. H. Griffith.

R. B. Dunn to Mary C. Davenport, 21 Nov 1863;married by Rev.
Saml. C. Pharr.

W. A. Davis to Amelia Honsucker, 11 Aug 1864; married by T. W.
Dewey, J. P.

A. B. Downes to N. R. Griffith, 24 March 1864; married by Rev.
R. Z. Johnston.

C. A. Davis to Margt. Goens, 17 May 1865; married by Rev. J. F.
Butt.

M. L. Davis to Julia J. Davis, 29 May 1865.

J. B. Deaton to Mary A. Parks, 18 Dec 1865; married by J. L.
Jetton, J. P.

T. M. C. Dodd to Mattie E. Torrence, 12 Sept 1865; married by
A. McIver, J. P.

W. H. Downes, to M. S. Coffey, 11 Nov 1865; married by Rev. R.
Z. Johnston.

J. T. A. Davis to Mary J. Whisnant, 30 April 1866; married by
Rev. W. C. Power.

J. B. Deaton to Nancy J. Park, 6 June 1866.

Charles DeCamp, to S. A. Johnston, 19 Feb 1866; married by Rev.
R. H. Griffith.

Wm. N. Dickey to Mary Jane Brown, 23 July 1866; married by Rev.
S. L. Watson.

Wm. DeLaney to Anna Smith, 10 Jan 1867; married by John Walker,
J. P.

D. H. Dulin to Mary Dulin, 7 Feb 1867, married by F. M. Ross,
J. P.

Peter Engle to Amelia Williamson, 31 Aug 1861, married by J.
P. Ross, J. P.

S. C. Earnhardt to Mary J. Earnhardt, 31 May 1866; married by
Rev. J. G. McLaughlin.

R. M. Emmerson to M. E. Tye, 23 Nov 1866; married by Rev. T. E.
Davis.

John Ensfield to Martha Camden, 11 June 1866; married by Rev.
R. H. Griffith.

A. R. Erwin to Mattie E. Erwin, 10 Dec 1866; married by Rev.
Jno. Douglas.

J. Lee Erwin to Magie E. Alexander, 5 Dec 1866; married by Rev.
R. Z. Johnston.

S. N. Fincher to Eveline Harget, 7 March 1864; married by Robt McEwan, J. P.

R. J. Ferguson to H. L. Brown, 28 May 1866; married by Rev. John Hunter.

Fite, Robert D. to Angeline Jordan, 21 April 1866, married by Rev. W. S. Pharr.

Wm. Folley to Elizabeth Maxwell, 2 May 1866; married by Rev. J. G. McLaughlin.

M. L. Frazier to Sarah J. Reglar, 26 Nov 1866; married by Rev. R. H. Griffith.

J. N. Fincher to Hannah Rea, 21 Feb 1867; married by J. S. Reid, J. P.

Robert H. Flow to Mary A. Alexander, 22 Jan 1867; married by Rev. J. G. McLaughlin.

B. A. Grier to Sarah L. Davidson, 9 Dec 1862; married by R. Z. Johnston.

W. W. Gray to Martha A. Thomason, 7 Dec 1866; married by Rev. W. S. Pharr.

Thomas J. Grier to M. D. Withers, 24 Dec 1866; married by Rev. John Douglas.

R. W. Garrison to Mattie E. Earnhardt, 3 Nov 1866; married by Rev. J. G. McLaughlin.

David Gibson to Mary Parks, 29 May 1866; married by R. F. Blythe, J. P.

J. C. Goodrum to Laura T. McGahey, 4 Oct 1866; married by Rev. A. Ranson.

E. W. Groot to Delia Joyce, 26 Dec 1866; married by Rev. J. J. OConnel.

Dr. S. W. Hutchison to Mary Adeline Parks, 17 May 1852; married by Cyrus Johnston, minister.

James I. Hagan to Sabina Skinner, 7 Nov 1854; married by J. P. Ross, J. P.

J. M. Herron to Margt. E. Williamson, 3 Oct 1854; married by Rev. A. M. Watson.

Abraham Hester to Martha J. Simpson, 22 Dec 1854.

S. L. Hoover to Nancy M. Blankenship, 19 Dec 1854; married by P. Nicholson.

John M. Houston to Elizabeth E. Sample, 28 March 1854; married by Rev. H. B. Cunningham.

Wm. L. Howie to Margt. A. Houston, 14 Nov 1854; married by Rev. S. C. Pharr.

Hugh D. Houston to Dorey E. Stewart, 30 Jan 1855; married by H. B. Cunningham.

Gaskin E. Hipp to Amelia Lawing, 14 Nov 1857; married by G. S. Campbell, J. P.

A. J. Hood to Isabella Biggers, 27 Oct 1857; married by L. L. Stewart.

W. H. Howie to M. J. White, 27 Feb 1857; married by Danl. A. Penick.

Wm. B. Harry to Sarah A. Lawing, 18 Dec 1858; married by Rev. S. C. Pharr.

James M. Hutchison to Elizabeth J. Morrow, 15 April 1858.

John N. Hanna to Mary V. Caruthers, 28 Nov 1859; married by Rev. J. B. Watt.

Wm. A. Hannon to Sophronia Henry, 10 Nov 1859; married by J. C. Chalmers.

James P. Henderson to Margaret S. Patterson, 9 August 1859.

J. N. Howie to Sophia Cruse, 26 Dec 1859; married by Alex Phillipi.

Thomas J. Hancock to Sophronia Sanders, 29 May 1850; married by Rev. J. W. Miller.

H. M. Hunter to M. J. Hunter, 3 Oct 1860; married by A. Ranson.

James Harty to Emma E.Ross, 17 April 1861.

James Hunt to Jane Lee, 30 Dec 1861; married by J. C. Chalmers.

Joshua Harkey to Sarah A. Harget, 7 July 1862; married by E. C. Moretz.

Field A. Hawkins, to Martha A. Todd, 19 June 1862; married by C. Overman, J. P.

Thomas Hawley to Sally Hudson, 4 Jan 1862; married by J. C. Nicholson, J. P.

J. N. Hunter to Mattie A. Brown, 20 March 1862; married by E. F. Rockwell, V. D. M.

W. H. Hall to Martha J. Parks, 3 March 1862.

A. J. Hall to Esther White, 18 Dec 1865; married by J. R. Gillespie, J. P.

J. F. Hall to J. A. Williamson, 4 Sept 1865; married by Rev. J. C. Chalmers.

P. C. Harkey to Sarah R. Gingles, 12 Oct 1865; married by Rev. John Hunter.

James T. Heart to R. R. McCall, 25 Jan 1865; married by R. McEwan, J. P.

Horea Helms to Evaline Helms, 17 Oct 1865; married by J. S. Reid, J. P.

Jackson Helms to Prudy Yandle, 2 Oct 1865.

R. M. Herron to Eugenia Cathey, 9 Dec 1865; married by Rev. J. F. Butt.

John R. Hood to Mary A. Hunter, 22 Dec 1865; married by Rev. John Hunter.

John Huie to E. S. Werringer, 10 Aug 1865; married by T. M. Alexander, J. P.

M. B. Hunter to Nancy Flowe, 17 Aug 1865; married by Rev. W. McDonald.

W. C. Hutson to Sarah Hinson, 21 Oct 1865; married by Rev. J. D. Carpenter.

Jacob Harkey to Mary Spoiller, 1 March 1866; married by C. Overman, J. P.

Thomas M. Harkey to M. A. Adams, 28 Nov 1866; married by Rev. J. C. Chalmers.

C. M. Harris to Sarah A. Stockton, 28 July 1866; married by C. Overman, J. P.

W. C. Harris to A. A. Query, 16 Oct 1866; married by Rev. J. G. McLaughlin.

Wm. P. Hartis to M. A. Byrum, 8 Aug 1866; married by J. S. Reid, J. P.

S. H. Helton to M. A. Jackson, 8 Dec 1866; married by Rev. N. Aldrich.

J. E. Hennigan to M. R. Watt, 31 July 1866; married by Rev. J. C. Chalmers.

Wm. P. Hipp to M. A. Cathy, 30 July 1866.

W. L. Hood to M. M. Rusell, 29 Dec 1866; married by Rev. Jas. Stacey.

A. D. Hoover to M. L. Hipp, 18 Dec 1866.

William H. Hoover to S. A. Smith, 13 Dec 1866.

Seth Hotchiss to Lucinda Steele, 17 Feb 1866; married by Rev. J. C. Chalmers.

A. J. Hunter to Harriet Sample, 17 Oct 1866; married by Rev. A. Ransom.

D. P. Hunter to Martha Barnett, 4 July 1866; married by Rev. J. F. Butt.

Thomas Hamilton to Mary Wriston, 10 Jan 1867; married by Rev. J. F. Butt.

Milas Heist to Caroline Mullis, 8 March 1867; married by Rev. J. F. Butt.

Wm Irvin to Mary Ann Wilson, 8 March 1854; married by Isaac Wilson, J. P.

John Ingard to Ann Young, 1 Dec 1865; married by Rev. Jno F. Butt.

Martin Icehour to J. E. Reid, 8 Oct 1866. married by Rev. A. Aldrich.

J. M. Johnston to Miriam C. Wallace, 29 April 1863; married by John Wallace, J. P.

T. N. Johnston to Elizabeth S. Alexander, 13 April 1866; married by J. G.McLaughlin.

Solomon Jordan to Mary C. T. Ferrill, 5 May 1866; married by Rev. W. S. Pharr.

J. M. Johnston to Lydia E. Wallace, 8 Jan 1867; married by Rev. John Hunter.

M. H. Jordan to J. M. Young, 1 Feb 1867.

John F. Kinsell to Margt. Collins (no date 1855)

M. E. Kistler to Jane F. Love, 16 Feb 1857; married by Stephen Wilson, J. P.

G. W. Kisiah to Lucinda White, 18 July 1862.

John L. Kiser to Mary Jane Weant, 27 Dec 1864; married by J. C. Chalmers.

D. P. Kelly to Sarah J. Price, 1 Aug 1866; married by Solomon Sifford, J. P.

John T. Kerr to Mary L. Hoover, 29 May 1866; married by Rev. John F. Butt.

Thomas R. Kerr Jr. to Harriet R. McIntosh, 1 May 1866; married by Rev. W. M. Kerr.

J. H. Killian to Catherine E. Taylor, 13 Nov 1866; married by Rev. R. Burwell.

Thomas Love to Martha C. Kerr, 27 Dec 1853; married by Alex Cooper, J. P.

D. F. Lawing to Sarah D. Robinson, 4 Oct 1864; Married by Wm. S. Norment, J. P.

E. L. Ligon to R. A. Coser, 18 March 1865; married by Rev. R. H. Griffith.

G. A. Lawing to Mary J. Vance, 14 June 1866; married by W. M. Kerr.

J. M. Lee to Lizzie J. Smith, 27 Oct 1866; married by Rev. R. H. Griffith.

Andrew Leeper to Martha Cathey, 27 Oct 1866; married by Rev. J. D. Hall.

R. L. Long to Margaret E. Black, 27 Sept 1866; married by Rev. C. C. Williams.

Isaac H. Moore to Martha Parks, 22 July 1854; married by Rev. Cyrus Johnston.

James C. Moon to Mary J. McCorcle, 1 May 1855.

B. F. Morrow to E. A. Stitt, 21 Jan 1857.

John G. Marks to Susan Deaton, 21 Dec 1858; married by J. B. Watt, minister.

John W. Moon to Margt E. McRea, 28 Jan 1858; married by Rev. R. H. Lafferty.

Wm. G. Morris to Mary E. Dennis, 1 Feb 1858; married by Wm. P. Maxwell, J. P.

Robert W. Miller to Elizabeth Pucket, 27 Feb 1860; married by Rev. S. C. Pharr

B. H. Moore to Catharine Byles, 2 Aug 1860; married by R. Y. Russell.

John R. Morris to Emma C. Watson, 19 Nov 1860; Rev. R. H. Lafferty.

Marion Moss to Minerva Wheeler, 25 Jan 1860; married by W. S. Norment, J. P.

Harvey L. Mulwee to Effize Beaty, 7 Aug 1860; married by William Boyles, J. P.

Ptolemy P. Maxwell to Margaret C.Hunter, 25 April 1861; married by Rev. E. F. Rockwell.

Wilson H. Mock to Mary A. Cashon, 12 June 1861; married by Rev. John E. Presly.

M. A. Moon to S. A. Sandifer, 14 May 1861.

C. P. Mungo to I. A. Blair, 3 Dec 1861; married by Rev.H. N. Pharr.

David G. Maxwell to Margt. E. Watson, 26 Oct 1863; married by Rev. Wm. McDonald.

H. S. Miller to Elizabeth Hembrill, 7 May 1863; married by Wm. S. Norment, J. P.

Wm. Lee Manson to E. A. Rea, 14 Dec 1866; married by Rev. R. Z. Johnston.

Jas. A. Marshall to Mary E. Wearn, 31 Dec 1866; married by Rev. S. C. Pharr.

J. B. Meacham to S. M. Williams, 14 May 1866; married by Rev. A. W. Miller.

James B. Miller to Fanny Armstrong, 26 July 1866; married by C. Overman, J. P.

H. L. D. Montieth to Margt. T.Alexander, 31 Oct 1866; married by Rev. H. B. Platt.

James Monteith to M. A. Orr, 14 Nov 1866; married by Rev. W. S. Pharr.

A. Moony to Sarah J. Abernathy, 20 Jan 1866;married by T. W. Davey, J. P.

James Moran to Charlotte McCracken, 13 Feb 1866.

Phileman W. Morris to Mary Deemster, 10 April 1866; married by D. G. Maxwell, J. P.

Daniel N. McCauley to Margt. R. Bell, 22 Feb 1853; married by Rev. R. F. Taylor.

David L. McCord to Mary Bigham, 5 Jan 1853; married by J. P. Ross, J. P.

John McDonald to Sarah Elwood, (no date 1854).

Wm. D. McCuiag to Susan Alexander, 6 Oct 1856; married by G. D. Parks.

Robt F. McGinn to Jane P. Herron, 28 Nov 1857; married by G. S. Campbell, J. P.

Wm. R. McLean to Margt. A. Kerr, 31 Aug 1857; married by Jas. C. Nicholson.

A. W. McCuaig to Elizabeth McElhenny, 12 Dec 1860; married by William C. Owens.

B. W. McLean to Mary A. Hayes, 11 Aug 1860; married by J. Walker, J. P.

E. A. McLeod to Eveline E. Alexander, 8 Nov 1860; married by Rev. A. Sinclair.

John C. McCauly to Ann C. Reid, 6 Aug 1861; married by A. Ranson.

James A. McGahey to Martha McLure, 20 Aug 1861; married by Walter S. Pharr.

J. F. McGinn to Amelia S. Ledwell, 2 Dec 1861; married by Wm. Means, J. P.

H. B. McLean to Mary S. Caldwell, 16 Dec 1861; married by Walter S. Pharr.

Joseph M. McAllister to Martha E. Phifer, 25 Oct 1862; married by J. C. Nicholson, J. P.

James C. McCall to Margt. M. Smith, 2 Dec 1862.

E. A. McKee to M. J. Reed, 19 Oct 1863; married by R. Z. Johnston.

J. F. McGuire to C. M. Capps, 15 Nov 1865

J. H. McAllister to Martha Clark, 31 May 1866; married by Rev. J. F. Butt.

A. McCoy to Catherine Potts, 19 Sept 1866; married by Rev. E. F. Rockwell.

Isaac L. McIntosh to Sarah J. Alexander, 22 Dec 1866; married by Rev. T. E. Davis.

John G. McConnell to Elizabeth J. Robinson, 13 Feb 1867; married by Rev. J. C. McLaughlin.

W. McGarres to Margaret Clark, 10 Jan 1867.

J. P. McGinnes to Mollie E. Matthews, 27 Feb 1867; married by R. McEwan, J. P.

J. Cooper Nesbitt to M. E. Young, 27 June 1866; married by Rev. A. W. Miller.

Wm. B. Neil to Lilly Henderson, 14 Jan 1867.

J. J. Noles to Mary L. Blair, 17 Jan 1867; married by F. M. Ross, J. P.

J. J. Norman to Elizabeth Hutchison, 7 Jan 1867.

John A. Osment to Mary L. Collier, 18 Dec 1855.

M. S. Osmint to Mary Warren, 11 July 1860; married by Rev. J. W. Miller.

J. E. Orman to M. J. Walker, 20 Aug 1866; married by S. J. Berry-hill, J. P.

David K. Orr to Martha C. Biggers, 28 May 1866; married by Robt McEwan, J. P.

Joseph L. Orr to Margt. J. Wilson, 8 Nov 1866; married by Rev. A. W. Miller.

J. F. Osborne to Catherine Wallace, 1 May 1866; married by Rev. J. F. Butt.

John L. Osborne to Nancy A. Henderson, 24 Jan 18671 married by Rev. Aldrich.

R. D. Parks to Mary M. Miller, 20 Oct 1854; married by James Johnston, J. P.

Will M. Prather to Harriet M. Hayes, 4 Sept 1861; married by J. C. Chalmers.

Hugh Pigg to S. T. Taylor, 2 May 1865.

Gaston Paul to Adda McCrany, 16 Oct 1866.

T. W. Phelan to Anna E.Rozzle, 31 Oct 1866; married by Rev. W. C. Power.

J. Z. Porter to S. A. Coffey, 8 Nov 1866; married by Rev. R. Z. Johnston.

E. M. Pucket to M. J. P. Wilson, 3 Sept 1866; married by Rev. E. F. Rockwell.

W. C. Pucket to M. M. Hawkins, 22 Nov 1866; married by Rev. J. F. Butt.

Francis Platt to Mary Smith, 21 Dec 1867; married by Rev. J. J. Prather.

Leander Query to N. E. Query, 30 Oct 1866; married by Rev. J. G. McLaughlin.

Hugh K. Reid to Eliza Alexander, 18 Nov 1865; married by Rev. R. Z. Johnston.

Dallis M. Riglar to Mary J. Archer, 15 May 1866; married by Rev. R. H. Griffeth.

C. H. Riglar to Mary D. McKenzie, 23 April 1866; married by Rev. R. H. Griffith.

Edwin Rogers to M. A. Black, 16 Sept 1866; married by A. McIvor, J. P.

J. W. Reed to M. J. McDowell, 23 Feb 1867; married by Rev. J. F. Butt.

Elisha Robinson to Vina Robinson, 4 April 1867; married by Rev. J. F. Butt.

Wm. R. Sternes to Ann Darnell, 15 June 1854.

Moses Steuffer to Margaret Shuman, 25 Jan 1854; married by Alex. Springs, J. P.

H. W. Stinton to Ellen A. Harris, 22 July 1857; married by Rev. Jno S. Harris.

Wm. H. Shuman to Margaret Beaty, 28 Sept 1858; married by J. H. Grier, J. P.

Alex Sinclair to Mary L. Davidson, 10 Aug 1858; married by Rev. James Sinclair.

H. C. Severs to M. R. Prim, 26 June 1865; married by W. M. Kerr.

R. C. Stricklen to Martha C. Hunter, 18 Dec 1865; married by Rev. J. G. McLaughlin.

R. A. Sharp to Elizabeth Lawing, 8 June 1866; married by Rev. J. F. Butt.

James Shields to Lucenda Thomas, 24 Dec 1866; married by D. G. Maxwell, J. P.

A. D. N. Smith to Hannah Ledwell, 15 Aug 1866; married by Rev. J. F. Butt.

David J. Smith to Nancy J. Cathey, 14 Sept 1866.

George Smith to Louiza McLean, 28 July 1866.

T. N. Steele to M. C. Query, 30 Oct 1866; married by Rev. J. G. McLaughlin.

D. H. Stokes to Mary J. Mullis, 7 June 1866; married by Rev. J. G. McLaughlin.

J. M. Simmerman to Maria Propst, 5 Feb 1867; married by Rev. J. F. Butt.

John Simpson to Eliza McLure, 13 Feb 1867; married by S. Sifford, J. P.

W. A. Sing to Jane E. Marshall, 6 March 1867; married by S. J. Berryhill, J. P.

A. A. Stewart to M. M. Griffith, 20 Feb 1867; married by Rev. John Hunter.

Frank Taylor to Esther Michael, 28 Aug 1861.

John P. Taylor to Amanda Roberts, 1 April 1861; married by Thomas W. Query, J. P.

John Tuloar(?) to Margaret L. Riglar, 19 March 1861; married by Richd. H. Griffith, Minister of the Gospel.

W. H. G. Tysor to Caroline Berryhill, 12 Sept 1861; married by J. C. Nicholson, J. P.

William Todd to Caroline Todd, 20 Feb 1862; married by J. P. Ross, J. P.

J. C. Taylor to D. A. Noles, 8 Aug 1866; married by Rev. F. B. Anderson.

Andrew L. Thomas to Nancy Ashly, 19 Nov 1866; married by Rev. J. M. Garrison

James Thomas to Cintha Mitchel, 13 Oct 1866; married by Rev. J. F. Butt.

C. B. Todd to Susan J. Berryhill, 22 Aug 1866; married by Rev. J. J. Prather.

L. N. Todd to Sarah L. Marshall, 24 April 1866; married by S. J. Berryhill.

D. F. Troutman to L. R. Price, 9 July 1866; married by Rev. F. B. Andrews.

Wm Turner to Fanny Strickland, 5 Nov 1866; married by Rev. J. F. Butt.

H. M. Thornburg to S. A. Orr, 11 Feb 1867; married by Rev. W. K. Milton.

B. F. Teye(?) to N. A. Morris, __ March 1867; married by Rev. W. McDonald.

David J. Vance to Elizabeth Vance, 23 July 1860; married by John S. Means, J. P.

John Vogel to Laura Vogel, 1 June 1861; married by Rev. G. D. Bernheim.

W. B. Vance to Lizzie Bethune, 4 Dec 1866; married by Rev. W. C. Power.

B. H. White to Jane Flow, 17 Feb 1853; married by Casper Harget, J. P.

Wm. Worsham to E. J. Cashon, 15 Dec 1853; married by James M. Garrison.

James B. Watt to A. Louisa Neel, 28 June 1854; married by J. Monroe Anderson.

R. A. Ward to Martha A. Johnson, 12 Aug 1856; married by Alex Cooper, J. P.

George H. Warren to Mary E. McDonald, 5 March 1856; married by Rev. H. B. Cunningham.

M. L. Wriston to Mary E. Springs, 2 April 1856; married by Rev. A. W. Miller.

Joseph Wenterlo to Charlotte Balthasar, 1 Sept 1858; married by E. J. Meynardie, Pastor M. E. Church.

John Mc. Wilson to Jane O. Sloan, 23 Dec 1858; married by Rev. E. F. Rockwell.

L. S. Williams to Delia S. White, 30 April 1861; married by Rev. A. Sinclair.

Branch A. Worsham to N. A. E. Johnston, 23 Dec 1861; married by Walter S. Pharr.

M. L. Wallis to M. M. Russell, 9 Nov 1863.

N. J. Walker to C. E. Berryhill, 20 June 1864; married by G. C. Cathey, J. P.

John W. Warner to Sarah E. Taylor, 3 Feb 1865; married by W. McDonald, J. P.

J. L. Wicks to Maggie R. Robinson, 14 June 1865; married by Rev. R. Z. Johnston.

L. J. Walker to Dorcus C. Marshall, 24 April 1866; married by S. J. Berryhill.

J. B. Wallace to M. J. Oehler, 28 Nov 1866; married by Rev. W. S. Pharr.

R. P. Waring to Annie E. Aldrich, 8 May 1866; married by Rev. N. Aldrich.

J. D. Watts to N. A. Davis, 8 Oct 1866; married by Rev. W. S. Pharr.

J. N. White to E. C. Finch, 15 Dec 1866; married by R. F. Blythe, J. P.

M. D. Whitesides to M. E. Christenbury, 18 Oct 1866; married by Rev. J. Douglas.

John Wilson to Mary A. Brown, 29 Oct 1866; married by R. McEwan, J. P.

M. A. Wilson to Jane E. McCombs, 9 Oct 1866; married by Rev. J. G. McLaughlin.

W. M. Wilson to S. A. Shaw, 16 Feb 1866; married by Rev. A. W. Miller.

W. A. Wallace to W. B. McCall, 4 Feb 1867; married by John Walker, J. P.

A. S. White to Sarah C. Burns, 7 Feb 1867; married by Rev. W. C. Power.

C. C. Wingate to Jane Kelley, 18 Jan 1867.

Wm. J. Yates to Sarah A. Springs, 23 Nov 1857; married by Rev. Alex Sinclair.

P. C. Yandle to M. D. C. Erwin, 9 Oct 1866; married by Rev. B. J. Jones.

Prepared by Miss Karon Mac Smith

Alexander Cont.
R.B. 225
R.D. 6, 77, 100, 206,
  209, 225
Rebecca C. 9, 31
Rebekah 102, 207
R.H. 225
Robert D. 179
Robt. W. 43
Rosana E. 105
Rufus L. 5, 7, 90,
  153, 172
Ruth 4, 16, 123, 182
Ruthe 89, 121, 210
Ruth J. 194
Ruth Jane 33
Ruthy 11, 19, 30, 38,
  64, 110(2), 116,
  134, 136, 146, 166,
  172, 206
R.W. 86
S. 134
Saml./Samuel P. 4, 7,
  26, 168, 169
Sarah 3, 206
Sarah J. 236
Sarah Jane 50
Sarah N. 173
Satirah H. 220
S.C. 12, 108, 221,
  224(2)
Silas 58, 110
Silas W. 142
Sinai 23, 216
Sophia 143
S.P. 66, 119, 183,195
Stannope W. 2
Stephen 32
Susan 2, 5, 145, 150,
  153, 236
Susan M. 120
Susan R. 161
Susan Marander 35
Susannah 73
Susan R. 8, 59, 98,
  135
S.W. 28, 106, 214
Telemacus 114, 206
Telemans 75
Terissa 157
Terza 163
Thomas 4, 167
Thos. H. 91, 218
Thos./Thomas M. 6,
  184, 204
Tho./Thomas N. 72, 77,
  130
Thos. S. 209
Tirza 186
T.N. 137, 141, 194
T.P. 225
Ulyses C. 106
Ulysses L. 204
Violet 102
Violet D. 157
Violet E.L. 216
Virginia C. 136
W.F. 59, 63, 73, 90,
  189
W.H. 45
William 7, 25, 42, 77,
  88, 89(2), 149,
  167, 206
William Junr. 6
Wm. B. 24, 32, 109,
  146, 158, 159, 179,
  221

Alexander Cont.
Wm. F. 8, 24, 35, 64,
  91, 104
Wm. H. 63, 80
William N. 173
William S. 184
Wm. S.D. 225
Wm. T. 16, 63, 76
W.J. 64
W.S. 105
W.W. 40
Zeras 147
Alison, John 74
Allen, Agness F. 151
Amz. W. 96
Andrew J. 45
Ann 73, 76
Cornelia 214
David 4, 64, 123, 221
Eleanor 46
Eliza 53
Elizabeth 23, 194
H.W. 225
James L. 225
J.B. 225
John 8, 76, 184
John N. 138
Margaret 45
Margaret E. 52
Margaret H. 5
Mary 4, 55
Mary J. 216
Rebeca 98
Robert 151
Samuel 34
Sara 116
Sarah 45, 138
Thomas 46
Wm. G. 225
W.W. 195
Alley, Roze 177
Allison, Ann L. 145
David 204
Elizabeth R. 42
J.A. 11
Jane E. 145
Jno. 32, 35, 43, 84,
  138, 152, 207, 208,
Joseph 42
Margaret 66, 106
Rebecca S. 94
R.M. 191
R.W. Jr. 86
Sarah M. 53
Susan R. 128
Thomas C. 33, 84
William 3, 42, 170,
  175
Anatham, Theresa 226
Anderson, Adam C. 57
Elizabeth 106
F.B. 239
Jane 186
J. Monroe 151, 239
Mary 103
Mary Ann 197
Milas J. 154
Milly 141
M.J. 57, 185
Nicholas 61, 106, 141
Thomas 105
Andrews, Elizabeth 23
Wm. 33(2)
Anderson, W.J. 225
Andrews, F.B. 239
Anton, John 73
Archer, Betsey 78

Archer Cont.
Cyrus A. 63
Francis 201
Margaret E. 63
Mary J. 238
Rebecca 201
Archey(?), Emma C. 52
Archie, D. 20
Ardry, Mary J. 16
W.C. 225
Ardrey, M.R. 155
Arman(?), R.L.D. 26
Armon, R.L.D. 3, 55
Armond, Sabina 183
Samuel J. 148
Armor, Mary M. 226
R.L.D. 26, 28, 40(2)
Armour, Louiza 72
Arms, Emily E. 17
Armstrong, Arthur 83, 84
Cynthia 15
Fanny 235
Arnes, E.E. 227
Arnold, Mary 188
Arrowood, Emeline 56
Arthurs, Rebekah 3
Arwood, Martha E. 125
Asbury, Daniel 126
Ashley, Frances 192
Moses 52
Ashly, Nancy 239
Atchison, Peggy 125
Atkinson, Sarah 13
Auten, Peter 9
Robert F. 119
Auton, E.J. 113
Elizabeth Adley 109
H.R. 225
Jane 13
Jemima P. 192
John 106, 174
John W. 30, 225
Margaret 209
Margaret N. 161
Powell S. 225
Robert F. 9, 113
Sarah 73
Sarah J. 109
William 109
Wm. M. 38
Avery, T.L. 99
Aydlott, M.J. 225

Baaton, Isaac 201
Badger, S.J. 211
Baer, Griffith 10
Bagget, Chesy 183
Bailes, Martha 219
Baily, Betsey 220
Sally 209
Bain, Eliza 44
Jane H. 99
John 10
Margaret 107
Polly 101
Baine, Sarah 201
Baird, Samuel A. 23
Baker, ___ 41
Aaron 21
Abel 202
Amanda 71
Amelia 117
Charles M. 11, 171
Dorcas 63
Elijah Senr. 10
Elizabeth 168, 208

245

Baker Cont.
Elizah 117
Elizebeth 7
George 109, 132
George F. 172
Hannah 46
Harriet 4
Isaac A. 127
Jacob 9, 41
James 205
James W. 108
Jane 37, 198, 204
Jane C, 10
Jane Lenora 71
J.E. 172
Jepthah 29, 31
John M. 227
Jonathan 71, 168
Kessander W. 49
Lucinda 157
Mary F. 26
Matilda 164
M.E. 71
Rachel 46
Rebekah 132
Roxana A. 72
Sarah 75, 224
Sarah H. 129
Susannah 127
Wm. F. 7
Baldridge, Elizabeth 82
Baldwin, Allen 36
Mary C. 166
Ballard, Margaret 174
Nancy 61
Baller, J.T. 226
Balthasar, Charlotte 220, 240
Bankes, Sophia 84
Barkley, H.S. 227
Barckly, John 92
Bargman, George 202
Barker, Mary 141
Barkley, Elenor 92
H.S. 83
Barnes, Elizabeth 164
Barnet, James G. 99
Wm. G. 224
Barnett, Abbey M. 5
Abigal 166
Amos 34
Anna 27
Catharine 83
David 184
David E. 213
Elizabeth 185
E.L.S. 27
Esther 34
James G. 102
Jas. M. 125
Jane 102, 178
Jane M. 154
J.D. 145
J. Lee 12
John 13, 103, 204
John D. 14, 227
John S. 150
John W. 227
J.S. 227
J.W. 216
Levicy C. 48
Malinda 174
Martha 233
Martha A. 229
Martha C. 226
Mary 44, 109, 196
Mary E. 54

Barnett Cont.
M.E. 98
Patsey 174
Peggy Curry 206
Robert 12
Robert F. 173
Susanna 181
Thomas 144, 206
Thomas 6, 27, 206
T.L. 226
Vincent 196
W.G. 56, 63, 176, 187, 189, 224
Wm. G. 54
W.S. 175
Zelia 69
Barnette, Wm. P. 147
Barnhardt, Margaret 187
Barnhill, Betsey 9
Caroline 179
Harriet 37
John 108, 207
John H. 13, 71
John W. 227
Mary 174
Peggy 207
Rachael 35
Barnycastle, Sarah 53
Barr, John C. 15
Mary 66
Nancy 59
Polly 194
Barr(?), Wm. V. 22
Barringer, Martin L. 105
M.L. 56, 158, 201
M.S. 226
Barry, Andrew M. 154
Ann 70
Dovy 180
Eleanor R. 94
Hugh 131
Jane L. 173
Mary 94
Violet 131
Bartlett, James 226
J.H. 227
William 219
Bates, Harriet Ann 37
Bath, Jane Hunter 6
Baxter, Frances 90
Rachel 155
Beam, John C.M. 226
Bean, William 182
Beard, E.A. 16
J.F. 150
John C. 227
Joseph H. 28
Leonora 145
Lucy 41
M.A.M. 54
Margt. E. 227
R.C. 208
Robert 14, 38, 227
Sally 164
Beatey, Cynthia 171
Moses L. 226
Wm. 69
Beatty, Wm. F. 227
Beaty, Agness 8
Alexander 217
Anderson 14
Andrew M. 167
Betsey 84
Celina 168
Clarrissa C. 119
Cornelia R. 61
Cresy 101

Beaty Cont.
Cynthia C. 118
Effize 235
Eleanor 40
Esther 145
Frances 119
Francis M. 40
Isaac 31
Isabella 15, 108, 189
James M. 152, 228
Jane 119, 205
John 31, 193
John Jr. 80
John W. 15
Jonathan 14
Laura 10
Lavina 80
Margaret 216, 238
Martha 177
Mary 147, 193
Mary A. 18
M.E. 4
M.G. 225
Milly 159
Moses 80
Nancy 41, 104
Nancy Caroline 15
Nathan 104
Ruth 180
Smith 30
Thos. L. 142
Wm./William 8, 19, 21, 60, 99, 131, 147, 180, 207
William C. 90
Wm. Frank 101
Becket, Jane 149
Samuel 15
Belk, James P. 15
Sam. E. 67, 130
S.D. 86
Bell, Elizabeth D. 67
John 107, 129, 156
Margt. R. 236
Mary 95
M.W. 16
Rachel E. 65
Robert C. 25, 100, 205
Robert E. 139
Sarah 116
Walter 128
Wm. A. 117, 139
Benedict, John J. 16
Benfield, Amanda 171
Benham(?), John 67
Bennitt, John 161
Bentley, Elizabeth 114
Sarah 4
Benton, Eliza Ann 150
Berean, Jane Adaline 95
Bernheim, G.D. 138, 143, 160, 198, 239
Berry, Ann A. 78
Elizabeth 25
John 66
Robert 16
Berryhill, A.A. 168
Alford A. 17
Amanda A. 194
Andrew 141
Betsey 17
Caroline 239
C.E. 203, 240
Dorcas 119
Elizabeth C. 3
Hannah 160
Jas. S. 226

Berryhill Cont.
James S. 8
Jas. W. 225
Joseph 28, 38
Joseph J. 112, 199
K.W. 44, 53, 96, 97,
 100, 176, 180, 186,
 208
Margt./Margaret 9, 163
Margaret B. 19
Margaret E. 168, 209
Martha J. 62
Mary 176, 199
Mary E. 12
Matilda 21
Peggy Ann 16
Pinkney 168
Pinckny 162
Rachel H. 180
Rachel S. 178
Saml./Samuel 9, 16, 17,
 61, 119, 199, 200
Sarah 163
S.J. 168, 237, 238,
 239, 240
S.P. 62, 147
Stephen T. 19
Su---- 47
Susan J. 239
Thomas 17
Thos. P. 215
Wallace 180
Wm./William R. 17, 33,
 161, 197
William W.E. 10
W.R. 227
Bethune, A. 15
 Lizzie 239
Bevins, Moses 17
 Union 118
Bibb, Betsey 175
 Nancy 94
Bibby, Elizabeth 44
Bicket, Margarett 133
Biggart, Clementine A.
 214
 James 214
 Margaret 80
Bigger, Allison H. 206
 Francis A. 131
 James 18
 Joseph 86
 Mary C. 167
Biggers, Elizabeth 206
 F.A. 209, 216
 Francis A. 73
 Isabella 232
 John A. 226
 Martha C. 237
 Sarah H. 18
 Susannah J. 87
 William 209
Biggert, Wm. S. 227
Bigham, Elizabeth 170,
 184, 219
 Fanny 193
 James 18, 33
 Jane 140
 Jane L. 150
 Joseph W. 92
 Margaret E. 162
 Margaret J. 193
 Mary 92, 236
 Mathew 69
 Nancy E. 64
 Peggy 194

Bigham Cont.
 Robert 184
 Robt. N. 123
 Saml./Samuel 18, 41,
 140, 185, 194
 Sarah 17, 18
 W.C. 162
 William 124
 Wm./William M. 128,154
Bighers, Mary Ann 207
Bighim, Samuel 172
Bill, Wm. 27(2)
Binton, Mary S. 86
Biram, John 19
Bird, John 19
 Mary 163
Biren, Abram 19
Bissell, E.H. 195
Black, Absalom 143
 A.M. 26
 Amelia 21
 Ann 35
 Betsey 34
 Caroline 91
 Celia 219
 Christina 106
 Cynthia 45, 70
 Cyrus 75, 117
 Deborah 63
 Eli O. 1
 Elizabeth 116, 129,
 156, 215
 Esther 203(2)
 Hamilton 116
 H.W. 47, 90
 James 70, 131
 James M. 97, 130, 178,
 226
 Jane 92, 218
 J.B. 98
 Jean 220
 Jensey 79
 John 20, 33, 80, 98,
 115, 160, 183, 226
 John S. 187
 Joseph P. 97
 Louiza 151
 Lucy 103
 Margaret 115
 M.A. 238
 Margaret E. 234
 Margaret K. 20
 Margaret T. 97
 Martha 115
 Mary 99, 211, 226
 Mary Caroline 207
 Mary A.J. 29
 Nancy 146
 Narcissa 210
 Peggy 20, 63
 Rosanah E. 158
 Rosanna 204
 Sam 100
 Saml./Samuel 20, 73,
 115(2)
 Sarah Ann 183
 Seeley 94
 Sophia J. 133
 Thos. M. 20, 115
 T.J. 227
 W.A. 47, 227
 William 105, 115, 204
 William J. 184
 William L. 21
Blackburn, Louisa 162
Blackledge, Rich. 227

Blackminister, Jas. J. 45
Blackwelder, David M. 22
 Elizabeth 198
 John 198
 Mary Ann 198
Blackwood, Ann 22
 Betsey 208
 Joseph 6, 8, 22, 81,
 109
 Marget 46
 Mary 25
 William 113
Blades, Elizabeth 57
Blair, Adaline 39, 228
 A.M. 52
 Amzi W. 92
 A.W. 48, 51
 Clarinda J. 88
 Elizabeth C. 89
 I.A. 235
 Isabel 115
 John 74
 John W. 50, 144, 154
 J.W. 33, 67
 Margaret C. 28
 Martha 99
 Mary L. 237
 Patsey 42
 Samuel 22, 56
 Washington 22
Blake, H. Josephine 229
 Jas. H. 19
Blakely, Hugh 23
 Mary Jane 194
 Thos. H. 226
 Wm. 225
 W.J. 227
Blalock, Almina L. 64
 Margaret A. 194
Blanchard, Caroline 212
 Mary 38
 Rosanah 4
 Thomas 207
 William 10
Blanchart, Mary 207
Blankenship, Malvina 53
 Nancy M. 231
 Polly 165
 S.A. 226
Blankenshipp, Sally 108
Blanset, Tersa M. 45
Blear, Milton 184
Bloom, John F. 196, 198
Blount, Eliza A. 86
 Jane 123
 J.M. 226
 John 164
 Matilda 118
Blyth, C.N. 214
 Saml./Samuel 172, 204
 Ann 128
Blythe, Buck 213
 Elen 13
 John N. 226
 John N. 3
 K.F. 6
 Margaret R. 62
 Mary 205
 Rebecca 172
 R.F. 3, 26(2), 27, 28,
 65(3), 107, 118,
 132, 169, 200, 208,
 211(2), 213, 214,
 225, 231, 240
 Robert 202
 Samuel 226

Clonts, Jacob 42
  John A. 73
Clontz, Cartharine M. 27
  Jeremiah 25
  Mary E. 73
Cnup, Mary 51
Coal, Thomas 182
Coble, Joel 179
Coburn, Azariah 110
Cochran, A.H. 42
  A.J.D. 228
  Alexander H. 158
  Azeriah 44
  Barbara P. 43
  Cena 44
  C.N. 33
  Dorcas M. 7
  Eli 197
  E.P. 34
  Eliza J. 34
  Francis 140
  J.A. 225
  Joseph L. 158
  Levi 42
  Lucinda 136
  Margaret 7
  Martha 33
  Mary J.C. 204
  Mijah 43
  Moses 119
  Nancy B. 144
  Polly 17
  R.C. 75
  R.M. 44
  Robert 43
  Robert C. 92
  Robert W. 43
  Sally 19, 114
  Sarah 158
  Sarah E. 86
  Sarah M. 158
  Terressa ,Jane 186
  Thomas 43(2)
  Virginia C. 83
  Wm. 132
  Wm. B. 44
  William R. 43
Cochrane, Robert E. 106
Cochron, Elizabeth M.
    178
  Rachel 165
Cofer, R.A. 112
Coffey, Abdon A. 137
  Margaret M. 185
  Mary A. 185
  M.S. 230
  S.A. 237
Cohen, Carrie 52
Coldins, Jane V.C. 9
Coldiron, Jacob 112
  Sarah A. 104
Cole, Ann 186
  Caroline 38
  Isabella 1
  M. 158
  Martha 3
  Thomas 16, 101
Coleman, James 221
  W.H. 228
Colley, Jane 74
  Margaret 45
  Thomas 45
Collie, Bannister 228
Collier, Mary C. 42
  Mary L. 145, 237
  W.J. 213
Collins, Isabella 61

Collins Cont.
  James S. 45, 61
  Jane 87
  J.S. 2, 44, 66
  Marg./Margaret 105,
    110, 234
  Martha J.D. 225
  Mary 209
  Robert 44
  Robert D. 209
  W.J. 39
Colthrap, Eliza Jane 80
  Martha 92
Colthrop, Rhoda 92
Colvard, Sallie A. 163
Combs, Margaret J. 69
Comstock, William 80
Conder, Elizabeth 202
  Elizabeth 189
  Lewis 202
  Mary 216
  Harriet E. 190
Condre, Mary 31
Condor, Ann Jane 106
Coner, Torence 135
Conger, Susannah 205
Conly, John W. 14
Connel, Elizabeth 131
Connelly, John 221
  Mary 221
Connely, Mortimer 42
Connell, Thomas H. 131
Conner, Caroline 188
  Catherine 135
  Elizabeth 13
  Jas. 91, 135, 149,
    192(2)
  Henry 29, 37, 152, 176
  Henry W. 32(2)
  Henry W.M. 26, 218
  Jas. 16, 33, 34, 37,
    152, 156, 176, 178,
    212
  Margaret J. 26
Conner(?), Jas. 28
  William 34, 105
Connor, Elizebeth E. 68
Cook, Austin 7
  A.W. 43
  Caroline 168
  Catherine 163
  Chas./Charles 45, 46,
    67, 148
  Daniel 83
  Eliza 144
  Elizabeth 10, 72, 226
  Eleanor C. 216
  James 7
  John 209
  Katharine 31
  Margaret 83, 130
  Margaret M. 7
  Martha J. 71
  Mary 10, 31, 137, 148
  Mary E. 11
  Mary J. 23, 227
  Nancy 221
  Polly 184
  Powel 10
  Rachel 138
  Rachel R. 96
  Robert 31, 72
  Sarah 14
  W.A. 45
  William 31, 45, 46
  Z. 122
Cooke, Joseph 56

Cooper, A. 31, 42, 46,
    62, 73, 89, 97, 99,
    106, 111, 167(2)
  Adam 44, 52, 81, 146
  Alex./Alexander 8, 17,
    22(2), 31, 79, 104,
    155, 197, 210, 229,
    234, 239
  A.M. 83
  Harriet E. 82
  John A. 7, 74, 82
  L.C. 166
  Mary A. 46
  Mary P. 224
  Nancy 81
  Nancy C. 162
  Nancy E. 215
  Nancy Sarah 7
  Patsey 126
  Sarah Jane 179
  Thomas 46
  Thomas S. 166
  William 7
  Wm./William 117, 167
Cooper(?), Alex 34
Coover, Jane 72
Corlett, Robert 76
Corum, Polly 168
  William 166
  Wm./William C. 5, 186,
    210
Coser, R.A. 234
Cosey, Hubart 47
Cottrell, John B. 114
Couchrane, Thomas 165
Coughorn, Robert 47
Coughran, Thomas 109
Coughren, John 25
Courier, James 118
Cowan, Abel 184
Cowan, David 14, 108,
    113, 218
  David F. 62
  Elizabeth J. 184
  John 48
  Margaret 45
  Martha 183
  Lvm. C. 63
  William George Wash-
    ington 143
Cowen, Ann S. 62
  John T. 42
Cox,   55
  Harriet Matilda 196
  J. 98
  Jane 23
  Jane P. 108
  John 95
  Pressley M. 55
  Sara 86
  Sarah A. 97
  Sarah E. 188
  Sarah M. 108
Coxe, Will G. 198
Crage, Wm. 50
Craig, Alexander 91
  Elizabeth 68
  James D. 201
  Manda 123
  Mary L. 57
  M.J. 71
Craige, Margret 91
Crammond, Jas. 228
Craton(?), Sarah 16
Crawfor_, Nancy 84
Crawford, Joseph 34
  Martha 131

251

Davis Cont.
Samuel A. cont.
  207, 219
Sarah E. 116
Sinthy 218
S.W. 195, 229
T.E. 230, 236
Terza 147
Thomas 52, 156
Thomas W. 151
W.A. 230
Davison, Sarah 31
Daw, Eliza 124
Dawkins, R.S. 2
Deans, J.C. 59
Dearman/DeArman, Abigail
  S. 52
Dearman, Richard L. 52
Dearmon/DeArmon, Richard
  L. 68
  R.L. 69, 92, 97, 102,
    225, 226, 228
  R.L. 213
  Wm. W. 7, 109
Dearmond/DeArmond,
  Amelia 175
  A.L. 228
  E.H. 229
  E.M. 51
  James 104, 182
  James B. 228
  Martha A. 84
De Armor, R.L. 40
Deaton, Delila A. 156
  James A. 27
  James C. 71, 189
  James R. 175
  J.B. 230(2)
  J.C. 107
  J.L. 229
  John L. 185
  John Z. 229
  Sarah A.K. 175
  Susan 149, 235
  Wm. 71
Deberry, George 229
DeCamp, Charles 190, 230
Deenster, Mary 236
Delane, A. 89
DeLaney, Wm. 230
Dellipoe, Sarah 156
Dempsey, Sarah 147
Denkins, Lewis 218
  Margaret 165
  Polly 215
Dennis, Charles 64, 128
  James T. 229
  John C. 229
  Mary E. 235
Denny, Eli 159
Denton, James 209
Dermond, Jane 165
  Mary 104
Dewease, Hellan 211
Dewese, Abigail 97
  Amanda 213
  Annis 97
  Calvin T. 208
  Caroline 127
  Catharine 37
  C.T. 187, 229
  Elizabeth E. 8
  Henritta 84
  Jane 196
  John A. 97
  Jonathan 10
  Margaret 162

Dewese Cont.
Nancy A. 213
Sarah J. 225
Dewey, Tho./Thos. 44, 90,
  188
  T.W. 9, 23, 24, 85,
    87, 133, 230
  Zedick 111
De Wolfe, F.S. 183
Dick, James W. 180
Dickey, Moses 68
  Wm. N. 230
Dickson, Elizabeth 124
  Harriet T. 82
  Hugh M. 82
  James 2
  Mary 211
Dillard, John R. 228
Dillerman(?), Jordan 46
Dillin, Thos. Jo. 159
Dillon, Wm. 57
Dilyard, Dolly 16
Dinkins, Alex. H. 152
  Dorcas H. 101
  E.J. 130
  Emily C. 208
  James 88
  Jno./John 26, 209
  K.D. 24
  K.J. 26
  K.S. 13, 17(2), 21
  Lewis 101
  Lucinda 179
  Mary Ann 136
  Richd./Richard S. 4,
    80, 114, 145
  R.J. 46, 53, 56, 57,
    58(2), 61, 68, 88,
    89, 98, 102(2),107,
    111, 127, 141, 145,
    148(2), 156, 164,
    165, 170
  Robert J. 31
  R.S. 30, 41, 62, 82
    (2), 93, 119, 123,
    133, 155
  Sarah 26
  S.C. 69
Dinkins(?), K.D. 5
Dixon, David E. 228
  Elvira M. 180
  George D. 224
  Hugh M. 196
  James A. 124
  James W. 229
  Jane 212
  Jane E. 86
  John 228
  John R. 211
  Lucinda 114
  Margaret 124
  Mary 33
  Sarah 41
Dobbin, Alexander 77
Dobson, Jane 141
Doby, Martin P. 229
  M.P. 229
  W.C. 229
Dodd, T.M.C. 230
Doherty, Anne 30
  Elizabeth B. 10
  Hannah 82
  J. 10, 16, 74, 117,
    140, 179, 221
  James 84, 116, 179,
    184
  Mary 159

Doherty Cont.
Minth 125
Rebekah 3
Susanna 159
Donaldson, C.L. 47
  Robert 22
Donnell, George 224
Dorrier, John 224
Doster, Cloey 177
  Hannah 220
  Milley 221
Doubt, William 229
Dogherty, David 187
  Polley 184
Douglas, J. 240
  Jno./John 59, 139,154,
    228, 230, 231
  Samuel A. 228
Douglass, Catharine E. 66
  Ja./James 187, 221
  Joseph 12
  Marshel H. 200
  Thomas 229
Doulin, Nancy 59
Dow, Amelia 109
  Isabella 124
  Margarett 142
  Susannah 10
  William 124
Dowdle, Jane 154
Dowell, Nancy 101
Downes, A.B. 230
  Caroline 50
  Mary A. 139
  W.H. 230
Downs, A.B. 71, 157
  John T. 58, 149
  Jonathan 128
  J. Thomas 123
  Larkin 148(2)
  Louiza 157
  Mary T. 226
Downs(?), Wm. 177
Dozier, Edward 56
Drew, Peggy 75
Drury, Patsey 209
Ducas, Rachel 73
Duckworth, Geo. 51
  John 66, 84, 96
  John Junr. 16
  Mary 91
  Polly 219
  William 37
Ducworth, Nelly 156
Dudley, M.A. 145
Duese, Eveline 10
  Margaret M. 12
Duest, Mary 123
Duffey, Elizabeth 123
  Mary 57
  Robert 182
  Jane 19
  John 19
  Robert 59
Douglass, Jinny 114
  Jo 121
  Jno. 48
Dulah(?), Cathren 43
Dulen, Reuben 111
Dulin, Ambrose 224
  Amy 152
  Cyntha 103
  Daniel 152
  D.H. 230
  Emaline 85
  Janes J. 142
  Margaret 197

254

Ferrell Cont.
James 29, 127
James F. 180
Jane C. 40
Melissa 37
Polly 28
Telitha 40
William 28, 55
William W. 26, 40
Ferril, Sarah A. 228
Ferrill, Mary C.T. 234
Polly 67
Fesperman, Frederick 56
John C. 6
Festerman, Betsey 171
Eady R. 43
Elizabeth 130
Fanny 89
Julia 62
Levi 130
Mary G. 229
Polly 90
Precila 47
Fewell, Wm. B., Dr. 56
Fidler, Adaline 108
Fields, Green 11
Fieser, Levina 29
Fifer, James 134
Finch, Betsey 192
E.C. 240
Eliza 97
Jenny 16
Fincher, Betsey T. 192
Eliza 30
J.N. 231
Jonathen 170
Joseph 57, 192(2)
Kissander 151
Kiziah 125
McCuen 152
Mary R. 70
Miles R. 151
Nancy 103, 220
Sarah 170
S.N. 231
Finey, Ervin 51
John 113
Molley 113
Finley, Charles 57
Finney, Elisabeth 76
Ervin 100
John 219
Finny, Rachel 219
Sarah 75
Fisher, Amy 167
Elizabeth 187
Fite, Anna 156
George 145
G.F. 110
Green P. 118
John 57
Louisa Cawan 113
Peter 39, 57, 113
R.D.R. 183
Robert D. 231
Zekiel 78
Fitten, Jno. 161
Flanagan, Margaret L. 215
Mary 183
Flangan, Mary 94
Flanigan, Elizabeth 145
John O. 189
M.A. 55
Samuel 175
Flaniken, John 174
Flannagan, Elizabeth 30
John B. 28

Flannagan Cont.
Mary A. 162
Mary Jane 169
Robert C. 144
Sarah M. 106
Sarah P. 225
Fleniken, David 144
Jane R. 160
Flenneken, Martha 58
Flenniken, Frances 204
Isaac 58
Flennikin, Ann 205
James G. 29
Flin, William 15, 143
Flinn, Eliezer 36
Eliza C. 94
Wm. M.B. 94, 216
Flow, Ceclia 75
David 59
David W. 73
Dorcas 59
Elizabeth L. 126
Elizabeth M. 218
Ellen C. 77
Harriet H. 157
James 157, 197
Jas./James C. 58, 178, 206
Jane 211, 239
J.C. 129
J.M.W. 214
John 3, 58, 102
Margaret A. 2
Margaret E. 15
Matildy 21
Mary E.J. 218
Polly 185
Rachel 73
Robert H. 231
Sarah 172
Flowe, Nancy 233
Flowers, Rachel 70
Foard, Elizabeth 60
John 59
Nancy 133
Rachel 197
S.H. 86(2)
William 221
Folger, William H. 48, 85
Folley, Wm. 231
Folsom, Darias 193
Forbes, Archabald 48
Ford, Chas. A. 100
Geo./George 26, 219
Henry 174
Fore, Lawson 59
Forster, Alex. M. 55
Forsythe, Elizabeth 216
Mary 67
Foster, Andrew 137
Betsy 88
Cornelia 82
Dorcas 75
Elizabeth 34
Evelina W. 75
Henry 76
John 145
Joseph 161, 162
Margaret 182
Fowler, Apsey 49
Fox, Abraham M. 162
A.M. 166
Cynthia 214
Daniel 59
H.E.A. 9
H.M. 42
J.A. 73

Fox Cont.
J. Alexander 26
Margaret P. 200
Mary A. 214
Matilda 85
Philadelphia H. 217
Franklin, Margaret 162, 171
Polly 58
Fraser, Esther 119
Jas. H. 60
Frasure, Sinthey 12
Frazer, Cynthia 153
J.C.C. 52
John T. 60(2)
Frazier, M.L. 231
Freasure, John C. 177
Joseph A. 111
Freeman, Charles T. 18
Eliza 114
Elizabeth 105
Elizabeth M. 84
James F.W. 144
James T. 61, 205
John 17, 110
Mary 41, 162, 214
Mary J. 38
M.E. 228
Michael 214
Michael W. 61
M.W. 29
Nancy 179
Nancy Ann 41
Nancy P. 28
Peggy 181
Peggy Ann 17
Robert A. 39
Sally 83
Sarah J. 28
Thomas Jefferson 173
William A. 38
French, Polly 149
Frew, Archibald 177
Baldwin 52
William 15
Friday, Jackson 62
Sidney 120
Friedman, Charles 13
Fulenwider, A.C. 122
Fullum, Martha A. 202
Fullwood, J.M. 219
Furr, Elizabeth 60
Elizabeth L. 100
Sarah 208

Gadberry, Haly 88
Gainer, Jane 9
Gaines A. 148
Galbraith, Martha 204
Gallant, Nancy 31
S.M. 58
Gallent, Daniel 94
Galloway, Daniel 63
Deborah 97
Elizabeth E. 150
Elizabeth W. 63
Henry H. 44, 124
Hugh 63
Margaret 44
Martha 117
Martha E. 56
Mary C. 230
Nancy 63
Sidney E. 80
Thomas H. 63
Gallway, Josiah 177

256

Hunter Cont.
Martha A. 204
Martha C. 238
Martha E. 139
Martha N. 63
Martha S. 143, 154
Mary 196
Mary A. 233
Mary Ann 63, 195
Mary C. 154
Mary E. 81
Mary M. 18
M.C. 190
M.H. 63
M.J. 141, 232
Nancy C. 64, 139
Nancy Jane 172
Olivia M. 205
Rebecca A. 64
Robert 63(2)
Robert B. 51
Robert C. 204
Rosanna E.J. 139
Rossannah D. 24
Sarah 187
Sarah A. 63
Sarah Ann 24
Silus(?) C. 6
Thomas 63, 204
Thos. J. 43
T.J. 83
William 73
William B. 91
Huson, Richard 82
Sarah 117
Huster, Taripa 23
Huston, Joseph 139
William 173
Hutchinson, A.J. 189
Hutchison, Charles 93,
128, 161
Chas. L. 124
Cynthia J. 37
Elizabeth 199, 237
E.N. 182
E. Nye 13, 98, 176,
209, 214
Esther 77
James 116, 128
James H. 105
James M. 25, 37, 64,
136, 232
James R. 117
J.M. 16, 17
Jno./John 92, 121,
164, 179
Jno./John B. 93, 200,
Louisa 9
M.A. 227
Margaret 197
Mary C. 121
Mary G. 142
Mary C. 133
Matthew H. 92
Peggy 2
Samuel T. 172
S.N., Dr. 224
S. Nye 179, 216
S.W., Dr. 231
Thos. 8
Thomas L. 11, 93, 96,
199
Violet 54
Wm./William 5, 120,
172
Wm. M. 52
Hutchson, James 93

Hutson, Mesel 19
Peggy 215
Sarah S. 1
W. C. 233
Hux, D. W. 59
Isaac 93
John N. 224
Martha 130
Samuel 130
Susan 59
Hyams, Isaac 58, 63
Hyatt, Salina C. 195
Hypp, Margaret 97

Icehour, Martin 8, 234
Ingard, John 233
Ingram, Alexander H. 206
John M. 198
Irvin, Batte 96
Wm. 233
Irwin, Batte 118, 214
Cordela A. L. 81
Cynthia 60
Eliza 79
Francis 59, 128
James 94, 129, 205
Jane 24
John 10, 42, 88, 94(2)
John T. 135
Jos. H. 91
Margaret S. 41
Martha 169, 196
Mary 19, 21, 58
Mary A. 8
Mary Ann 135
Mary L. 176
Nancy 63, 120
Nicey 60
Octaria E. 99
Peggy 120
Ralph E. 40
Reuben M. 180
Robert 58
Sarah 8, 94, 172
S. E. 104
Selia 21
Thomas 94
William 100, 120
Ivy, G. W. 166

Jackson, M. A. 233
Nancy 124
Polly 19
Sarah 113
Zebulon 95
Jamason, Mary 27
Jameson, Arthur 17, 88
Jane 52
Jamison, E. C. 124
E. J. 229
Elizabeth D. 197
Eliza J. 9
Harriet M. 141
Isabel 82
James 39, 134, 200
Jane 122
John 28, 29
Katharine 29
M. A. 69
Margaret E. 61
Mary 13, 15
Mary Ann 49
Nancy 53
Nancy C. 27
Rachel 47

Jamison Cont.
Robert Mc. 27, 38, 97
Sally 48
Sarah 71
Sarah A. 177
Sarah Adeline 173
Sarah C. 181
Sarah Jane 193
Thomas 15
Thomas J. 95
Wm./William 99, 193,
199
Wm./William J. 27, 30,
95
Janes, Peggy 49
Jarrett, Esther 132
Jemison, Andrew 82
Isabella 199
Jean 28
Jenkins, E. D. 212, 217
Lucy 64
Madulsy 68
Jennings, Eliza 112
George W. 186
Julia 148
Richard 165
Jeteen, Nancy 6
Jetton, A. B. 16, 27, 32,
85, 109, 111, 117,
118, 127, 176(2),
178, 211
Alexander B. 112
Alex. R. 24
E. S. 90
J. L. 230
John 200
Lewis 26
Martha N. 107
Nelly 100
Sarah S. 3
Jetun, Jane 112
Jimmeson, Nancy 12
Jingles, Elizabeth 120
John, Ruth A. 72
Johnson, Andrew 37, 172
Angus 156
Cornelia C. 148
Dianna 75
Ezekiel 89, 129
I. A. 79
James 47
Margaret B. 85
Martha A. 239
Mary 67, 113
Milas W. 217
Nancy P. 170
Peter 166
Samuel 158, 208
Sarah 206
S. H. 35
Thomas A. 170
Johnston, Abigail 182
Adaline 186
A. N. 206
Ann 41
B. A. 98
C. 180
Caroline 121
Catharine 65
Catharine J. C. 7, 225
Cyrus 87, 102, 129,
138, 155, 216, 217,
218, 224, 225, 228,
231, 234
Eliz./Elizabeth 15, 20,
96, 192, 197, 221
Emma A. 155

Johnston Cont.
Ezekiel 130
Ezekil 129
Francis 214
Henry 65
Isabella 83
Isobel 95
Izabella 86
Jas./James 7, 8, 9,
  14, 21, 23(2), 24,
  37, 38(2), 51, 65,
  66, 78, 79, 82, 84,
  88, 97, 98, 107(4),
  119, 127, 128,
  137(2), 138, 146(2),
  155, 162, 169, 176,
  193(2), 200, 202,
  208, 211, 213, 214,
  218, 221, 225, 237
Jas./James A. 52, 77,
  87(2), 90, 102, 124
  145(2), 162, 170,
  201
James C. 164
Jane 98, 158
Jane C. 131
Jane Delitha 40
Jane E. 102
Jane S. 194
J. C. 39
Jesse B. 98
J. M. 234(2)
Joe 98
Jno./John 13, 76, 95,
  133(2), 146, 197
Joseph 99
J. W. 138
Lucy 174
Lucy B. 207
Mc. 135
Margaret 136
Margaret M. 207
Martha 166
Martha E. 38
Martha T. 182
Mary 5, 136
Mary A. 34, 86, 201
Mary Anne 21
Mary C. 98, 227
Mary E. 130
Mary J. 95
Matilda 184
M. E. 219
N. 32
N. A. E. 240
Nancy 52, 109
Nancy A. E. 208
Nancy M. 149
Nathaniel 97
Patrick 45, 135
Patsey 12
Polly 96
Prissilla 157
R. 65
Rachael 97
Rachel 88
Rachel C. 50
Rachel M. 39
R. B. 225
Robt./Robert 122, 174,
  205
Robert H. 79
Robert P. 12
R. Z. 6, 13, 17, 21,
  30, 52(2), 54, 55,
  70, 71, 98, 120,
  122, 158, 161, 175,

Johnston Cont.
R. Z. cont. 210, 230
  (3), 231, 235, 236,
  237(2), 240
S. A. 230
Samuel 99
Sarah 34
Sarah H. 30
Swen 100
Syntha 134
Thomas F. 193
Thos./Thomas T. 15, 21,
  46, 57, 121
T. N. 234
Will 214
Wm./William 21, 67, 89,
  93, 97, 106, 136,
  147
Johns(t)on, William 11
Jolly, Nancy 119
Jones, B. C. 227
  B. G. 108
  B. J. 241
  Elizabeth 137
  Harriet N. 226
  Isaac F. 88, 174
  Jos. W. 145
  Julia C. 30
  Julius A. 205
  Mary E. 228
  Minerva 174
  R. B. 20, 51, 79
  R. W. 92
  Sarah R. 218
  William W. 1
Jordan, Ananias 208
  Angeline 231
  George 111
  Mary Ann 195
  M. H. 234
  Richard 40, 93
  Solomon 234
Jorden, Jean 110
Josey, Dianah 152
  Laura 17
Joster(?), Rebecah 68
Joyce, Delic 231
Julan, Mary 170
Julian, Hannah 207
  Jacob J. 100
  Peggy 144
Julien, Jacob 16
Julin, Sarah Ann 64

Kanady, A. A. 5, 93
Karter, Elizabeth L. 197
Kee, M. E. 52
Keeker, Patsey 209
Keliah, Mary 141
Kelley, Jane 240
Kellough, J. W. 46
Kelly, Alexander 211
  Andrew A. 85
  D. P. 234
  Drusilla J. 33
  Elizabeth C. 169
  Hamie E. 116
  Margt. 164
  Margaret J. 95
  Sarah 85
Kenady, Aron Alexander 5
Kendrick, Ephraim 24, 159,
  173, 188
  Green 81, 96
  Margaret 159
Kenedy, F. Milton 226

Kenedy Cont.
Thomas 84, 182, 192
Kennady, Robert 16
Kennedy, A. J. 122
  Alexander 210
  Amelia Sophia 110
  Andrew 210
  David 201
  F. Milton 73, 207
  Hanah 118
  James 118
  Jane 210
  Margaret 118
  Martha 182
  Martha Ann 134
  M. J. 225
  Nancy R. 180
  Rebecca Jane 182
  Samuel 101
  Thomas 3, 4, 5, 66
  William 101, 102
Kennerley, E. W. 211
Kenon, Mary 90
Ker, Martha A. S. 32
Kern, David Stewart 34
Kernes, Margaret 1
  Martha V. 227
  William 221
Kerns, James H. 148, 157
  Jane A. 207
  Robert 176
  Robert V. 117
  R. V. 207
  Sarah E. 179
  Thomas 92
  Thos. M. 66
Kerr, Ann 22, 161
  Catharin 69
  Catherine L. 31
  Dorcas 211
  Eliza 9, 60
  Elizabeth 160
  E. R. 58
  Esther 119
  George W. 112
  Hannah 128
  Helena 137
  Isabella 11, 112
  James 54
  James H. 41
  James M. 128, 149
  Jane 44, 142
  Jane E. 44
  J. B. 17, 41, 94, 156,
    173, 200
  John 36, 128, 201
  Jno./John N. 50, 74(2),
    102, 103
  John T. 234
  Joseph 34, 116
  Josephine E. 179
  Laura E. 51
  Louisa 148
  Manica 29
  Margaret 100
  Margt./Margaret A.
    178, 236
  Margaret E. 102
  Margaret J. 176
  Martha 33, 224
  Martha C. 234
  Mary 150
  Mary C. 171
  Moses 114
  Nancy J. 226
  Peggy 128
  Rachel 116

Lees Cont.
  Thomas N. 101
Leggett, Wm. 110
Leiser, J.G. 138
Lemmond, Eleanor 49
  Elizabeth 5
  Jane 204
  John Q. 22
  Margaret A. 172
  Martha C. 190
  Rachel 197
  Wm. Q. 178(2)
Lemmonds, Anne 140
Lemons, Nancy M. 8
Lensing, Rebekah 212
Lentile, Jane 34
  Sabrina 172
  Shadrick 172
Lepher, Caroline 36
Lesley, Hannah 76
Letters, Sarah 26
Leviston, Mary 46
Lewallen, Hardy 194
  Jesse 133
Lewelen, Hardy C. 90
Lewellen, Jesey R. 111
Lewing, Biddy 135
  Nancy 174
Lewis, Catharine 31
  Elizabeth 216
  F.L. 126
  Francis 31
  Franklin 24
  Isabella 131
  James J. 153
  James M. 216
  Jonathan 112
  Keziah 168
  Martha 215
  Miriam 158
  Patsey 189
  Rachel 141
  Sally 212
  Thos./Thomas 143, 218
Lide, William W. 137
Ligett, James 177
Liggett, Charles S. 160
Ligon, E.L. 234
Lindsay, Darcas 42
  Robert 154, 162
Lineberry, A.W. 59
Lingo, Elisabeth 89
Linsay, Jacob 124
Linsing, Sally 36
Lintele, Ellen 14
Lithcoe, William M. 146
Litle, James 120
Litten, Francis T. 107
Little, A. 37
  Alfred B. 112
  I.F. 114
  James 48(2)
  Jane 59
  Jane E. 141
  Lewis M. 185
  L.M. 66
  Nelly 68
  Sherod 107
  William 112
  Wm. P. 113, 131
Locke, Elizabeth C. 77
  George A. 104, 176
Locky, Robert 181
Long, Ann 48
  Catharine 152
  George A. 73
  Henry Jr. 113

Long Cont.
  Jacob Jr. 103
  Joel 161
  John E. 113
  J.R. 65
  Katherine 49
  Mary 109, 194
  Melinda 95
  Polly 111
  Richd. 69
  R.L. 234
Looker, John C. 127
Lorance, Elisabeth 36
Loughrey, William 196
Louis, Rebecky 111
Lourie, Peggy 46
  P.J. 201
  S. 42
  Saml. 26
  Saml. G. 14
  Sam./Saml J. 2(2), 26
    (2), 27, 36, 46(2),
    50, 51, 52, 53, 58,
    60, 63(2), 70, 74,
    79, 91, 94, 95, 96,
    99, 104(2), 106,
    112, 115(2), 116
    (2), 121, 123, 124,
    127, 128, 130, 133,
    134, 142, 144, 145,
    150(2), 151(2),
    152, 154, 156, 157,
    159, 160, 162(2),
    163(2), 164, 166,
    167, 168(3), 171
    (2), 174, 175, 179,
    181, 182, 183, 184,
    193, 194, 196, 198
    (2), 199, 200(2),
    203, 204, 206, 207,
    208(2), 215, 216,
    220
  S.J. 12, 30, 43, 51,
    54, 57, 64, 70, 86,
    116, 124(2), 133,
    149, 174, 220
  S.S. 30
Love, David 98
  E.J. 47
  Elisabeth 91
  Henry A. 97
  Jane F. 234
  Jane T. 101
  Joseph 195
  Joseph T. 9
  Polly S. 199
  Thomas 159, 234
Lowe, Mary Ann 71
  Thos. L. 198
Lowenstein, Isaac 52
Lowrie, Ann 107
  Louisa 115
  Lydia M. 142
  Robert J.A. 201
  Saml. 13
Lowry, Mary 125
Lowther, Robert 152
Lucas, Hugh 198
  Jane C.M. 210
  Martha 198
Luckey, Catharine 138
  Robert 206
  William 12, 53
  William Junr. 27
Lucky, Darcus E. 99
  Mary 71
  Wm. 146, 168

Mc_____, Esther 42
McAlexander, James 119
McAlister, Eliza 163
  John W. 41
  Sarah J. 195
McAll, Elizebeth 49
McAllister, James 163,205
  J.H. 114, 236
  Joseph M. 236
  J.W. 41, 114
  W.C. 148
M'/McAulay, Deborah 180
  Hugh 12, 181
  Isabella 106
M'/McAuley, Daniel 20, 21
  Elizabeth 20
  William 160
McBride, Nancy 88
  Stevon D. 214
McCacharn, John 153
McCachren, John M.W. 116
McCain, Hance 25, 116
  Hosea 75
  Hugh J. 115
  Margaret 115
McCaleb, Jane O. 65
  Sarah S. 44
M'/McCall, Eli 20, 87
  Eliza 126
  James C. 164, 236
  Jane L. Mina 143
  John A. 115, 123
  Josiah F. 115
  Margaret C. 157
  Mary 78
  Mary Ann 75
  Milas W. 142
  R.R. 78, 232
  Samuel M. 19
  Sarah A. 115
  Sarah Jane 169
  S.M. 183
  Thomas 20, 183
  W.B. 240
  Wm. 29, 56, 76, 165
McCallester, Jas. 220
McCaner(?), A.W. 17
McCappin, Dorcas 110
McCarty, Mary 225
McCarver, Eli P. 35
McCauley, A.E. 21
  ·Daniel N. 236
  E. Rixley 27
McCauly, John C. 236
McCawley, Zachariah 52
McCay, Esther 24
  Mary 57
McCibbins, Jane 191
McClain, Joseph H. 59
Maclean, Thos. B. 91
M'/McCleary, Abigail 44
  Eleanor 133
  Michl./Michael 167,
    176, 191
  William 78, 114
McClelan, Thomas 42
McClellan, John 130
  Wm. R. 141
McClenachan, Alexander
    113
McClenahan, Mary 113
McCloud, Esther C. 84
  Sarah 67
McClung, Jean 129
M'/McClure, Alexander 122
  Betsy 184
  Cyurs 86

M'/McClure Cont.
Elizabeth 77
James 12, 15
Jane 95
Malinda 5
Mary 91
Moses 116, 176
Moses Jr. 117
McCoard, John H. 93
Margaret 202
Martha K. 120
Matthew R. 109
Patsey 156
Robert C. 119
Thomas 101, 202
Thomas T. 61
McCoart, Elam T. 198
McCollugh, Jon: 74
McCollum, Catharine 50
Daniel 141
Poly 56
M'/McComb, Alvira 20
Elizabeth 186
Elisa P. 136
James 136
Jane 53, 121
Jane N. 32
Joseph 186
Margaret 136
Mary 87, 154, 214
Matilda 216
Nehemiah H. 186
Rachel 172
Sally 20
Samuel 210
Wm./William 56, 59,
221(2)
McCombs, Jane E. 240
Margaret E. 144
Mary 70
Mintey 135
Robert 70, 96, 180
Sarah 96
William 181
McConnaughey, Mary Ann
125
McConnaughy, Joseph 117
McConnel, James 117, 171
Martha E. 92
Thomas 117
McConnell, Elizabeth 151
J.H. 49
John G. 236
John L. 216
Thomas Y. 54
McCorcle, Mary J. 134,
234
McCord, David L. 236
Dorcas 197
Elizabeth 176
Elizabeth A.B. 120
Jane C. 121
John 15, 123, 193
Margaret A. 127
Margaret E. 61
Martha 193
Martha C. 157
Nancy L. 121
Rachel A. 193
Rosanna B. 96
Sarah A. 199
McCorell, John 133
McCorkel, John 90
McCorkl, Isabell 14
McCorkle, Eliza 126
Hanah 125
Hannah 160

McCorkle Cont.
H.P. 78
Jane 3
J.G. 120
Joel 14
John 118, 125
Mary D. 143
Nancy 89
Sarah M. 41
Thomas 14
Thos. J. 157
McCormick, Eliz. 105
Rebekah 121
Robert 121
William 80
William C. 74
McCorguodale, Allan 22
McCowin, Elizabeth 106
McCown, Elizabeth 186
McCoy, A. 13, 236
Abegail 146
Beaty 24, 146
Columbus W. 92
C.W. 102
D.W. 226
Eli H. 85, 163
Esther S. 213
James A. 209, 215
J.C. 215
Jennett S. 125
J.G. 194
Jno. 153
Jno. H. 215(2)
John W. 109, 127
J.W. 23, 72, 103
Kitty 114
Margaret T. 92
Marsall 102
Marshal R. 102
Martha E. 118
Mary P. 215
Sarah V. 198
Violet L. 215
McCracken, Ann 188
Barbara M. 33
Charlotte 236
George 14
James M. 199
Jane 143
Jane E. 54
Martha L. 146
Mary 14, 171
Mary A. 122
Wm. D. 54, 146
M'Craken, Betsy 6
McCrary, Adda 237
J.M. 108
McCraven, John 75
McCreary, Jordan 89, 224
McCredie, Andrew 184
McCreery, Mary 43
McCrery, Samuel 125
McCrum, Eliz. 217
McCuaig, A.W. 236
McCubbins, Nancy 129
McCuiag, Wm. D. 236
McCuie, Nancy A.C. 57
Maculla(McCullough?),
Polly 14
McCulloch, Isaac 119
John 46
Margaret C. 155
Margaret 54
Martha D. 215
Melissa A. 147
William 148
Esther 137

McCulloh, Jenny 137
Jno. 119
Margaret 213
Mary 147
McCullough, Mary M. 112
McCuloch, Amos 137
McCurdy, Saml. 213
McDay, Philip 128
M Donald, Wm. 130
McDonald, C.W. 87
David 36, 205
D.W. 176
Elizabeth 99
G. 60
G.F.H. 220
Geo./George W. 127(2),
198
G.W. 227
Hannah 200
Hannah P. 179
John 236
Joseph B. 10
Margaret J. 87
Martha J. 176
Mary C. 228
Mary E. 239
Matilda 176
Peggy 124
Susanna 56
W. 233, 239, 240
Wm. 74, 134, 183, 190,
207, 209, 212
McDowal, Eliza R. 178
McDowell, Dolly 19
Esther Y. 156
Hugh 8, 209
I.H. 120
Jane 140
Jane P. 162
Jno. D. Jr. 185
John H. 120, 154
Mary Ann 156
Mary B. 112
M.J. 238
Permillia 53
Robert W. 53, 120
R.W. 6, 162
McDugald, Sarah 203
McElhenny, Elizabeth 236
McEmmerson, David 35
McEwan, R. 232, 237, 240
Robt. 231, 237
Sarah 147
McEwen, A.A. 58
Darcus(?) 43
Duncan 115
Ellen 134
Leanah 160
Margarett 170
P. 115(2)
R. 18, 50, 61, 73, 78,
103, 228
Robert 50, 94, 170,
174
Robert M. 75
Ruth 187
Samuel 134
Sarah 19
Selina 122
McWin, Dorcas 189
McFall, Mary 212
McFalls, Hanah 106
McFarlin, Abigail 2
McFarlin, Elizabeth 81
Jacob 2
McGahey, James A. 236
Laura T. 231

265

McGahey Cont.
Margaret C. 29
Martha 12
McGahy, Milton 121
William T. 29
McGarrar, Mary 40
McGarres, W. 236
McGathey, Sarah J. 51
Thaddeus C. 9
McGaw, Mattie 80
McGee, Catharine 4
Charlotte E. 129
Eliza 15
Emily 161
Mary A. 108
Thos. 121
McGill, Esther 124
John 72
McGilvary, M.J. 44
Sarah P. 89
McGilvray(?), Jane
Pemella 41
McGilvrary, David 49
McGin, Christian 163
John 163
William A. 190
McGinis, Barbra 147
McGinn, Amz: 81
Anne E. 179
Betsy C. 199
Christine L. 198
Elizabeth 95
George L. 15
James H. 121
James W. 42, 121
J.F. 236
J.H. 193
John 35
Laura 114
Mary 124
Polly 199
Robt./Robert F. 118,
198, 236
T.F. 179
W.A. 17
McGinnes, J.P. 237
McGinney, Jenny 105
McGinnis, Agnes M. 53
Caroline 183
D. 126
Elizabeth E. 158
Jane E. 158
J.H. 19
J.P. 97
J.W. 158
Margery 45
Martha 4
Martha M. 43
Mary G. 42
R.C. 43, 99
McGinniss, Eliza 43
Sarah 114
McGinty, Alex 131
Mary 102
McGlaughlin, Samuel 122
McGuin, James 199
McGuire, J.F. 236
McGuirt, David 80
Mary 80
McGuyer, Nancy 183
McHunter, James 91, 154,
204, 205
McIlwann, Wm. 44
McIntire, Sarah C. 171
McIntosh, Harriet R. 234
Henrietta 29
Isaac L. 236

McIver, A. 200, 230
McIvor, A. 238
McKaven(McKown?),
Elisebeth 57
McKee, Amelia S. 194
E.A. 236
Elias A. 158, 194
Elizabeth 187
Hannah 163
James 171
John 85, 104
Margaret C. 173
Martha 83
Mary 125, 191
Nancy C. 191
Ruthy 132
Samuel 216, 217
Susanah 15
Thomas 15
Thos. B. 106
Wm./William 68, 83,
163, 177
William E. 11
Winslow 93
McKelvy, Caroline 124
James T. 59
Jane D. 119
McKenzie, Isabella M. 1
J.M. 1
Mary D. 238
Robert 36, 37
Robt., Dr. 170
McKibben, Betsey 56
Marcus Alexander 123
McKibbens, Margaret 128
Rebekah 131
McKibbon, Thomas S. 213
McKinish, Rebekah 100
McKinley, Agness 191
Ann 121
Eliza 74
Elizabeth 191
John 180
Margaret 212
Robt./Robert 139,
212(2)
McKinney, George W. 87
Jesse 123
Mary 78, 138
Sarah 87
Wm. 224
McKinny, Hannah 73
McKiny, George W. 122
McKnight, Ann 103
Catherine C. 43
Catharine L. 126
David 156
Hannah J. 30
James 43, 48, 103,
146, 171
James M. 43, 163
Jane 102
Jane C. 153
Margaret J. 102
Martha V. 102
Mary 48
Mary Ann 89, 110
Mary L. 117
Nancy 19
Robert 19
Rosannah 157
McKorkel(McCorkle),
John 48
McKorkl, Margt. 5
McKorkle, Joel 123
McKory, Robert S. 141
McKoy, Marshall R. 12

McLain, John A. 4
Pruda 48
McLane, Jno./John 10, 51,
137, 208, 214
McLarty, Alexander 207,
218
Archibald 188
Catharine 207
Elizabeth 140
George W. 135, 203
John 140, 212
Margaret 129
Mary 212
Polley C. 135
Samuel W. 169
McLaughlin, A.M. 70
I.G. 132
I.S. 80, 89, 90, 92,
149, 165, 183, 184,
190(3), 206
Isaac G. 43
Isaac S. 86
James 178
J.B. 175
J.C. 233, 236
J.G. 16, 33(2), 43(2),
44(2), 52, 63, 68,
230, 231(3), 234,
237, 238(3), 240
J.J. 81
Wm. L. 159
McLean, Agness 156
B.W. 236
H.B. 236
Jno. D. 150
John M. 33, 144
Louiza 238
Martha A. 164
Matilda 4
Patsey 165
R.G. 198
Wm. R. 236
Maclean, Richard S. 68
McLeary, Amelia 37
Ann 197
James 111
Isabella 9
John W. 124
M. 47, 78
Martha 167
Michl. 14, 18, 85, 98,
111, 211(2)
Milissa 171
Samuel 44
S.E. 136
Wm./William H. 104,
190
McLeen(?), Sarah Jane 28
McLellan, Martha 155
McLelland, Laney 111
McLeod, Alexander 3
Christian 138
E.A. 74, 165, 182,
236
James 190, 210
M.C.L. 24
M.D. 81
M. Del. 91, 109, 124
M.D.L. 58, 70, 78,
105, 110, 212
M'Linzy, M. 6
McLoud, James A. 57
Jane 58
Marquis D.L. 215
Mary 112
McLure, C.S. 124
Eliza 238

269

Porter Cont.
Peggy 31
Peter 70
Polly 118
Precilla 81
Robert 19, 31(2), 92
Samuel 119, 155
Susana 170, 202
Tho./Thos./Thomas F.
  78, 104, 118, 145
William 125
Wm. M. 55, 104, 127(2)
Potter, Gordon 155
Ira L. 72
Jesse 191
Mary 30
Rosannah B. 91
Potts, A.C. 20
Ann R. 155
Catherine 236
Charles S. 155
Edwin 20, 73, 74, 82,
  113, 169
Elizabeth C.M. 148
Eloisa 121
James A.G. 88
Jane L. 36
Jenny 119
J.H. 178
J.M. 99
Jont. 156
John M. 155, 166
John W. 4, 191
Lewis 64
Lucinda 12(2)
Lydia 68
Lydia L. 50
Mary 156
Mary A. 148
Nancy E. 66
Nancy F. 50(2)
Nancy H. 205
Peggy 202
Robert C. 137
Spencer 110
Thos./Thomas 132, 200
Wm. 48, 146
Zelinda 82
Power, W.C. 225, 230,
  237, 239, 240
William C. 183
William W. 173
Powers, Elisabeth 137
Patsy 37
Sally 137
Suckey 37(2)
Prater, Mary 163
Prather, J.J. 237, 239
Nathan 163, 170
Sarah V.V. 154
Silas F. 155
Wm. S. 185
Will. M. 237
Pratt, Eliza 143
H.B. 27, 32, 81(2),
  123
Presley, Polly 35
Presly, John E. 235
Preson, Cynthia 155
Pressley, Betsey 168
Wm B. 56
David A. 215
Pressly, J.E. 80
John E. 182
Prestan, Thomas 80
Price, Ann G. 107
Caroline 108

Price Cont.
Charles N. 90, 175
Eliza 165
Elizabeth 106, 108
Elizabeth D. 146
Elizabeth T.A. 171
Esther 139
E.Y. 93
Isaac 83
Isaac J. 140
Isabella 188
James 139
James D. 73
Jane 213
Jane J. 107
Jane M. 140
J.G. 155
J.J. 12
John 156
Keziah 112
L.R. 239
Margaret 107
Martha 83
Martha M. 120, 139
Mary A. 139
Mary E. 202
Nannie R. 6
Pamelia R. 206
Polly 76
Rachel 3, 15
Rebecca E. 78
Reece 107, 166
Robert 15, 188
Robert S. 119, 175
Sarah J. 234
Thos./Thomas B. 100,
  156
Valentin 200
William W. 25
Prichard, H.M. 69
Prim, Betheney 68
Eliza 124
Harriet R. 225
Joseph 72
Margt. 150
Mary Ann 218
Matilda 177
M.R. 238
Prime, O.A. 192
Propst, Maria 238
Pucket, Elizabeth 131,
  235
E.M. 237
Mary 16
Mary Ann 118
Sarah 211
W.C. 237
Puckett, McCamy 192
Milas F. 86
Sidney 157
Puckette, Nancy R. 86
Pullen, Turner 184
Purser, Dorcus 183
Elisabeth 130
John 130
Purveance, Martha 49
Purviance, Eliza 73
Nancy 75
Purvines, Margaret 188
Putman,. Sarah 29
Pyrant, Elizabeth 49
William 49
Pyron, Clarinda 218
Jas./James 110
J.H. 149
J.M. 183
John M. 178

Pyron Cont.
Margaret D. 183
Matilda 36
Milly 174
Wm./William 80, 103(2),
  126, 174, 183(2),
  186, 189, 194

Quay, A. Foster 43
Queery, Cyrus 218
Querie, Nancy 63
Querry, Margaret M. 32
Query, A.A. 233
A.J. 22
Calvin M. 158
Caroline 63
Elisabeth C. 43
Francis G. 67
Francis N. 2(2), 43
Jane 19
Jane A. 20
Jane C. 33
John G. 147, 162
Leander 237
Lucius 20
Margaret 22
Mary A. 33
Mary E. 77
Mary Elizabeth 154
M/C. 238
Melinda L. 115
N.E. 237
Robert 5
Thomas W. 239
Quiery, Ann 202
Quinn, Wm./William W. 14,
  35, 49, 96, 174,
  196, 208
W.W. 90
Quirey, Elizabeth 17

Raben(?), Adam M. 65
Radish, Dorins 56
Rainey, H.H. 97
John W. 60, 213
Ramsey, Agness 122
James 62
William 122
Randolph, Margaret 24
Rankin, A.M. 181
Ephraim L. 163
John D. 57
P.A. 15
Richard 159
R.J. 122
Robert 117
Sarah E. 159
Ransom, A. 227(3), 233
Ranson, A. 12, 14, 30, 43,
  54, 63, 107, 133,
  155, 196, 206, 231,
  232, 236
Alexr. 94
Rape, John 90
Mary 220
Sally 190
Ratchford, Joseph 126
Rawdon, Andrew 38
Elizabeth 113
Harriet Judith 168
James J. 166
John 159
Minton H. 17
Polly 78
William 72

Reid Cont.
W.K. 201(2), 202(2),
  203, 204(4), 205
  (3), 206(3), 207,
  208(2), 209(4),
  210(3), 211, 212
  (2), 213(3), 214(2),
  215, 216(2), 217(3),
  218(2), 219(4), 220
  (4), 221, 222
Reives, Mary T. 196
Rese(Rise), George 50
Rheimds, Antinett 156
Rhodes, Mary 170
Rice, Catherine 157
  Jane 16
  Jared 210
  Jarrod 178
  Juny 227
  Mary M. 178
  Rachel 187
  Valentine W. 106
  William 158
  Wm. A. 16
Rich, Annie 225
  Isaac 75
Richards, L.J.G. 36
Richardson, Edward 142,
  152, 164
  Elizabeth E. 219
  Jane K. 71
  Mary 15
  Mason 186
  Susannah 174
Richmond, Lavine 10
Riglar, C.H. 238
  Dallis M. 238
  Margaret L. 201, 239
  Mary E. 8
  Dallas M. 161
Rigler, C.H. 81
Riley, Andrew 155
  Franklin 134
  Harriet 208
  Jane 155
  Mary R. 125
  Sally 171
Rily, James R. 165
  Jno. M. 164
Rise, Easter 210
Ritch, Betsy 80
  Charrity 39
  Edey 190
  Edmond 80, 200
  Edmond 200
  Elijah 203
  Georg. W. 164
  James 45, 64
  James S. 189(2)
  Jno./John 68, 75, 108,
    112
  John P. 195
  Jos./Joseph 200
  Mary S. 195
  Olleary 187
  Polly 160
Ritche, Rachel 203
Ritchison, Betsey 152
Rives, Ann R. 183
  Wm. 6
Roach, Patsey 16
Roan, Cathrine 80
  Herbert 165
Roark, William 50, 179,
  187, 189
Robards, Mary D. 90
Robarts, John 165

Robb, Jane 86, 186
  Margaret 77
Robberson, Mathew A. 168
Roberson, John 138
  Nancy 2
  Osborne 100
Roberts, Amanda 239
  Amy 172
  Joseph 101
  Joseph M. 123
  Mary L. 184
  Philip 45, 172
  Polly 173
Robertson, Marey 48
  Recinda 155
  Thomas 193
Robeson, Alexd. 62
  Cynthia 24
  Ellen 203
  Frances 12
  Isabella 146
  Jane 97
  Robert 12
  Susanna 109
Robinett, Margaret 20
Robinson, D.M. 119
  Dovey L. 123
  Elisha 238
  Elizabeth J. 236
  Hannah 159
  Jas. B. 123
  Jno./John 167
  John L. 151
  Maggie R. 210, 240
  Martha 119, 173, 192
  Mary 80, 207
  Mary M. 225
  M.E. 185
  Milly L. 50
  M.W. 15
  Rebecca 18
  Sarah D. 114, 234
  Susan S. 130
  Vina 238
  William T. 66
  Winslow 37
Robison, Alexander 168
  Ann 194
  Charlotte 8
  Clarissa 14
  Daniel 57
  D.C. 116
  D.H. 122
  Elim 7
  Elisabeth 112
  Elizabeth 166, 173,
    207
  Elizabeth W. 41
  Esther M. 162
  Ezel./Ezekiel 5, 6,
    180
  James 68
  Jane 133
  Jane D. 88
  John 12, 81(2), 133,
    143, 166, 173
  Jno./John P. 168
  Martha 6, 166
  Mary 40, 111
  Mary N. 8
  Matthew A. 168
  M.W. 87, 97, 150, 159,
    201, 209
  Nancy 69
  Nancy H. 127
  Patsey 3
  Polly 138, 156

Robison Cont.
  Polly B. 107
  Rachel C. 10
  Rebecka E. 75
  Robert 117
  Robert C. 61
  Ruhama 193
  Sally 147
  Sarah 61, 180
  Sarah A. 26
  Sarah J. 41
  S.W. 51
  Wallis 119
  William 90(2), 167
  Wm. Taylor 113
  Wm. W. 127
Rockwell, E.F. 4, 21, 24,
  26, 31, 41, 72, 104,
  154, 176, 220, 232,
  235, 236, 237, 240.
  Harriet S. 41
Rodden, Benjamin 159
  Catherine 134
  Dicey 159
  Elizabeth 17
  Evaline 112
  Hannah R. 168
  Jacob 134
  Judy 9, 74
  Kezia 153
  Margaret C. 193
  Mary E. 17
  R.H.E. 69
  Rosanna 23
  Susan E. 167
  William 23, 268(2)
  Wm. G. 167
Roddin, Jane 168
Roden, Bengmin 168
Rodgers, Betsey 208
  Cherine 69
  David 158
  Eliza 219
  Elizabeth 111
  Harriet 187
  Hugh W. 129
  Hugh Wilson 129
  James 169, 211
  Jno./John W. 77, 120
    (2), 126, 153
  Joseph 85
  Julius D. 67
  Louisa 129
  Lucretia 74
  Martha R. 91
  Mary A. 64
  Matilda P. 126
  Samuel H. 131
  Sarah 144, 208, 225
  Sarah H. 126
  Thomas 169
  Thomas P. 169
  Wm. 133
Rodin, Adalin 165
Roediger, Charles 110
  Wm. 202
Roeseler, J. 209
Rogers, _____ 170
  Ann 179
  Betsey 211
  Dolly 136
  Edwin 238
  Elsey 72
  Hannah 169
  Isabella 120
  Jn. 95, 113, 170, 201,
    217

275

277

Todd Cont.
Sarah 139
Sarah J. 123
Sarah Jane 84
Sarah L. 95
Silas 199
Sophia R. 200
Sophina 163
Susan 42
Susan A. 39
Susannah 9
W.A. 2
Wm./William 17, 163
Wm./William A. 26,
  95(2), 139, 174,
  185, 193, 239
William H. 193
Wm. L. 149
William N. 200
Tolbert, Sarah 229
Tomberlin, Elizabeth 178
  Reubin 142, 202
Tonkin, Jane 189
Torrance, Isabella 182
Torrence, Adam 53
  Alexander H. 211
  An B. 217
  Camilla C. 108
  Delia R. 98
  Hugh 108
  Jas. C. 217
  J.H. 169
  Letitia A. 26
  Mary 53
  Mattie E. 230
  N.C. 155
  Sarah J. 64
Torrince, Stephen 129
Towle, Jane M. 184
  Lydia E. 43
Towns, Elis. 201
  Elisha 201
Townsend, James H. 201
  Martha 143
Traderick, Margaret J.79
Tradenick, Sarah Ann 97
  N.P. 219
Tredennick, J.R. 149
Tredinnick, Nicholas 138,
  189
  Richard 77
Treese, Nancy 99
Treelase, Richard 131
Trelour, John 42
Trexler, Susan 201
Triplett, T.L. 47
Troll, Jane 146
Trotter, Anna 218
  Emma 213
  Joshua 106
  Thomas 81
Trout, Rachael 199
Troutman, D.F. 239
Tucker, Dolley 37
Tuloar(?), John 239
Tunstall, Wm. H. 53
Turner, H.P. 189
  Jane 35
  Joanna N. 188
  Mary A. 160
  Wm. 239
  Wm. S. 1
Turrentin, Wm. H. 192
Tye, Betsey 78
  John 45
  Lewis M. 151
  L.M. 165

Tye Cont.
M.E. 230
Saline 215
Tyer, M.M. 4
Tysor, W.H.G. 239

Underwood, Christian C.
  38
  S.E. 202
Urie, Frances 172

Vail, Abigail 184
Vance, Catharine 229
  David J. 239
  Elizabeth 239
  Janie 198
  John 198
  Mary J. 234
  Samuel 218
  W.B. 239
Vanpelt, Ann 175
  Mary 80
  Simon 18
Varner, Elizabeth 202
  Jane 121
  John 96, 121
  Sally 67
Varnor, Rebecca 132
Vary, Mary 201
Vaynes(?), D.C. 38
Vealn, Esther 14
Vence, Feltte 187
Vickry, Mary 48
Vince, Esther 187
Vinson, Agnes 142
Vinty, Margaret 31
Vinty(Vintz), Valentine
  31
Viporell, Jane 131
Vizie, Mary 143
Vogel, John 239
  Laura 239
  Mary 110

Waddell, Ester 38
  Jane 14
  M.H. 38
  Peggy 109
  William H. 108
Waddington, Hannah 178
  Robert 203
Waddle, Archibald 41
  Cynthia 210
  Frances 47
  George 39
Wade, Julia 175
Wadsworth, John W. 191
  J.W. 70, 150
Waggoner, Nancy 178
Wagstaff, George Wash-
  ington 170
  Mary 170
Waine, Edw. 19, 80, 158
Wains, Edw. 139
Waisner, Lavina 90
Walker, Adaline 127
  Agness 28, 121
  Andw./Andrew 3, 15,
  48(2), 120, 142,
  152, 154, 158, 168,
  181, 184
  Ann 40, 161
  Caroline 205
  Catharine M. 217

Walker Cont.
Deborah 76, 204
Editha R.S.A. 53
E.G. 181
Elizabeth 88, 110,154
Elizabeth J. 175, 212
Ephraim A. 204
Esther 63
Esther E. 63
Henry J. 79
Hugh 28, 65
J. 7, 11, 24, 62, 142,
  173, 204, 206, 214,
  236
Jas./James 181, 193,
  214
James H. 92
James M. 72(2), 93(2),
  228
Jane 161
Jane R. 58
Jean 62
J.M. 5, 21, 24, 51,72,
  89, 92, 139, 140,
  160(2), 204, 228
Jno./John 5(2), 11,20,
  62, 68, 71, 75, 97
  (2), 116, 121, 142,
  171, 188, 190, 203,
  204, 207, 219, 220,
  230, 240
John E. 172
Joseph 23, 172
Joseph C. 43
L.A. 219
L.J. 240
M.A. 140
Margaret 128, 214
Margaret C. 155
Margret B. 200
Martha 22
Mary 20, 148, 160,
  205(2)
Mary E. 204
Missouri 101
M.J. 106, 237
Moses 55
Nancy 31, 172
Nancy E.J. 204
N.J. 240
Patsey 100
Peggy H. 92
Robert 133
Rosanna A. 92
Sarah 18, 186
Sarah E. 24
Suckey 209
Thompson 96, 120, 122
T.J. 14
William 28, 58, 94,
  116, 131, 161, 165,
  203, 205
Walkup, Ann Eliza 59
  Emily 25
  Martha 191
Wall, J.B. 7
  Minsegey 192
Wallace, Alexr. 129
  Andrew 146
  Catherine 237
  Elizabeth 206
  Eveline 134
  Harriett 81
  Jack 191
  Jackson 77
  James 12, 64
  Jane 97

281

White Cont.
Elizabeth 102
Esther 232
Givens 178
Hugh 185
Isabella 84
Jas./James 192, 205,
  212
James P. 47
James T. 101
Jane 190
Jane A. 93
J. Harvey 50
J.N. 240
Jno./John M. 161(2)
Lucinda 103, 234
Margaret 107
Margt./Margaret E. 15,
  226
Mary Jane 91
Mary L. 107
M.J. 232
McCamy A. 18
Nancy S. 82
N.V. 200
R.M. 14, 17, 32(3),
  80. 96, 115, 122,
  134, 149, 155, 171,
  177, 184, 204, 205,
  207, 208(2), 210,
  214, 220
Samuel D. 75
Sarah C. 220
Sarah Jane 200
Sarah L. 7
Susy 67
Sylva 177
Zenas 123
Whiteside, E.A. 106
Eliz. 107
Joseph 47
Samuel 74, 107, 212
Samuel M. 107, 140
Thomas 89
Whitesides, John N. 18
Margaret 62
M.D. 240
Rachel L. 140
Samuel M. 36
Whitley, Decature 65
Robert D. 118
Whitlow, Elam W. 40
E.W. 3
Whitty, Mary J. 113
Wiatt, Mary Ann 87
Mitchel 89
Wicks, J.L. 240
Mary E. 102
Wier, Agness 20
Wiggins, Patsey 132
Tillitha 132
Wiley, Agness 123
Esther 167
Even L. 125
James 10
Jane 174
Leah 152
Margaret M. 166
Mary 10, 133
Robert P. 157
R.P. 208
Sarah C. 16
Sarah E. 180
Wilkerson, T.J. 44
Wilkinson, E.J. 217
Esther A. 130
Nancy G. 201

Wilkinson Cont.
Neil 27
Neill 27, 218
William 213
Wilks, Julia 132
Williams, Agness 186
Andrew Jackson 207
Angeline 193
Betsey 168
C.C. 234
Clement 125
Dicey 114
E.C. 55, 56, 197, 198,
  214
Elisabeth 162
Elizabeth 162
Godfrey 153, 221
Godphrey 168
Hannah 16, 168
Harriet L. 174
H.B. 70, 168
Henry B. 32, 67, 189
James H. 4
James J. 100
Jane R. 150
Jean 30
John R. 19
Kate J. 166
Lewis S. 1, 157
L.S. 120, 240
Martha 36
Martha Ann 122
Martha E. 55
Mary 113
Mary Ann 37, 114
Polly 168
Rhoda 80
Sally 186
Sarah 137
S.M. 235
Susanna 131
Thomas W. 187
Unity 192
Urrisa 157
W.P. 198
Williamson, A.C. 62
Amelia 94, 230
Amzi L. 160
Christian 119
Cynthia A. 46
David 215
Dawson 41
Elisabeth M. 207
George W. 31
Godfrey W. 111, 204
G.W. 177, 215
Hannah 31
J.A. 232
John 58, 196(2), 197
J.R. 155
Levina 35
M.A. 149
Margt. E. 231
Martha S.F. 142
Mary 72
Matilda 124
M.E. 216
S. 110
Sally 31
Sarah A. 32
Sarah R. 35
Thomas J. 19
Violet S. 84
Willson, Debrah 48
James 160
Samuel 206
Wilson, _____ 38

Wilson Cont.
Addeline 130
Albert 32, 216
Anabella 60
Anabella J. 113
Andrew 194, 219
Anne 200
Ann M. 173
Benece P. 126
Benjamin 16
Caroline H. 105
Catharine 77
Catherine 95
Charles 117
Charles B. 176(2)
Cornelia A. 6
David V. 73
Dinah 31
Eliza 45
Elizabeth 14, 66, 135,
  218
Elvira Catherine 7
George 130
Hannah 133
Hannah K. 2
Harriet A. 37, 202
  iley, 45
Isaac 40, 88, 93, 99,
  147, 192, 211, 233
Isabella 146(2)
J. 29
James 5, 14, 15, 90,
  99
Jas. C. 218
James D. 203
James W. 147
Jane 131
Jane R. 191
Jethro 9
J.H. Jr. 136
Jinsy 200
J.L. 215
John 13, 150, 217, 240
Jno./John M. 144, 173,
  217
John Mc. 240
John N. 192
John N.D. 146
Jno. R. 158
John W. 207
Jordon 133
Joseph 39, 216
Joseph H. 144
Josephine E. 158
Joseph R. 2
J.P. 225
L.G. H. 82
L.H. 213
Louisa 147
Lucretia J. 2
M.A. 70, 240
Marg./Margaret 23, 24
Margaret E. 32, 107
Margt./Margaret J. 25,
  237
Margaret M. 147
Margaret S. 210
Margarett M. 130
Martha 55, 174
Martha A. 224
Martha J. 32
Mary 70, 216
Mary Ann 22, 36, 233
Mary C. 182
Mary L. 4, 170
M.J.P. 237
Nancy L. 134

www.ingramcontent.com/pod-product-compliance
Lightning Source LLC
Chambersburg PA
CBHW071843270326
41929CB00013B/2090